THE ROMANTIC PERFORMATIVE

The Romantic Performative

Language and Action in British and German Romanticism

Angela Esterhammer

STANFORD UNIVERSITY PRESS
STANFORD, CALIFORNIA

Stanford University Press
Stanford, California
© 2000 by the Board of Trustees of the
Leland Stanford Junior University
Printed in the United States of America

Library of Congress Cataloging-in-Publication Data

Esterhammer, Angela
　　The romantic performative : language and action in British and German romanticism / Angela Esterhammer.
　　　p.　cm.
　　Includes bibliographical references (p.) and index.
　　ISBN 0-8047-3914-5 (alk. paper)
　　　1. English literature—19th century—History and criticism.
2. Romanticism—Great Britain.　3. English literature—18th century—History and criticism.　4. German literature—18th century—History and criticism.　5. German literature—19th century—History and criticism.　6. Literature, Comparative—English and German.
7. Literature, Comparative—German and English.　8. Performative (Philosophy).　9. Speech acts (Linguistics).　10. Romanticism—Germany.　I. Title.
PR457.E88　　2000
820.9'145—dc21　　　　　　　　　　　　　　　　　　　　　00-057324

This book is printed on acid-free, archival-quality paper.

Original printing 2000

Last figure below indicates year of this printing:
09　08　07　06　05　04　03　02　01　00

Designed and typeset by John Feneron in 9.5/12.5 Trump Mediaeval

for John

Acknowledgments

Most of this book was written during a research leave in Berlin, and I would like to express my sincere gratitude to the foundations and individuals who made that stay possible: the Alexander von Humboldt Foundation, which awarded a fellowship for the project; the Social Sciences and Humanities Research Council of Canada, which supported earlier and later stages of the research; the University of Western Ontario, for a generous leave arrangement; Winfried Menninghaus, for a hospitable welcome at the Institut für Allgemeine und Vergleichende Literaturwissenschaft of the Freie Universität Berlin; and Jürgen Trabant, for expert advice and assistance throughout the writing of the book. I benefitted enormously from the comments of other friends and colleagues who read all or parts of the manuscript-in-progress: David L. Clark, Alex Dick, Cyrus Hamlin, Alice Kuzniar, Mary Anne Perkins, Tilottama Rajan, and the Stanford University Press readers. I am also grateful for invitations to present my research between 1995 and 1998 at the University of British Columbia, Cambridge University, the Freie Universität Berlin, the University of Groningen, and the University of Leiden; for the helpful comments and critiques of audiences who heard excerpts from the project presented at the "Romanticism in Theory" conference in Copenhagen, the Coleridge Summer Conference, meetings of the International Comparative Literature Association's Literary Theory Committee, and conferences of the British Association for Romantic Studies and the North American Society for the Study of Romanticism. The students in my graduate seminar on "Romanticism and Performativity" in 1998–99 allowed me to test the "uptake" of my ideas in a dialogic situation and guided me toward some important revisions. Special thanks to Haley R. Bordo for tireless assistance in preparing the manuscript and index.

An earlier version of my research on Humboldt appeared in *The Wordsworth Circle* as "Wilhelm von Humboldt, the Dialogic Situation, and Speech as Act"; this material is reprinted by permission of *The Wordsworth Circle*. Part of chapter 1 appeared as "Of Promises, Contracts, and Constitutions: Reid and Bentham on Language as Social Action" in *Romanticism* 6.1 and is reprinted here by permission of the editors; part of chapter 5 appeared as "Hölderlin and the Inter/Subjective Speech Act" in a volume of *Amsterdamer Beiträge zur neueren Germanistik* entitled *Rereading Romanticism*; and a part of chapter 6 appeared as "'The Duel': Kleist's Scandal of the Speaking Body" in *European Romantic Review* 10.1. Finally, I gratefully acknowledge the assistance of Kathleen Okruhlik, Dean of Arts, with regard to a grant in aid of publication from the University of Western Ontario, J. B. Smallman Fund.

Contents

Preface   xi
A Note on Translations and Abbreviations   xvii

Introduction: Locating the Romantic Performative   1
Romanticism and Linguistic Pragmatics, 2   Introducing the Romantic Performative, 7   The Romantic Performative and Speech-Act Theory (Austin, Searle), 10   The Romantic Performative and Universal Pragmatics (Habermas), 13   Fabulous Retroactivity (Derrida), 16   Performativity, History, and the Romantic Text, 19

1. Of Promises, Contracts, and Constitutions: Speech-Act Philosophies and Practices in Britain, 1775–1800   23
   The French Revolution and Linguistic Acts, 24   The British Background: Hobbes, Hume, and the Social Contract, 29   Thomas Reid: Illocutionary Acts in the Eighteenth Century, 33   Jeremy Bentham: Laws, Oaths, and Fictions, 41   Burke and Paine: What's in a Constitution?, 51   Binding Terms, 56   God and the Social Contract, 61

2. Kant, German Idealism, and Philosophies of Language in Action   68
   Kant's *Satz*, 70   Herder's *Ursprung der Sprache*: Cognition, Communication, and Words of Power, 76   Herder's *Metakritik*: Permutations of Being in Language, 78   Revolutionary Grammar, 81   Fichte's *Setzen*, 83   Fichte on the Origin of Language, 86   Bernhardi and Fichtean Linguistics, 89   Real Being and Represented Being, 93   Schelling and the I, 96   The Problem of Subjectivity: From Natural Philosophy to Literary Theory, 100

3. The Performative Humboldt   106
   Energeia and *Kraft*, 109   Humboldt's Linguistic Turn, 112   The Humboldtian Speech Act: Mind and Materiality, 114   Synthesis in Humboldt and Kant, 117   The Midpoint of

Language: Verbs, 120   Pragmatic Orientations: Humboldt, Searle, Benveniste, 124   The Hinges of Language: Pronouns, 128   Grammar and Reference: Humboldt, Hegel, de Man, 131   Cognitive and Communicative Dialogue, 136   The Paradox of the Performative, 138   Humboldt and Romantic Literature, 142

4. The Performative Coleridge … 144

The Hollow Speech Acts of the 1790s, 146   "Fears in Solitude": The Sermon in the Dell, 151   The *Lay Sermons*: Positing an Ideal Performative, 155   The Language of Energy and the Energy of Language, 162   Performative Frames: *Aids to Reflection*, 165   "Hymn before Sun-Rise": Locating the Voice of Nature, 169   Cognitive and Verbal Acts in the *Logic*, 173   "Frost at Midnight": The Fluttering Film, 180   Mathematics, Christianity, and Performativity, 184

5. Subjective and Intersubjective Speech Acts in Hölderlin's Work … 187

Hyperion: The Failure of Performative Utterance, 191   *Der Tod des Empedokles*: Utterance, Uptake, and Identity, 203   The Dialogic Hölderlin, 217   "Germanien": Uptake?, 221   "Friedensfeier": The Social Hölderlin, 225   "Patmos" and the Apostrophic Coda, 233

6. Kleist and the Fragile Performative Order of the World … 240

The Constitutions of the Schroffensteins, the Amazons, and the Prussians, 243   *Amphitryon* and the "I Am," 254   Speaking, Thinking, and the Body, 263   *Michael Kohlhaas*: Coal-Black Horses and the White Page, 267   Conventions, Contingencies, and the Will of God in "Der Zweikampf," 279

7. Godwin's Philosophy and Fiction: The Resistance to Performatives … 289

Political Justice, Promises, and Phantom Limbs, 290   The Progeny of Promises, 295   *Caleb Williams*: Truth and Performatives, 298   Marriage and the Disintegration of Discourse (*Deloraine, Fleetwood*), 313   The Fetters of Superstition: Promises and Secrets (*Deloraine, St. Leon*), 316   Identity as Institutional Fact (*Deloraine, Cloudesley*), 320   Fiction as Testimony and Testament, 326

Conclusion … 329

Bibliography … 335
Index … 351

Preface

The title of this book, *The Romantic Performative*, risks two contentious words. New historicist criticism has linked the term "Romantic" with an "ideology" that we must get beyond in order to recognize the period around 1800 as a field of competing discourses, and to recover writers, since marginalized, who played crucial roles in the era's conflicted culture. Some British writers who figure prominently in this book, such as Reid, Bentham, and Godwin, present a challenge even to broadened definitions of "Romantic"; and German literary history offers a variation on the problem by resolutely assimilating Humboldt and Hölderlin to the "Classical" rather than the "Romantic" tradition.

"Romantic," here, is in the first instance a heuristic term for the historical period covered by this study—approximately 1785 to 1835. Thus, "Romantic writers" replaces the impossible phrase "writers of the late eighteenth and early nineteenth centuries," and the still awkward "Romantic-period writers." But "Romantic" in my formulation "Romantic philosophy of language" has polemical import as well. The understanding of language as a form of action is so pervasive, turning up in different but recognizable guises in such a wide range of late-eighteenth- and early-nineteenth-century writing, that it needs to be identified as the prevailing way of thinking and using language during this period. The analysis of language in terms of utterance, speech, dialogue, power, energy, and continuous activity is, if not precisely a new Romantic *ideology*, nevertheless so widespread and so profoundly theorized a concept that it deserves to be synthesized under a prominent and even provocative name.

If "Romantic" is contested, "performative" is notoriously resistant to clear explication. In the phrase "Romantic performative," it is also consciously anachronistic, and does not correspond exactly to any one theorist's definition. Rather, I draw on recurring structures of thought that have prompted theorists from J. L. Austin to Judith Butler to adopt the term "performative," and I attempt to delineate parallels (not exact equivalents) in Romantic-period philosophy of language. The most crucial of these recurring concepts is that something *happens* when words are spoken. Verbal utterances have an effect on the addressee, the speaker, and the speech situation that needs to be described not just in terms of rhetoric or persuasion, but as the actual founding of the subject-positions of speaker and hearer, the establishment of their relationships to one another and to the external world. My use of the term "performative" relies heavily on the meaning it carries within modern philosophies of language: Austin's concept of utterances that perform actions rather than describing the world; Benveniste's more rigorous identification of sentences that name the action they accomplish when they are uttered; Habermas's sociological application of the performative to describe those elements of discursive interactions that establish and regulate the speech situation itself. But because I am seeking to contextualize the Romantic performative within the philosophical and political climate of the late eighteenth century, I also draw on recent applications of the term in less obviously linguistic contexts. In this extended sense, the identity of an individual or a group can be called performative if that identity is established through the very process of practising it—so that doing and being, or saying and being, or becoming and being, are indistinguishable. Bourdieu's suggestion that the meaning of certain social acts can be summed up in their implicit decree to the participating individual to "Become what you are" is another thought-provoking indication of what the social performative might involve. Conversely, this definition of performativity also harks back to the Aristotelian definition of *energeia*, suggesting an action that contains its end within itself, or an acting that does not stop when some external terminus is reached. The act or practice is thus constitutive of the fact or state that results from it.

As a term that has profoundly influenced literary and cultural theory, "performative" is now frequently applied to individual Romantic figures and texts, though it has not heretofore been used in a systematic approach to the language of Romanticism. My presentation of Romantic philosophy *as* a theory of the performative, and of Romantic literature in terms of that theory, is meant to open up two avenues for re-thinking Romanticism and the philosophy of language. First, I would like to contribute to recent scholarship that is uncovering the historical roots of twentieth-century speech-act theory, even when it has tried to sever itself from those roots. Secondly, I hope to show that certain themes and structures in Romantic literature and philosophy can be analyzed more precisely by using the vocabulary and the models for comparison that modern theories of the performative have made available.

Both these motives for bringing together Romantic philosophy of language and twentieth-century linguistic pragmatics are discussed in the introductory chapter, where I attempt a preliminary presentation of the "Romantic performative" by comparing Romantic concepts of utterance, action, subjectivity, and dialogue with various twentieth-century models of the performative, including both Anglo-American and German-Continental theories. The Introduction provides an overview of topics that are treated in much more detail in the first, philosophical half of the book. Chapter 1 presents theories of language as action in late-eighteenth-century Britain, as they developed within the overlapping fields of moral, legal, and political philosophy and in the context of the debates engendered by the French Revolution. Key moments here are Reid's theory of social acts and Bentham's theory of fictions, as well as the public debate between Burke and Paine with its intentional and its unconscious messages about the language of contracts and constitutions. Chapter 2 introduces the German philosophical context by examining the response of linguistic thinkers to transcendental idealism. As Kant and the Idealists assign the mind a creative role in the representation of reality, linguistic philosophers identify language as the medium in which this creative power manifests itself. Fichte and Schelling, as well as Herder and Bernhardi, develop action-centered theories of language and systems of grammar in which the verb functions as the central part of speech, and the verb "to be," as the linguistic form of the concept of being, is endowed with the power of constructing an "ideal reality" or "represented reality" distinct from things-in-themselves. Chapter 3 presents Humboldt as the consummate representative of these linguistic theories and the foremost spokesperson for the Romantic performative, a speech act that paradoxically founds the conditions within which it operates in the very moment when it is uttered.

The discussion of Coleridge in Chapter 4 brings together Kantian philosophy, the political and social discourses of 1790s Britain, and literary texts. Coleridge's suspicion that the rhetoric of the revolutionary age brought about an over-reliance on the *effect* of words and a neglect of their *meaning* led him to search for a compensatory language that would be both meaningful and effective. He found it in the Logos or "I am," the foundational principle of grammar, logic, and theology, a principle that grounds all language in the coexistence of being and action. Poems such as "Fears in Solitude," "Frost at Midnight," and "Hymn before Sun-rise" illustrate Coleridge's performative linguistics by showing how language posits speaking subjects, objects, addressees, and contexts, and by calling attention to the difference that poetic utterance *might* make in the world—while also admitting that its effect remains tenuous and uncertain. Chapter 5 shifts to Hölderlin who, in the context of Coleridge's conversation poems and German Romantic philosophy of language, may be re-read as a strikingly dialogic and intersubjective poet. His novel *Hyperion* and his drama *Der Tod des Empedokles* feature important confrontations between institutionally authorized speech acts and the performative utterances that derive from the individual creative mind, while poems like "Germanien," "Patmos," and "Friedensfeier" reveal the poet's identity to be dependent on dialogic address and the potential uptake or acknowledgment of an addressee.

Chapters 6 and 7, respectively, examine the drama and fiction of Kleist and the novels of Godwin, two authors who turn out to have much in common when read with attention to public and private identity, declarations and legal documents, and the disturbing parallels between sociopolitical and fictional utterances. Kleist's *Amphitryon* unsettles the concept of subjectivity by showing how a person's identity may depend on dialogic response and even public consensus. His drama *Penthesilea*, and his stories *Michael Kohlhaas* and "Der Zweikampf," demonstrate the extent to which society is established and perpetuated by laws, petitions, declarations, edicts, and oaths, but they also reveal the weak points of a social order founded on verbal constructs, especially its inability to accommodate the divine or the supernatural. The effectiveness and the destructiveness of public speech acts are also central concerns of Godwin's *Caleb Williams*, while his subsequent novels pick up and intensify individual speech-act issues raised in *Caleb Williams*, such as the danger of predicating one's behavior on promises and secrets, or the contrast between subjective identity and identity as a legal or textual construct. Although in his essays Godwin seems to reject the idea of performative language outright, promoting the conviction that language should always be the instrument of truth and sincerity, his novels are in fact superlative examples of the way not only legal and institutional utterance, but fiction itself as a speech act, exerts a formative influence on what we know as reality.

"Alles ist Rede gegen Rede, die sich gegenseitig aufhebt," wrote Hölderlin in response to *Oedipus the King* (StA 5: 201). Once again, most of his terms are debatable ones; but a plausible translation might be: "everything is speech against speech, which mutually sublimates [or 'cancels,' or 'preserves'] itself." Although Hölderlin is referring to the dialogic structure of Greek tragedy, the phrase seems equally applicable to the process of critical debate. It is also, as I will argue, emblematic of the new understanding of language advocated by Hölderlin and his contemporaries, where the emphasis is on speech or discourse, action and interaction, positing and opposition. I hope that calling attention to this concept of language may help fill in a neglected part of the background to Romantic texts, and that it may stimulate further *Rede*—if of the oppositional kind, then with the Romantic understanding that opposition involves the recognition of a common origin and a common goal, and that it is a form of true friendship.

A Note on Translations and Abbreviations

English translations are provided for all quotations from German texts; the German original is also given for quotations of poetry, and where it is essential to the discussion. Published translations are cited when available; otherwise, translations are my own. Titles of German works are given in German, except in cases where the English version is very well known (e.g., *Critique of Pure Reason*). A translation of the German title—using the title of the published English translation when it is quoted here, otherwise a heuristic translation—is provided the first time a work is mentioned.

Frequently quoted works are identified by abbreviations of their titles; all abbreviations can be found in the bibliography, listed under the name of the author.

THE ROMANTIC PERFORMATIVE

Introduction:
Locating the Romantic Performative

"The status of literature is the weakest point of theories of language—what they have on their conscience," writes the linguistic and literary theorist Henri Meschonnic (194). For the field of Romantic studies, if not in general, one might reverse his proposition: "The status of language is the weakest point of theories of literature—what *they* have on *their* conscience." The thesis of this book, however, is that certain philosophies of language have an untapped potential to inform and illuminate literary texts of the Romantic period.

"Philosophy of language" refers, here, to the branch of thought—sometimes adjoined to philosophy, sometimes to linguistics—that poses vital questions about the relationships among speakers, hearers, language, and the world. "What do we do with words?" and "How do words relate to the world?" are its central concerns. The Romantic period did not assign a specific intellectual or academic space to inquiries of this kind. Rather, they were addressed by thinkers whom we would label philosophers (Fichte, Schelling, or Reid) and by those we would call linguists (Humboldt) or grammarians (Bernhardi), as well as by writers known primarily for their political philosophy (Godwin), their legal theory (Bentham), or their engagement with literature (Coleridge). Many of the writers discussed in this book worked in all of the not-yet-segregated domains of philosophy, philology, and literary criticism. These same people, along with their friends and contemporaries, produced works of poetry, fiction, and drama that bear directly on the interaction among language, language-users, and the world. The following chapters examine aspects of that interaction, and what it means for the reading of English and German Romantic literature.

The phrase "philosophy of language" has also gained currency as the term for a branch of twentieth-century philosophy—although it has thereby achieved greater ambivalence rather than greater clarity. Some would argue that all twentieth-century philosophy is, in effect, philosophy of language. During the first half of the century, the work of Frege, Russell, Wittgenstein, Husserl, and Heidegger redirected many of the traditional philosophical questions toward an analysis of the language in which philosophical questions are formulated, indeed toward the nature of language as an instrument that connects thought with objects of thought and minds with other minds. But a more specific field called philosophy of language was established within analytic philosophy during the second half of this century, primarily by J. L. Austin and John R. Searle. The two questions I cited above—"What do we do with words?" and "How do words relate to the world?"—echo the title of Austin's seminal work (*How to Do Things with Words*) and the opening sentence of Searle's *Speech Acts*, respectively. They testify to the concern of these philosophers with an action-centered theory of utterance, which would later evolve into a pragmatics of language. One ongoing theme of the following chapters is the unacknowledged resonance between Austin's and Searle's speech-act theory and the ideas of Romantic-period writers about language as action in the world.

ROMANTICISM AND LINGUISTIC PRAGMATICS

The work that was done in the philosophy of language from 1785 to 1835 forms as important a background to the literature of that period as the better-known texts of idealist philosophy, late-eighteenth-century political theory, and Romantic literary criticism. This is all the more true because philosophy of language was so often being written by the same people who were writing poetry and fiction, or else by their close friends and collaborators. August Ferdinand Bernhardi is now known (if known at all) as the foremost grammarian of his day, but he was also an intimate of the Jena circle of Romantic writers and philosophers, a contributor to the Schlegels' journal *Athenäum*, a close friend of both Tieck and Fichte, an acquaintance of Humboldt, and an author of fiction (albeit a not very successful one). Typically for linguists in his day, he devotes substantial sections of both his major books on grammar to the use of language in literature and other arts and sciences. Grammar, in fact, is for him an adjunct to aesthetics. Similarly, in his influential Berlin lectures of 1801–2 on literature and art, A. W. Schlegel gives poetry pride of place among the arts—and then begins his presentation of poetic theory with a long piece "On Language." He regards poetry and systems of language as parallel expressions of human creativity: poetry "already presupposes language, the invention of which belongs, after all, to the poetic disposition, for language itself is a poem of the entire human race, ever becoming and changing, never complete" (A. W. Schlegel 388). His brother Friedrich's famous program for Romantic literature as a "progressive universal poetry" in *Athenäum* Fragment 116 also begins with the explicit mandate to "bring poetry into contact with philosophy and rhetoric" (*KFSA* 2: 182).

Scholars who read Romantic philosophy of language find the links between it and literature inescapable. Kurt Müller-Vollmer pleads for them as follows:

> It is characteristic of early Romantic theory that it directs attention at the poetic medium itself and that it conceives of a necessary relation between the nature of language and that of literature and poetry.... We will find therefore that at the core of the Romantic theories of literature and of poetry there is an explicit or implicit concept of the nature of language. In fact, the conceptions of poetry and of language are mutually interdependent.... Thus to understand the literary ideas of the Romantics one has to consider them in conjunction with the corresponding concept of language. On the other hand, the Romantic idea of language cannot be grasped in isolation from those literary and poetic concepts with which it forms a continuous field of meaning. ("From Poetics to Linguistics" 196)

Despite this interdependence, I will *not* be arguing here for direct relationships of influence between linguistic philosophers and poets. While in some cases such relationships seem inevitable (Coleridge, for instance, continued to revise his early poetry in light of his developing philosophy of language), in other cases they are unlikely, and the search for them is always restrictive. But it is not necessary to rely on a condition as vague as the "spirit of the age" either. A more accurate way of characterizing the historical perspective of this book is to say that certain events, among which the publication of Kant's epistemology and the political debates unleashed by the French Revolution are paramount, created an environment in which both theoretical and creative writers reached an attenuated awareness of the problematic relationship between language and the world. They became preoccupied with questions about the relation of language-users to language that Kantian philosophy raised but did not solve, and with the power of utterance to affect both individual cognition and sociopolitical relations. It is not a matter of philosophy or linguistics providing a theory of language which poets then apply. Rather, *both* linguistic and poetic texts are *both* analyses of language as action and instances of language as action.

As it becomes more evident how much importance Romantic-period writers attached to the philosophy of language, scholars have begun commenting on the need to know more about the linguistic thought of these years; in fact, Romantic philosophy of language seems recently to have acquired the status of an "unduly neglected" field of study. "The early Romantic theory of language is still virtually unknown," Ernst Behler wrote in the early 1990s. The prevailing cliché that the Romantics were interested only in the origins of language and in historical-comparative linguistics "has obscured the profounder reflections on language in the writings and fragments of the early [German] Romantics, particularly with regard to the importance of language for poetry, the process of understanding in human communication, and the interaction of human beings with the world" (E. Behler 263). Somewhat confusingly, the linguistic thinkers who were most instrumental in developing a concept of language as action also laid the groundwork for the historical-comparative study of language that would later displace this concept. Nineteenth-century historical linguistics is often said to have been founded on Humboldt's immensely wide-ranging studies of grammatical systems, Friedrich Schlegel's rediscovery of Sanskrit in *Über die Sprache und Weisheit der Indier* (On the language and wisdom of the Indians, 1808), and the work of their Romantic contemporaries Franz Bopp and Jacob Grimm. But the historical and comparative linguistics of Schlegel and, especially, Humboldt must be read in the context of their insistence that language, conceived of as energy and activity, is constitutive of both cognition and interpersonal relationships.

In Britain, too, where the sources of linguistic philosophy are more diverse, Romanticists have overlooked important dimensions of linguistic thought and their relevance to literature. Hans Aarsleff established the modern view of British Romantic linguistics when he described it as being completely dominated, and fossilized, by the linguist John Horne Tooke and his idiosyncratic method of tracing all words back to roots that refer to concrete objects: "for thirty years it [Tooke's *Diversions of Purley*] kept England immune to the new philology until the results and methods finally had to be imported from the Continent in the 1830's" (*Study of Language in England* 73). Aarsleff's picture of Romantic linguistics as being obsessed with etymology has itself been ensconced for thirty years and more, but it needs to be supplemented both by a recognition of the sociopolitical context of Tooke's linguistics, and by studies of other linguistic thinkers. In light of his celebrated political radicalism, Tooke's etymological approach needs to be seen as an attempt to show people that language can act to change an unjust society, rather than perpetuate the status quo. Tooke strives to demonstrate that all words derive from simple, concrete facts precisely in order to undermine the abstract language used by those in power to hoodwink a linguistically unsophisticated public. Olivia Smith's *The Politics of Language 1791–1819* opens up this context, and along with recent, revisionary studies of eighteenth-century philosophy and law (such as Stephen K. Land's *The Philosophy of Language in Britain* and John Barrell's *English Literature in History, 1730–80*), lays the groundwork for an account of speech acts in late-eighteenth-century Britain. Only when all these disciplines are brought together does the concept of language as action, energy, force, and creative power emerge in the formidable dimensions it assumed during this period. Alongside Tooke and the linguistic theorists contemporary with him, writers who were ostensibly concerned with political or moral philosophy—with constitutions, oaths, social contracts, or (like Coleridge) with the interpretation of the Bible—were thereby also analyzing the uses and effects of language in the world.

Historically as well as intellectually, then, the ideas of Reid, Bentham, Herder, Humboldt, Coleridge, and others inhabit a space between the linguistic preoccupations of the eighteenth century (universal grammar and the origin of language) and those of the later nineteenth century (historical and comparative linguistics). The generation of linguistic philosophers writing around 1800 posed fundamental questions that the work of their predecessors implied and that of their descendants depended on, yet generally ignored. In posing these questions, Romantic-period writers made the philosophy of language integral to both the politics and the literature of their age in a way that it has not been before or since.

This book begins by examining what British and German thinkers of the late eighteenth and early nineteenth centuries claim, and what they imply, about speakers and language. Although I discuss these theories here with the specific view of relating them to certain literary texts in the second half of the book, they amply merit attention for their own sake. Both philosophers of language and historians of linguistics have recently begun to recognize this, and some now write about an early flowering of linguistic pragmatics from the 1780s until the 1820s. "Pragmatics" is used here in its modern linguistic sense, deriving from the tripartite division of semiotics proposed by Charles Morris in 1938, whereby *syntax* (or "syntactics") studies the relation of signs to other signs, *semantics* the relation of signs to their objects, and *pragmatics* the relation of signs to their users or interpreters. Pragmatics is, in other words, the branch of linguistic thought that complements syntax and semantics by focusing on speakers, hearers, and contexts, or on the use of language in specific temporal and spatial settings. Its philosophical correlative is speech-act theory.

In talking about a pragmatic moment in European linguistics around 1800, then, philosophers and linguists have begun to trace the history of linguistic pragmatics—and, more specifically, speech-act theory—back to the Romantic period. In their contributions to the volume *Speech Acts, Meaning and Intentions* (1990), Armin Burkhardt, John F. Crosby, and Barry Smith propose a new genealogy for speech-act theory. Here and in other essays, Smith argues the importance of Thomas Reid as an eighteenth-century progenitor, but the main thesis of this volume is that speech-act philosophy was born very early in the twentieth century: "the core of speech act theory," according to Burkhardt, "undoubtedly originates from the works of the Austro-German phenomenologists within the Brentano-Husserl tradition" (2). In her introduction to the 1995 volume *Speech Acts and Linguistic Research*, the Italian linguist Elisabetta Fava cites Burkhardt's view as the now-standard genealogy of speech-act theory. But Brigitte Nerlich counters, in the first essay of the same collection, with the claim, "it all started in 1795, the year which is generally regarded as marking the beginning of the early Romantic movement" (1). The case for a Romantic-period origin for linguistic pragmatics is most expansively and systematically presented by Nerlich and David D. Clarke in their 1996 book *Language, Action, and Context: The Early History of Pragmatics in Europe and America, 1780–1930*. "The notion of a speech act, and the theory of speech acts in general, could only appear to be revolutionary because speech-act theorists ignored what had been written earlier," Nerlich and Clarke claim (440). Twentieth-century versions of pragmatic theory "have been blind to their own history, and have cut themselves off from a wealth of ideas which were developed during the 19th century, about how language and the mind work" (442).

Nerlich and Clarke choose to begin their story, as they put it, with John Locke, who effected a linguistic turn in European philosophy by devoting the third book of his *Essay Concerning Human Understanding*—entitled "On Words"—to the role of language in epistemology. Since my own "story" is not a history of linguistic pragmatics per se, but an account of the way pragmatic concerns emerge in Romantic literature and theory, the starting points of this book are the political and intellectual watersheds of the late eighteenth century: the French Revolution and Kant's "Copernican revolution" in philosophy. In beginning with both a

Introduction: Locating the Romantic Performative 7

philosophical and a political event, I hope to provide a foundation for discussing both subjective and intersubjective (i.e., interpersonal or social) tendencies in the Romantic view of language and its effects. Romantic writers are concerned with speech acts not only as phenomenological interactions between mind and world, but also as sociopolitical interactions between individuals and institutions. My presentation of their linguistic philosophy focuses on issues that are especially relevant to the reading of literary texts: the expression or creation of subjectivity in language; the way authoritative utterances determine social relations; the dialogic interaction of speaker and hearer, as a basis for the interaction between fictional characters, between poet and addressee, or between author and audience. Moreover, my reading of philosophers and philologists involves not just a presentation of their ideas, but a text-critical inquiry into the figural language with which these ideas are expressed.

Perhaps these differences in origin, aim, and perspective account for the fact that, after surveying some of the same dialogue- and context-oriented theories in early-nineteenth-century linguistics that are treated here, Nerlich and Clarke come to a diametrically opposed conclusion. Although "the Romantic conception of language has many aspects in common with modern pragmatics, especially the exploration of communicative interaction and dialogue," they claim, Romanticism completely lacks a concept of the performative: "What is still missing in the Romantic conception of language is an insight into the performativity of language. The view that language is the expression of thought still dominated a burgeoning theory of language and communication" (*Language, Action, and Context* 60). By contrast, this book aims to introduce precisely the concept of a *Romantic performative*, and to indicate its differences from the twentieth-century performative while arguing its importance for the reading of Romantic literature.

INTRODUCING THE ROMANTIC PERFORMATIVE

Nerlich's and Clarke's conclusion about the absence of performativity from Romantic theory stems in part from their restricted definition of the term "performative." Distinguishing, in general, between theories of language oriented toward cognition or representation and those oriented toward communication or pragmatics, they associate cognitive-representational theories with "the view that language is the expression of thought," and imply that "performative" insights are found only when communicative-pragmatic concerns predominate over cognitive-representational ones. But what makes the Romantic conception of the speech act unique and powerful, I will argue, is precisely that it fuses the two classical contexts for the understanding of language—*cognition* and *communication*. For the thinkers discussed here, the effect of utterances in an interpersonal context follows ineluctably from the way words operate in the private context of the mind's encounter with the world. Oral speech and dialogue with other individuals stand at the center of Romantic theories of language, precisely because individual cognitive process is itself conceived as a dialogue with the otherness of external reality. Herder's claim for the primacy of dialogue, from his influential essay of 1770 on the origin of language, is typically passionate:

> I cannot think the first human thought, I cannot align the first reflective argument without dialoguing in my soul or without striving to dialogue. The first human thought is hence in its very essence a preparation for the possibility of dialoguing with others! The first characteristic mark which I conceive is a characteristic word for me and a word of communication for others! (*EOL* 128)

Subjectivity, even *being* itself, begins to be defined as a series of verbal or, at the very least, responsive relationships to objects and to other subjects. This book therefore pays a good deal of attention to Romantic reevaluations of the verb "to be," to modes of subjective and social being, and to the relationship between being and representation. For the interpretation of "to be" as a verb-substantive, thus as both an act and a state—and thus as a phenomenon that resembles *becoming* or even *performance*—lies at the heart of the Romantic speech act.

Coleridge, principal spokesperson for the verb-substantive, preferred to cite it using the more elegant one-word Latin and Greek equivalents *sum* and *eimi*, and in English rendered it as "I am": "the verb substantive ('am', *sum*, εἰμι) expresses the identity or coinherence of being and act. It is the act of being" (*L* 16–17). The German language also provides a provocative verb-substantive in the word *sein*, which can translate as the infinitive "to be" or (especially when capitalized) the noun "being." But the expression "verb-substantive," oxymoronic in any language, points to a key paradox within the Romantic speech act. Just as the proposition *ich bin* or "I am" designates, for German idealist philosophers, the state of existence but *simultaneously* the act of positing existence, for Romantic linguists words refer to already existing objects or states in the world, but also in some sense bring those objects or states into existence in the first place. Subjectivity and objectivity are redefined as processes rather than givens. The Romantic speech act is typically an utterance that articulates a portion of reality and makes it into an object of thought, that instantiates the relationship between speaker and hearer, and thereby even establishes the subjectivity of the speaker *in the very moment when the utterance occurs*. Whereas twentieth-century speech-act theory generally analyzes an utterance in relation to a stable context and in terms of pre-existing conventions for discourse, the concept of utterance that recurs throughout the work of Romantic linguists is both more disturbing and more exhilarating. They discern that utterances themselves create contexts and alter conventions. Their speech acts somehow *posit the conditions for their own effectiveness*—an idea that makes the Romantic version of the performative a paradoxical, yet peculiarly appropriate, model for analyzing the relationship between speaker and addressee, or the speaking subject and the objective world, in Romantic poetry and fiction.

Wilhelm von Humboldt, the supreme spokesperson for the Romantic performative, appropriates the Kantian term *Synthesis* and the Fichtean term *setzen* 'posit' in describing the operation of language. The act that takes place "immediately on uttering the word" is an "act of *spontaneous positing* by bringing-together (synthesis)" (Act des selbstthätigen Setzens durch Zusammenfassung [Synthesis]). Originary and responsive at once, verbal utterance is an event by which "the mind creates, but by the same act opposes itself to the created, and allows this, as object, to react back upon it" (*OL* 184/*GS* 7: 213). Speaking, then, is simultaneously an act of "positing" (i.e., a creation ex nihilo) and an act of "synthesis" (i.e., a combination of already existing elements). In uttering a word or a sentence, the mind creates an object, but "the same act" of creation also embodies the mind's response to that object—as if the object (and the mind-object relation) were both in existence and not yet in existence at the moment the utterance occurs. Far from being unique, this temporal paradox is typical of the account of language offered by Humboldt's contemporaries, and overdetermined by his philosophical context. The foundation of existence and knowledge within idealist philosophy, as exemplified by Fichte's account of self-positing, manifests an identical structure:

> The *self posits itself*, and by virtue of this mere self-assertion it *exists*; and conversely, the self *exists* and *posits* its own existence by virtue of merely existing. It is at once the agent and the product of action; the active, and what the activity brings about; action and deed are one and the same, and hence the 'I am' expresses an Act, and the only one possible. ... (*Science of Knowledge* 97)

The act is equivalent to the fact or state that results from it: this is the fundamental enigma—and the deeply performative principle—that marks the idealist philosophy and the linguistic thought of Humboldt's age.

THE ROMANTIC PERFORMATIVE AND SPEECH-ACT THEORY (AUSTIN, SEARLE)

By contrast, the aim of contemporary speech-act theories, especially their Anglo-American incarnations, has been to systematize a pragmatic approach to language. In the seminal text of this philosophical movement, the lectures presented by J. L. Austin in 1955 and published after his death as *How to Do Things with Words*, Austin critiques philosophy's obsession with the "constative" or referential dimension of language and the criteria of truth and falsity. He identifies many instances in ordinary language where an utterance cannot be judged true or false, but must be evaluated in terms of its "felicity" or success in achieving an effect or performing an action. After isolating this type of utterance as "performative," he pursues several attempts at a systematic analysis of performative force: by identifying the social conventions necessary in order for performatives to operate; by isolating grammatical criteria by which they may be recognized; by distinguishing among "locutionary," "illocutionary," and "perlocutionary" dimensions of an utterance; and finally by proposing lists of individual verbs that have various types of illocutionary force. When none of these analyses proves conclusive, Austin's attempt to distinguish between constative and performative breaks down, famously, into an admission of the indivisibility and interdependence of the two categories.

Despite Austin's ironic mode of presenting his hypotheses and his habit of dismantling them once made, *How to Do Things with Words* keeps returning to the idea that the performative might be isolated according to formal or semantic criteria and defined within a comprehensive theory of action. John R. Searle is even more determined to complete Austin's unfinished project by developing a reliable analytic model, and his book *Speech Acts* is grounded in the definition of language as a "rule-governed form of behavior" (12). Using the promise as his central example, Searle pursues a formalized analysis of the rules, relationships, and expectations that must obtain on the part of speaker and hearer in order for an utterance to count as a promise. In the essay "A Taxonomy of Illocutionary Acts," the most influential of Searle's writings among literary scholars, he extends this formal analysis by subsuming the promise and all other illocutionary acts under the categories of assertives, directives, commissives, expressives, and declarations.

Both Austin and Searle assume that the speaker acts on the world in a way that is made possible by the rules of language and other pre-existing institutional conventions. The success of the speech act depends on the hearer's ability and willingness to recognize the type of illocution the speaker is making and the conventions that govern it. The speaker's privileged, indeed idealized, role in the whole scenario becomes increasingly clear in Searle's later work, where he integrates his philosophy of language into a more general philosophy of mind and action and defines the speech act as the speaker's communication of "his" "Intentional state." When Searle revises his earlier speech-act theory in the book *Intentionality*, he also distinguishes explicitly between the "representing intention" and the "communication intention" involved in illocutionary acts (165–66). His assertion that a "clear distinction between representation and communication" is necessary in order to explain how illocution works reveals a basic difference from Romantic philosophy of language, which regards representation and communication as inseparable aspects of verbal utterance. Anglo-American speech-act theory is essentially a theory of the way utterances act on the hearer and the world—on those elements of the context that are external to the speaking subject, who is conceived of as a fully formed, independent, responsible agent, in possession of (according to Searle) a pre-existing Intentional state.

It is true that the assumptions of Austin and Searle differ from those of Romantic linguistic philosophers because the goals of their inquiry are different; even were these goals the same, the disparity in their philosophical contexts would inevitably make for a different kind of analysis. Nevertheless, since all these philosophers are searching for ways to analyze the effects of verbal utterance, and all are calling attention to language as a medium by which speakers and hearers interact with one another, it is revealing to compare the different conceptual frames they adopt for this enterprise. Austin's and Searle's attempt to discover and enumerate the rules that govern linguistic behavior inevitably raises the question of whether the infinitely variable speakers and contexts that are the raison d'être of a pragmatic theory of language are of such a nature that they operate according to rules in the first place. Most of the critiques that have been leveled against Austin's and Searle's speech-act theory attack, in one way or another, their assumption that the speaker is a stable and apparently unchanging subject. Ethnologists have a particular problem with the metaphysical or universalized concept of the speaker assumed by speech-act theory, pointing out that it is itself specific to Western culture. What if, Michelle Z. Rosaldo asks, using the example of the Ilongot people of the Philippines to argue that speech-act categories are not uniform across cultures, we are confronted by a society that indeed regards speech as action, but lacks the Western concept of speech or action as "the achievement of autonomous selves" (204)? Mary Louise Pratt, one of the first critics to bring speech-act theory to bear on the interpretation of literature, questions the assumption that (even Western) speakers are "authentic, self-consistent, essential" subjects; in reality, "people always speak from and in a socially constituted position," a position that is constantly shifting (62–63). In their introduction to the volume *Performativity and Performance,* Andrew Parker and Eve Kosofsky Sedgwick invoke postmodern critiques of the concept of agency to show that Austin over-simplified the roles of both speaker and hearer, and they conclude that "Austin tends to treat the speaker as if s/he were all but coextensive—at least, continuous—with the power by which the individual speech act is initiated and authorized and may be enforced" (7). Arguably, though, this is less a critique of Austin than a restatement of his assumptions. He is interested not in historical, cultural, or even philosophical problems of subjectivity, but in a systematic account of speech and action. In fact, G. J. Warnock's sympathetic account of Austin's philosophy concludes with the observation that Austin actually says next to nothing about language itself, for a speaker in unproblematic possession of language is his starting point:

> [Austin] simply takes it for granted that, as a basic resource for his performance of speech-acts, a speaker has a language at his command, a vocabulary and a grammar, enabling him to produce sentences which express 'what he means' and which will (he hopes) be appropriately understood by his audience.... He was willing simply to assume that we have 'got' a language, with a view to getting on to the question: what do we *do* with it? (151)

The Romantics, on the other hand, begin their inquiry into the relationship of speakers and language elsewhere: with the problem of subjectivity itself. Eighteenth-century empirical philosophy, especially the work of Hume, undermined the idea of a metaphysical subjectivity and instead made the mind subject *to* impressions or sensations of a physical world. In attempting a compromise between empiricism and idealism that would reassert the autonomy of the mind as distinct from physical perceptions, Kant disquieted his contemporaries even further. As Philippe Lacoue-Labarthe and Jean-Luc Nancy have stressed, Kant offered only an empty and substanceless version of the Cartesian *cogito*: "all that remains of the subject is the 'I' as an 'empty form' (a pure logical necessity, said Kant; a grammatical exigency, Nietzsche will say) that 'accompanies my representations'" (30; cf. Kant, *CPR* 331/B 404). For those philosophers and poets who set themselves the task of working out the role of language in a Kantian universe, a vulnerable subject is the point of departure. From here they develop various phenomenological and relational models of subjectivity—models in which the phenomena themselves, and the relations between mind and phenomena, are at least partially constituted by words.

In attributing a constitutive role to words, post-Kantian writers anticipate the basic orientation of twentieth-century philosophy: they begin to articulate the idea that individual consciousness may be subordinate to the structures or the internal form of language. But this idea appears inconsistently. The typical position adopted by Romantic linguists is that individual speakers do things with language *while* language *also* does things to individual speakers. Accordingly, the speaking subject tends to be a much more fluid entity for them than it is in twentieth-century speech-act theory—neither a function of the power that linguistic rules and societal conventions assign to certain utterances, nor an independent agent exerting control over the external world, but a mind negotiating its position with respect to language, nature, and society. Romantic writers are concerned not only with the effect of an utterance on the hearer and the surrounding environment, but also, or even primarily, with its effect on the speaker. This "effect" is something far more basic than what Austin addresses when he notes that the perlocutionary or persuasive force of an utterance may "produce certain consequential effects upon the feelings, thoughts, or actions of . . . the speaker" (101). What the Romantics mean is that speakers are only defined—which is to say they only come to occupy an I-position in relation to a You, to other subjects, to the divine, to nature—in and through the act of speaking. Rather than taking the status of the speaker for granted, a Romantic speech-act theory considers utterance as an event that before all else shapes the subject's consciousness, determines the subject's relationship to the world and the hearer, and changes the environment that surrounds, and includes, the one who speaks.

THE ROMANTIC PERFORMATIVE AND UNIVERSAL PRAGMATICS (HABERMAS)

Yet Austin and Searle are not the only twentieth-century philosophers with whom Romantic linguistics can be brought into dialogue, and Continental European approaches to linguistic pragmatics maintain a closer affiliation with the phenomenologically oriented theories of the Romantics. Nerlich and Clarke usefully summarize the major directions of pragmatic theory in England, France, and Germany during the twentieth century: English (and American) philosophy of language is dominated by the ordinary-language approach, particularly speech-act theory; France, by a theory of enunciation best represented by Emile Benveniste; Germany, by universal pragmatics as represented by Jürgen Habermas ("Language, Action and Context" 439). French theories of *énonciation* and *énoncé* tend to reflect the Romantic interest in the interaction between speaking as process and speech as product, and there are some particularly striking parallels between Humboldt and Benveniste, the structuralist linguist who developed a concept of the performative independently of but at the same time as Austin. Benveniste shares with Humboldt the conviction that dialogue and subjectivity are the key elements of discourse, and his echoes of Humboldt (to be discussed further in Chapter 3) are so marked that they probably indicate direct influence.

For Habermas, the encounter with Anglo-American speech-act theory forms part of his attempt to develop a "universal pragmatics"—a sociological theory of communicative processes based on the assumption that speakers and hearers share basic norms of rational behavior, but must find their way to shared norms in each dialogic interaction. In his *Theorie des kommunikativen Handelns* (*The Theory of Communicative Action*), Habermas begins his examination of speech-act theories with a general critique of "the analytic theory of action developed in the Anglo-Saxon world," because it puts too much stress on purposive agency:

> It conceptualizes action on the presupposition of exactly one world of existing states of affairs and neglects those actor-world relations that are essential to social interaction. As actions are reduced to purposive interventions in the objective world, the rationality of means-ends relations stands in the foreground. (*TCA* 1: 273–74)

As a sociologist interested in an empirical account of discourse in society, rather than a philosophical idealization of fundamental concepts, Habermas directs attention away from the independent agency of the speaker and toward the *Lebenswelt* or life-world of shared concepts that allows participants in communicative processes to interact with one another in the first place. Within the *Lebenswelt*, the conditions for each discursive interaction must be negotiated anew when the interaction takes place. Habermas redefines Austin's term "illocutionary force" so as to line it up with his own phrase "communicative action": for him, illocutionary force refers to the aspect of discourse that specifies *how* semantic content is to be conveyed and understood. Habermas outlines a tripartite division of frames of reference and "validity claims" for the participants in a discourse: the *objective* world elicits a claim to *truth*; the *subjective* or *interior* world elicits a claim to *sincerity*; and the *intersubjective* or *social* world elicits a claim to *rightness*. Given this structure, the illocutionary force of the discourse determines "which validity claim [i.e., truth, sincerity, or rightness] a speaker is raising with his utterance, how he is raising it, and for what" (*TCA* 1: 278). This definition of illocutionary force means that the conditions for responding to an utterance are negotiated anew in each instance. Instead of being set by preexisting conventions, "these conditions for accepting the linguistic claim, and thus for agreement between *S[peaker]* and *H[earer]*, *spring from* the meaning of the illocutionary act itself" (*TCA* 1: 301).

In contrast to Austin and Searle, Habermas explicitly traces his philosophy of language back to Humboldt, and with some reservations joins his colleague Karl-Otto Apel in working with and extending the Kantian framework of transcendental philosophy. As Nerlich and Clarke note, both Habermas and Apel stress "interaction, intersubjectivity and understanding more than rules and conventions" ("Language, Action and Context" 454). Their language has explicit Kantian resonances; Habermas, for instance, demonstrates that certain components of a discourse bring about the "conditions of possibility" for discourse in the first place, by defining an intersubjective realm and a realm of possible referents. Identifying five categories of words or grammatical forms that count as "pragmatic universals" (including deictics, performative verbs, etc.), Habermas claims that

> we can only use sentences in utterances by first producing, with the help of the pragmatic universals, the *conditions of possibility for communication* and thereby the speech situation—namely, the level of intersubjectivity, on which people enter into dialogic relationships and thus are able to appear as subjects capable of speech and action; and the level of objects, on which the real can be depicted as an object of possible utterances. ("Vorbereitende Bemerkungen" 110)

Elsewhere, he describes the process of exercising communicative competence in an even more Humboldtian way, suggesting that "language is the medium through which speakers and hearers realize certain fundamental demarcations":

> The subject demarcates himself: (1) from an environment that he objectifies in the third-person attitude of an observer; (2) from an environment that he conforms to or deviates from in the ego-alter attitude of a participant; (3) from his own subjectivity that he expresses or conceals in a

first-person attitude; and finally (4) from the medium of language itself. ("What Is Universal Pragmatics?" 66)

From the recognition that speakers use language to adopt a position with respect to both objects and other subjects, to the notion that this positioning happens *as* people speak, to the idea that the activity of speaking is also an interaction with the medium of language itself, this formulation echoes very closely what is going on in the Romantic performative. The ambiguity by which the performative simultaneously claims to create and to refer, finally, is reflected in Habermas's description of utterances in terms of the slippery but significant Romantic term *Darstellung* '(re)presentation': "In a certain way, every explicitly performative utterance both establishes and represents an interpersonal relation" (Jede explizit performative Äußerung *stellt* in gewisser Weise eine Interaktionsbeziehung zwischen mindestens zwei sprach- und handlungsfähigen Subjekten zugleich *her* und *dar* ["What Is Universal Pragmatics?" 34/"Was heißt Universalpragmatik?" 216]).

Yet I would like to claim for the Romantic performative a still greater fluidity and creativity than is allowed for in Habermas's theory. Although the point of his concept of communicative competence is that participants in discourse can and do re-create the conditions for the possibility of discourse in each instance, they still do so according to laid-down norms: "All communicative actions satisfy or violate normative expectations or conventions" ("What Is Universal Pragmatics?" 35). Habermas's analysis of communicative action provides a useful point of reference, because he shares the Romantics' assumption of a transcendental framework combined with an empirical interest in the way language-users negotiate their life-world. But the Romantics base their exploration of interpersonal speech acts on a phenomenology of utterance, or on the individual encounter of mind, word, and object, rather than on the Habermasian substructure of shared rationality and social norms. Romantic theorists are unwilling to separate the pragmatic and communicative dimension of language from language's inalienable role in cognition.

FABULOUS RETROACTIVITY (DERRIDA)

Whereas the basic unit of discourse in Habermas's theory, as in Searle's, is the sentence, Romantic philosophers locate a performative dimension in words themselves. Words establish the relationship between speaker and world, altering both these terms in the process. From this phenomenological nexus, Romantic writers extrapolate to the act-character of sentences and texts, to the effect of utterances in a dialogic context and in the sociopolitical world. Herder and Humboldt address the role of language in forming communities and nations, while literary texts from Hölderlin's *Der Tod des Empedokles* to Godwin's *Cloudesley* explore the way public utterances shape people's identities, which in turn determine how their words will be received by their fellow citizens. Yet even on the sociopolitical side of Romantic philosophy of language, the "rules" by which language forms social identity continue to be in flux. Verbal utterances bring social or political conventions into existence in the first place, even if the utterances "then" behave according to those same conventions. A version of the hermeneutic circle seems ever-present in the principles of Romantic philosophy of language and in the readings of Romantic literature that those principles generate: among the effects of every speech act is, at least potentially, the founding of new conditions according to which speech *does* act.

This enigma of the utterance that seems to collapse temporality, or to create the conditions of its own possibility, gives rise to one further comparison between Romantic and modern analyses of performative language. Poststructuralist philosophers and critics, including Paul de Man, Jacques Derrida, and Jean-François Lyotard, tend to regard the self-referentiality of the speech act—that is, the fact that it refers to a state that it itself creates—as an aporia that disrupts the purity of language as a sign-system. In de Man's reading of Romantic literature and philosophy, the simultaneously cognitive and performative nature of language causes texts to deconstruct themselves: their "grammatical" appeal to general or abstract knowledge is incompatible with their "rhetorical" claim to creation or instantiation in a specific instance of reading (*Allegories of Reading* 270). Poststructuralist philosophers expose the way speech acts derive their legitimacy from conditions that they themselves found—or, to put it differently, the way performative utterances derive their ability to act from the fact that they *do* act. Derrida writes of the scandal, violence, and "fabulous retroactivity" of the performative. In numerous analyses, he exposes the way laws and constitutions use performative utterance so as to found their legitimacy on the existence of conditions that only come into existence through the utterance itself. The phrase "fabulous retroactivity" comes from Derrida's reading of the American Declaration of Independence, from which he concludes that the text of the Declaration creates and guarantees its own signatories at the same time that the signatories create and guarantee the Declaration ("Declarations of Independence" 10). Derrida locates the same structure of retroactivity in the South African constitution ("Admiration de Nelson Mandela" 457–59), and analyzes the founding of law in an act of performative violence in the essay "Force of Law," while Lyotard remarks on a similar paradox in the French Declaration of 1789 (146). In other words, declarations pretend that the situation they aim to bring about already exists, retroactively, before the words are spoken, written, or signed; they maintain a necessary undecidability between constative and performative. Similarly, though not in a deconstructionist frame of reference, Elaine Scarry undertakes a text-critical analysis of the declarations of war issued by the American Congress in the course of its history, and draws a powerful conclusion about the way performatives legitimate themselves by deliberately misrepresenting temporal sequence: "A performative utterance that camouflages itself as a descriptive utterance transposes into the past the material reality that it itself first produces; it back-dates it" (296).

For Romantic-period writers, fabulous retroactivity is the normal condition of language. It is remarkable how often the various forms of the Romantic performative that appear in philosophical and literary texts take account of the retroactive and self-referential structures, the vulnerability and the potential for failure that poststructuralist philosophy has exposed in its critique of the performative. Postmodern theorists, focusing on fabulous retroactivity as a feature of the texts that maintain sociopolitical power structures, typically describe it in terms of disruption, dissimulation, and repression: Derrida's usual terms are "violence" and "scandal"; Lyotard, in *The Differend*, identifies the "torts" and "damages" that result from the conflicting claims of different language games; Pierre Bourdieu writes of the "misrecognition" and "imposture" involved in the authorization of discourse (109–13). Romantic writers like Humboldt and (especially) Bentham are equally aware of the dynamics of language and power in authoritative utterances, yet for them, fabulous retroactivity is a profound and pervasive characteristic of all language—something that "only language can do," and without which "all true thinking, is impossible" (Humboldt, *OL* 56). They tend to describe the paradoxical temporality of declarative statements, not as a scandal, but as something like a miracle—a characteristic of human language that can be observed but not fully explained. Accordingly, Romantic theorists themselves are never too surprised when their attempts to analyze the operation of language run into ambiguities, gaps, or self-contradiction.

Introduction: Locating the Romantic Performative 19

PERFORMATIVITY, HISTORY, AND THE
ROMANTIC TEXT

Although performativity is not a historical moment in language, in the sense that one could call the language of one era "more performative" than that of another, it does seem to attain a more conscious awareness in some periods than in others. The twentieth-century development of speech-act theory, beginning with Frege, Husserl, and Wittgenstein, continuing with lesser-known German phenomenologists and legal theorists such as Adolf Reinach, and culminating in Austin, Searle, and Habermas, constitutes one such period. But the late eighteenth and early nineteenth century is another. In comparing and contrasting these two moments, my aim has also been to arrive at a theory of language that can be applied sensitively to the reading of Romantic literary texts so as to highlight the interaction of speakers and contexts and yield a more precise analysis of the way language acts in and on the world. What speech-act theory contributes to this amalgam is a helpful vocabulary and a more fully developed awareness of the different kinds of action performed by verbal utterances. Having introduced terms such as performative, constative, illocution, and uptake, modern speech-act theory is useful for gathering together Romantic ideas about language as action and presenting them from a perspective that was not available to the Romantics themselves, but that reveals for us the path-breaking aspects of their thought. However, rather than assimilate Romantic philosophy of language to speech-act theory, I maintain that Romantic theory can provide a necessary critique of speech-act theory as it has been formulated by twentieth-century analytic philosophers. It does this because of its greater and, in the literal sense of the word, wonderful attention to the speaking subject as a subject-in-process.

The juxtaposition of twentieth-century and Romantic philosophies of language also highlights the modernity of the latter, showing that several "contemporary" perspectives begin to enter linguistic philosophy around 1800. These include *constructivism*, reflected (for instance) in Bentham's insistence on the "fictional" character of abstract nouns and social norms, and in the ambivalence of German thinkers over whether linguistic representation involves a reflection, or an actual construction, of external reality. *Dialogism* is absolutely central to Romantic philosophy of language, and constantly suggests correlations with more recent and better known dialogic theories from Bakhtin's multivocality to Levinas's ethical confrontation between self and Other. Most important, though, is the way Romantic-period philosophers typically conflate the cognitive and communicative functions of language. Knowledge of the world (cognition) occurs through dialogue with its objects (communication); conversely, interpersonal dialogue involves positioning oneself relative to other speakers by responding to the acts of cognition embodied in one another's speech acts. The products of these dialogic processes—that is, the self and the external world—are thus conceived of, not as given, but as *intersubjectively experienced* through a series of discursive interactions.

One corollary of the Romantic performative, then, would be an experiential sense of history, according to which the formation of subjectivity takes place through utterances and responses to utterances, generating a continual readjustment of the speaker's relation to other speakers, to objects, and to language itself. Different as it is from the materialist sense of history that has influenced Romantic studies powerfully in recent years, this definition of history may have something to contribute to new historicism, by helping it to think in terms of action rather than static representation. Alan Liu has recently examined how concepts of "literary action"—including research on the politics of language and on processes of publication and dissemination, and studies of politics as a regulated activity—have made their way from deconstruction into cultural criticism. The result, he claims, is "a mode that might be called a *new rhetorical historicism* . . . a method that views cultural discourse less as symbolic representation or figure than as performative act" (66). Learning to think in terms of action, activity, and active representation, rather than in terms of "the literary Subject contained within history-as-representation," Liu argues, is essential to new historicism and cultural criticism if they are to break through their self-imposed limits (62–63).

By the same token, the Romantic performative may shed new light on questions that are central to cultural critique. Issues such as the performativity of personal and social identity, the construction of political and literary authority, and the achievement or denial of the right to speak have a vital place in gender-based, cultural-studies, and post-colonial readings of Romantic texts. When performativity is invoked within such readings, it is normally done in terms of a poststructuralist, postmodern paradigm within which power is seen as circulating through verbal or semiotic discourses, such as the stereotypes attached to race and gender. This influential model of performativity derives primarily from the work of Judith Butler, whose notion of discourse involves adaptations of the Derridean concept of iterability and the Foucauldian circulation of power. Butler's analyses relocate agency, not just into language, but into the very iterability or repetition of the speech act. The notion of a "sovereign subject" who creates and takes responsibility for his or her utterances is merely a fantasy of our desire to attribute agency. Instead, in a version of fabulous retroactivity, the subject who cites a performative is, for Butler, "temporarily produced" as the "belated and fictive" origin of it (49).

While the iterated, power-generating performative offers one way to counteract the straitjacket of history-as-representation, it can itself be supplemented by the Romantic concept of speech as action, which is characterized by the inseparability of the political and the epistemological—where the ability of specific utterances to shape sociopolitical reality depends on the universal function of language in shaping cognitive reality. Starting from the Romantics' own notion of language as inherently pragmatic and dialogic, we may analyze how they represent the self and the world as products of linguistic processes. This approach generates a notion of history, and of performativity, that is intrinsic rather than extrinsic to Romantic texts. The project of this book, therefore, is to read the language of Romanticism as performative *and* to recognize among its achievements the historical founding of the discourse of performativity itself.

1

Of Promises, Contracts, and Constitutions: Speech-Act Philosophies and Practices in Britain, 1775–1800

Writers of the English Romantic period inhabited an environment marked by a new awareness of the bond between language and action. The extent of this awareness can only be appreciated when several discourses are brought together—at a minimum, those of moral, political, and legal philosophy. "What effect do words have on the world?" is a question as relevant to participants in the debate over revolution, constitutions, and censorship as it is to late-eighteenth-century moral philosophers—or, for that matter, to writers like Blake, Wollstonecraft, Godwin, Inchbald, and Coleridge. In contrast to Germany, therefore, where Kant and the Idealists constituted by far the most important influence on an emerging philosophy of speech acts, linguistic theory in Britain developed both within academic philosophy and in the sphere of public political debate. Changing ideas about the relationship between language and reality, in both these contexts, are the subject of several recent studies.[1] The purpose of this chapter is to bring together pragmatic elements of both linguistic and sociopolitical thought that form an important background to early Romantic literature.

The notion that language is not merely descriptive of reality, but that it affects, shapes, alters, or even creates reality, underlies several interrelated currents of theory and practice from the 1780s onward. The events

---

[1] The pragmatically oriented studies of Land and (especially) Nerlich and Clarke constitute a rewriting of the history of linguistic thought in Britain during the Romantic period, and may be contrasted with the strikingly different emphases of the classic studies by Funke and Aarsleff that first opened up this field. All these histories of philosophy and linguistics follow a different course from Olivia Smith, who demonstrates that knowledge or lack of knowledge of "educated" language was used to control access to political power, and that theories of language proliferated both among those who wanted to preserve that language barrier and those who sought to dismantle it.

of the French Revolution itself provide some of the most dramatic examples, and I will begin with a survey of these events and the way they relate to an emerging awareness of the performative. But scholarship on the French Revolution in connection with linguistic philosophy has been centered on (as well as in) France and Germany, and in order to analyze the pragmatics of language in Britain in the 1790s another tradition needs to be brought into play: the theory of contracts, promises, and constitutions that leads from Hobbes and Hume to late-eighteenth-century philosophers. Of the latter, I will concentrate in this chapter on Thomas Reid and Jeremy Bentham, each of whom developed an analysis of nonpropositional utterances that it is hard not to call a theory of illocutionary acts. Against the background of the pragmatic discourses of the French Revolution and the British preoccupation with issues of contract and obligation, I will conclude with an account of performativity as both a theoretical and a practical concern in Edmund Burke's and Thomas Paine's conflicting claims about constitutions.

THE FRENCH REVOLUTION AND LINGUISTIC ACTS

The events of the French Revolution offer some striking indications of the significance of the performative to the late-eighteenth-century context. When the revolutionaries undertook to create a new social order in 1790s France, they did so by giving new names to its citizens, places, dates, weights, measures, and institutions. By decree of the National Assembly, the titles of the nobility were abolished in 1790 and even *monsieur* was replaced by the universal *citoyen*; the Constitution of 1791 transformed Louis XVI from "the French king" to "the king of the French"; in the Republican calendar, the months and years received new names. New procedures governed the most important of officially sanctioned performative utterances: marriage ceremonies and divorce proceedings, wills and bequests, courtroom oaths. More aggressively, the revolutionaries engaged in a project of unifying the country by standardizing the French language, which involved suppressing dialects and local vernacular languages. Their campaign, virtually a form of linguistic terrorism, included proposals that it be made a punishable crime to utter words that threatened to cause controversy among the revolutionary forces—including "Jacobins," "moderates," or "alarmists," but also "Mountain," "Plain," or "Marsh," since these words had come to be associated with political factions (Ozouf 170).

What is significant is not just that these large-scale exhibitions of the potency of language took place, but that they led to reflection on the nature of language and the effects of utterance, both at the time of the revolution itself and in our own day. Especially during the wave of revisionist scholarship that accompanied and followed the bicentennial of the French Revolution, historians and critics concentrated more and more on issues of language and signification, analyzing the discourses that shaped or even caused the revolution as well as the discourses by which it entered into historical consciousness. Two prime examples are the revisionist histories of the revolution produced by François Furet and Mona Ozouf in the late 1970s. Furet's influential *Interpreting the French Revolution* (1978; English 1981) challenged traditional Marxist historiography by examining the competing and fragmented cultural discourses of the revolutionary period alongside the consolidating narratives of nineteenth-century historians. In 1789, according to Furet, "language was substituted for power" (48). "The Revolution replaced the conflict of interests for power with a competition of discourses for the appropriation of legitimacy," he continues (49), shifting emphasis from the events themselves as manifestations of class conflict to the strategies of representation and interpretation employed during the revolution as well as by later historians.[2]

Mona Ozouf's *Festivals and the French Revolution* (1976; English 1988) casts the revolution as a cultural and semiotic event by interpreting it through its festivals, staged public occasions that center on verbal acts. Not only did the festivals of 1789 to 1799 constitute performances in which speeches, declarations, invocations, and scripted banners played a major role, but many of them featured explicit, public performatives such as the swearing of an oath. Ozouf documents the dramatic effect oath-taking had on some participants, causing them to evade the ceremony if possible, to inhibit the performative power of the utterance by altering its words, or to faint or succumb to temporary paralysis (178, 193). Approaching a linguistic-philosophical analysis of the phenomenon, she theorizes that these reluctant oath-takers intuited the overwhelming illocutionary force of the oath and its controversial aim: to confer irreversibility on contemporary acts by projecting the revolution

---

[2]For the adoption and consolidation of this viewpoint among British literary scholars, see the report of the University of East Anglia English Studies Group at a conference commemorating 1789: "the French Revolution marks a convenient point from which to study a new formation of discourse and power, in the sense that it confronted society directly with an immense work of representation, and substantial parts of this work devolved on the intellectual, the spokesman and the apologist. The society emerging from the Revolution was prepared to yield part of its political power to those who were able to represent the world in discourses which both defined and opened up the channels of power" (Barker et al. 85).

"into the eternity of discourse"; to "den[y] . . . time, in its corrupting dimension"; to "perpetuate an unfruitful present" (168, 178). The oath of the revolutionary festivals—which was sworn, moreover, on another verbal construct, the constitution—is one example of the rapid ascendancy, the complex interrelation, and the widespread awareness of explicit performative utterances in 1790s France. In the wake of new sociological theories, especially those of Jürgen Habermas, on the late-eighteenth-century transformation of the public sphere, research has focused on a wide range of other speech acts in which the revolution was represented and enacted, from theater and song to new print media that brought about something like mass communication.

Most recently, collaboration between historians and linguists in Germany and France has produced extensive work on the way a *theory* as well as a practice of linguistic pragmatics developed at the time of the French Revolution. At the center of this scholarly enterprise are Brigitte Schlieben-Lange, a linguistic historian specializing in pragmatic approaches, and Jacques Guilhaumou, a social historian influenced by discourse analysis. In her 1981 overview of the state of scholarship on the French Revolution and language, Schlieben-Lange summarizes transformations in both the use and the study of language that took place during the revolutionary years. These include changes in the vocabulary and phonetics of the French language, which in turn generated new dictionaries, lexica, and studies of neologisms and linguistic change. Politically, the revolution marks the first major instance of state interference in the development of a language, as the National Assembly sought control over the different languages and dialects spoken in France. This state involvement extended to a new institutionalization of linguistic theory and research; institutes and clubs were formed and journals grounded for the purpose of discussing linguistic questions. As language and the uses of language changed, so did the study of literacy, education, and linguistics. Schlieben-Lange stresses, above all, the way revolutionary events turned the linguistic theory of the Enlightenment in a political and pragmatic direction. She proposes that speech-act theory might help analyze this development, and that the theory might itself benefit from engagement with this particularly fruitful historical example:

> some of the grave innovations concern not so much language as speech—that is, the level of verbal actions and of the complex patterns of verbal action in texts. . . . After all, speech-act theory has until now, because of its provenance in the philosophy of language, proceeded largely in a universalizing manner, so that a historicizing of it in the case of such an interesting object would also be extremely productive for the further

development of speech-act theory. ("Französische Revolution und die Sprache" 107)

A few years after Schlieben-Lange's call for linguistic-pragmatic studies of the French Revolution, the challenge was met by Jacques Guilhaumou's *La langue politique et la Révolution Française* (French 1988; German 1989). Guilhaumou succeeds in re-enlivening Marxist and sociocultural analysis of the revolution through a study of its oral and written texts and their conditions of production. His sources range from speeches, declarations, broadsheets, popular satires, and scholarly texts on language and grammar to specialized genres spawned by revolutionary events, such as the *Cahiers de doléances*[3] that gave official expression to regional grievances, or the autobiographies produced by political prisoners during the 1790s in order to justify their actions. These texts show language being put to new uses, as well as a new awareness of the uses to which it can be put. Guilhaumou argues that the concept of a "political language" may be traced to 1789 (20), but the events, publications, and public utterances of the succeeding years document a process of working out what this concept means. They allow us to watch the evolution of "a particular historical formation of the subject of enunciation" (22), during which the new concept of "citizen" comes to be defined as one whose right to speak is equal to that of others in society. Most importantly, the revolution is a process of inventing a "language of freedom" that will be the experiential version of the "proclaimed natural rights" actualized in the constitution. On the basis that "at the time of the French Revolution the speech act stands at the center of the discourse of public assembly" (173), Guilhaumou develops the concept of the revolution as a particular "speech economy" that embraces new assumptions and practices: "As a preliminary approximation, the speech economy may be defined as the totality of speech acts that, on the one hand, are continually determined by the behavior of the people, and, on the other hand, correspond to the proclaimed natural rights" (150).

Guilhaumou's history of the revolution, together with Schlieben-Lange's history of linguistic pragmatics, consolidate the idea that the speech acts of the revolutionary age are essential to understanding its ideology and its heritage. At the same time, they show that the revolutionary years marked a new *philosophical* preoccupation with the context and force of verbal utterances. The onomastic reform of the revolu-

---

[3]A subcategory of linguistic scholarship on the French Revolution specifically engages in speech-act analysis of the *Cahiers de doléances*; see Slakta and Zimmermann.

tionaries gave practical expression to the belief of eighteenth-century *idéologues*, beginning with Condillac, that language is not just the expression of thought, but that thought depends on language (and thus on names, titles, and verbal formulas). By 1796–97, France's Institut National publicized a topic for its annual essay competition—"Déterminer l'influence des signes sur la formation des idées"—which *assumed* that signs influence the formation of ideas, and was framed so as to elicit scientific confirmation of this belief. The campaign to suppress dialects and unify the French language also drew heavily on a philosophical tenet—namely, the idea that the language of a people shapes its worldview, so that speakers of different languages actually experience the world differently. This thesis, too, gained greater impetus after the revolution and is now most famously associated with Humboldt and other German thinkers of the early nineteenth century as the idea of linguistic relativity or the *Weltbild der Sprache*.[4]

This research on the linguistic events of the French Revolution has not yet crossed into English scholarship or literary theory, despite a large number of new-historicist studies concerning the impact of the revolution on ideology, nationalist consciousness, radical movements, and individual writers of the English Romantic age. Most scholarship dealing with the revolution's influence on language in England is of an older school, oriented toward the rhetoric and style of political prose; connections between the French Revolution and British philosophy of language remain largely unexplored.[5] Yet a similar interweaving of philosophy and political practice obtains in Britain. The most famous English linguist of the age, John Horne Tooke, was even more famous for his radical political activities. During his 1777 trial for sedition, he successfully defended himself by making a linguistic argument about the interpretation of the word "that" in the phrase, "She knowing that Crooke had been indicted for forgery...."[6] The incident, a media sensa-

---

[4]Christmann traces the *Weltbild* theory of the German Romantics back to the Enlightenment and through its political uses during the French Revolution, then into German thought by way of a little-known treatise by Carl August Göriz.

[5]On the rhetoric of political prose, see Boulton. For more recent English-language studies of the speech acts of the French Revolution, see Petrey's Austinian analysis of revolutionary events (17–51) and Blakemore's work on Burke and other writers of the revolutionary age. To varying degrees, Blakemore finds, British journalists and philosophers became aware that the revolution debate was a battle over language, meaning, and representation; he identifies a "special linguistic self-consciousness" that shaped contemporary views of the revolution and rendered it, even at the time, "an astonishing linguistic event" ("Revolution in Language" 4).

[6]Like performatives in general, a dictum introduced by "that" cannot be classified as true or false; thus, the given statement does not affirm anything about Crooke's

tion in late-eighteenth-century England, provides a dramatic counterpoint to Tooke's later publication of his etymological and materialist linguistics—a theory of language based on his profound belief that words alter people's opinions and behavior. Many British texts of the 1790s reveal an awareness of speech and its effects that can be located within a long tradition of political philosophy, but is intensified by the urgent political situation. To take one example, the legal definition of public utterance as an actionable crime, through the King's Proclamation against Seditious Writings in May 1792 and the Two Acts in December 1795, testifies that oral and written utterance is increasingly regarded as action in the world. These pieces of legislation, in turn, generate further debate over their mode of operation as sociopolitical speech acts, the authority and the context that validate them, and the assumptions about speech and publication that underlie them. In England during the 1790s, censorship laws, tractate literature, and political debate all reflect—and promote—a new awareness, fed by the events of the French Revolution, of what utterance accomplishes and what it might accomplish.

THE BRITISH BACKGROUND: HOBBES, HUME, AND THE SOCIAL CONTRACT

British philosophy of language in the late 1700s was also developing within a context of moral and political philosophy that had been given its direction during the previous century. While Locke is credited with a crucial development in the history of linguistics for his theory that words are signs for ideas, not things, Thomas Hobbes also developed an extensive, anthropologically oriented philosophy of language that considers the impact of passions, power, and context on the meaning and use of verbal expressions.[7] More important still, for the history of speech-act theory, is Hobbes's incorporation of a central speech act into his theory of government and society. In *Leviathan* (1651), he claims that society is founded on a universal covenant by which people give up their power to a sovereign:

---

indictment for forgery, but only about the speaker's belief. The interpretation of "that" is a recurrent topic in twentieth-century philosophy of language; similar examples come up in philosophers like Wittgenstein and Benveniste as they illustrate that we do not necessarily use language to describe the world, but rather to situate ourselves within a discourse or play various language games.

[7] For a recent study of pragmatic elements in Hobbes's philosophy of language, see Isermann, especially Chapters 6 and 7.

> This is more than Consent, or Concord; it is a reall Unitie of them all, in one and the same Person, made by Covenant of every man with every man, in such manner, as if every man should say to every man, *I Authorise and give up my Right of Governing my selfe, to this Man, or to this Assembly of men, on this condition, that thou give up thy Right to him, and Authorise all his Actions in like manner.* (120)

This covenant, which constitutes the basis for all other sociopolitical speech acts, is itself an echo of divine *fiat*: "the *Pacts* and *Covenants*, by which the parts of this Body Politique were at first made, set together, and united, resemble that *Fiat*, or the *Let us make man*, pronounced by God in the Creation" (9–10). Hobbes's theory of a mutual, founding promise sets the act of promising at the center of British thought about language and its relation to mind and society. Even writers who are not centrally concerned with language, like Shaftesbury or Hume, pick up the discussion of a universal or social contract, and it is no accident that when a full-fledged speech-act theory was developed in the twentieth century, by Oxford philosophers working within the tradition of British moral philosophy, the promise became its central paradigm.

In his *Treatise of Human Nature* (1739–40), David Hume disagrees with Hobbes's attempt to link political behavior, such as the subject's obedience to the sovereign's commands, to an original covenant or promise. The duty of allegiance, Hume maintains, might "be at first grafted on the obligation of promises" when a government is originally established, but in general, allegiance "has an original obligation and authority, independent of all contracts" (542). Hume's contention that the promise is a separate, private matter, distinct from the public issue of allegiance, leads him to a separate analysis of promises in book 3, section 5 of the *Treatise*, a chapter that inspired much late-eighteenth-century discussion of verbal acts. Either through sympathy with Hume's argument, or through disagreement with it, philosophers were motivated to find new ways of discussing the promise, and often other speech acts along with it.

Hume sets out to show that "the rule of morality, which enjoins the performance of promises, is not *natural*"; rather, "promises are human inventions, founded on the necessities and interests of society" (516, 519). In proving this claim, he does not yet treat the promise as a performative utterance, but instead seeks the "act of the mind" expressed by the "certain form of words" that we call a promise. "We cannot readily conceive," he admits, "how the making use of a certain form of words shou'd be able to cause any material difference" (523). Despite these anti-performative assumptions, Hume's conclusion that the promise is

Of Promises, Contracts, and Constitutions 31

not actually identifiable with an act of the mind—and therefore is "not *natural*"—leads him to admit that the spoken words themselves are, in fact, the "principal part of the promise" (523). He continues with a series of observations about the conditions that validate or invalidate promises as utterances people address to one another. These observations are worth quoting at length, because they show up throughout later theories of speech acts, including, especially, Austin's:

> 'Tis evident, that the will alone is never suppos'd to cause the obligation, but must be express'd by words or signs, in order to impose a tye upon any man. The expression being once brought in as subservient to the will, soon becomes the principal part of the promise; nor will a man be less bound by his word, tho' he secretly give a different direction to his intention, and with-hold himself both from a resolution, and from willing an obligation [1]. But tho' the expression makes on most occasions the whole of the promise, yet it does not always so; and one, who shou'd make use of any expression, of which he knows not the meaning, and which he uses without any intention of binding himself, wou'd not certainly be bound by it [2]. Nay, tho' he knows its meaning, yet if he uses it in jest only, and with such signs as shew evidently he has no serious intention of binding himself, he wou'd not lie under any obligation of performance [3]. . . . All these contradictions are easily accounted for, if the obligation of promises be merely a human invention for the convenience of society; but will never be explain'd, if it be something *real* and *natural*, arising from any action of the mind or body. (523-24)

These insights echo uncannily as Austin begins to list the main characteristics of what he calls performative utterances:

> [1] since performatives do not express "fictitious inward acts," the utterance "I promise that . . ." confers an obligation even if the person uttering it does not have the appropriate intention (Austin 9-11);
>
> [2] if a speaker uses an expression without knowledge of its meaning, and thus unintentionally or accidentally, the performative will be "void," because "extenuating circumstances" of this kind render any act unsatisfactory (Austin 21);
>
> [3] speaking in jest, or otherwise non-seriously, also renders an utterance "hollow and void" (Austin 9, 21-22).

If these observations reappear in Austin, who does not make any reference to Hume in *How to Do Things with Words*,[8] they also reappear in

---

[8]Nerlich notes the significant intermediary role of Austin's colleague, the Oxford philosopher Harold A. Prichard, who published on Hume, promises, and obligation during the 1940s. According to Nerlich, the impetus for *How to Do Things with Words* came from Austin's correspondence with Prichard about the nature of promising ("The 1930s—at the Birth of a Pragmatic Conception of Language" 325; "Einführ-

the work of earlier philosophers who *are* specifically responding to Hume's account of promises. Hume opens the debate over original covenants and social contracts to more specific considerations of the actions performed by certain forms of words.

As a focal point for the more general issue of nature versus culture, the question of an original contract has a central place in eighteenth-century moral philosophy. Philosophers lined up on either side of the issue that Hume addresses so forcefully: whether humans have a natural inclination toward responsibility, duty, and mutual co-operation, and are therefore meant to take their cue from "natural law" and "natural right," or whether they are naturally motivated only by necessity and self-interest, and can only escape from the state of nature with the help of artificial agreements. Within the nature-culture debate, the origin and role of language becomes a more specific point of controversy, as philosophers, especially in Enlightenment France, argue over whether the origins of language lie in the state of nature or mark the beginning of civilization.

The issues of language and original contract coalesce into theories of utterance as social action in the work of two late-eighteenth-century philosophers: Reid and Bentham. As is evident in Bentham's work, from the 1770s onward events in America and France caused the traditional debate over *contracts* to evolve into a debate over *constitutions*. But Reid's and Bentham's pragmatic ideas about language, and the constitution controversy of the 1790s, have a shared background in seventeenth- and eighteenth-century debates over the social contract. The influence of this background may still be discerned in Anglo-American speech-act theory, with its recurring focus on the promise as the paradigmatic performative. As a limited monarchy, the political structure in Britain depends on an agreement between sovereign and people that manifests itself, over the centuries, in various public performatives: in Magna Carta and the 1689 Declaration of Rights, in oaths of allegiance and investiture, and more ambiguously in the "unwritten" or common law. These verbal acts and the conditions that validate them cannot but become the focus of theoretical reflection. By what authority can laws and declarations be passed, and by what authority can they be altered? Are oaths binding on only those individuals who make them, or on their descendants too? Must laws and constitutions be written down, and who must sign them? These questions, equally relevant to late-eighteenth-

---

ung in die Geschichte der Pragmatik" 415; Nerlich and Clarke, *Language, Action, and Context* 99–100).

century philosophical and political thought and twentieth-century speech-act theory, may in fact constitute the historical link between the two.

THOMAS REID: ILLOCUTIONARY ACTS IN
THE EIGHTEENTH CENTURY

Reid, the leading philosopher of the Scottish "Common Sense" school, advanced a theory of utterance as social action during the later eighteenth century. Reid's primary concern is the action of the mind as it apprehends the world, but his philosophy of mind intersects with philosophy of language in several ways. Throughout his career, and increasingly in his later work, Reid derives his conclusions about the way the mind works from an examination of the way language works: "Language being the express image of human thought, the analysis of the one must correspond to that of the other.... The philosophy of grammar, and that of the human understanding, are more nearly allied than is commonly imagined" (2: 691–92; cf. 1: 233). This is entirely in line with the principles of eighteenth-century universal grammar. Yet Reid stresses the particular importance of *everyday* language, appealing constantly to the conclusions that common sense must draw based on ordinary linguistic usage, for "the authority of common use... in matters of language, is great" (2: 676). His starting point is the same as that of Austin and Searle, who take their impetus from the ordinary-language movement in analytic philosophy—a movement that, in fact, likely derives from the reception of Reid at Cambridge and Oxford during the early twentieth century (Nerlich and Clarke, *Language, Action, and Context* 105–6).

Like speech-act theorists, Reid believes that the whole range of uses of language deserves to be studied, not just the one type of sentence to which philosophy has always devoted its attention: the true-false proposition. This prejudice dates from Aristotle, who noted the existence of non-propositional utterances such as requests and prayers—but only in order to relegate them to rhetoric or poetics, and designate the truth-bearing statement as the focus of serious philosophical inquiry. In his *Account of Aristotle's Logic* (1774), Reid moves to recover these banished, non-propositional forms:

> He [Aristotle] observes justly, that, besides that kind of speech called a *proposition*, which is always either true or false, there are other kinds which are neither true nor false, such as a prayer or wish; to which we may add, a question, a command, a promise, a contract, and many others. These Aristotle pronounces to have nothing to do with his subject,

and remits them to oratory or poetry; and so they have remained banished from the regions of philosophy to this day; yet I apprehend that an analysis of such speeches, and of the operations of mind which they express, would be of real use, and perhaps would discover how imperfect an enumeration the logicians have given of the powers of human understanding, when they reduce them to Simple Apprehension, Judgment, and Reasoning. (2: 692)

This observation, versions of which can be found throughout Reid's work, establishes a clear connection between his interests and those of Austin and Searle, and historians of linguistics and philosophy are increasingly coming to regard Reid as a forerunner of speech-act theory.[9] What has not been noted, though, is that Reid's attention to "banished," marginal, or parasitic forms, in order to expose the "imperfect" state of mainstream philosophy, is a deconstructive move that links up with other deconstructionist tendencies in his philosophy of language. Reid's work reveals the range of perspectives on language that was available within late-eighteenth-century philosophy, embracing not only an awareness of performativity but even the deconstructionist critique of the performative.

Having identified a range of illocutionary acts, Reid establishes the basis for an analysis of them in his *Essays on the Intellectual Powers of Man* (1785) by proposing a distinction between "solitary operations" of the mind (such as judging, reasoning, willing, or desiring) and "social operations" of language (such as asking, promising, commanding, contracting, or plighting faith). In *Essays on the Active Powers of the Human Mind* (1788), he renames the categories "solitary acts" and "social acts." These divisions coincide fairly well with what we now know as constative and performative, although within Reid's eighteenth-century context they correspond to the traditional distinction between the powers of understanding and the powers of will, or the contemplative and active faculties, respectively. The most innovative aspect of Reid's theory is his characterization of social acts, which anticipates both the pragmatic turn in Romantic linguistics and, more distantly, speech-act theory.

---

[9] See Nerlich and Clarke, who devote the largest part of their chapter on "Protopragmatics in England" to Reid (*Language, Action, and Context* 103–11), and Land, who ends his *Philosophy of Language in Britain* with a comparison of Reid's "social acts" to Austin's illocutionary acts. Schuhmann and Smith provide a concise discussion of the major points on which Reid anticipates speech-act theory and an evaluation of how the history of pragmatics should be amended in light of Reid's ideas and those of the early twentieth-century legal philosopher Adolf Reinach, whom the authors consider the first thinker to have proposed a full-fledged theory of speech acts.

Social acts are inherently interpersonal: "in the social operations, the expression is essential. They cannot exist without being expressed by words or signs, and known to the other party" (2: 664). To put it in modern terms, the act is identical with the utterance. This means that social acts are not simply the spoken versions of solitary acts, but basic ethical actions in their own right. A command, for instance, is not simply an expression of a desire; rather, "a command is a social act of the mind. It can have no existence but by a communication of thought to some intelligent being; and therefore implies a belief that there is such a being, and that we can communicate our thoughts to him" (2: 532). Reid anticipates Austin's denial, at the beginning of *How to Do Things with Words*, that there is a "real" internal act going on "behind" the performative utterance. He stresses that the command encompasses the entire mental act of recognizing one's position in a social context, recognizing the presence and the capacities of an interlocutor, and intending, within these circumstances, to make an utterance that will count as a distinct social operation, separate from any cognitive act of wishing, judging, or intending.

Social acts, as described by Reid, are inherently *contextual* in that they are determined by the circumstances in which they are uttered: the presence of another person; my evaluation of the relationship between myself and that person, and of our respective potential for future action; my common-sense familiarity with social acts as they are habitually performed. In the first of his *Essays on the Active Powers*, Reid uses the very existence of social acts as proof that the human mind possesses "active powers"—that is, that there is such a thing as free will, and that, contrary to idealist and empiricist claims, the mind can make contact with real objects, not merely with ideas or impressions of objects. Since everyday verbal interactions can only work if people possess active powers (such as "will"), and since these interactions clearly *do* work, both speakers and addressees must in fact possess free will: "our exertions, our deliberations, our purposes, our promises, are only in things that depend upon our will. Our advices, exhortations, and commands, are only in things that depend upon the will of those to whom they are addressed" (2: 619). Given the extent of Reid's response to Hume (of which more below), it is not surprising that his most extended illustration of this principle concerns the familiar example of promises:

> If a man promises to pay me a sum of money to-morrow, without believing that it will then be in his power, he is not an honest man; and, if I did not believe that it will then be in his power, I should have no dependence on his promise. . . . No man can be certain of the continuance of any of

> his powers of body or mind for a moment; and, therefore, in every promise, there is a condition understood—to wit, if we live, if we retain that health of body and soundness of mind which is necessary to the performance, and if nothing happen, in the providence of God, which puts it out of our power. The rudest savages are taught by nature to admit these conditions in all promises, whether they be expressed or not; and no man is charged with breach of promise, when he fails through the failure of these conditions. (2: 517)

The universal practice of making promises assumes common-sense knowledge of the world and the possibility of action in it, by ourselves and by others. Reid goes on to argue that it also implies free will: under a system of necessity, promising would not work, and one might as well promise on behalf of someone else as on one's own behalf.

But Reid's argument about promises changes direction part-way through—and thereby takes on a certain similarity to the deconstructionist critique of the performative. He begins with the idea that since social acts (e.g., promises to pay money) are in common use, and since they depend on our common assumption that certain things (e.g., paying money) are within our power, therefore we must in fact possess the powers we assume. But then he reverses the logical order of assumption and utterance, and calls the assumption itself into question. "Therefore, in every promise, there is a condition understood": promises now seem to *depend on* (rather than testify to) a universal, but precarious, assumption that what is currently within our power will continue to be so. Every promise or other social act, by this argument, becomes conditional, for it is founded on a positing of the conditions that we take to be essential for its successful performance. If the potential for failure or incapacity is "understood" in Reid's promise, the "possibility of the negative" becomes, in effect, a "structural possibility"—just as it does in Derrida's deconstructionist model of the performative (*Limited Inc* 15).

De Man's version of a similar deconstruction emerges from his reading of Rousseau's *Social Contract*, where he maintains that the illocution contained in Rousseau's text—a promise—depends on a prolepsis by which the present is projected into the future: "Considered performatively, the speech act of the contractual text never refers to a situation that exists in the present, but signals toward a hypothetical future" (*Allegories of Reading* 273). This "hypothetical future" is what Reid brings into the promise when he makes explicit its assumptions about the time of fulfilment: "*if* we live," *if* divine providence does not intervene to make fulfilment impossible. The corollary, according to de Man, is that neither promises, nor other speech acts that imply temporal and causal prolepsis, could be made without assuming a "transcendental principle of signification" (*Allegories of Reading* 276)—an omniscient principle that could guarantee that the present promise will in fact correspond to a future state of affairs. De Man identifies this guarantor of meaning, which enters tacitly and therefore illicitly into Rousseau's *Social Contract*, as God. Reid's assumption of a transcendent guarantor for social acts, on the other hand, is quite explicit. As he puts it elsewhere in *Essays on the Active Powers*, "There is a condition implied in every promise, *if we live* and *if God continue with us the power which he hath given us*" (2: 617). Reid's approach resembles a "common-sense deconstruction" of the language of contracts, which acknowledges the role of language in constructing social relationships, but also recognizes that temporality and experience impose on language an ever-present possibility of failure.

Reid's account of the intersubjective nature of social acts spans the range of ideas from eighteenth-century moral philosophy to Austin's concept of uptake—and beyond, to touch on a Derridean notion of the iterability of performatives. As their name suggests, social acts "necessarily imply social intercourse with some other intelligent being who bears a part in them" (2: 664). Not only must a social act be "expressed by words or signs," not only must it be "known to the other party," but it must be *understood*: it belongs to the nature of a contract that both sides understand it (2: 667), and a legal text can only have meaning if it applies to an accountable being who "*understand[s] the law to which he is bound, and his obligation to obey it*" (2: 620). Reid bases his belief that people are capable of morally responsible uptake on faith in human nature. In contrast to Hume, he maintains that humans are naturally able to understand the concept of obligation because they are naturally oriented toward responsibility, fidelity, and honor. Yet Reid's common-sense argumentation and the examples he provides also imply that social acts work because of convention and iteration, or at least because of repeated experience. We recognize and respond to promises or laws because we know they are used all the time, and we have a common-sense understanding of how they operate.

Reid's comments on the social act of "testimony," which he wants to distinguish from the solitary act of "judgment" (i.e., cognition), provide the most interesting example of the role of experience. Testimony is, first of all, identifiable as a social act because it can only exist as utterance: "it is essential to it to be expressed by words or signs" (1: 413). Yet an act of testimony tends to look the same as the verbal expression of a solitary act of judgment. Both normally take the form of a propositional sentence—such as, perhaps, "I saw him; it was a large man dressed in red, with white hair and a beard." We are accustomed to distinguishing testimony from judgment, however, on the basis of context and common sense, for we recognize that testimony conventionally occurs in a courtroom between a witness and a judge. What identifies an utterance as testimony is context and convention; in modern terms, we might say that the act of testifying is *iterable*, deriving its authority from being repeated in a recognizable institutional context. Reid also acknowledges that exactly the same words might be uttered in a different context (say, between two friends who meet in the street), in which case they would not count as testimony, but probably as the expression of a solitary act of mental judgment. We recognize a sentence as an act of testimony, then, because of its pragmatic similarity to other utterances repeated in a courtroom, as well as by its difference from utterances that sound identical, but count as different acts because they occur in different situations.

Most interestingly of all, Reid goes on to imply that the social acts that take place in the conventional context of a courtroom are prior to the corresponding solitary acts. He speculates that the very term "judgment," used of a mental act, is borrowed from the courtroom situation: "As a judge, after taking the proper evidence, passes sentence in a cause, and that sentence is called his judgment, so the mind, with regard to whatever is true or false, passes sentence, or determines according to the evidence that appears" (1: 413). The speculation that mental acts (or at least their names) derive from institutional, public acts is radical for an eighteenth-century moral philosopher, but it is supported by Reid's conviction that the *primary* use of language is communication and the construction of interpersonal relationships. Linking his philosophy of mind to universal grammar, Reid observes that major elements of the linguistic system—second-person verbs and pronouns, for instance, and the vocative case—exist entirely for the sake of social acts (1: 245). He argues that the presence of these elements in all languages shows that the "primary and direct intention of language" is to perform social operations. Its use in solitary operations of the mind (e.g., helping us get "a firmer hold" on our thoughts) is secondary and unessential. The social act attains a certain priority over the solitary act—just as performatives do over constatives at the end of *How to Do Things with Words*, where Austin suggests that the latter may be just a special case of the former (145–47).

Modern as Reid's philosophy of language often seems, all his arguments are framed within an eighteenth-century context: their points of reference are universal grammar, the Aristotelian and Cartesian traditions, the empiricism of Hume and the idealism of Berkeley. His most fully developed and most "modern" analysis of the speech act occurs, in fact, in the context of an argument specifically directed against Hume's analysis of promises. Reid refutes Hume's claim that obligation (like other moral virtues) is conventional rather than natural by arguing that Hume confuses the intention to *enter into* a contract or promise with the intention to *perform* that which is promised. Hume maintains that, prior to the establishment of societal conventions, a promise or contract would neither be intelligible nor confer an obligation to perform that which is promised. But Reid answers that it is impossible that anyone could enter into a contract without the intention to contract and thus to take on obligation. In other words, the idea of a pre-conventional but non-functioning "contract," which Hume invents only in order to refute it, is a red herring; entering into a contract *is* expressing an intention to assume an obligation. However, it is perfectly possible that people either in a state of nature, or in society, may enter into a contract without any intention of doing that which they promise to do:

> But it ought to be observed, that the will, which is essential to a contract, is only a will to engage, or to become bound. We must beware of confounding this will with a will to perform what we have engaged. . . . But the intention to perform the promise, or not to perform it, whether the intention be known to the other party or not, makes no part of the promise—it is a solitary act of the mind, and can neither constitute nor dissolve an obligation. What makes a promise is, that it be expressed to the other party with understanding, and with an intention to become bound, and that it be accepted by him. . . . And as there can be no promise without knowledge and will to engage, is it marvellous that words which are not understood, or words spoken in jest, and without any intention to become bound, should not have the effect of a promise? (2: 667–70)

It is debatable whether, by defining the contract as a social act and thus as an act that *necessarily* involves understanding and the taking on of obligation, Reid has satisfactorily refuted Hume's argument. Yet his account does address exactly the issue that has raised ongoing problems with Austin's and Searle's speech-act theory: the role of intentionality and sincerity in defining the existence and the felicity of a promise. More clearly than modern theorists, Reid distinguishes the "will to engage" from the "will to perform what we have engaged." The intention to promise, along with the understanding of the promise on the part of the addressee, is an essential condition of the social act of promising; the intention to fulfil the promise is a solitary mental act, and therefore separate and unessential. Here again, in defining the essential conditions of a promise, Reid includes the possibility of failure. Either the hearer (if there is lack of understanding), or the speaker (in the case of a jest), may fail to recognize that an act of promising is taking place, in which case the act is void.

Rooted in eighteenth-century moral philosophy, the work of Reid demonstrates that ideas about speech as social action form a vital part of the philosophical response to British empiricism. Reid's unwillingness to believe that the mind's relation to reality is as counter-intuitive and problematic as either Hume or Berkeley suggests leads him to call on the authority of common sense and ordinary language. Consequently, language is important to him because of the ways it is habitually used, especially in interpersonal contexts where it mirrors our assumptions about ourselves and one another as moral agents. Because Reid is convinced that the primary purpose of language is communication, he finds a theory of social acts necessary in order to account for the very existence of language. Solitary mental acts alone do not require it, and Reid claims that language would never have developed if humans lived in isolation. This idea stands in striking contrast to Herder's almost contemporaneous assertion, in his essay on the origin of language, that language is so thoroughly dialogic that even solitary human beings would have had to develop it in order to interact cognitively with their surroundings. A revealing contrast between the British and German traditions emerges. For the Germans (including Herder, Humboldt, and Bernhardi), language is essentially dialogic because cognition is essentially dialogic. For Reid, language is essentially dialogic—but precisely this distinguishes it from cognition and renders it essential to the existence of human beings as social creatures. To some extent, the difference corresponds to a distinction between the performative as phenomenological act (theorized mainly by the Germans, as a response to transcendental philosophy) and the performative as sociopolitical act (theorized mainly by the British, as a response to the empiricist tradition combined with the impact of the French Revolution). Both roads lead to the pragmatic linguistics characteristic of the Romantic period.

The lack of a fully developed speech-act theory in Reid's writings is counterbalanced by the fact that his ideas about social acts are expressed consistently and repeatedly in different parts of his oeuvre. Reid's *Essays* of the 1780s summarize the concepts he developed and discussed over the course of his long career. These are ideas to which a large community of philosophers and students were exposed through Reid's role as a public intellectual in Aberdeen and Glasgow throughout the second half of the eighteenth century. In the dedication printed in *Essays on the Intellectual Powers of Man,* Reid confirms that he has been lecturing on the ideas presented in the volume for well over twenty years.

This dedication is addressed to two younger philosophers who studied with Reid at Glasgow, one of whom, Dugald Stewart, sustained the speech-act tendency of Reid's work during the Romantic period. Although he does not seem to have picked up Reid's theory of social acts, the influential Stewart embraced the argument that the meaning of verbal expressions is not abstract and objective, but intersubjective and context-dependent. Like Reid, he insisted that the study of language—including non-propositional uses of language—should form a standard part of logic and philosophy. The handbook Stewart published in 1793 for the use of his students at the University of Edinburgh, which contains the kernel of his later and longer works, puts the case for a philosophy of language succinctly: "As it is by language alone, that we are rendered capable of general reasoning, one of the most valuable branches of logic is that which relates to the use of words. Too little attention has hitherto been bestowed on this subject" (41).

JEREMY BENTHAM: LAWS, OATHS, AND FICTIONS

If logicians failed to bestow enough attention on the use of words, a contemporary legal philosopher helped remedy the situation. Between 1775 and 1830, Bentham published numerous works that develop at greater length and in greater detail than Reid a theory of what people do with words, especially in the public sphere of the law. His manuscripts include long essays on logic, language, and universal grammar, which resemble the work of contemporaries like Reid in emphasizing the use of language in interpersonal relations. Bentham's "Essay on Language," for instance, repeats Reid's hierarchical distinction between the "social" use of language, which is primary, and its "solitary" use, which is secondary (*Works* 8: 301). The same essay discusses at length the properties that language should possess in order to fulfill its communicative function—properties like "clearness," "correctness," "completeness," "non-redundance," and so on, that strongly resemble the "conversational maxims" H. Paul Grice would later introduce as the basis for his version of speech-act theory. But in his legal and philosophical writings, Bentham goes further than modern speech-act philosophers in exploring the grave importance of these linguistic issues to the principles on which society is founded: constitutions, common and positive law, punishment, oaths, and testimony. Writing in 1931, at the centenary of Bentham's death, the philosopher C. K. Ogden identified Bentham's theory of language as the aspect of his work that is most neglected, yet most merits attention (Bentham, *Theory of Legislation* xi). Well over half a century later, his philosophy of language has still not been much studied. Bentham remains known to Romanticists mainly as the standard-bearer of utilitarianism, even though he also developed the most important theory of his time about the way language shapes reality.

Despite their training in different disciplines, Bentham and Reid share the same starting points for a theory of language: a critique of Aristotle and a response to Hume. Bentham traces deficiencies in the understanding of both logic and jurisprudence to Aristotle, alluding to the passage in *De Interpretatione* (17a: 1–7) in which Aristotle identifies a range of speech acts but then dismisses all except the statement-making sentence from present consideration. Like Reid, Bentham regrets that virtually all Western philosophers have followed Aristotle's lead in ignoring what Bentham calls "sentences of volition," which include illocutionary acts such as commanding and interrogating. Had Aristotle and others taken this branch of logic more seriously, the science of jurisprudence might be much further ahead than it is (*Introduction* 299n–300n). While Bentham's response to Aristotle thus leads him in a similar direction to Reid, and both simultaneously develop theories of non-propositional utterances, Bentham's philosophy of language is also shaped by his utilitarian ideas, which were inspired by a sympathetic reading of Hume. Bentham relates in his influential 1775 text *A Fragment on Government* how the reading of Hume convinced him to abandon faith in the notion of an original contract and to base his ideas about governance on the principle of utility. Accordingly, Bentham's major works on jurisprudence—most explicitly, the *Introduction to the Principles of Morals and Legislation* (1780)—are founded on the idea that pleasure and pain are the sole realities motivating human behavior, and the proper basis for systems of governance and legislation. It may seem that this founding principle would lead Bentham to a theory of action rather than a theory of language, but in fact the one forms an essential complement to the other in his work. For the major corollary of his idea that pleasure and pain are the only realities is that all the other things people take to be realities are actually *fictions* created by language.

The critique of Aristotle and the response to Hume thus generate two complementary currents in Bentham's philosophy of language. First, he recognizes the importance of non-propositional sentences in the science of law and government. Attempting to supplement the Aristotelian tradition by taking these sentences into account, Bentham articulates a range of speech-act principles, exploring issues of authority, uptake, felicity and infelicity in sociopolitical discourse. This pragmatic orientation is complemented by the more phenomenological approach to language embodied in his theory of linguistic fictions. In what follows, I will discuss Bentham's theory of illocutionary acts and his theory of fictions in that order, concluding with his specific analysis of contemporary issues such as oaths and constitutions that bring his entire philosophy of performative language into play.

Distinguishing between Aristotelian "sentences of assertion" and the hitherto neglected "sentences of volition," Bentham picks up the terminology used by James Harris in his influential treatise on universal grammar, *Hermes* (1751). At the beginning of *Hermes*, Harris claims that, since the powers of the soul fall into the two classes of perception and volition, "EVERY SENTENCE WILL BE EITHER A SENTENCE OF ASSERTION, OR A SENTENCE OF VOLITION" (17).[10] But Bentham also recognizes that the categories of assertion and volition—which correspond nicely to Austin's constative and performative—are not mutually exclusive. All sentences, including sentences of volition, assert something; conversely, all sentences of assertion actually contain an element of volition, in that they imply the speaker's attitude toward the assertion. The utterance "The robber is killed" really comprises "I *understand* or I believe that the robber is killed" (Bentham, *Introduction* 300n; cf. Austin 133–39).

The notion of illocutionary force that Bentham here identifies affects his legal theory in a variety of ways. To begin with, he correlates different illocutions with different relationships of power and status between speakers. Whether volition is expressed as a prayer, a request, a demand, or a command depends on whether the speaker stands in a relationship of inferiority, equality, or superiority to the addressee (*Bentham's Political Thought* 148–49). This observation comes in the context of a polemical definition of law, where Bentham insists that law be recognized as a particular kind of illocution addressed by a superior to an inferior: "a law is a *command*" (*Bentham's Political Thought* 150), and not a custom, a resolution, a divine revelation, a law of nature, etc. The particular form of words in which a law is framed is not a determining factor, as long as

---

[10]Harris further distinguishes the different "species of sentences": "who is there so ignorant, as if we address him in his Mother-Tongue, not to know when 'tis we *assert*, and when we *question*; when 'tis we *command*, and when we *pray* or *wish*?" (12). As his rhetoric suggests, though, Harris treats these illocutionary distinctions as obvious and preliminary to grammatical analysis, so that they do not play a major role in the rest of his work.

the illocutionary force comes across; different forms of words can convey a law's crucial "imperative quality" or "imperation" (*Introduction* 305).

Bentham's definition of law as a command has dramatic implications for politics and jurisprudence. It makes law-giving into an interpersonal act whose success or failure depends on relational and contextual factors. Defining law as a command draws attention to its contingency, to the fact that it is dependent on particular circumstances and individuals, rather than being divinely given or else collectively agreed. For Bentham, the most important issues raised by this situation are how the authority to issue laws gets established, and the possibility that laws might fail to be obeyed. As he realizes, the success of the law-as-command depends on the authority of the law-giver, but the authority of the law-giver depends equally on the pragmatic success of the law-as-command. Not only do the law-giver and the law stand and fall together, but the authority of the one and the success of the other necessarily depend on language, which injects its peculiar fallibilities into the machinery of the system.

At various junctures in his work, Bentham points out that anyone can write a book of law. But there is a discrete difference between the book written by someone who is authorized to make law, and the book written by someone who (like Bentham himself) is not, and who can therefore only publicize, critique, or otherwise write *about* the law:

> A book of expository jurisprudence is either *authoritative* or *unauthoritative*. It is styled authoritative, when it is composed by him who, by representing the state of the law to be so and so, causeth it so to be; that is, of the legislator himself: unauthoritative, when it is the work of any other person at large. (*Introduction* 294)

Conversely, if a non-authorized person cannot make anything into law, an authorized law-giver can make everything, even non-law, into law: "whatever is given for law by the person or persons recognized as possessing the power of making laws, is *law*. The Metamorphoses of Ovid, if thus given, would be law" (*Introduction* 301). But the power of making laws is itself granted by legislation. Identifying the different types of laws that combine to make a complete legal code (imperative, punitory, and discoercive or permissive), Bentham asserts that a body of law must also contain constitutional law that empowers the law-givers themselves:

> The constitutional branch is chiefly employed in conferring, on particular classes of persons, *powers*, to be exercised for the good of the whole society, or of considerable parts of it, and prescribing *duties* to the persons invested with those powers. (*Introduction* 307)

These power-granting sentences are themselves "discoercive" laws—that is, specially granted exemptions to the general imperative code. In Bentham's theory (as will be discussed below), rights and duties are only ever created by illocutionary utterances in the form of laws, which in this case leads to a regression from illocution to illocution: the right to make laws is conferred by a law that exempts law-makers from certain of the laws that apply to the public in general.

This circularity does not present a particular problem for Bentham, yet he does realize that the authority of the law-giver needs to be both established and acknowledged—and therein lies the possibility of failure. In *Of Laws in General*, a manuscript written in 1782 as a sequel to the *Introduction to the Principles of Morals and Legislation* from which the above comments on authority are drawn, Bentham enumerates various risks related to the exercise of authority. If a would-be law is not issued by a properly authorized law-giver, or "sovereign," it is (of course) an illegal mandate, and an offense. But it may also be the case that the issuer of the law is a properly authorized sovereign, yet the law is addressed to a party over whom that sovereign has no power, with the result that the would-be law again turns out to be void (*Of Laws* 18–20). This is a fairly straightforward case if, for instance, the law-giver is the sovereign of England whereas the addressee is a citizen of France, but it becomes more problematic if the addressees are citizens of England who have decided to *exempt themselves* from subjection to the English sovereign:

> in point of fact, I say, the ultimate efficient cause of all power of imperation over persons is a disposition on the part of those persons to obey: the efficient cause then of the power of the sovereign is neither more nor less than the disposition to obedience on the part of the people. Now this disposition it is obvious may admit of innumerable modifications—and that even while it is constant; besides that it may change from day to day. (*Of Laws* 18n)

This observation represents a radical turn within the theory of authority and legal utterance that Bentham develops. It finds a much later parallel in the postmodern critique of the performative by Jean-François Lyotard, who maintains that performativity is self-validating. The authority to issue a performative is only confirmed by the uptake it receives: *if* a command, declaration, or act of excommunication succeeds in bringing about the state of affairs it describes, *then* the speaker has the requisite authority to produce it (Lyotard 82). Authority might be theoretically determined by the constitutional branch of the law code, and citizens might be required by this law code to accept the illocutionary acts issued by persons so authorized, but Bentham recognizes—at least in a footnote—that the pragmatic response of the addressee adds an unpredictable qualification to the functioning of written law.

Most intriguingly, Bentham reveals that the "deficiencies" to which legislation is exposed are directly related to the fact that legislation is expressed in language—even though it can *only* be expressed in language. Written laws may, in theory, be either singular or general; that is, they may apply to specifically named or designated persons, or to groups of people and classes of acts. The first option is obviously unworkable, since it is impossible for the sovereign to have detailed enough knowledge of individual circumstances, not to mention the fact that singular laws could not be made at all so as to apply to an unknown future. This leaves the option of legislating according to classes, the way that virtually all laws do in fact operate. But here the law-maker is foiled by language, which drastically limits the number of ways people or things can be classed: "the legislator in the grouping of the persons things and acts which he takes for the subjects and objects of his laws is limited to such parcels as correspond to the generic names which are furnished by the language" (*Of Laws* 82).

This limitation takes some of the authority out of the hands of the sovereign, investing it not only in the structure of language, but also in the citizen, who can now take advantage of the space for interpretation created by a language that does not express the sovereign's will completely and precisely. If there is inexactness in the definition of the "grouping," and ambiguity as to who belongs to it, the person to whom the law is addressed will exercise his or her power of interpretation to determine whether the law applies in his or her case. Bentham refers to these qualifications to the sovereign's power as a "chasm" (*Of Laws* 92), a term that finds an odd echo in Derrida's characterization of the risk of abuse as an "abyss" or "ditch" that surrounds the Austinian performative (*Limited Inc* 17). Like Derrida, and like Reid, Bentham recognizes that the ever-present possibility of failure or abuse is part of what constitutes even the successful speech act.

While Bentham's most explicit comments on the infelicities that threaten legislative acts appear in *Of Laws in General*, which was not published until 1945, his awareness of the fallibility of authoritative language colors the theory of legal discourse articulated throughout the works published during his lifetime.[11] Identifying legislation as a particu-

---

[11] See also Bentham's enumeration of various infelicities that can invalidate the ceremony of oath-swearing in Chapter 6 of his 1813 tract *"Swear Not at All"* (*Works* 5: 187–229), of which Austin's analysis of infelicities in lectures 2 and 3 of *How to Do Things with Words* is strongly reminiscent.

lar kind of verbal act, Bentham acknowledges the need to define this act within a pragmatically oriented theory that specifies who has the right to perform it and the conditions under which it is valid. Beyond this, he recognizes dangers brought about by the *verbal* nature of the act: that language and experience often fail to correspond exactly, that the system of language itself exerts control over the language-user, and that the necessity of uptake and interpretation qualifies any authority the sovereign speaker may possess.

In his later work, Bentham develops another, more phenomenological insight into the nature of language, from which he draws further conclusions about the use of language in sociopolitical contexts. Convinced that pleasure and pain are the only realities, he exposes all other principles that help to shape the social order as "fictions" created by words. Combining the lists of such entities that Bentham provides in different works yields a catalogue of the most important sociopolitical fictions: obligation (the primary one, from which many others derive), right, liberty, power, property, command, duty, prohibition, exemption, privilege, license, and judgment. But there are also a host of nonpolitical fictions: the philosophical notion of faculty (and all of the Aristotelian predicaments), relation, motion, impossibility, even existence itself.

It might appear as if "fiction" is simply another term for "abstract noun," but to Bentham fictions are crucial evidence of the constitutive power of language. Language and fictitious entities require one another: "To language, then—to language alone—it is, that fictitious entities owe their existence—their impossible, yet indispensable, existence" (*Works* 8: 198). But language only works—or even, as Bentham puts it, only *exists*—because it places fictitious entities alongside real entities and treats the two equivalently: "the supposition of a sort of *verbal* reality, so to speak, as belonging to these fictitious entities, is a supposition, without which the matter of language could never have been formed" (*Works* 8: 126). When we use language, we constantly mix real entities with fictitious ones; but while the names of real entities can, if necessary, be connected with a referent in the external world, the names of fictitious entities are *only* names for cognitive constructs. "Of fictitious entities, whatsoever is predicated is not, consistently with strict truth, predicated (it then appears) of anything but their respective names" (*Works* 8: 199)—and yet, in ordinary speech and grammatical usage, we treat both kinds of nouns equally. The danger, and the reason that Bentham develops his theory, is that language-users may forget or fail to recognize the crucial distinction between the two types of nouns they are using. Confusion between real and fictitious entities is responsible for most of the errors that plague society.

Bentham's theory of fictions occupies a unique middle ground between British linguistics of the late eighteenth century, and German Romantic philosophy of language (although Bentham mentions neither school specifically). On the one hand, his belief that the concrete or "real" noun is the basic element of language, and the concomitant idea that every immaterial term likely has its origin in a material term (*Works* 8: 327–29), are strongly reminiscent of Horne Tooke. If Bentham does not pursue the elaborate etymological research that Tooke does to show that all words can be traced back to concrete perceptions, he does echo Tooke's philosophical and moral suspicion of attempts to pass off abstract entities as real entities. Yet Bentham's theory also embraces the principle that haunts Tooke's system as an unexpressed corollary, but lies at the heart of Humboldt's, Herder's, or Bernhardi's philosophies: that language does in fact succeed in creating immaterial objects and endowing them with at least a mode of reality. "To speak of an object by its name, its universally known name, is to ascribe existence to it," Bentham writes (*Works* 8: 328). Indeed, "existence" is itself one of the fictitious entities created by the use of language (*Works* 3: 210–11).

As fictions are brought into being by words, what they express relates to the structure of language and thought, not to material reality. The only way the fictitious entity "impossibility" can be explained, for example, is in terms of two contradictory propositions: the rules of logic and language teach us that the situation in which two propositions contradict one another is what is called impossibility (*Works* 8: 211). Possibility, impossibility, certainty, and uncertainty are not qualities of real entities, but rather terms that relate to what is proper or improper in the verbal expression of thought. Here, Bentham brings his theory of fictions into play in order to address misconceptions that infect public speech acts like testimony or judgment. When we think we are making assertions about real things, we are actually conveying our opinion of or persuasion about those things, and it is the linguistically expressed *opinion*, not the things themselves, to which terms like "certainty" apply: "neither improbability and impossibility on the one hand, nor their opposites, probability and certainty, on the other, have any real place in the nature of the things themselves" (*Works* 7: 77). Bentham's theory of fictitious entities links up at this point with his theory that all sentences of assertion conceal sentences of volition, because they contain the opinion, judgment, belief, or other psychological attitude of the speaker. "The robber is killed" really means "I *understand* or I believe that the robber is killed" (*Introduction* 300n); and certainty is a category that applies only to my belief about the event, not to the event itself.

Bentham's most explicit analyses of fictitious entities and the uses of language are contained in manuscripts that remained unpublished during his lifetime, but the implications of his theory of language show up in all of his works.¹² Linguistic fictions come in a range of forms, from the "serious" fiction of the logician (who recognizes that fictitious entities are essential for communicating ideas), to the harmless fiction of the poet (who uses fictitious entities for purposes of amusement), to the fiction of the priest or the lawyer (which Bentham terms "mischievous immorality") (*Works* 8: 199). His attitude toward fictions changes depending on context, but Bentham usually regards fictions as a necessary evil, without which we could neither communicate nor make and maintain laws, for all the conditions brought about by law—obligation, right, property, and so on—are fictitious entities. What is essential is that they be recognized as such. Bentham is adamant that fictitious entities should not be allowed to masquerade as real entities (for instance, right or obligation should not be put in the same category with pleasure and pain), and that once fictions have outlived their usefulness, they should be abandoned.

The most pernicious of outdated fictions, Bentham claims in *A Fragment on Government*, is the so-called original contract. It is time that the relationship between sovereign and people be put on a firmer basis than the notion of an illusory, mutual promise made in some distant past. Moreover, the fiction of an original contract has spawned two related fictitious entities, which have duped both sides in the political debates of the late eighteenth century. One is "natural right," appealed to by radicals and supposedly codified in edicts such as the French Declaration of 1789. The other fiction, which misleads the conservatives, is "common law," against which Bentham carries on a campaign throughout his writings on jurisprudence: "It appears then, that the customary law [i.e., the unwritten or common law] is a fiction from beginning to end: and it is in the way of fiction if at all that we must speak of it" (*Of Laws* 193). The entire import of Bentham's theory of fictions weighs against the idea of customary or common law, and it is perhaps even in

---

¹²Ogden points out that Bentham's French editor removed most of the theoretical passages on language when translating those manuscripts, like the *Theory of Legislation*, that appeared only in French versions during Bentham's lifetime (Bentham, *Theory of Legislation* xi). Nevertheless, briefer summaries of the linguistic underpinnings of his theory of fictions surface in most of Bentham's major works, from *A Fragment on Government* (1775) to *The Constitutional Code* (1830).

order to combat this notion of law that he developed his theory of language in this direction. Again and again, Bentham stresses that obligations, rights, and all other abstract principles to which people lay claim are actually fictions constructed by law—that is, by an authoritative verbal act. Defining a law as a command, and a command as a "statement of volition" determined by a relationship of unequal power between addressor and addressee, and recognizing that laws must rely on the capacity of language to group or classify terms, he concludes that all laws can really do is prohibit certain types of behavior. His model of society involves an original state of barbarism in which rights are only constructed negatively by authoritative commands: by ordering you not to murder me and not to steal my dinner, the law implicitly grants me the right to security and to property.

Since laws are commands, it follows that they must be expressed; they must be made known to the people who are meant to be governed by them. In the British and European context, this means that they must be written and positive rather than unwritten and customary, for "written law is the law for civilized nations" (*Of Laws* 153). Bentham adds that common or "unwritten" law may also get written down—in the sense, perhaps, in which Burke articulates some of the tenets of the English common law in his *Reflections on the Revolution in France*—but the crucial difference is that they are not written by the authorized legislator. Not only should the public be able to tell what the laws are, but it should be made aware of how laws are constituted by authoritative language. Only by learning to distinguish the fictitious entities created by language from real entities, and the law-as-command issued by the authorized legislator from other versions of "law" circulated by unauthorized parties, will people be able to prevent corrupt authorities from imposing on them.

Bentham's linguistically grounded jurisprudence positions him uniquely between conservatives and revolutionaries in the late-eighteenth-century political debates. Recognizing the dependence of law on language, he mounts a two-pronged campaign for reform of the legal system: he seeks to abolish the dependence on unwritten or common law, but also to eliminate the errors caused by ambiguous terminology in written law. The first campaign sets him against conservatives like Burke, who (as will be discussed below) reacted to the increasing political effectiveness of declarative speech acts by placing his faith in a kind of eternal, transcendent contract as the origin of both common law and natural rights. The second campaign, against the faulty use of language in written or positive law, makes Bentham into a fierce critic of contemporary constitutions. He develops something of a sub-specialty in critiquing official declarations, attacking the North Carolina Declaration of Rights (and implicitly also the declarations issued by other states, along with the Declaration of Independence) in a long note added to the 1789 edition of the *Introduction to the Principles of Morals and Legislation*, and penning critiques of the various declarations issued by the French National Assembly. Bentham's critiques tend to be very close readings of the language of these texts, in which he shows that, if the words are assumed to bring into being exactly the reality they describe, the result is absurdity or self-contradiction. It is absurd of the French Declaration of Rights of 1791, for instance, to be "asserting rights of any kind, acknowledging them at the same time not to be recognized by government" (*Bentham's Political Thought* 289), since "rights" are only created through laws issued by authoritative law-givers—that is, by government. Rights not created, let alone "recognized," by government simply do not exist. Indeed, Bentham refuses to accept the principle that unauthorized delegates, as he takes the framers of declarations to be, can decree limits on legislative power in the name of illusory "rights" that exist before rights have been created by authorized laws. His theory of linguistic fictions makes him equally critical of the original social contract *and* of its traditional contrary, natural rights: "What I mean to attack is ... all *ante*-legal and *anti*-legal rights of man, all declarations of such rights" (*Bentham's Political Thought* 285). It is no longer just a matter of "improprieties in language"; in the context of public declarations that purport to decree a legislative order to all future generations, verbal inexactitude becomes a moral and quasi-legal crime. Due to changes in the role of public utterance that came about at the time of the French Revolution, and due to Bentham's own analysis of language and law, the perceived relationship of language and sociopolitical reality has dramatically altered.

BURKE AND PAINE: WHAT'S IN A CONSTITUTION?

The world-altering documents of the late eighteenth century—including the American Declaration of Independence and the French Declarations of 1789, 1791, and 1795—drew the attention of many others besides Bentham to the relationship among verbal texts, abstract principles, and the material conditions of existence. Until the Pitt government placed severer restrictions on radical publishing in 1795, English readers experienced a passionate public debate over the existence, form, value, and definition of a constitution, in which Edmund Burke and Thomas Paine were the most notorious participants. It has often been noted that this debate was a struggle for the control of political language, in that each author's rhetorical style, as well as the price and method of distribution of his texts, was calculated to win the allegiance of certain groups and classes of readers (Klancher 103–11; O. Smith 35–67). Paine, especially, succeeded in gaining legitimacy for an epigrammatic, violent, and popular language of political debate.

But the Burke-Paine controversy may also stand as a reference point for a new awareness of verbal performativity, which emerges first of all in the different meanings the two writers attach to the word "constitution." In *Reflections on the Revolution in France*, Burke relies on a traditional definition of "constitution" as "mode of organization." According to this definition, it makes sense to talk of an "unwritten constitution"; and, to the extent that aspects of a nation's constitution *are* embodied in written documents, these texts describe a relation that already exists between the nation's government and its people. As Blakemore notes, this pre-Romantic definition of the word is confirmed by Johnson's dictionary and the Oxford English Dictionary: "A nation's constitution is everything that 'is' part of the nation's constituted reality, and the *is* reflects and reaffirms the *was* of the nation's past" (*Burke and the Fall of Language* 7). But Paine, in *The Rights of Man*, champions an emerging counter-definition of the word by insisting that the constitution is a document that establishes the terms "government" and "people," and their relationship, in the first place. John Quincy Adams confirms the novelty of this definition in his *Answer to Pain's Rights of Man*, where he recognizes that Paine must "endeavour to bring about a revolution in language" in order to have his definition of "constitution" prevail (quoted in O. Smith 45).

The language of Burke's constitution, in other words, is descriptive or constative, referring to a state of affairs in the world, while the language of Paine's constitution is performative, since it does not refer, but instead brings a new state of affairs into existence. "Paine's argument is, in effect, essentially linguistic," Blakemore notes (*Burke and the Fall of Language* 13), for Paine takes Burke's own realization that the French Revolution involves a revolution in language and turns it against him by showing that declarative language, as used by the revolutionaries and by Paine himself, is a more potent force than Burke imagined. In part 1 of *The Rights of Man*, Paine repeatedly accuses Burke of focusing on "men" when he should focus on "principles." Burke writes as if the French Revolution were a revolt against a specific individual, Louis XVI; but Paine counters that the revolution was about principles, and principles should form the crux of the debate as well. His own text therefore turns to logical, universalizing arguments that are often arguments about the relation of words and the world.

Yet it would be too simplistic to claim that Burke stands for constative language and Paine for the up-and-coming performative. Rather, an anxiety over the relation of words to the world cuts across the revolution debate, causing both sides to champion certain forms of language that are (or should be) referential, and other forms of language that do (or should) alter existing circumstances. Paine's redefinition of the term "constitution" turns out to be qualified by his belief that constitutions only bring rights into being *on a sociopolitical level*—for there is another, "natural" level on which rights already exist independently of the language that gives expression to them. His rhetoric implies, though, that this sphere of independently existing principles can be, and needs to be, delimited by Paine himself; for in all matters that do not belong to the sphere of natural rights he assumes the power to declare existing forms of expression invalid and articulate the principles by which society should operate. Burke, for his part, upholds tradition and the unwritten law, yet habitually solidifies his principles around speech-act metaphors—most famously, the notion that society is a contract. A reading of Burke and Paine with attention to the way they allude to explicit performatives, and the way they themselves use performative language, reveals that *both* writers actually base their arguments on the assumption of an original contract. Yet each abrogates to himself the ability to discern the conditions of this contract and its relevance to the present state of society.

Paine discerns the performative aspect of a constitution clearly (even if not under that name), stressing that is a material document as well as a specific order of words:

> A constitution is not a thing in name only, but in fact. It has not an ideal, but a real existence; and wherever it cannot be produced in a visible form, there is none. A constitution is a thing *antecedent* to a government, and a government is only the creature of a constitution. (1: 278)

Constitutions create governments, but they also create the fundamental values of the state. Using a linguistic analogy, Paine credits the state and federal constitutions in America with constructing principles such as liberty: "The American Constitutions were to liberty, what a grammar is to language: they define its parts of speech, and practically construct them into syntax" (1: 300). But if constitutions create governments, and even construct the public form of abstract principles, Paine is careful to limit their performative power to the sociopolitical sphere. In the 1795

Dissertation on First Principles of Government, he states just as adamantly that declarations do *not* create principles, since there exist natural (one might say "extra-linguistic") rights that cannot be granted or taken away by documents:

> A declaration of rights is not a creation of them, nor a donation of them. It is a manifest of the principle by which they exist, followed by a detail of what the rights are; for every civil right has a natural right for its foundation, and it includes the principle of a reciprocal guarantee of those rights from man to man. (2: 583)

The key distinction here is between "civil right" and "natural right." Declarations do not create the latter; but by expressing natural rights in a public context, in a document ratified by the representatives of the people, they re-create natural rights as civil rights. In analyzing the causes of the French and American Revolutions in *Rights of Man*, Paine stresses the interdependence of "facts" (by which he means historical events) and "principles." Documents such as "the declaration of American independence" or "the treaty of alliance between France and America" are both facts *and* principles, since they embody independently existing principles but also, as historical events, bring about the establishment of those principles in given sociopolitical contexts (1: 300).

Paine's analysis of charters—which he distinguishes from constitutions—confirms his notion of verbal acts as phenomena that do not create the essential identity of human beings, but do establish a sociopolitical form of identity. Like Blake in "London," Paine describes charters as restrictive instruments; rather than creating rights, they take away the natural rights of the many so as to leave them to the few. Charters articulate limits and distinctions: "they make a difference in favor of A, by taking away the rights of B" (1: 408). In effect, Paine's account of charters is the reverse of Bentham's account of laws, and the rift between them opens along the fault-line of the traditional nature-culture debate. Bentham claims that laws restrict the natural inclination to act according to one's own interest on one side, thereby creating rights on the other side. Paine, believing that rights (and not only self-interest) are natural, claims that charters restrict already existing rights on one side, and thus create artificial and unfair privileges on the other side.

With Paine's assertion that natural rights cannot be created or given, but only restricted or confirmed, by sociopolitical speech acts, the stage is set for his comparison of the French and British constitutions. The French Declaration of the Rights of Man and Citizen can now be favorably contrasted with Magna Carta and the 1689 Declaration of Rights. When people refer to Magna Carta as a constitution, Paine claims, they pretend that it bestowed rights and created a government; but in fact it does not deserve the name "constitution," because it only placed some limits on the power that the Norman monarchs and their government had already assumed. The 1689 Declaration of Rights, too, was nothing but "a bargain, which the parts of government made with each other to divide powers, profits and privileges" (1: 383). Paine distinguishes between legitimate constitutions, which are performative inasmuch as they precede the existence of a government, and other speech acts such as charters and legislation (e.g., the 1689 Declaration) that proceed from an already-existing government, albeit one that wields power illegitimately because it has not been brought into existence by a constitution. The Parliament of 1688, according to Paine, is "a few persons got together" who "called themselves by that name" (1: 383). Representation or delegation becomes the key factor in determining whether speech acts have the proper authority behind them: a legitimate constitution is one proclaimed by an assembly of elected delegates. Delegated authority depends, in turn, on the prior existence of the natural right of man to judge for himself and, by extension, to nominate a representative who will express this judgment for him. Thus the French Third Estate, as an elected constituent assembly and the hero of natural rights, legitimately and successfully "declared themselves ... THE REPRESENTATIVES OF THE NATION" in June 1789, even though they were not authorized by the existing system to make such a declaration (1: 308–9). However, when the First Estate lays claim to a traditional name that offends against the natural right of equality, it commits the illegitimate speech act of "styling itself the Nobles" (1: 309).

According to Paine's theory of how declarative language operates, the potentially ambiguous opening statement of the 1789 Declaration of the Rights of Man and Citizen, in which the National Assembly "recognizes *and* declares" these rights, is literally accurate. The Declaration (constatively) recognizes the prior existence of rights on an essential level, as "rights of man," and (performatively) declares them into existence on the sociopolitical level, as "rights of citizens." By consistently and deliberately preserving a level on which human identity seems untouched by language, Paine justifies the performative-constative undecidability that Derrida later locates in all declarations, as they gloss over their own performative claims by pretending that the rights they are in the process of positing have existed all along ("Declarations of Independence" 9–10). But Paine's concept of rights thereby becomes vulnerable to another postmodern critique of political declarations. Paine shares the assumption of the authors of the 1789 Declaration that the "philosophical universe" of natural rights and the "historical-political universe" of civil rights specific to the French Republic, as Lyotard has called them, can unproblematically be identified with one another. The linguistic event of the French Revolution, for Lyotard, is embodied in the equivocation by which the Declaration of 1789 invokes the philosophical or speculative "Idea of Man" as the guarantee of its validity, and yet simultaneously authorizes itself by appealing to a historical-political signatory, the "representatives of the French people" (147). So Paine, too, assumes an equivalence between the natural rights of men and the declared rights of citizens, and thereby evades difficult questions about whether "natural rights"—or at least any individual's perception of them—are not also subject to historical and verbal construction.

BINDING TERMS

Derrida's and Lyotard's readings of constitutions and declarations arguably reflect the postmodern notion that identity is always implicated in language and networks of power, an idea that eighteenth-century writers did not necessarily share. Nevertheless, there is evidence that Paine's attempt, careful as it is, to define separate spheres for what is natural and what is declared or constructed, ultimately fails. For one thing, his own language, even as it aims for a new directness and transparency, often resembles the sociopolitical performative in the way it assumes power and challenges the validity of previous speech acts. Its illocutionary force is determined in part by the dialogic context of the revolutionary debate, in which the speech acts of all the participants compete against those of their opponents in the struggle to validate assertions about the political and social order. The language of the 1790s tracts, in other words, makes no secret of its pragmatic commitments. Burke's *Reflections* are framed as advice addressed to a young Frenchman; Paine's *Rights of Man*, which he held off writing until it could be presented as a reply to the *Reflections*, is addressed to Burke; the many published responses to both works generally address either Burke or Paine directly. Pragmatic questions about the source of the writer's authority, the identity or the construction of the addressee, and the way meaning is affected by dialogic context, lie very close to the surface.

The competitive context into which *The Rights of Man* enters takes on particular importance when Paine calls attention to the arbitrariness of terminology and definition. Expressions like "what is called . . ." or "what is styled . . ." are common enough in the rhetoric of the 1790s in any case, but seem especially conspicuous in Paine's writing.[13] By referring to "the Elector of Hanover, sometimes styled King of England" (1: 247), to "what is called the British Constitution" (1: 452), to "what is called a king" and "what, in Europe, is called the executive" (1: 394), he exposes variations in terminology in different political jurisdictions and among different factions. More truculently, he casts suspicion on the terms used by his opponents; more abstractly, he reveals that diction always depends on context and on the prejudices of the speaker. At the same time, Paine asserts his own right and ability to reassign terms so as to restore their proper meaning. Importunate references to King George III as "the Hessian" and "the Hanoverian" in part 2 of *The Rights of Man* earned him charges of libel and sedition. This is more than a rhetorical device (though it is that), since one of Paine's fundamental contentions, as he says in the preface to the French edition, is that "truth has always been suppressed in England" and "this insult to public morals has received the name of *law*" (1: 248). Just as natural rights exist prior to declarations, truth exists prior to the fictitious names that people have imposed. Paine puts himself forward as one who can, by measuring the declarative language of different parties in the revolution against independently existing rights, expose linguistic and onomastic falsity, and restore to men their natural rights by restoring to words their natural meaning. What goes unexplained is how one gains access to the extralinguistic sphere of natural rights, and why—if not because of his experience in the thoroughly verbal realms of reading, writing, and debating—Paine can claim to be the best knower of it. Paine's book will, by renaming things, restore their original names; it will, like Blakean prophecy, melt linguistic surfaces away and display the infinite which was hid; but to do so, must it not be something other than a linguistic medium? In fact, Paine's title might be read as an attempt to claim for his text a paradoxical, pre-linguistic status. It is not, like the text of Burke's to which it responds, an individual's "reflections," but the thing itself, the original which was hid: the "Rights of Man."

The declarative force of Paine's onomastic rhetoric comes even closer to the surface when he analyzes the language of declarations themselves.

---

[13]For Paine's emphasis on naming, calling, and "styling" in *The Age of Reason*, see Esterhammer, "Calling into Existence." The power of language to rename and redefine was also employed against Paine; see Olivia Smith's account of his arraignment under the King's Proclamation against Seditious Writings in May 1792, which, as Smith puts it, "conjured a new character of Thomas Paine to suit the purpose of prosecution" (63).

The opening section of *The Rights of Man* centers on official speech acts and their limitations, and addresses the most famous issue in the Burke-Paine confrontation: whether verbal agreements should be considered binding on future generations. In his *Reflections*, Burke cites and relies heavily on the language of the Declaration of Rights, which he identifies as the cornerstone of the British constitution. Burke maintains that the English have always looked to the past for evidence of their established rights, and that present-day Englishmen are bound by the declaration that was made for them a century ago to accept their political structure as it stands. Paine vehemently opposes these principles:

> I am contending for the rights of the *living*, and against their being willed away, and controlled and contracted for, by the manuscript assumed authority of the dead; and Mr. Burke is contending for the authority of the dead over the rights and freedom of the living. (1: 252)

The idea that the words of past generations should not be binding on the present was already something of a commonplace by the time Paine used it; the argument was articulated by Rousseau and Kant, and continued to be made in various contexts throughout the Romantic period. Bentham, too, affirms the absurdity of using legal language to control the legislative power of future generations, most explicitly in his 1813 tract *"Swear Not at All"*. Here, his main objection to the use of oaths in the legal system—for example, at the investiture of secular and religious governors—is that they prevent innovation, and thus perpetuate existing abuses: the mischievous assumption behind legislation sustained by oaths is "that, for the governance of the *living*, the proper heads and hands are—not those of the *living* but those of the *dead*" (*Works* 5: 207). Yet it is not only conservative regimes against which Bentham levels this charge. His primary critique of the French Declaration of Rights of 1791 is that it attempts to bind the hands of future governments by declaring the rights it articulates to be imprescriptible for all future generations (*Bentham's Political Thought* 270).

But Paine's argument about the "manuscript assumed authority of the dead" also raises general linguistic-pragmatic questions, and indeed is surprisingly close to the argument that Austin would make for the infelicity of a performative. Paine affirms:

1. That Parliament did not have the right to make a declaration binding on future generations, since it had not been given a mandate by future generations but had only "assumed" the power to speak for them. "A cannot make a will to take from B the property of B, and

give it to C" (1: 325); in other words, the speaker does not have the requisite authority.
2. That the descendants of those who made the declaration were not present to give or withhold consent, or even to recognize the document as a declaration. "The preclusion of consent is despotism" (1: 323); in other words, the speaker failed to secure uptake.
3. That written utterances are more problematic, in terms of their effects, than spoken ones.

The last of these points corresponds to Austin's parenthetical caveat, in *How to Do Things with Words*, that "written utterances are not tethered to their origin in the way spoken ones are" (61). In Paine's case, the same mistrust of the written reveals itself when he asserts the "rights of the *living*" over "the manuscript assumed authority of the dead," his double adjective linking the illegitimacy of authority ("assumed") to the fact of its being expressed in writing ("manuscript").

Paine's arguments aim at one fundamental principle: that only the person who enters into a contract can be bound by it (or, conversely, that only the person who will be bound by a contract has the authority to enact it). The cornerstone of a theory of moral agency, this principle is common to Austin's speech-act philosophy and Paine's discourse of natural rights. Yet Paine's formal reply to what he considers Parliament's illegitimate assumption of authority over the future adds an ironic twist to his critique. He himself claims, at some level, the authority to legislate over anyone who would legislate for future generations:

> There never did, there never will, and there never can exist a parliament, or any description of men, or any generation of men, in any country, possessed of the right or the power of binding and controlling posterity to the *"end of time,"* or of commanding forever how the world shall be governed, or who shall govern it; and therefore, all such clauses, acts or declarations, by which the makers of them attempt to do what they have neither the right nor the power to do, nor the power to execute, are in themselves null and void. (1: 251)

Paine's language is deliberately legalistic, in its attempt to predict and exclude qualifications or conditions, and explicitly declarative, especially in the final clause that proclaims the excluded "clauses, acts or declarations" "null and void." More than that, however, it is a statute that enacts its own rupture, when it asserts that there "*never* will" and "*never* can" exist a speaker qualified or able to make a declaration binding on future governments. In outlawing the type of government that might, in some future state of entirely different composition, have the right to make laws binding on posterity, Paine himself would seem to be giving in to "the vanity and presumption of governing beyond the grave," even while he denounces this as "the most ridiculous and insolent of all tyrannies" (1: 251). In abrogating such a right to himself while declaring a statement of exactly the kind he is making "null and void," can we assume that Paine is demonstrating, through parody, the absurdity of trying to make an eternally valid declaration? Is he simply unaware of the irony in his attempt to counter a sociopolitical speech act with another of the same kind? Or is he intimating that his utterance is of another order: that it possesses a kind of authority that goes beyond the authority delegated to governments by democratic process, because it is sanctioned by natural rights?

Paine's echo of Kant's essay "Was Ist Aufklärung?" ("What Is Enlightenment?"), published seven years before *The Rights of Man*, supports the idea that both writers are claiming a new basis for verbal authority, outside of and higher than the declarative authority of governing institutions. To the suggestion that it might seem prudent for a public body, such as a church, to bind itself "by oath" (eidlich) to some permanent system, Kant responds:

> I say that this is quite impossible. Such a contract, concluded to keep all further enlightenment away from the human race forever, is absolutely null and void, even if it were ratified by the supreme power, by imperial diets and by the most solemn peace treaties. One age cannot bind itself and conspire to put the following one into such a condition that it would be impossible for it to enlarge its cognitions (especially in such urgent matters) and to purify them of errors, and generally to make further progress in enlightenment. This would be a crime against human nature, whose original vocation lies precisely in such progress; and succeeding generations are therefore perfectly authorized to reject such decisions as unauthorized and made sacrilegiously. ("Answer" 19-20)

In maintaining that the attempt to hold future generations back from enlightenment is a crime against human nature itself, Kant, like Paine, challenges the power of institutions on the basis of innate or natural rights. These rights are embodied in the individual and expressed by an utterance that derives its power from individual reason and will rather than institutional authority. Beginning with a forceful "I say that," Kant emphasizes the opposition between his single voice and the hypothetical consensus of traditional authorities. At the same time, this rhetorical device makes explicit the illocutionary force of the passage as the claim of a specific speaker in a specific historical context. Given the biblical cadences of eighteenth-century rhetoric, not to mention the fact that

Kant is writing about the Church, it is likely that a biblical paradigm lies behind these appeals to the authority of individual voice: the cry of the Hebrew prophets in the wilderness, or the rhetorical position of Jesus, who, in a public performance like the Sermon on the Mount, repeatedly opposes an abstract corporate voice ("ye have heard it said") with his individual utterance ("but I say unto you").

GOD AND THE SOCIAL CONTRACT

The tension between these two forms of verbal authority—the declarations and laws issued by political institutions, and the voice of the individual who claims the right to void official declarations in the name of an authority that is other and higher—surfaces repeatedly among political and literary authors of the 1790s. Besides being shared by pro-revolutionary and counter-revolutionary writers, this duality of institutional and individual voice cuts across the more simplistic distinctions by which it would appear, for instance, that Paine supports a performative and Burke a constative language, or that Paine always maintains a strict division between pre-linguistic "natural rights" and the speech acts that bring these rights into existence as political principles. Both Burke and Paine recognize the *de facto* authority of sociopolitical performatives and place alongside them some alternative authority, which may be that of tradition (as with Burke) or that of natural rights (as with Paine). Yet both writers also figure this alternative authority as verbal and performative, even as both derive it from the divine.

At the beginning of *The Rights of Man*, Paine accuses Burke of ascribing the power of Parliament to divine authority:

> Under how many subtilties, or absurdities, has the divine right to govern been imposed on the credulity of mankind!
> Mr. Burke has discovered a new one, and he has shortened his journey to Rome, by appealing to the power of this infallible Parliament of former days; and he produces what it has done, as of divine authority; for that power must certainly be more than human, which no human power to the end of time can alter. (1: 252–53)

Paine's comment is doubly ironic: first, because Burke quite explicitly derives parliamentary authority from the will of God, so that Paine's exposure of the assumption is hardly needed; secondly, because Paine himself also appeals to the divine as the ultimate guarantor of legitimate political declarations. Both of them posit God as the first source of the social contract; they differ, though, in their idea of how authority devolves from a divine source, and on the terms of that original contract. According to Burke, the unwritten British constitution corresponds to the universal social contract, which Burke characterizes as the proper foundation for the contracts that make up individual societies:

> Society is indeed a contract. Subordinate contracts for objects of mere occasional interest may be dissolved at pleasure—but the state ought not to be considered as nothing better than a partnership agreement in a trade of pepper and coffee, callico or tobacco, or some other such low concern, to be taken up for a little temporary interest, and to be dissolved by the fancy of the parties. It is to be looked on with other reverence; because it is not a partnership in things subservient only to the gross animal existence of a temporary and perishable nature. It is a partnership in all science; a partnership in all art; a partnership in every virtue, and in all perfection. As the ends of such a partnership cannot be obtained in many generations, it becomes a partnership not only between those who are living, but between those who are living, those who are dead, and those who are to be born. Each contract of each particular state is but a clause in the great primaeval contract of eternal society, linking the lower with the higher natures, connecting the visible and invisible world, according to a fixed compact sanctioned by the inviolable oath which holds all physical and all moral natures, each in their appointed place. (*Writings* 8: 146–47)

Describing the state's power as an extension and reflection of God's power, Burke makes the performative instruments "contract" and "oath" into metaphors. He deliberately dissociates these terms from the familiar, verbal transactions carried out between humans, such as contracts for trade in material goods, in order to apply them to a universal and apparently pre-linguistic realm that embraces the great chain of being, the moral order of the cosmos, and the transcendent power of God as legislator and sovereign.

But when Burke specifies the relationship between this transcendent agreement and human, social transactions, the metaphorical contract gets translated back into the actual speech acts that mediate the relationship between ruler and ruled. Throughout the *Reflections*, Burke challenges the French revolutionaries on the grounds that their speech acts are invalid, unsuccessful, or both, because the revolution has destroyed the chain of authority that renders utterances effective. Having rejected the "emanations" of hereditary authority, the revolutionary government has relinquished any paradigm that might make its commands operative, creating a state in which language will no longer exert any control over physical force:

> they have their residence in a city whose constitution has emanated neither from the charter of their king, nor from their legislative power.

> There they are surrounded by an army not raised either by the authority of their crown, or by their command; and which, if they should order to dissolve itself, would instantly dissolve them. (*Writings* 8: 118)

Later, Burke takes up the question of military discipline in France in greater detail. As an institution in which strict conventions govern the effectiveness of speech acts, and verbal power manifestly controls physical power, the military provides a focal point for his invective against the revolutionaries. He derides them for relying on performatives that have lost their validity and their effect:

> After they had been told that the soldiery trampled upon the decrees of the assembly promulgated by the King, the assembly pass new decrees; and they authorise the King to make new proclamations. After the Secretary at War had stated that the regiments had paid no regard to oaths *prêtés avec la plus imposante solemnité*—they propose—what? More oaths. They renew decrees and proclamations as they experience their insufficiency, and they multiply oaths in proportion as they weaken, in the minds of men, the sanctions of religion. (*Writings* 8: 261)

Not only have the religious sanctions that would incline inferiors to obey the commands of their superiors been abandoned, but the revolutionaries have undermined their own authority by telling the soldiers that they possess the rights of man—including, disastrously, the right to govern themselves. Burke is convinced that declaring the rights of man is incompatible with the proper operation of the speech acts that uphold civil society: commands, laws, and oaths. In this he has the agreement of Bentham, at least insofar as Bentham believes that the French Declaration of Rights, which literally, permanently, and without qualification enshrines liberty and property as rights of the individual, actually makes all legislation and good government impossible. As Burke and Bentham half realize, on its most abstract level the problem is the incommensurability of theory and practice. In theory, all men including soldiers possess the right to liberty, but in practice this right must be qualified by the obligation to obey the orders of a superior officer; in theory, civil rights may be absolute and perennial, but in practice, it must be possible to legislate about matters such as personal liberty and property. The incompatibility between theory and practice repeats the tenuous relationship between general will and individual will that Rousseau identified in his *Social Contract*, according to which the general desire for the "happiness of each" is inevitably founded on self-interest: "there is no one who does not apply the word *each* to himself, and is not thinking of himself when he votes for all" (Rousseau 68). In a document guaranteeing inalienable individual rights, each reader's tendency to interpret in reference to a subjective "I" is both necessary and antagonistic to the concept of a society in which all (abstract, objective) citizens possess equal rights.[14]

Paine's concept of declarations and the other speech acts that constitute society and government, however, is based precisely on the existence of individual, natural rights. What is more, these rights are ultimately God-given via an original contract. Paine's first discussion of the social contract in *The Rights of Man*, a critique of Burke's exposition of original contract in the *Reflections*, displaces the contract from the context of ruler and ruled to the context of an agreement among private individuals. In other words, he returns directly to the Hobbesian model of a "covenant of every man with every man":

> It has been thought a considerable advance toward establishing the principles of freedom, to say, that government is a compact between those who govern and those who are governed: but this cannot be true, because it is putting the effect before the cause; for as a man must have existed before governments existed, there necessarily was a time when governments did not exist, and consequently there could originally exist no governors to form such a compact with.
>
> The fact therefore must be, that the *individuals themselves*, each in his own personal and sovereign right, *entered into a compact with each other* to produce a government: and this is the only mode in which governments have a right to arise, and the only principle on which they have a right to exist. (1: 277–78)

But the "personal and sovereign right" of individuals to contract with one another was also derived from somewhere, and Paine implies that it was from an even more fundamental contract between God and man. In his observations on the Declaration of 1789, Paine expresses reservations about Article 10, which attempts to guarantee freedom of conscience in religion, on the grounds that any attempt to legislate with regard to the relationship between humans and the divine might offend against this primeval contract:

> before any human institutions of government were known in the world, there existed, if I may so express it, a compact between God and man, from the beginning of time; and . . . all laws must conform themselves to this prior existing compact, and not assume to make the compact conform to the laws, which, besides being human, are subsequent thereto. (1: 316n)

---

[14]De Man's deconstructionist extension of this argument from Rousseau's *Social Contract* to the tension between grammar and rhetoric in the language of every text (*Allegories of Reading* 246–77) is particularly relevant in the case of Bentham, whose "Critical Examination of the Declaration of Rights" (*Bentham's Political Thought* 257–90) also intuits the linguistic or textual basis of the political dilemma.

Both Burke and Paine ultimately derive the rights of man—be they corporate rights, as for Burke, or individual rights, as for Paine—from a contract between man and God. This representation of the relationship between humans and the divine in the form of an originary speech act has an important archetype in the biblical image of covenant, that evolves from Yahweh's agreement with Abraham in the Book of Genesis to its radical re-interpretation in the New Testament. The notion of covenant can be brought in on any side of the debate: it supports both the idea that rights are inalienable, and the idea that the most fundamental laws are unwritten; it has the authority of tradition and canonicity, yet the canonical text can always be interpreted anew. For Burke, the covenant is perpetuated in the ordinances of government together with the unwritten constitution, as he suggests by affirming his faith in these institutions in language that echoes the Bible: "I never desire . . . to read in the declaration of right any mysteries unknown to those whose penetrating style has engraved in our ordinances, and in our hearts, the words and spirit of that immortal law" (*Writings* 8: 70–71). In Jeremiah 31.33, a passage that is particularly important for New Testament writers arguing for the authority of a spiritual covenant that supersedes the Israelite law, Yahweh promises to make a new covenant with his people: "I will put my law in their inward parts, and write it in their hearts." Like the covenant of God, engraved on tablets of stone at Sinai but also, more significantly, written on the heart, the British constitution is embodied in the 1689 Declaration of Rights and other legal ordinances, but its better part is the spiritual, immortal, unwritten law. In both cases, the penetrating effect of the ordinances is guaranteed by a divine authority higher than sociopolitical convention.

Paine, not surprisingly, takes a different route back to the immortal covenant. When he considers the contest between political writers to derive rights from different historical declarations, he recognizes that "it is authority against authority all the way"—but the progression of authorities ends at "the divine origin of the rights of man, at the Creation" (1: 273). The principle that Paine derives from the biblical account of creation, which "admit[s] of no controversy," is that of "*the unity or equality of man*" (1: 274). Because of its divine origin, this principle has exactly the power that parliamentary decrees do not have, of binding succeeding generations: it "relates not only to the living individuals, but to generations of men succeeding each other." Paine argues that men are separated from the fundamental truth of their origin as equals by a series of "turnpike gates," which (quoting from Burke) he identifies as kings, parliament, magistrates, priests, and nobility, along with the duties and relationships that the citizen is bound to maintain with each of them. In place of these many duties, Paine would put only "duty to God, which every man must feel; and with respect to his neighbor, to do as he would be done by" (1: 275). He is, in effect, repeating Christ's distillation of the law into one great commandment, the New Testament's redefinition of the Mosaic covenant: "Therefore all things whatsoever ye would that men should do to you, do ye even so to them: for this is the law and the prophets" (Matthew 7.12).

Both of the major participants in the revolution debate concern themselves with the operation and legitimation of the speech acts by which society is established, maintained, and altered, including contracts, constitutions, declarations, commands, oaths, and laws. Both of them appeal ultimately to God as the authority who, by an *ur*-performative figured as a contract or covenant, sanctioned future sociopolitical speech acts as long as they do not violate the original, transcendent agreement. For Burke, though, this agreement binds humans to one another and to the rest of the cosmos in a compact that can only ever be corporate, collective, and hierarchical. For Paine, it is a contract between God and the individual, affirmed at the creation and confirmed by the New Testament's golden rule. *His* transcendent covenant grants each man equality with others, as a natural right that human constitutions must honor or risk being declared invalid.

While the entire debate was occasioned by urgent, material realities—how government would be structured, who would hold property, and who would have power to command whom in the monarchies and new republics of the late eighteenth century—metaphysical questions about the power of language are also at stake. Foremost among these is the validity of speech acts over time. Not only because of their beliefs about declarations and constitutions, but because they are themselves authors of public documents, both Burke and Paine need to uphold the lasting effect of words on the world. Yet, at other times, both also need to defend the ability of present speech acts to prevail over the speech acts of the past. Without the latter, their own utterances (one thinks especially of Paine's attempt to supersede established names and terms) could not have an effect at all; without the former (one thinks of Burke's appeal to the 1689 Declaration as the legitimation of his own words), they could have no lasting effect. The power of language in the face of the power of time is the fundamental issue behind the controversy over the "manuscript assumed authority of the dead," and behind the appeal of both writers to an original, transcendent contract—which, however, each claims to be able to define anew.

As will be discussed in the next two chapters, Continental philosophy took a different view of the problem of speech acts and temporality, and produced the idea, recurrent throughout German Romantic philosophy of language, of a performative that anticipates itself, so that the parameters within which it operates both are and are not already in place at the time of utterance. But in Britain during the early Romantic period, reflections on the relation between language and world stand under the influence of a far-reaching social-contract debate, beyond which can be glimpsed the more ancient image of divine covenant. Reid and Bentham respond to this tradition by exploring the linguistic-pragmatic basis of contracts, promises, and laws as contextualized, interpersonal speech acts. There is significant evidence that Reid, in particular, represents the same line of thought that later led to Austin's engagement with promises and his theorization of the performative. If Burke and Paine are less consciously concerned with the philosophy of language, their texts are nevertheless responsible for instituting new ways of reading, writing, and thinking the declarations that make up the social order. For the first generation of Romantic poets, engaged in what has been called a "piecemeal search for a new linguistic theory that could serve the poetry of a republican politic" (Turner 52), the texts of Burke and Paine contributed both in theory and in practice to an engagement with public speech acts. Theories of the original social contract, combined with the response to empiricist philosophy and the experience of the French Revolution, compelled these writers to think about language in a pragmatic context, and brought about the conditions for an intersection of politics, philosophy of language, and literature.

2

Kant, German Idealism, and Philosophies of Language in Action

For poets and philosophers of language, the intellectual revolution inaugurated by Kant's *Critique of Pure Reason* in 1781 provided a new basis on which to relate perception, cognition, and language. The mind, in Kant's philosophy, is no longer passive and receptive in its relationship with the external world, as in an empiricist epistemology; rather, it is actively and creatively engaged in forming representations of reality, albeit according to necessary, *a priori* categories. The work of Kant's younger contemporaries, Fichte and Schelling, turns this paradigm in an idealist direction by extending exactly those aspects of Kant's philosophy that have the greatest relevance for a philosophy of the performative: the primacy of the subject or "I," and the characterization of the I as an active principle. Kant's proposal of a new foundation for knowledge, combined with Fichte's and Schelling's idealist revisions, provides Romantic thinkers with the epistemological background for a philosophy of language that centers on subjectivity, intersubjectivity, identity, and existence itself as conditions constructed by the word.

It is nevertheless well known among intellectual historians, perhaps even infamous among historians of linguistics, that Kant did not concern himself with language per se in his investigation into the conditions of possibility for human knowledge. Modern scholarship is divided on the question of whether there is at least an *implicit* Kantian philosophy of language—that is, whether the absence of explicit reflections on language in Kant's work betokens a lack of interest in linguistic questions, or a repression of them. "The theory of language and action has not (despite Humboldt) found its Kant," Habermas claims ("What Is Universal Pragmatics?" 23). But even while denying that Kant provides a distinct foundation for theories of language, Habermas implies that followers like Humboldt turned his work in this direction—and he cautiously backs the efforts of scholars like Karl-Otto Apel to develop a "transcendental hermeneutics" and a "transcendental pragmatics" by pursuing philosophy of language within a Kantian framework. More programmatically, the Austrian philosopher Erich Heintel maintains that "the *fundamental* formulations of Hamann, Herder, and Humboldt signify nothing other than the *linguistic-philosophical form of the basic problematic of transcendental philosophy*" ("Einleitung" xx–xxi). By reflecting on the conditions of knowledge, Heintel argues, Kant established a vital foundation for philosophy of language by transforming the objective (gegenständliche) world into a logos-like (logosartige) world—that is, a world that exists for us not in terms of simple objects, but in terms of meanings and intentions. The Kantian understanding, which is constitutive of objects (gegenstandskonstitutiv), yet also limited in its constitutive role by the prior existence of objects created by the divine Logos, is for Heintel not only "characteristic of our entire Western tradition," but also easily translatable into a philosophy of language ("Einleitung" xxxii). From the perspective of linguistic historians, Nerlich and Clarke reach a similar conclusion: that transcendental philosophy may be considered a fundamentally linguistic enterprise, inasmuch as the Kantian forms of thought can be regarded as a "grammar" (*Language, Action, and Context* 14–15). Kant himself alludes to a parallel between his concept of logic and universal grammar in the *Logik* (*Introduction to Logic*), implying that he recognizes a connection between his project and that of eighteenth-century philologists.

Despite occasional hints like this on Kant's part, his contemporaries and followers wondered at his general neglect of language, and speculated that he might have taken his analysis of the understanding further had he considered its role. A younger generation of philosophers and philologists accordingly set to work translating key Kantian principles into linguistic principles. Various aspects of this transmutation of Kantian philosophy into philosophy of language have been studied,[1] though not Kant's relevance for the development of a concept of performative language. It is not often noted that, in the opening pages of *How to Do Things with Words*, Austin twice credits Kant with being "among the pioneers" in showing that many statements do things other than simply imparting factual information (2–3). Yet the immense influence of the performative in twentieth-century linguistic, literary, and cultural the-

---

[1] See Streitberg on the responses of Kant's contemporaries to his apparent disregard for language, and their attempts to compensate for it. Markis argues that Kant's philosophy of language exists only in traces of a repressed awareness that language plays a crucial role in the formation of ideas, and that Kant's followers, drawing out these traces, use his work to make the transition from a nomenclature-based theory to a theory that language generates ideas.

ory may actually be due to the fact that Austin and Searle only gave explicit and systematic form to a concept that is deeply rooted in Kantian and post-Kantian philosophy, as well as in German idealism and Romanticism.

KANT'S 'SATZ'

Kant's *Critique of Pure Reason* keeps linguistic questions in the background, apparently assuming that words play a purely secondary role as representations of phenomena that exist independently of and prior to them. But the reader of the First Critique occasionally stumbles over passages like the following, from Kant's concluding note on the analysis of the understanding:

> the transcendental object which may be the ground of this appearance that we call matter is a mere something of which we should not understand what it is, even if someone were in a position to tell us. For we can understand only that which brings with it, in intuition, something corresponding to our words. (CPR 286/B333)

This is a disturbing passage, twice over. First it surprises and provokes by implying that words *might* have a role in the epistemological process (i.e., we might be able to grasp the transcendental object "if someone were in a position to tell us"), even though neither reason nor sensory perception (as Kant is here lamenting) seems able to penetrate to the ground behind the appearance of matter. But this suggestion is immediately deflated when we realize that understanding only occurs by way of intuitions that "correspond to" words—that is, that language is only a nomenclature after all, since words always stand for "something." Just as the mind's construction of representations is limited by the presence of a real, if inaccessible, world of things-in-themselves, so the performativity of language is limited by the presence of referents to which linguistic signs are secondary.

Yet Kant's epistemology foreshadows a concept of the performative at a deeper level, through a linguistic figure for which the German language and philosophical tradition are perhaps responsible, but which Kant puts to significant use. This is the ambivalence of the noun *Satz*, meaning both logical proposition or judgment, and grammatical sentence.[2] Kant

---

[2]English terminology provides a certain parallel, inasmuch as "proposition" (the Latinate equivalent of *Satz*) refers to both a logical entity and a grammatical entity. But the ambiguity is more significant in German, where the philosophical term *Satz* (plural *Sätze*) is Kant's normal word for logical or intellectual judgment (though it has a near-synonym in *Urteil* 'judgment'), as well as being the only word available in

is, of course, interested in the first, "philosophical" definition of *Satz* throughout the *Critique of Pure Reason*, and particularly in the section on the operations of the understanding, the faculty responsible for making judgments or forming logical propositions. But Kant's elucidation of the logical *Satz*, and his frequent use of such *Sätze* as examples, provides a bridge to linguistic philosophers' recasting of Kant using *grammatical* examples. Friedrich Schlegel, for one, achieves a clear insight into the interdependence of the logical and the grammatical *Satz*, and thereby into the interdependence of philosophy and universal grammar: "The grammatical sentence has an exact relation to the logical [proposition]. The two clarify each other reciprocally" (Der grammatische Satz hat eine genaue Beziehung auf den logischen. Beide erklären sich gegenseitig [*KFSA* 13: 303]). Where Kant considers the logical aspect of propositions, then, linguistically oriented readers of Kant, like Humboldt and Coleridge, tend to shift the focus onto their grammatical dimension. Twentieth-century speech-act theory, moreover, which begins with the sentence-as-utterance, frequently reaches conclusions about it that are already anticipated in Kant's analysis of the logical *Satz*.

A few examples of this progression from the logical proposition, to the grammatical sentence, to the speech-act utterance, may be helpful. When analyzing the different kinds of judgments (Urteile) the understanding can make, Kant provides as an example the hypothetical proposition (hypothetische Satz), "If there is a perfect justice, the obstinately wicked are punished." He then breaks this down into two related propositions (Sätze)—"there is a perfect justice," and "the obstinately wicked are punished"—and notes, as a principle of logic, that the hypothetical proposition concerns the relationship of two or more propositions without regard to their individual truth (*CPR* 109/B98). For Humboldt, the linking of two *Sätze* becomes a basic mental act; indeed, it is one illustration of what he regards as the most important creative act of the mind, calling it, in significantly Kantian terms, the "act of *spontaneous positing* by bringing-together (synthesis)" (*OL* 184). But Humboldt describes this "activity of the . . . language-forming mind" as an act that is inseparable from its grammatical manifestations. In the above example, for instance, synthesis is brought about by the conjunction ("if"), in such a manner that "the preceding clause [is] kept hovering long enough before the mind for its successor to impart complete determinacy to the total utterance" (*OL* 200). Humboldt's shift of attention to the use of lan-

---

German for the grammatical sentence, phrase, or clause. The cognate verb *setzen* 'to posit' is also more conspicuous in German, whereas in English the relationship of "proposition" to "posit" or "propose" lies semi-concealed in Latin roots.

guage itself as that which forges the relationship between two propositions is completed in speech-act philosophy. An analysis of the way language joins propositions to one another, thereby abstracting from their truth in relation to reality, leads Austin and Searle to preliminary definitions of the performative. "I am stating that John is running" is one of Austin's examples, and he examines the relationship of entailment between "I am stating" and "John is running" in his attempt to pin down the "difference" between constative and performative statements (54–55). Searle, finally, uses (as Kant did) a hypothetical sentence—"If Sam smokes habitually, he will not live long"—to introduce his redefinition of propositions in the context of speech-act philosophy (*Speech Acts* 29). While Kant regarded the joining of two propositions as a *logical* act, Searle describes it as one of many *illocutionary* acts we perform in using language.

Kant continues to provide a basis for later definitions of the performative when he picks up the same, hypothetical example again in the following paragraph. His theme here is modality, or the distinction between optional, assertive, and apodeictic (i.e., necessary) judgments. Noting the different values, uses, or implications a proposition can have, depending on whether it is "thought only as . . . optional," or "stated assertorically," he points out that, "In the above example, the proposition, 'There is a perfect justice,' is not stated assertorically, but is thought only as an optional judgement, which it is possible to assume; it is only the logical sequence which is assertoric" (*CPR* 110/B100). This observation appears in the context of a discussion on how even a "problematic" judgment, or one whose objective truth is by no means proven or even likely, can nevertheless contribute to the discovery of a true proposition: "The problematic proposition is therefore that which expresses only logical (which is not objective) possibility—a free choice of admitting such a proposition, and a purely optional admission of it into the understanding" (*CPR* 110/B101). Even a proposition that cannot be *asserted* in its own right can be *used* to advance toward the realms of truth and necessity; and as Kant hierarchizes the modalities (from possible up to apodeictic), he also temporalizes them as successive "moments of thought." But when Coleridge repeats the same point in his *Logic* (a treatise that, as will be discussed in Chapter 4, enacts a linguistic turn on Kant's philosophy), the meaning of *Satz* shifts from "judgment" to "sentence" as the focus shifts from modality to referentiality. Coleridge's point is that the mind has the ability to form an infinite number of propositions prior to and independently of their reference to reality. To illustrate this, he indicates that the sentence "The house is white" constitutes the same kind of mental act as "Cerberus is three-headed" (*L* 76–77)—and his conspicuous choice of a mythical creature as an example turns the argument toward questions of reference and fictionality. Searle locates the issue of modality even more clearly in the context of linguistic philosophy. He distinguishes relentlessly between a "neutral" (or "possible") proposition and an assertion: "*a proposition is to be sharply distinguished from an assertion or statement of it,*" since "an assertion is a (very special kind of) commitment to the truth of a proposition" (*Speech Acts* 29). Searle's pragmatically oriented version of Kant's distinction of modalities is fundamental to the concept of performativity. It makes room for the necessary distinction between the neutral, abstract, or idealized *proposition* and the contextualized *illocutionary act*—that is, the same proposition as uttered by a speaker in a specific context so as to convey commitment to it or uncertainty about it. When Kant's distinction between optional and assertoric propositions is carried over onto the level of language, in other words, it effectively becomes a concept of illocutionary force.

The significance of the Kantian *Satz* is bound up with cognates and compounds that appear frequently in the *Critique of Pure Reason*, including *Grundsatz* 'principle,' *Gegensatz* 'opposite,' *Gesetz* 'law,' and especially *setzen* 'to posit.' The verb *setzen* comes to be of utmost importance to Fichte's adaptation of Kant's system, as well as to the concept of the performative, since speech-act theory is centrally concerned with the ability of language to posit rather than describe reality. For Kant's nineteenth-century followers, no less than for twentieth-century readers, the act of positing in the First Critique is inseparable from what Kant calls *synthesis*, and describes as the fundamental operation of the understanding. Defined in general as "the act of putting different representations together, and of grasping what is manifold in them in one [act of] knowledge" (*CPR* 111/B103), synthesis is the operation by which the mind gathers scattered intuitions of the world and unifies them into concepts. If the act-character of this central operation of the mind is not as radical for Kant as it will be for Fichte, Kant nevertheless leaves no doubt but that synthesis *is* an act, calling it a *Handlung* and an *Actus*. He also describes it as a *creative* act, particularly when he stresses that synthesis is necessary for the production of objects as we experience them:

> The synthetic unity of consciousness is, therefore, an objective condition of all knowledge. It is not merely a condition that I myself require in knowing an object, but is a condition under which every intuition must stand in order *to become an object for me*. (*CPR* 156/B138)

The mind's act of synthesis needs to be distinguished from the hypothetical operation of a divine mind that would create *things*, not just represented objects; one could imagine, Kant says, "a divine understanding which should not represent to itself given objects, but through whose representation the objects should themselves be given or produced" (*CPR* 161/B145). Nevertheless, Kant's central hypothesis of the synthetic power of the human mind introduces a moment of creative action, construction, or positing into the cognitive process that could be seen as the germ of the Romantic performative.

Kant's act of synthesis is divided up among various faculties of the mind. The imagination or *Einbildungskraft*, always in the First Critique a problematic and imprecisely located faculty, is responsible for all synthesis that brings together the manifold of intuitions apprehended by sensory perception. But it is the "second" synthesis performed by the understanding (Verstand) that brings these forms to order under *concepts*, thus creating them as objects for us and making knowledge or recognition (Erkenntnis) possible. The highest form of synthesis brought about by the understanding is that which has been called the Kantian *cogito*. It is the "transcendental unity of apperception" or, alternatively, the "transcendental unity of self-consciousness"—the subject's awareness of *its own* unity as that which bestows unity on manifold intuitions. This act of synthesis, based on the proposition of transcendental unity, represents the summit of logic and the essential activity of the understanding:

> Combination . . . is an affair of the understanding alone, which itself is nothing but the faculty of combining *a priori*, and of bringing the manifold of given representations under the unity of apperception. The principle of apperception is the highest principle [Grundsatz] in the whole sphere of human knowledge. (*CPR* 154/B135)

Kant's most famous formulation of the principle of transcendental unity is phrased, thought-provokingly if not self-consciously, in terms of verbal expressions ("the 'I think'") and utterances ("I call them . . . *my* representations"):

> It must be possible for the 'I think' to accompany all my representations; for otherwise something would be represented in me which could not be thought at all, and that is equivalent to saying that the representation would be impossible or at least would be nothing to me. That representation which can be given prior to all thought is entitled intuition. All the manifold of intuition has, therefore, a necessary relation to the 'I think' in the same subject in which this manifold is found. . . . I am conscious of the self as identical in respect of the manifold of representations that are

given to me in an intuition, because I call them one and all *my* representations, and so apprehend them as constituting *one* intuition. This amounts to saying, that I am conscious to myself *a priori* of a necessary synthesis of representations—to be entitled the original synthetic unity of apperception—under which all representations that are given to me must stand, but under which they have also first to be brought by means of a synthesis. (*CPR* 152–55/B131–35)

There is an intriguing structural parallel between Kant's claim that "I think" accompanies all our mental representations, and can always potentially be made explicit, and Austin's claim that "I state that..." implicitly accompanies all our verbal representations, whether or not it is actually articulated (135). Making the "I think" explicit reveals the active role of the understanding in forming representations; making the "I state" explicit reveals the active role of the speaker in forming sentences. In both cases, the act-character of the (cognitive or verbal) judgment is bound up with a reference to the first-person subject—and the centrality and asymmetry of the first person in both speech-act philosophy and Kantian-Romantic theories of cognition is a key issue for a theory of the Romantic performative.

For philosophers of language, Humboldt and Coleridge especially, Kant's concept of synthesis will serve to redefine the function of the copula, or the relationship between subject and predicate in a sentence. Kant himself refers only in passing to the fact that the copula "is" (das Verhältniswörtchen *ist* [*KrV* 142/*CPR* 159/B142]) is the correlate in language, or at least in the linguistic expression of propositions, of the act of judgment performed by the understanding. For Kant, "is" conveys the *objective* unity of representations that accompanies a synthesis made by the understanding, as opposed to the *subjective* unity bestowed by the imagination (i.e., the difference between the objective proposition "Bodies *are* heavy" and the subjective observation "If I support a body, I feel an impression of weight"). The opening sentences of his 1762 essay "Die falsche Spitzfindigkeit der vier syllogistischen Figuren erwiesen" ("The False Subtlety of the Four Syllogistic Figures") provide a little more detail on the subject-predicate relationship. Here, Kant explicates the act of judging as the act of (re)marking or noting a distinguishing feature of the object:

> To compare something as a characteristic mark [Merkmal] with a thing is *to judge*. The thing itself is the subject; the characteristic mark is the predicate. The comparison is expressed by means of the copula *is* or *are*. When used absolutely, the copula designates the predicate as a characteristic mark of the subject. ("False Subtlety" 89)

For Kant, the act of judgment itself merits analysis; the language in which propositions are expressed is secondary, and he mentions it only for purposes of clarification. But his priorities are reversed by the following generation of linguistic philosophers, for whom "is" becomes the central word and concept in a theory of language, and who account for its centrality by tracing it back to the Kantian analytic of the understanding.

HERDER'S 'URSPRUNG DER SPRACHE': COGNITION, COMMUNICATION, AND WORDS OF POWER

Two bold attempts to "correct" Kantian epistemology, by arguing that language (and not a nebulous transcendental schema) provides the organizing principles for our experience, came from Kant's contemporaries Johann Georg Hamann and Johann Gottfried Herder, each of whom produced his own *Metakritik* of the *Critique of Pure Reason*. But Herder's more important contribution to a performative concept of language began a decade before the First Critique, with the publication of his influential *Abhandlung über den Ursprung der Sprache* (*Essay on the Origin of Language*) in 1772. A critique of previous accounts of the origin of language produced by the French and German Enlightenment, Herder's essay insists on the inalienable role of language in cognition. The linguistic sign is implicated in the mind's initial act of *noting* and *reflecting on* a specific feature in the chaos of perceptions that surrounds it:

> Man manifests reflection when the force of his soul acts in such freedom that, in the vast ocean of sensations which permeates it through all the channels of the senses, it can, if I may say so, single out one wave, arrest it, concentrate its attention on it, and be conscious of being attentive. (*EOL* 115)

The act of paying attention (aufmerken) to one particular sensation is the "first act of... acknowledgment" and the "first judgment of the soul"; it produces a "clear concept" and a distinctive word with which the concept can be recalled and communicated (*EOL* 116). When Herder refers to the distinctive sensation as a "word of the soul" (Wort der Seele), "word" is both figurative and literal: this is at once the action of a mental faculty that operates like speech, and the origin of an actual, interpersonal language that externalizes mental action. "The first characteristic mark which I conceive," Herder emphasizes, "is a characteristic word for me and a word of communication for others!" (*EOL* 128).

From the moment of its origin, language is bound up with both cognition and communication, as Herder illustrates in a memorable account of the birth of language in a human being's encounter with a sheep. Confronted by indefinite sensations of whiteness and woolliness, the human subject cannot make sense of the sheep until it bleats, and thereby offers a distinctive mark (Merkmal) or word (Merkwort). The sound it produces imprints itself on the mind of the listener as a mark by which it can be recognized again, as a verb signifying its distinctive activity, and as a name that can be communicated to others. Essentially a "speech" act, the sheep's bleating alters the world as the listener perceives it and gives the sheep itself an identity within that world. The account of cognition advanced in the language-origin essay, which grounds all of Herder's thinking on epistemology and philology, is that of a living, acting, speaking world (these being one and the same) that, in a series of dynamic encounters, marks the human intellect. While sound and oral language set the pattern for the mind-world engagement in which language originates, silent impressions work analogously to sounds. Thus an encounter with lightning (presented in Herder's essay in a literally "dramatic" context, using a quotation from Shakespeare's *A Midsummer Night's Dream*) produces the word *Blitz* 'lightning,' a sound that reenacts for the ear the impression of "the ultimately sudden and quick" (des Urplötzlichschnellen) that lightning originally made on the eye (*SS* 40). Herder's insistence that the verb was the original part of speech adds to the dynamism of his account of language, especially when he describes verbs as the "first elements of power" (*EOL* 132). We experience the world, he maintains, as a series of encounters with "sounding acts" (diese tönenden Handlungen) rather than with things. Paradoxically, these acts exist for us prior to agents; and because the structure of language mirrors the developmental process of the human spirit, it follows that verbs exist for us prior to nouns (*SS* 33–34).

If this phenomenological model of language as action seems far from Austin's convention-governed context for illocutionary acts, or Searle's rule-governed one, Herder approaches a more modern sense of performativity when he carries his concept of creative utterance over into a societal context. The second part of his language-origin essay turns from the individual and cognitive context to the social and communicative world, tracing the development of language through increasingly larger societies of family, community, nation, and human race. Here a negative contrary to Herder's creative, energetic account of language-origin emerges when he suggests that speech acts might limit or constrain the linguistic universe of future speakers. Referring mainly to Rousseau, Herder notes that other philosophers believe the speech acts of our ancestors have marked the world with errors and misleading concepts:

> Before we were able to think, we were taught to fall down before verbal concepts as before statues, instead of being allowed to see them wander like living bodies in nature, and study them; and there arise—as Bacon, the most powerful sensibility with regard to this wound of humanity, calls them—idols of the guilds, idols from dark caverns, idols that are the seduction of the marketplace and the spectacle of the stage—and that are all perpetuated by nothing so much as by language. There stand the rules and the laws that we must think according to our fathers' analogies and not according to nature, that we must read the images of the universe in the distorting mirror of tradition, and not in nature. There lie the forms of that cave in which the inventors of language and all their descendants thought, the plastic figures of those small worlds from which they looked out into the larger one.... (SS 72)

Yet clearing all of this historical-linguistic detritus away, Herder warns, would leave us naked in a wilderness. The best course is to proceed with caution, with an awareness that the creative power of language also brings with it the power to perpetuate a worldview or to make judgments (Urteile) into prejudices (Vorurteile). Even if Herder is trying to counter the pro-nature, anti-culture bias of the Rousseauist tradition with his own picture of a genial world of family and community, in which the language just barely invented by the fathers is passed on, together with its freshly formed worldview, to their sons, it is hard not to feel that his account of verbal prejudice represents the darker intimation of his own theory of creative language. If language is both means of cognition and means of communication, it may well shape the worldview not only of the speaking subject and the immediate listener, but of their descendants and society at large. Momentarily, Herder's language-origin essay anticipates the more political, more modern, and more threatening aspect of the performative as a phenomenon that perpetuates rules, laws, and power structures "by nothing so much as by language."

HERDER'S 'METAKRITIK': PERMUTATIONS OF BEING IN LANGUAGE

Given his conviction that language is, quite simply, the mind's way of relating to the world, Herder is highly critical of the Kantian system, which he regards as neglecting language yet postulating esoteric schemas and categories that the mind uses without knowing that it is using them. He complains of not being able to understand the First Critique, and accuses Kant and the transcendental idealists of hyper-cleverness: through the unfounded invention of new terminology, they set up a phantom realm of things-in-themselves and human-faculties-in-themselves that obscures the actual world in which we exist, and the means by which we understand it. Besides misusing language to describe their nebulous categories, transcendental philosophers also marginalize the crucial role of language in a theory of knowledge. If properly developed, Herder boldly declares, metaphysics would actually turn out to be identical with a philosophy of language: "Mithin wird Metaphysik eine *Philosophie der menschlichen Sprache"* (SS 184).

In his 1799 *Metakritik zur Kritik der reinen Vernunft* (Metacritique of the *Critique of Pure Reason*), Herder tries to restore language to a central position and thereby restore clarity to an account of human cognition. He presents an intriguing, if not consistently worked out, philosophy of language as the organ of reason—that is, a philosophy in which language plays a performative role in shaping the speaker, the speaker's environment, and the relation between the two. In his *Metakritik*, Herder associates the thesis of his language-origin essay, according to which cognition involves the subject's identification of a distinctive mark by which the object can be recognized and named, with Kant's account of cognition as the subject's creation of a unified concept from scattered intuitions. Apparently regarding the parallel as so obvious that he assumes it more than he explicates it, Herder concludes that language is actually equivalent to cognition: "What does it mean *to think? To speak inwardly*, that is, to pronounce for oneself the features [Merkmale] that have been internalized; to speak means to think aloud" (SS 189). Because Kant fails to realize this, he relegates language to a secondary role: he regards it merely as an instrument used by the philosopher to formulate categories and schemas by which the operations of the understanding are (belatedly) explained. In reality, Herder counters, language is the means by which the understanding operates in the first place:

> Since the assembled categories are themselves no magic formula, but rather the *action (actus purus)* of the effective understanding, language as a whole must be an expression of the cognitive understanding, not only in classes and types of explanation, but in the formation of the concepts themselves, and as such it must prove itself as a living form. (SS 212)

Herder demonstrates what it would mean to regard language as "living form" by literally rewriting Kant's four categories, or "pure concepts of the understanding" (i.e., quantity, quality, relation, modality [CPR 113/B106]). In Herder's version, the categories are founded on *being* as the basic concept of human reason, which is also the basic concept of language. His verb-centered theory of language corresponds to a theory of cognition in which *being existent*—moreover, being or existence conceived of as an *active power of continuing*—is the key feature in the mind's apprehension of objects. Thus, the Kantian categories translate into different aspects of the verb *sein* 'to be': [3] existence ("is" = exists [in reality]); attribution ("is" connects the subject to predicates or attributes); becoming ("is" indicates occurrence, cause, and effect); and measurement ("is" in a mathematical sense, also represented by the symbols =, +, −, or x).

These distinctions between different inflections of *sein* are only one of several possible rewritings of the Kantian categories that Herder proposes in the *Metakritik*. All of them are encompassed within the basic schema he offers for the concepts of the understanding (Verstandsbegriffe), which are again based on the modalities of being:

Sein [being = existence]

Dasein [being in space, presence]   *Dauer* [being in time, duration]

Kraft [power]   (SS 189)

These rubrics can also serve to categorize the grammatical parts of speech, as follows:

1. *Sein*—Independent words, along with indications of relation (i.e., nouns with prepositions);
2. *Dasein*—Properties (i.e., adjectives);
3. *Dauer*—Powers (i.e., verbs);
4. *Kraft*—Measures (i.e., expressions of number, size, gradation) (SS 213)

Whether these categories are fully consistent, and whether they are (at least in the relatively undeveloped form in which Herder presents them) directly useful for the analysis of discourse as the "*type of a coherent act of the effective understanding*" (Typus eines zusammenhängenden Akts des wirkenden Verstandes [SS 213]), is questionable. Important for the concept of the Romantic performative, though, is that Herder proposes a metacritique of Kant's *Critique* in which cognition works by means of language and in terms of grammatical categories. Different forms of intellectual apprehension are identified with the different ways language expresses existence. Existence itself, moreover, has both "static" aspects (Sein, Dasein) and "active" aspects (Dauer, Kraft). Herder emphasizes the latter: he regards being as an active appropriation of space or time, as

[3] As with the term *Satz*, the common ground shared by transcendental philosophy and linguistic philosophy is somewhat more evident in German, where "being" as an ontological and epistemological principle (Sein) and "to be" as a verbal infinitive (sein) are the same word, possibly (but not consistently) distinguished by capitalization.

effective causality, or as becoming. His permutations of the verb "to be" open up a performative dimension within being itself, that finds its counterpart in a performative account of discourse.

REVOLUTIONARY GRAMMAR

Herder's *Metakritik* represents an attempt to link Kant's First Critique with universal grammar—the study of parts of speech in terms of universal logical categories, rather than in relation to specific natural languages, that formed the prevailing mode of linguistic scholarship during the eighteenth century. As such, the *Metakritik* constitutes one example of a revolutionary perspective on grammar that also appears in numerous other grammatical treatises dating from the same period, in France as well as in Germany. Brigitte Schlieben-Lange has shown that grammar books began to be written differently around 1800—that is, after Kant and after the French Revolution. These new grammar texts take account of new theories of the origin of language; they tend to put the verb (rather than the noun) first, regarding it as the most important part of speech; and they pay new attention to relational words like pronouns, conjunctions, and relative pronouns, showing how these words function in dialogue and discourse. In general, they "understand speaking as an activity" and "grant a special role to the historical situation of a speaking subject" (Schlieben-Lange, "Elemente" 81). In other words, as Schlieben-Lange notes, at the end of the eighteenth century Continental grammars shifted noticeably toward a *pragmatic* understanding of language in terms of speaker, addressee, and speech situation.

The analysis of the verb as that which gives "life" or "soul" to discourse is crucial to the new grammar (Schlieben-Lange, "Elemente" 81). Even more important is its reinterpretation of the verb "to be"—for in this case the animating force of the verb seems to reach beyond the realm of discourse entirely and become a determining factor in the very existence of subject and object. Where Kant analyzed the status of representations produced by the understanding, post-Kantian linguistic philosophers analyze the status of representations to which language attaches the predicate "is." By marrying universal grammar with transcendental philosophy, these linguistic thinkers produce a revolutionary interpretation of the copula that has profound implications for the understanding of both ordinary and literary language.

On the one hand, the unique status of "to be" is a commonplace in the history of philological thought; such authorities as Aristotle and the seventeenth-century grammarians of Port Royal already assigned this verb a unique place in the structure of language. Following Aristotelian tradition, eighteenth-century universal grammarians categorized parts of speech according to the presence or absence of the verb "is." Thus, the two kinds of predicates, adjectives and verbs, differ in that the adjective lacks the element "to be" (e.g., "asleep"), while the verb contains it (e.g., adjective "asleep" + copula "is" = verb "sleeps"). Similarly, grammarians described "to be" as the only true verb, since all other verbs are formed from a static predicate plus "is": thus, the verb "sings" breaks down into "is" plus "singing," "thirsts" breaks down into "is" plus "thirsting," and so on. This eighteenth-century interpretation of the copula is typified by Johann Werner Meiner, whom Herder refers to both respectfully and critically as one of the leading contemporary grammarians. In his very formal and classificatory grammatical handbook of 1781, *Versuch einer an der menschlichen Sprache abgebildeten Vernunftlehre oder philosophische und allgemeine Sprachlehre* (An attempt at a doctrine of reason modeled on human language, or philosophical and universal grammar), Meiner articulates the commonplace distinction of verbs from adjectives: while both are predicates and therefore dependent parts of speech, verbs contain in themselves the *copula propositionis* (i.e., "is"), while adjectives do not (80–81). Although, as the title of Meiner's book indicates, he too sees himself as mediating between philosophy and grammar, this is the full extent of his commentary on the verb-substantive as the basis of all verbs.

But for Herder, "to be" is the original *Machtwort* or "word of power."[4] It expresses the basic concept in which cognition inheres, and once we recognize its different modalities, it allows us to distinguish between the claims of the understanding and the real existence of objects (die Behauptungen des Verstandes von *Wirklichkeit der Dinge* unterscheiden [*SS* 215]). Based on his conviction that language originates in and as an act that is at once cognitive (because it allows the human subject to recog-

---

[4]The literary criticism of Johann Jacob Breitinger provides an eighteenth-century definition of *Machtwort* (literally "power-word"), a term that now survives only in the German expression "to make a decision" (*ein Machtwort sprechen* = to exercise one's authority, decide the matter). According to Breitinger, the *Machtwort* condenses many concepts into one expression, causing the reader to think intently; such words "give a thing to be understood with particular emphasis" (50). The term *Machtwort* appears again in Herder's fragmentary writings on language, where he claims that German is particularly rich in words of power, although these words were even more plentiful in an older form of the language, and are retained in a greater number in Swiss German (*SS* 111). When language was still closer to poetry, it contained the strongest words of power (*SS* 119), yet power still inheres fundamentally in all languages through their expression of the central and original *Machtwort*: the verb-substantive "to be."

nize the sheep and place himself in relation to it) and communicative (because it gives him a representative word with which to express his experience of the sheep, and even because it is a kind of communicative experience *with* the sheep), Herder tries to correct and supplement Kant's analytic of the understanding. The result is a theory of language as an active and efficient medium, by which subjects locate themselves within a world that is only knowable through discourse. The verb, which stands at the midpoint of Herder's theory of language, is a figure for the way external objects express their nature (e.g., by bleating) and are grasped by the intellect; the intellect, in turn, apprehends this distinguishing feature of the object as an actual verb ("you bleat!"), the basis for both a concept of the object and a name by which it can be recalled to memory and communicated. The verb *sein*, a special word of power, anchors the universal form of language, and of cognition, by expressing existence, presence, duration, and power as the categories under which we experience phenomena.

Among linguists who are more receptive to transcendental idealism than Herder, the re-evaluation of the copula goes even further. Fichte's elucidation of being as an active principle, and Schelling's presentation of being as a self-reflexive principle, prompt linguistic thinkers to elevate "to be" into the central operator in their philosophy of language. It becomes the basis of Humboldt's concept of synthesis, Coleridge's concept of the verb-substantive, and Bernhardi's concept of the verbal representation of reality. In all three cases, forms like "is," "am," and "are" somehow contain an active element that allows *being* to be regarded (in ways that still need to be examined more closely) as an *act of being*. The analysis of the copula in Romantic philosophy thus achieves something analogous to the project that speech-act theory later undertakes—that is, a redefinition of the standard proposition as a performative act.

FICHTE'S 'SETZEN'

Crucial to the re-evaluation of being in language is the work of Fichte, who re-interprets the Kantian system so as to render it both dynamic and idealistic, and thereby locates being, acting, and positing at the heart of the philosophical enterprise. By insisting on the primacy of an act of positing, and with it the existence of the I as pure act, Fichte provides the ideal philosophical background for linguists who were beginning to regard language, too, as an activity of the mind in the world. Despite this, and despite the excitement that he and his work caused among early Romantic poets and theorists (including Humboldt, Bernhardi, the

Schlegels, Novalis, and Hölderlin), Fichte's impact on the philosophy of language is problematic. The brief essays that he devotes specifically to language are, ironically, among the handful of Romantic texts to argue the reactionary position that language has *no* role in cognition, but simply facilitates communication by providing signs for thoughts.

Fichte himself is a highly rhetorical speaker and writer, which is to say that the central texts of his idealist philosophy—the "Introductions" to the *Wissenschaftslehre* or *Science of Knowledge* published during the 1790s, and the *Wissenschaftslehre* itself, presented in several series of lectures in Jena and Berlin—are full of explicit speech acts. Important points in both his essays and his lectures are marked by an emphatic "I say that" or "I state." In other words, Fichte's own acts of positing as a speaker and writer conspicuously frame his story of the I that posits (setzt) itself as infinite activity, and posits as its contrary (Gegensatz) the Not-I or world. The Not-I then reflects back on the I, limiting it and bringing it to a reflective consciousness of itself as a representation, and as the activity of representation. Fichte's *Wissenschaftslehre* conflates being and doing, by making the existence of the self, and of all that the self conceives, dependent on its primary and definitive act of self-positing. Not substance, nor even existence, but rather activity and relation, occupy the center of this philosophical system.

Fichte insists that the I can only be understood as an activity that turns back on itself: "the I is nothing but a self-reverting acting, and a self-reverting acting is the I" (*Introductions* 117). He is careful to qualify even this formulation by noting that the I must not be conceived of as an agent performing an action. Rather, the agent itself is the *product* as well as the origin of the act of positing: "The intellect, for idealism, is an *act* [ein *Thun*], and absolutely nothing more; we should not even call it an *active* something [ein *Thätiges*], for this expression refers to something subsistent in which activity inheres" (*Science of Knowledge* 21). The paradox of a self-reflexive "acting" that generates its own agent serves as the basis, not only of Fichte's philosophy, but of the Romantic performative.[5] Humboldt nearly echoes Fichte's formulation when he describes synthesis—the key principle in his philosophy of language—as an "act-

---

[5] See also Gasché's argument that the performative act in general "has its roots in Fichte's idea of a self-positing self" (39). According to Gasché, speech-act theory, especially in its application to literary texts, remains bound to the Idealists' metaphysical conception of the speech act as a free act of the individual subject. Only de Man achieves a more fundamental notion of the performative by abandoning the horizon of metaphysics and characterizing the performative in terms of dissociation, disruption, and incompatibility with the constative (Gasché 41–46).

ing" rather than an "act" or "quality": "Since the synthesis we are speaking of is not a state [Beschaffenheit], not even properly a deed [Handlung], but itself a real action [Handeln], always passing with the moment, there can be no special *sign* for it in the words" (*OL* 184).

Being centered on an entity that, in effect, performs itself, Fichte's entire system takes on performative qualities. In his "Erste Einleitung zur Wissenschaftslehre" ("First Introduction to the Science of Knowledge," 1797), he describes his system as self-generating, denies that it can be judged true or false by reference to other philosophical propositions, and claims that its "felicity" lies in the reader's acknowledgment of its own postulates:

> My system can therefore be examined on its own basis alone, not on the presuppositions of some other philosophy; it is to agree only with itself, it can be explained, proved, or refuted in its own terms alone; one must accept or reject it as a whole. (*Science of Knowledge* 4–5)

Yet language per se plays an intermittent and problematic role in Fichte's system. It is only in the later versions of the *Wissenschaftslehre* that he presented in Berlin in the early 1800s that Fichte begins to address directly the relationship between the act of *setzen* and the verbal *Satz* that was implicitly present in Kant. The central term in his philosophy, elsewhere identified as I, self, being, or reason, is here also called "light," and Fichte presents the self-positing of the I as a virtual counterpart to the performative utterance by which God creates light in Genesis:

> The midpoint . . . was pure light. If we are actually to reach this, then the concept must be posited [gesetzt] and annihilated, and a being that is incomprehensible in itself must be posited [gesetzt]: *let us assume [gesetzt] that light is, then through this proposition everything that has been said is posited* [so ist durch diesen Satz alles das Gesagte gesetzt]. This we have now recognized; it is true, and expresses the fundamental principle [Grundgesetz] of all knowledge, and as such we can commit it to memory. (*Fichtes Werke* 10: 119)

This kind of passage (which is not at all out of the ordinary for the rhetoric of the *Wissenschaftslehre*) begins to approach rather closely to a concept of performative utterance. Fichte posits, through his own utterance or *Satz*, a mode of being that cannot be proven or even understood to exist, but that exists for us purely through an act of positing that also takes the form of a sentence (i.e., the *Satz* "let light be" [das Licht solle sein]). Through this verbal act, being-as-posited becomes the fundamental law or postulate (Grundgesetz) underlying all knowledge.

However, Fichte sees a fundamental contradiction between the immediate, subjective experience of intellectual activity to which he is trying to guide his hearers and readers, and the secondary, objective contemplation of phenomena that we undertake when we make use of words and concepts. He insists on a distinction between "doing" and "saying," and connects the latter with an inferior, belated experience of appearances rather than realities: "I say that in all derived knowledge whatsoever, or in appearance, there is a pure absolute contradiction between doing and saying: *propositio facto contraria*" (*Fichtes Werke* 10: 238).[6] Only the intellect or pure reason posited in Fichte's system achieves a form of knowing in which saying and doing are equivalent: "absolute reason will therefore distinguish itself from this relative knowledge in that what is expressed in reason is what it does, and it does what is expressed, in absolute qualitative indifference" (*Fichtes Werke* 10: 239). While insisting, then, that traditional philosophy and philosophical language split saying off from doing, Fichte complicates this distinction by adverting to the interrelationship between the fundamental activity of *setzen* and its (verbal) products—*Sätze* as acts of positing, principles, propositions, and laws. He reserves a performative prerogative for his own system of knowledge, based as it is on the experience of pure reason, for which saying and doing *are* equivalent. Presumably this equivalence holds for the language Fichte himself uses, as a spokesperson for the *Wissenschaftslehre*. According to his own account of the way he expects his teaching to be received, his emphatic "I say that . . ." pronouncements are acts that will bring about the re-creation of the *Wissenschaftslehre* in the minds of his hearers.

FICHTE ON THE ORIGIN OF LANGUAGE

In the essays that he devotes specifically to linguistic topics, Fichte again describes language as a second-order representation of thought. Indeed, he insists polemically on the separateness of thinking and speaking in defiance of the new linguistics of his time, which was enthusiastically promoting the idea that language plays an intrinsic role in the formation of thoughts. Herder's claim that thinking and speaking are interdepend-

---

[6]See also Fichte's aside on Schelling, whom he critiques for propounding a derivative philosophy, and specifically for merely "saying" that which the *Wissenschaftslehre* already "does": "This is the first nasty trick he encounters: *saying*, which always proceeds from subjectivity, and by its nature produces a dead object, is not at all more refined, but instead much more trivial, than doing, which stands between both at the midpoint of inner, vital being" (*Fichtes Werke* 10: 197).

ent met with general approval in late-eighteenth-century Germany. Hamann writes that "the whole ability to think rests on language" (224); Humboldt's first reflections on the nature of language appear in a series of theses entitled "Über Denken und Sprechen" (On thinking and speaking); Bernhardi and the Schlegels develop their own models of the interdependence of thought and language, which will be discussed below. "Thinking is speaking," Novalis writes with particular lucidity, then goes on to link both thinking and speaking to action: "Speaking and doing or making are a single, merely modified operation" (3: 297). Schleiermacher, finally, begins his lectures on hermeneutics with a powerful affirmation of the dependence of thought on language:

> language is the way and means by which thought becomes real. For there is no thought without speech. The utterance of the words relates only to the presence of another person, and in that sense is accidental. But no one can think without words. (77)

Against this consensus, however, Fichte programmatically defends the self-sufficiency of reason. Challenging the tradition of Condillac and, in particular, Herder's language-origin essay, he argues in "Von der Sprachfähigkeit und dem Ursprunge der Sprache" (On the linguistic capacity and the origin of language, 1795), and more obscurely also in "Über Geist und Buchstab in der Philosophie" (On spirit and letter in philosophy, 1794), that cognition is prior to and independent of language, and that language developed as a secondary ability for the sole purpose of communicating thoughts between reasoning beings. While the former of these two essays, Fichte's most explicit contribution to the late-eighteenth-century debate about language, is entirely leveled against the idea that thought depends on the ability to speak, he states his opposition most clearly in a strident footnote: "Language, I am convinced, has been held to be far too important when it was believed that without it no use of reason would have taken place at all" (*Fichtes Werke* 8: 309n).

Yet in denying language a creative role in cognition, Fichte aligns it, instead, with another sphere of human action. In his account of its origin and purpose, language is a thoroughly pragmatic phenomenon. Human beings are rational creatures who, in striving to guard the unity and integrity of their faculty of reason, do battle with nature because it appears antagonistic to reason; yet they seek to communicate their purposes to one another, because they recognize each other as fellow creatures endowed with reason. Language emerges as the most practically useful method by which I can give you to understand that I too am a reasoning creature, so that you and I, instead of seeking to eliminate one another, can work together in our purpose of extending rational control over the natural world. Specifically, Fichte believes that the oral medium of language developed as the most practical replacement for other possible ways of getting fellow humans to understand one's rational purpose—such as, for instance, gestures or pointing. Despite the fact that Fichte is at pains to distinguish linguistic signs from actions—signs are expressive, whereas actions are purposeful—the role of verbal utterances is to *replace* physical actions, and to participate in the larger activity of forging relationships among reason-endowed individuals. The tone of the essay is set by the repeated terms "purpose" (Zweck) and "act" (Handlung). As Jere Paul Surber writes in a thorough treatment of the political and sociological implications of this text for early Romantic thought, the originality of Fichte's argument lies in his treatment of language "as an issue intimately connected with the intersubjective origins of society" (41).

In the second part of "Von der Sprachfähigkeit und dem Ursprunge der Sprache," Fichte goes into more detail about the development of oral language, examining the logical necessity and relative priority of different grammatical forms. Although his accounts of the various parts of speech are brief and often less than convincing, he identifies concepts that will be important to his more linguistically oriented and linguistically trained contemporaries. For instance, Fichte's definition of the noun "thing" (ein Ding) in terms of the word *sein*, as "something existent" (ein Seyendes überhaupt) (*Fichtes Werke* 8: 319), could be regarded as the elementary form of Coleridge's and Bernhardi's conviction that all nouns also contain a verbal principle. Coleridge's idea of the verb-substantive is the most fully developed version of this grammatical ambiguity, and Fichte goes in the same direction as Coleridge will when he deduces that the original "words" must have been equivalent to entire sentences. "The first words contained within themselves a substantive and a verb" (*Fichtes Werke* 8: 325); only later did these separate into different parts of speech. Although Fichte fails to work out the larger linguistic implications of his own idealist philosophy, observations like these gesture toward the idea that an active principle not only underlies the origin of the I, but, even for Fichte, also underlies the origin of language.[7]

---

[7]Fichte later came to recognize a much more fundamental role for language in the processing of thought and the shaping of both individuals and nations, above all in the fourth of his *Reden an die deutsche Nation* (Addresses to the German nation) of 1808. As Gipper notes, this change of heart may have been influenced by the work of

BERNHARDI AND FICHTEAN LINGUISTICS

The real bridge between transcendental idealism and philosophy of language, and moreover between philosophy of language and literature, is the work of the literary critic, school reformer, and grammarian August Ferdinand Bernhardi. As Fichte's best friend in Berlin, an acquaintance of Humboldt, a contributor to the Schlegels' journal *Athenäum*, and brother-in-law of Ludwig Tieck, Bernhardi communicated with Fichte's philosophical circle as well as with the early Romantic literary community, "often serving as something of an emissary between them" (Surber 112). Bernhardi's mediation between transcendental idealism and Romantic literature took the form of linguistic philosophy, as expressed above all in his influential *Sprachlehre* (Grammar, 1801–3). In many respects the 130-page introduction to Bernhardi's *Sprachlehre* reads as an expanded, more detailed, and more competent version of Fichte's "Von der Sprachfähigkeit und dem Ursprunge der Sprache." Like Fichte, Bernhardi attempts to derive the necessary form of language from reason itself, based on the principle that reason must be conceived of as a unity that seeks to realize itself in the world-order. Bernhardi's account of the development of language out of the human being's relationship to nature and need to communicate with other humans is almost identical to Fichte's, and a large part of his introduction extends Fichte's comments on the derivation and development of the various parts of speech.

Yet Bernhardi repeatedly swerves away from Fichte's language-origin essay in his attempt to be more Fichtean than Fichte. He is concerned, as Fichte himself apparently was not, to bring "Von der Sprachfähigkeit und dem Ursprunge der Sprache" into dialogue with the *Wissenschaftslehre*—that is, to reconcile the implications about language as a form of *setzen* that derive from the latter with the secondary role that Fichte assigns to language in the former. To the extent that Bernhardi achieves a compromise between these positions, he does so by transmuting "communication," which Fichte identified as the purpose of language, into the more inclusive and imaginative concept of *Darstellung* 'representation': "then language would be the ability to represent our ideas [das Vermögen der Darstellung unserer Vorstellungen] through articulated sounds" (*Sprachlehre* 1: 16). Enhancing the definition of language by identifying it, not just as a means of transmitting information, but as the *only possible externalization of the activity of the intellect*, forces Bernhardi to complicate Fichte's separation of cognition from commu-

---

Humboldt, but it ultimately had little influence on the development of Fichte's philosophy ("Sprachphilosophie" 221–22).

nication, even though, in deference to Fichte, he attempts to affirm this separation at the outset of his *Sprachlehre*. "If it cannot be denied that the practice of reason and thought would also be possible without language," he begins, echoing Fichte's strident footnote—but immediately counters, "still it is evident on first sight that both would be limited to a high degree, that a language of words is the easiest of all means of connection among reasonable beings, and that it most fosters the development and cultivation of reason" (*Sprachlehre* 1: 4). Bernhardi adds an eloquent summary of the ways in which language *does* contribute to the development of reason, and language becomes more and more obviously bound up with the operations of the mind as his argument continues. Indeed, the imagery with which he describes the power of language hints at an almost cosmic creativity: "Whence does moving air have the power, when it falls into the ear as sound, to descend to the spirit and there stir up, like the wind on the water, sometimes a gentle rippling, other times wild waves?" (*Sprachlehre* 1: 6).

Like most post-Kantian linguists, Bernhardi regards language as a function of one particular mental faculty: the understanding. Both language and the understanding are engaged in producing representations, judgments, and concepts. Bernhardi generally explicates the connection and the distinction between epistemology and grammar with the help of the paired terms *Vorstellung* 'idea, presentation' and *Darstellung* 'representation,' whereby the *Vorstellung* is a mental concept that corresponds to a verbal *Darstellung*. When signs appear as "presentations" in the understanding, we call them "concepts," and when they appear as "representations" in an interpersonal context, we call them "words" (als Vorstellungen heißen sie Begriffe, als Darstellungen Wörter [*Sprachlehre* 1: 86]). Correspondingly, combinations of signs can be either mental "judgments" or linguistic "sentences" (daher entsteht als Vorstellung das Urtheil, als Darstellung der Satz).

This insight into the interdependence of mental and verbal representations—itself embodied in the etymological overlap between the terms *Vorstellung* and *Darstellung*—leads on to one of Bernhardi's most important contributions to the concept of a Romantic speech act: his analysis of the verb *sein*. Bernhardi's examination of the copula is twofold; it is part of an epistemology, but also part of a grammar. Epistemologically, Bernhardi demonstrates that *sein* is the principle by which the understanding performs its function of synthesizing "all substances, accidents, images, intuitions, and parts" (*Sprachlehre* 1: 33). The highest logical judgment the understanding can accomplish is that of identifying substance and accidents together as a *thing*, and thus concluding, "the thing is existing" (Das Ding ist seiend)—or, with Kant, A = A (*Sprachlehre* 1: 36). Being, in other words, is the highest condition of the objects of our knowledge:

> According to this, the thing, being, and the condition of existing [Ding, sein und seiend] would be the highest moments for the faculty of knowledge, and all three would finally resolve into *Being* itself [in das *Sein* überhaupt], as the highest condition of everything that is given and discovered. (*Sprachlehre* 1: 36)

As the most sophisticated logical judgment, the identification of an *existing thing* follows on two previous operations. The understanding first reveals itself as an autonomous (i.e., non-passive) faculty by choosing substances to join to predicates and thus forming concepts for itself. In this first stage, joining is itself the salient act. The real existence of the concept is thus far bracketed off as a separate question: "thus [the understanding] can join any accident it likes with any substance it likes into a judgment, subject to the condition that it gives up the connection of its judgment to reality and only concerns itself with a connection in its own right" (*Sprachlehre* 1: 33–34). In the second stage, the understanding progresses to an ordering of its concepts and a clearer distinction between substance and accident. Although qualities are first perceived as predicates (or accidents), the understanding *abstracts* so as to confer an ideal existence on them and make them into substances: "So what is sweet becomes sweetness, what is beautiful, beauty.... Every accident can become substance, although not the other way around" (*Sprachlehre* 1: 35).

Once the understanding has made arbitrary connections (first moment), then refined the status of substance and accident (second moment), it can proceed to the identification of certain substance-predicate combinations *as existing in reality* (third moment). This epistemological process provides a basis for Bernhardi's account of the development of language and specific parts of speech. He is unwilling to take a firm position on which single part of speech originated first, nor is he centrally concerned with the question of language-origin, although he turns to it in a few sections of the *Sprachlehre* as a question that had preoccupied most linguistic scholarship during the preceding decades. Although he tends to give precedence to the noun, Bernhardi's originary noun is one that is always imbued with the concept of *sein*, or the act of being. Thus, what he locates at the origin of language is really a noun-verb compound that, like Coleridge's verb-substantive, combines existence with action in a strikingly modern, and strikingly performative, manner.

Bernhardi's most extended account of the origin of language is a variant on Herder's more famous version of an originary scene: where Herder's primitive human encounters a sheep, Bernhardi's is confronted by a turtledove. Herder, in fact, also made passing reference to the turtledove and its cooing in his language-origin essay (*SS* 31), and Bernhardi apparently picks up on this example because it allow him to demonstrate more clearly how the bird's utterance ("tur tur") becomes its name (*turtur* being Latin for turtledove). More complex and significant, though, is Bernhardi's analysis of the bird's utterance as an originary "sentence" that fuses noun and verb, inasmuch as it designates the animal that produced the sound, the act of producing it, and also the entire mental event in which the human subject experiences the turtledove and forms a concept of it. Bernhardi identifies the two elements contained in the originary word "tur tur" as (1) the mental act of fusing qualities, or forming a judgment, and (2) the mental object produced by the act of judgment. "Both are fundamentally one," he claims, "and differ only according to one's perspective, so that the verb doubtless developed simultaneously with the noun; 'turtur' was not simply the name of the animal, but also designated the act of bringing forth this sound" (*Sprachlehre* 1: 67). This apprehension of the object *as it appears in a performative moment* ultimately makes the human subject aware of the category of *being* itself. Thus, in a not immediately intuitive and yet logical way, the apprehension of an existing object by means of a word effects the transition to the highest judgment of the understanding, a judgment that does not just combine qualities (first moment) but affirms the existence of the concept in reality (third moment). My experience of the turtledove's "tur tur" coincides with my designation of it by the name *turtur* and with my realization that this whole synthetic act is an engagement with being.

This entire process, finally, constitutes the invention of the proposition. Bernhardi describes the sound "tur tur" as the earliest form of sentence, since the second syllable is not simply a repetition of the first, but rather an affirmation of being—as if the first "tur" were a noun and the second "tur" a verb that confirms the turtledove's existence as an agent that defines itself through its activity. Presumably we have to understand the utterance "tur tur" as the abbreviated form of the proposition "the tur turs," or even "tur [the object] = tur [the object affirmed as existing]." "According to this," Bernhardi claims, "*tur tur* would be the example of the earliest kind of sentences, and the concept of being would lie in the latter *tur*" (*Sprachlehre* 1: 68).

Bernhardi's devotion to the sentence becomes even stronger in his second major treatise, *Anfangsgründe der Sprachwissenschaft* (Elementary principles of linguistics, 1805), a more pedagogically oriented continuation of the *Sprachlehre*. Here he describes the sentence as the real unit of linguistic communication: "Only with the sentence, one may say, is language invented, for simple lining-up and pointing are very incomplete forms of designation" (39). We might compare Bernhardi's preference for a sentence-based grammar with Gottlob Frege's renewed attention to the sentence in early-twentieth-century linguistic philosophy, which makes its way into speech-act theory when Searle quotes with approval Frege's dictum that "only in the context of a sentence do words mean something," and turns a sentence-based philosophy into an illocution-based philosophy (*Speech Acts* 25).

REAL BEING AND REPRESENTED BEING

All parts of speech can thus be derived from the elements that are contained in the originary "sentence" *tur tur*, which represents the object plus the mind's act of apprehending it, or the noun plus the verb "to be." The fact that the object is not conceived of as a "pure" noun (i.e., as a *Ding an sich*), but always accompanied by the mode of our perception (i.e., by the mind's concept of being), is the Kantian aspect of Bernhardi's grammar. The Fichtean aspect comes to the fore again when Bernhardi distinguishes between genuine existence and ideal or posited existence—and identifies the latter as the particular province of language. Although the mind may be aware of a concept of real being (reales Sein), in order to express real existence it must resort to "ideal being" (ideales Sein) or "the being of representation" (Sein der Darstellung). The word "is," Bernhardi claims, is "representative," yet the speaker "actually means to express real being" in using it (Dies Ist ist eigentlich darstellend; allein das darstellende Subjekt will eigentlich ein reales Sein damit ausdrücken [*Sprachlehre* 1: 214]). The way the mind confirms existence in reality is by *positing, representing, or idealizing existence in language*; as for Fichte, but now with a significant linguistic inflection, "being" exists because it is posited. When we use the word "is," we are referring to a perception mediated by our intellectual faculties, and thus to a representation rather than to a real thing. Nevertheless, we are all used to behaving as if this representation were an actual intuition:

> we bestow on the being of representation only the appearance of reality; this means, in other words, that a person treats representation as if it were an intuition. He posits a substance in space, the substantive; a sensation in time, the attributive; he joins both absolutely, and places them

in a certain relation to a knowing subject, and this he designates by means of being/to be [sein]. (*Sprachlehre* 1: 215)

In *Anfangsgründe der Sprachwissenschaft*, Bernhardi summarizes the representative status and the synthesizing function of *sein*:

> The being/to be [sein] of language ... is a copy, a reflection, a representation of the real one, and because it is meant to represent the unity and absolute fusion between intuition and feeling, it therefore possesses a copulating power, the ability to fuse substantive and predicate into a unity, the product of which is the ... sentence. (*Anfangsgründe* 1: 177)

As the cornerstone of Bernhardi's grammar, *sein* fulfils several interrelated functions: it is an implicit component of both verbs and nouns, it posits existence, and it joins subject and predicate into a sentence. This last function is again heavily involved with epistemology. The real object (a tree, say) exists as an amalgam of substance and attributes; yet we conceive of and represent the tree by mentally "deconstructing" it into a subject and a predicate, then reuniting these on the level of language. In other words, we abstract the concepts "tree" + "greenness" or "tree" + "growth," then bring these concepts together again in the predicating expressions "the tree is green" or "the tree grows" (*Sprachlehre* 1: 213). This means that objects in language are different from real objects, because they have in effect been *reconstructed*—even *re-created*—by our faculties of perception and synthesis. Bernhardi takes this process of recreation quite seriously. It is therefore possible to speak of a final performative moment in his theory of language—the moment in which, rather than simply restoring the original unity of the object, language *creates a new object*:

> in every judgment, not only is the reality of an intuition expressed, but also an entirely new, second substance is in fact acquired; every judgment (whether affirmative or negative is moot) creates a new subject of judgment, a new concept, and this immediately proves the infinite nature of the faculty of judgment; for now this new concept as such lies in my mind, and it can once again become the subject of a judgment, and my faculty of knowledge is again expanded by one concept, and so on to infinity.... Not only is a single substantive joined to a single predicate, at present and without further ado, through every sentence, but in fact a completely new sign is created, a new substantive, which can again become the subject of a new sentence. This, then, in the same manner, proves the infinite nature of representation in language. (*Sprachlehre* 1: 319)

By the time Bernhardi finishes analyzing the epistemological basis of the various parts of speech, he has left behind his original Fichtean identification of language with communication to develop a multi-faceted concept of language as a phenomenon that is entirely bound up with cognition, and that is as necessary to the solitary individual as to people wanting to communicate in a social context (*Sprachlehre* 1: 100–101). He develops a full-fledged theory of language as *Darstellung* of the operations of mental faculties, especially those faculties that Kant made responsible for the synthesizing of perceptions. "Language is understanding and judgment represented in articulated sound," Bernhardi writes; later, he adds imagination to this list of mental faculties as well (*Sprachlehre* 1: 86, 99).

The link with imagination deserves particular attention, for Bernhardi's account of the operations of language is ultimately directed toward the use of language in poetry and other arts. He devotes the entire second volume of his *Sprachlehre* to the analysis of language in art and philosophy, and *Anfangsgründe der Sprachwissenschaft* ends with a major section on "Applied Linguistics," the subject of which is again poetry, philosophy, the arts, and science. Most crucially, Bernhardi claims that although language in general *substitutes* ideal being for real being, these two aspects of being are *united* in poetry. Poetry is the fulfilment of our desire to consider representation as identical with a real intuition or with true being:

> Because represented being has the appearance [Schein] of real being, the possibility arises of actually mistaking it for real being, of thereby ascribing real existence to ideal substance, of taking the latter for an intuition [Anschauung], and of being deceived in this way. Now, this possibility is realized in poetry[.] (*Sprachlehre* 1: 215–16)

Poetic representations must be taken on their own terms as creating reality, and not as constructing referential copies of a reality that exists outside of themselves. This is Bernhardi's way of explaining the poet's traditional privilege of creative utterance, but what is crucial is that his account of poetic representation is entirely based on a detailed study of linguistic representation. Poetic theory is inseparable here from a theory of speech acts. "Daher," he concludes, "ist [die Poesie] in ihrer Form an der Sprachlehre abzuleiten": therefore the form of poetry is to be derived from the study of grammar (*Sprachlehre* 1: 216).

Based on the way Romantic-period philosophers and grammarians describe *sein* and other verbs as the central elements of language, we may formulate some preliminary conclusions about the nature of the Romantic performative. Taking their cue from Kant's analysis of the understanding as the faculty that creates representations of the world through synthesis, linguistic philosophers analyze language as a counterpart to the understanding that creates representations through its own synthetic process. They stress the way language not only represents but *recreates* being, where "being" is itself not a static but a dynamic principle, a constant coming-into-being. The result is a revised view of utterances, particularly propositions, that regards them not as (passively) referring to reality but as (actively) creating a represented reality, an ideal reality, or—in the most radical view, which is generally reserved for poetic utterance—simply *creating reality*. Romantic philosophers of language and modern speech-act philosophers, in other words, undertake a similar re-evaluation of the standard proposition, albeit from different angles. Whereas Austin elects to examine the types of utterances that are excluded by philosophy's focus on the proposition, the Romantics begin by re-positioning the proposition in the new framework opened up by transcendental philosophy. The proposition "A is B" already gains new meaning from Kant's account of synthesis as the construction of concepts by means of the mind's awareness of its own unity. "A is B" gains still more dynamism from Fichte's paradigm of the self-reflective act of positing as the ground of subjective identity, objective reality, and intersubjective relationships. Once reformulated by Herder, Bernhardi, Humboldt, and Coleridge as a *verbal* rather than purely logical act, the proposition not only mirrors the acts of the understanding, and not only participates in the understanding's construction of objects, but actually determines both mental action and the shape of reality.

SCHELLING AND THE I

The main consideration that still separates Romantic ideas about language and being, in the above account, from a modern analysis of the performative, is the speech-act theorist's attention to the role of a speaker in relation to a listener and a speech situation. Thus far, German Romantic philosophy of language has been associated with a re-evaluation of the proposition, but only indirectly with linguistic pragmatics. Yet the position of the speaking subject is precisely the other great discovery made by Romantic linguistics, and that which re-orients it toward a modern theory of speech acts. To the extent that this discovery involves an analysis of the dialogic situation as the paradigm for all uses of language, it will be discussed in the following chapter as Humboldt's major contribution. Here, a resume of Schelling's account of subjectivity in his early work may help to suggest how the Idealists' valorization of the I and its position in the world enters linguistic philosophy as a focus on the speaking subject.

The I of idealism is bound up with idealism's concept of being-as-activity. Schelling echoes Fichte's view of the I in his *System des transzendentalen Idealismus* (*System of Transcendental Idealism*, 1800), defining the I as "pure act, pure doing" that grounds all other knowledge and action because it is "the absolute ground of all positing" (2: 368, 403). Together with Fichte, Schelling intensifies the Kantian influence on philosophy of language by his stronger emphasis on the epistemological function of the I, as well as his increased attention to representations of the I in philosophical discourse. His response to Kant's "I think" as that which must accompany all my representations is to identify "I am" as the "absolute pre-judgment." Transcendental philosophy begins, according to Schelling, by separating the "I am" from the "it is" or the "there are [things]"—separating these propositions so that it can eventually reunite them. The dialectic of subject and object, one of the major themes of the *System des transzendentalen Idealismus*, is often framed in linguistic terms (i.e., Schelling evokes the act of *saying* "I am" or "it is"), which may be why Coleridge found it so useful in his own, still more discourse-oriented account of subjectivity and knowledge.

More than Kant or even Fichte, Schelling stresses the asymmetry of the I when compared with other (logical or grammatical) subjects. Propositions containing "I" break the rules that govern normal propositions—even though they also serve as the ground of those rules. Schelling illustrates this asymmetry in Kantian terms by noting that I = I, though it has the same form as the tautological proposition A = A, makes the latter into a synthetic proposition (i.e., a proposition that adds new information to the definition of the subject). It does this because the two terms it unites—namely, the I as subject and the I as object—are actually opposites:

> Through the proposition I = I, then, the proposition A = A is changed into a synthetic one, and we have found the point at which identical knowledge arises immediately out of synthetic knowledge, and synthetic out of identical.... In the proposition I = I, then, the principle of all knowledge must be expressed, because this very proposition is the *only possible* one that is simultaneously identical and synthetic. (Schelling 2: 372)

The uniqueness of I = I may be grasped more readily if the equation is rewritten in its less formal version, as "I am myself." Because of the self-reflexive motion of thought, the I produces itself as its own object; it is at once producer and product; the "knowing I" and the "being I" coincide. "I am myself" is therefore the only proposition that combines the foundation of logic (identity, or A = A) with the experience of reality (synthesis, or my experience of myself as existing). Moreover, Schelling stresses, I = I is better characterized, not as a proposition (Satz), but as an act (Akt). The central act of the *System des transzendentalen Idealismus*, and of Schelling's philosophy in general, is the I's act of making itself into an object; this is the act of self-consciousness itself and the basis of all knowledge.

Yet this key formulation covers over apparent fissures and ambiguities within the I in Schelling's earlier work. The *System des transzendentalen Idealismus* represents a sudden resolution to his struggle with the problem of how an I conceived of as absolute subject and first principle can enter into relation with a world of objects at all. In the 1795 treatise *Vom Ich als Princip der Philosophie* (Of the I as a principle of philosophy), Schelling strives, using a language he complains is inadequate, to establish the absolute I as the principle of knowledge and identity. In the process, he must constantly distinguish it from the finite, synthetic, logical, empirical, and objective forms of the I that appear in other systems of philosophy, or that are evoked by everyday uses of the pronoun. Foremost among these mediated I's is the I of Kant's "I think" as that which must accompany all my representations. For Schelling, the I of "I think" is a logical I striving to achieve the absolute identity of the absolute I, but it can only do so by clinging desperately to its own unity in relation to a multiplicity of objects. Even the Fichtean proposition I = I paradoxically objectifies the absolute I. "I think, I am" are "all analytic propositions"—yet transcendental dialectic, by recognizing the I that "is" as the object of something that "thinks," derives from these analytic sentences a synthetic proposition: "*that which* thinks, is; *that which* is thought *as* I, is I" (Schelling 1: 130).

Schelling defines the absolute I as that which is unconditioned, independent, identical, eternal, indivisible, unchanging, and free—and, above all, as that which can never become an object. That philosophy, as well as language, constantly *does* objectify the I, stems from people's confusion of the absolute I with the finite I, the latter being a term that could not exist apart from the postulate of an absolute I, but that is also conditioned by the Not-I, or objective existence. Indeed, "the whole business of theoretical and practical philosophy is nothing other than the solution of the contradiction between the pure and the empirically-conditioned I" (Schelling 1: 100). One of the sub-texts of Schelling's *Vom Ich* is that it is all but impossible for the absolute I to enter into language: "I am! is all that the I can state about itself" (1: 134). Even terms like *Dasein* (as opposed to absolute *Sein*), "existence," and "reality" lead to misunderstanding by imposing conditions on the absolute I. *Being*, however—absolute *Sein*—is inseparable from the I, which cannot be thought apart from it. Schelling's essay is, among other things, another formulation of the idealist principle that all philosophy is founded on a postulate of being.

The contradiction between the absolute and the finite I reappears in the *System des transzendentalen Idealismus*—but instead of causing Schelling's system to break down, it now becomes the driving force behind the system. For Schelling now identifies the source of philosophers' misleading statements about the I as a fundamental contradiction between ideal and real activity within the I itself, whereby the I limits itself and so sublimates its own infinite activity. "*All* the activity of the I proceeds from a contradiction within itself," he concludes, "and the continuation of all mental activity depends on the continuation, i.e., the constant re-emergence, of that contradiction" (2: 426). Schelling considered his recognition of the dual subject-object nature of the I one of his most important original contributions to philosophy; arguably, it is also his most important indirect contribution to the philosophy of language. Schelling's leap from identifying the problematic, asymmetrical, and paradoxical nature of the I, to placing this paradox at the heart of his system, is repeated by Romantic-period linguistics, and later again by speech-act philosophy. When Humboldt identifies the pronoun "I" as the hinge on which the linguistic system turns, and Coleridge grounds his theological and linguistic theory on the proposition "I am," both reconsider Schelling's paradox on the level of language. They, too, confront the contradictions between an absolute and a finite I, between an unmediated I and a mediating language, and especially between the I as subject and the I as object. Despite the gulf of time and differences of philosophical tradition between Schelling and speech-act philosophers, the asymmetry of first-person utterances that reappears so centrally in Austin's and Searle's definition of the performative might also be seen as an echo of this Schellingian-idealist problematic. When the term "I" enters into a discourse it breaks the rules of constative statement, deforming analytical sentences by introducing pragmatic issues such as the speaker's position, status, and frame of reference—which is precisely why speech-act philosophy adopts as its foundational utterance the explicit performative in the form "I promise," "I order," "I bet."

It is illustrative, though, that speech-act philosophers tend to *observe* the asymmetry of first-person forms and modify their analysis accordingly, without investigating the role of the I itself. The Romantic performative, on the other hand, grows out of a theorization of the I in its relation to being, objective reality, and other human subjects. It therefore focuses on utterances that not only (like the modern performative) alter the circumstances in which they are spoken, but also react back on the speaker, altering the I itself and its relation to hearer and context. More than this, the Romantic performative assimilates the self-reflexive movement of the I in Fichte's and Schelling's systems, so that the act of saying "I" founds, by positing, the identity of the I itself.

THE PROBLEM OF SUBJECTIVITY: FROM NATURAL PHILOSOPHY TO LITERARY THEORY

The Idealists' redefinition of the I, and their focus on the thinking, first-person subject, motivate a wide-ranging analysis of subjectivity whose effects can be felt in numerous disciplines—not only philosophy and linguistics, but also psychology and, certainly, literature and literary theory. As shown by the work of Herder, Bernhardi, and other late-eighteenth-century grammarians, grammar itself was conceived and taught differently by the end of the eighteenth century, reflecting a new emphasis on the way speakers use language to position themselves in a temporal and relational context. The work of Johann Jacob Wagner in natural philosophy, on the other hand, illustrates how important the role of language is even to a Romantic-period scientist when he analyzes mental processes like perception and cognition—and how closely related a scientific analysis of cognition can be, during this period, to linguistic and aesthetic analyses. Wagner's 1803 treatise *Von der Natur der Dinge* (On the nature of things), which has the avowed purpose of extending Schelling's *Naturphilosophie* into a universal system, ends with a section on "Psychology" or "Intellectual Nature," in which Wagner undertakes an extended analysis of the understanding as the faculty of forming ideas. He contributes to the translation of the Kantian system into a linguistic system by identifying the understanding as the producer of *concepts* and language as the corresponding producer of *judgments* (520–21). In other words, Wagner's psychological analysis is in sympathy with Bernhardi's linguistic analysis, as well as with the work of other linguists writing around 1800, such as Georg Michael Roth.[8] If Wagner stops short of assigning language as fundamental a role in cognition as Herder and Bernhardi do, he nevertheless regards language as homologous with cognition: developed by the will (Willkür) to give external

---

[8]Nerlich and Clarke discuss linguistic-pragmatic elements in Roth's *Antihermes* (1795), which also draws a parallel between the act of cognition in the mind and the act of communication in language: "Words thus represent concepts and sentences judgements; words and sentences as external actions have their equivalent in internal actions" (*Language, Action, and Context* 37).

form to what is in the understanding, language also shares the structure of the understanding (518). This correspondence means that parts of speech can be ordered according to the (Schellingian) contraries that structure the understanding's apprehension of objects: nouns are the expression of rest or stillness, verbs the expression of motion.

Taking Schelling's terminology further, Wagner characterizes nouns as "positive," because they are of themselves indefinite and therefore unlimited, and adjectives as "negative," since they have the effect of limiting nouns when joined to them as predicates. The verb "to be" fulfils the central function of linking these positive and negative principles:

> Furthermore: just as the understanding connects a positive and a negative, something that determines and something indeterminate, in every judgment—although this connection is not absolute, but rather is held within the limits of finitude by the necessity of all the other possible and actual connections—in the same way language divides naming words into nouns and adjectives, of which the former designate the indeterminate (positive), the latter the determining (negative), and through the verb *to be* both are connected, because this is the bearer of all oppositions in language, as the imagination is in the mind; and this copula of judgment never counts in an infinite sense either, because every judgment presupposes another, and determines a third, and the same copula must serve all of them. (520)

Joining together indeterminate and determining components, *sein* activates the linguistic system as a reflection of the cognitive process.

This dialectic of infinity and limitation, which Wagner arrives at by adapting Schelling's philosophy to a scientific study of cognition, parallels the account of language that Novalis arrives at by adapting Fichte's philosophy to aesthetics. In his *Fichte-Studien* (Fichte studies) of 1794–95, Novalis recognizes the copula as the verbal counterpart to Fichte's self-positing of the I: "The *is*-saying of language schematizes the *I-am*-positings of the Logos," as Wolfgang Janke puts it (176). Like the mind's "I am," the ability to say that something "is" (i.e., exists absolutely) opens up the realm of the sayable in the first place. Predication, or saying "A is B," on the other hand, constitutes an essential limitation or determination. In formulating sentences with the copula, then, we apply both a principle of potentialization and a principle of limitation, depending on whether we use "is" in an absolute or a predicative sense.

Wagner's account of the copula, above, ends with an observation about the way judgments or sentences depend on one another, so that each one both potentially and actually limits the infinite scope of the next. Although he does not develop this thought further, he gestures toward the role of speech acts in social interaction, noting that each utterance reacts on both the speaker and the listener:

> Every individual word that is uttered returns again to the utterer himself as a sensation, and in the same way the uttered word of another becomes a sensation and a concept for me, and thereby a stimulus for me to entrust my own inner thoughts to the word. (523)

For Wagner, this allusion to the interpersonal function of language leads directly to an analysis of the importance of language for the evolution of love and other social ties. His concept of language as dialogic and responsive finds a parallel in the work of many of his contemporaries, including the philologist Johann Severin Vater. Better known for his foundational work in historical linguistics and comparative grammar, Vater also proposed a theory of language in which the speaker, the hearer, intentionality, and uptake all have a significant place, as Nerlich and Clarke point out: "Vater distinguished between the goal or intention of the act of speaking and signifying and the success or uptake of this intention, which can be marked by a reply on the part of the hearer" (*Language, Action, and Context* 41).

The importance of uptake in the Romantic performative will be developed much further by Humboldt, but it also enters into the linguistic theory of those Romantic writers who most obviously bring the philosophy of language to bear on poetry: the Schlegel brothers. Both August Wilhelm and Friedrich Schlegel regard language as a (per)formative medium that is essential to the development of subjectivity and the apprehension of objects; both describe cognition as a communicative relationship between mind and world. For August Wilhelm, the role of language is best characterized as a combination of expression (Ausdruck) and representation (Darstellung), two functions that to some extent count as consecutive historical developments. In the account of the origin of language that he gives in the second letter of the *Briefe über Poesie, Silbenmaß und Sprache* (Letters on poetry, meter, and language, 1795), and again in the Berlin lectures on literature and art of 1801–4, he theorizes that language originates with the expression of self and progresses to the representation of external objects. Although even the representative function gets obscured once language develops further into a schema of logical, conventional signs for objects, both expression and representation remain crucial to our experience of ourselves as beings in the world:

> If something is to be designated by convention, it must first (even were it merely an impression of our condition) be externalized as an object, and

thus it follows that language is not only expression but representation. We express ourselves, but we represent objects. (A. W. Schlegel 250)

Friedrich Schlegel, too, regards the subject's expression of itself in language as the essence of the cognitive process. He reinterprets the dynamic, self-positing I of Fichte as the I that communicates itself (das *sich mitteilende Ich*), for the I-world relationship can only be comprehended as a verbal relationship: "language, as the empirical mid-point between I and object, becomes the paradigm of the reality that contains I and object" (Nüsse 27, 24–25). But while his brother focused on our representation of objects in language, Friedrich Schlegel affirms that the objects themselves speak to us. Especially in his Cologne lectures of 1804–5, he develops a radically dialogic philosophy of language and cognition. An external object—which he here designates as a "power"—can only become real to us if we recognize it as a You that speaks to us:

> Every power, as soon as it enters into a relationship with us—that is, as soon as we think, perceive, and attempt to investigate and penetrate it—becomes a *you*; this is what is real in intuition. The material is nothing in intuition. That which alone gives it reality is its essence, its meaning, its sense—is the language that obscurely addresses us, in which the *you* wants to make itself comprehensible to us. (KFSA 12: 338)

We perceive an object by accepting it as a You in dialogue with us; more importantly, though, this recognition of the You also involves a recognition that the object is part of ourselves. For the Not-I of Fichte, Friedrich Schlegel substitutes a "Counter-I" (Gegen-Ich) that, together with the I, forms part of the original I (Ur-Ich). "External things ... are not merely a dead, weak, empty, sensory reflection of the I," for we realize them as a vital and active counterpart of ourselves when they communicate with us: "The inner essence and the nature of the plants and animals are as it were the words and language that the distant, reserved You speaks to us" (KFSA 12: 338–39).

If language is inseparable from cognition, poetry, for the Schlegel brothers, is equally bound up with both. August Wilhelm regards poetry as the mode of language in which the natural connection between signifier and signified, which is gradually lost from sight as language becomes conventional, may be regained and re-experienced. Since language itself is "a poem of the entire human race, ever becoming and changing, never complete," he suggests that what we call literature is really meta-poetry, or "poetry of poetry" (388). Friedrich Schlegel, in the Cologne lectures where he develops his philosophy of language most fully, goes on to characterize poetry as a form of thinking that, like language itself, is dynamic and interactive, although it "*creates its own material, in a way, and is a ludic activity*" (*KFSA* 12: 371). It is Novalis who provides the most succinct affirmation of the interdependence of poetry and language, when he writes in *Das Allgemeine Brouillon* (Sketches for a general compendium, 1798–99), "Poetry refers immediately to language" (Poësie bezieht sich unmittelbar auf d[ie] Sprache [3: 399]). The similarity to Bernhardi's statement—"the form of poetry is to be derived from the study of grammar" (*Sprachlehre* 1: 216)—is worth noting: at the end of the eighteenth century in Germany, the poet and the philosophical linguist come to the same conclusion.

While the Schlegels, Novalis, Bernhardi, and others of their generation are often quite explicit about the interdependence they perceive between literature and linguistics, the unspoken parallels between their philosophies of language and the use of language in Romantic literature are still more significant. What post-Kantian linguists embark on as an explicit theoretical project, their contemporaries undertake as part of the task of writing poetry in a transcendental-idealist frame of reference: all face the challenge of understanding and using language as a medium that suddenly appears vital to the construction of reality. Anyone reflecting on the relationship between language and reality at the end of the eighteenth century seems obligated to redefine *language* in light of the way the Kantian system redefined *reality*. This may mean interpreting the Kantian categories as grammatical categories; or analyzing the way discourse locates speaker and listener within the Kantian transcendentals, space and time; or recognizing language as the medium by which the Kantian understanding performs its function of making scattered intuitions into unified concepts. Once Kant indicates that existence itself is a quality that the understanding *attributes to* phenomena, because the mind has no contact with the thing-in-itself, linguistic philosophers go on to identify existence (Sein) with the verb signifying existence (sein) and conclude that we attribute existence to objects *by verbally predicating something of them*. Fichte and Schelling, by identifying being with the I and affirming that both must be understood as active self-positing, strengthen the hypothesis that being is always an activity, a process, perhaps even a performance. The self-reflexive movement of thought in transcendental idealism, finally, by which the very existence of the I originates from the action performed by the I, shows up again in the Romantic performative as a paradoxical temporality. Utterance—for Herder, Bernhardi, or Humboldt—is an act that founds the cognitive relationship between I and world, yet language can only be understood in terms of the I-world relationship. This concept of an utterance that, to return to a Kantian formulation, *founds the conditions of its own possibility*, is the idea to be traced through various theoretical and literary manifestations in the following chapters.

3

The Performative Humboldt

The linguistic philosophy of Wilhelm von Humboldt strikes twentieth-century readers as both typically Romantic and peculiarly modern. A "Humboldt renaissance" has been underway since the 1930s, and one scholar notes that harkening back to Humboldt has "almost become the fashion in twentieth-century linguistics and philosophy of language" (C. Behler 2). What is more remarkable than the sheer number of references to Humboldt, though, is the wide range of application his ideas have found. He is seen as anticipating Saussure's concept of the linguistic system, the linguistic relativity of Sapir and Whorf, and Derrida's displacement of logocentrism and phonocentrism. He has been claimed as forefather of mid-twentieth-century "Neohumboldtians" like Leo Weisgerber, of Gadamer's hermeneutics, of Soviet linguistics and Marxist philosophy of language,[1] and (infamously) of Chomskian transformational grammar.[2] His remarkable modernity has, in general, been well documented by linguists and philosophers, and occasionally by literary critics.[3]

---

[1] This hypothesis derives mainly from the former East Germany, more specifically from Berlin's Humboldt University (founded by Humboldt himself, in the service of the Prussian government, as the University of Berlin), and the GDR's Academy of Sciences (the descendant of the Berlin Academy with which Humboldt was heavily involved). Members of this school stress the materialist, sociohistorical dimension of Humboldt's linguistic philosophy and his understanding of language as *energeia*, translated in this context as "activity" in the sense of "labor" (Arbeit) or even "technology" (Technik). See, for example, Neumann, "Über die Aktualität von Humboldts Sprachauffassung," and the collection edited by Welke.

[2] If referring to Humboldt is in itself "fashionable," the leading edge of this trend was, for a time, to critique Chomsky's recovery of Humboldt in *Cartesian Linguistics* (1966). Chomsky assimilates Humboldt into the rationalist, universalist, "Cartesian" study of language, a tradition that (according to Chomsky) reappears in modern linguistics as his own transformational grammar.

[3] See C. Behler, Bierwisch, Gipper ("Wilhelm von Humboldt als Begründer moderner Sprachforschung" and "Wilhelm von Humboldts Bedeutung für die moderne Sprachwissenschaft"), Müller-Vollmer ("Thinking and Speaking: Herder, Humboldt and Saussurean Semiotics"), and Neumann ("Über die Aktualität von Humboldts

Although the Anglo-American speech-act philosophers never mention him, Humboldt has also been linked with certain applications of speech-act theory. Habermas, for one, locates himself in the line of theorists influenced by Humboldt's view of language as intersubjective discourse (Gespräch). He credits Humboldt with opening up space for a theory of culture and society by envisioning a discursive relationship between an "Ego" and an "Alter Ego" that is recognized as being other, yet as having a common origin with the Ego. For Humboldt, as for Habermas, society is constituted by the speech acts that link individuals to one another: "Humboldt already understood speech acts to be linkages for interaction; he conceives of reaching understanding as the creative mechanism in socialization.... Language, world view and form of life are interwoven" (Habermas, "A Reply" 218). In Habermas's view, however, Humboldt is held back from a modern understanding of society by his residual Romantic commitment to a view of language as individual expression.[4] It is typical of Humboldt's disparate, often paradoxical legacy that a hermeneutic thinker like Paul Ricoeur values exactly this "Romantic" aspect of Humboldt as a model for his own notion of verbal performance. Ricoeur understands Humboldt's profoundly dynamic concept of language in terms of "the generation ... of the work of speech in each and every case" (84), and credits Humboldt with being one of the first to regard language as a process rather than a system. To understand language as actual discursive event, rather than as system *in potentia*, is, according to Ricoeur, the task of phenomenology:

> Phenomenology's task becomes more precise: this positing of the subject, which the entire tradition of the *cogito* invokes, must henceforth be performed in language and not alongside it.... This positing must be made to appear in the occurrence of discourse, that is, in the act by which the potential system of language becomes the actual event of speech. (256)

What Ricoeur describes as the enterprise of phenomenology is exactly Humboldt's enterprise: to analyze how the positing of the subject, as

---

Sprachauffassung"), to mention only essays where the modernity claimed for Humboldt is explicit in the title.

[4]For elaboration on this point, and on the Humboldt-Habermas relationship generally, see Trabant, "Habermas liest Humboldt." Focusing on Habermas's appeal to Humboldt, both in his dialogue with Charles Taylor and in his critique of Derrida, Trabant reveals Habermas's insight and his blindness with regard to Humboldt's understanding of the role of language. Trabant concentrates in particular on Habermas's tendency to separate the subjective, poetic, "world-creating" (welterschliessende) function of language from the intersubjective, discursive, problem-solving function—a separation that is foreign to Humboldt's philosophy of language.

well as the development of the subject's representations of the world and relationships to other individuals, occurs in language as a discursive act. What allows Ricoeur to enlist Humboldt into the project of phenomenology, while Habermas enlists him for his theory of communicative action, is that Humboldt's work encompasses a wide-ranging exploration of the way language performs identity within the interrelated realms of subjectivity, objective reality, and social or intersubjective experience.

This chapter will examine the points of contact between Humboldt's linguistic philosophy and speech-act theory, which are, I will argue, frequent enough to justify allusions to a "Humboldtian speech act," which is to say an exemplary form of the Romantic performative. At the same time, Humboldt's interpretation of verbal phenomena in terms of energy, power, dialogue, and intersubjective relations is fully consistent with the perspectives of his contemporaries; rather than being uniquely ahead of his time, he needs to be presented as the best exemplar of early-nineteenth-century ideas about language as action. Humboldt undertakes to redefine language in the wake of Kant's epistemological revolution in a manner akin to, but still more ambitious than, the projects of Herder or Bernhardi. His view of language as the operative principle that relates the mind to the world stems from his (and his contemporaries') understanding of mental faculties and natural processes alike as "energies" and "powers." Expressed in his earlier writings in the context of anthropology and literary criticism, this worldview gets transmuted, around 1800, into a philosophy of language typified by Humboldt's famous remark that language is ongoing activity and not a completed work—*energeia* and not *ergon*. This means not only that the linguistic system is in continual evolution, but that individual utterances must be understood in terms of a theory of action. Speech has definable effects: it conceptualizes aspects of reality as objects of cognition; it establishes the subjectivity of the speaker and the speaker's relation to an addressee; it reacts back on the system of language itself, altering the forms and conventions that provide a context for subsequent utterances. Humboldt's expression of these principles suggests that an awareness of utterance as action, of uptake, and of the importance of the speech situation was abundantly present among Romantic-period writers. But what Humboldt's version of linguistic performativity offers, in addition, is an insight into the fluidity of the rules by which utterances operate. Because he is dedicated to a social and anthropological frame of reference for his linguistic philosophy, and one that takes into account the way social relations change in time and history, his linguistics constantly interweaves the cognitive and communicative dimensions of language.

Humboldt's concept of speech as synthetic act, in which the speaking subject, the responsive addressee, the linguistic system, and the material world all have a formative influence on one another, offers a paradoxical, yet strangely illuminating background for the use of language in Romantic literary texts.

'ENERGEIA' AND 'KRAFT'

Humboldt's famous—perhaps even infamous—characterization of language as *energeia* triggers a preliminary connection with the idea of performativity. This is just the tip of the iceberg, but a point that has caused consternation for philosophers, linguists, and literary critics who assiduously debate the origins and connotations of Humboldt's Greek term. While the Neohumboldtians of the mid-twentieth century argue that *energeia* is absolutely central to Humboldt's view of language and, accordingly, make it the center of their own linguistics, others point out that Humboldt actually uses the term only once, parenthetically, in his major work, and argue that it is both overemphasized and wrongly understood by most interpreters, since it does not really correspond to the modern terms "energy" or *Energie*. To understand Humboldt's choice of the word *energeia*, it is argued, we must look at the specific senses in which the same word is used by eighteenth-century writers such as Leibniz and Herder, but also by Aristotle, for whom *en-ergeia* denotes "a doing that has its end within it, not posited outside of it."[5]

In fact, although *energeia* may call particular attention to itself as a foreign word in Humboldt's German text, the characterization of language as energy is an eighteenth-century commonplace. James Harris begins his influential treatise *Hermes* by describing speech as "the joint Energie of our best and noblest Faculties" (1), and his diction is echoed ever more frequently by British writers on language in the later eighteenth century (cf. Ulman 32, 34).[6] Both the Schlegel brothers discuss lan-

---

[5]*Nichomachean Ethics* 1098b33; see Böhler 248–49. Di Cesare provides a detailed account of Aristotelian terminology and its influence on Humboldt, from which she concludes that Humboldt, adopting and adapting Aristotelian ideas of *dynamis* 'potentiality' and *energeia* 'actuality, activity,' reverses the centuries-old priority of *langue* over *parole* in linguistic philosophy.

[6]Underwood contends that the term "energy" came into fashion in a wide range of disciplines and ideological contexts during the late eighteenth century, being used by Reid, Blake, Godwin, Wollstonecraft, Radcliffe, and Burke, among many others. He theorizes that the "vogue for energy" is politically motivated, inasmuch as the emerging bourgeoisie seeks to portray itself as "energetic" in contrast to the "inert" upper and lower classes.

guage as a form of energy (August Wilhelm in *Briefe über Poesie, Silbenmaß und Sprache* and Friedrich in the *Philosophische Fragmente* of 1798–99, for instance), showing that the idea also belongs in the conceptual sphere of early German Romanticism. Even if *energeia* appears a single time in the best-known text of Humboldt's maturity, *Über die Verschiedenheit des menschlichen Sprachbaues und ihren Einfluss auf die geistige Entwicklung des Menschengeschlechts*,[7] frequent references to energy throughout his work and the work of his contemporaries leave little doubt but that the concept is central to his view of human development. What is more, "energy" is only one term in a vocabulary of dynamism and power that is characteristic of Humboldt's writing, not only about language, but about the intellect, poetry, and the development of culture. Equally deserving of detailed study is his ubiquitous term *Kraft*—'power,' 'strength,' 'faculty,' or 'ability.'[8]

Humboldt regards the human mind as an energy or collection of energies striving to realize itself in a range of external and interpersonal activities, including language, art, politics, the nation, love and sex, science and exploration. In the anthropologically and sociologically oriented essay "Über den Geist der Menschheit" (On the spirit of humanity, 1797), he identifies the quality that makes some individuals extraordinary or outstanding as "the energy of a living power" (die Energie einer lebendigen Kraft [*GS* 2: 330]). The centrality of the terms *Energie* and *Kraft* is established in this early text when Humboldt explicitly uses them to define and justify the two key concepts named in his title, humanity (Menschheit) and spirit (Geist). "The concept of humanity," he claims, "is nothing other than the living power [lebendige Kraft] of the spirit that animates it, speaks from it, and shows itself active and effective within it" (*GS* 2: 332). "Spirit," he adds in a concluding note, is the appropriate term here precisely because it expresses the being (Wesen) of humanity as existence and power at once (als Wesen und Kraft selbst [*GS* 2: 332]). In other words, a performative principle—the identification of

---

[7] *On the Diversity of Human Language-Structure and Its Influence on the Mental Development of Mankind*, written in the early 1830s and published following Humboldt's death in 1834; the German text will be referred to by a short form of its title, *Über die Verschiedenheit des menschlichen Sprachbaues*. The main title of the English translation published in 1988 is *On Language* (here, *OL*). The text was edited posthumously from a long essay Humboldt intended as an introduction to his three-volume work *On the Kawi Language on the Island of Java* (the "Kawi-Werk").

[8] See Menze's comments on *Kraft* (96–105): claiming that "force is for Humboldt the fundamental principle of all existing things" (Kraft ist für Humboldt das Urprinzip alles Seienden [96]), he examines the concept in the context of Humboldt's philosophy of the human condition.

the entity's *activity* with its *essential being*—defines the realm of the human. In a letter of 1803, Humboldt reaffirms his commitment to "humanity" as the central, unifying term in his philosophy, equating it with what others would call "God," "universe," or "world soul." Here again, he identifies intellectual or spiritual power as the defining characteristic of humanity, while specifically re-interpreting Kant's *a priori* categories as *Kraft* and *Energie*: "The true *a priori*, I believe, must be the power in the individual that reproduces the real—but more complete—individual, but without application to some object or other, and as pure energy" (*Wilhelm von Humboldts Briefe* 155–56). But Humboldt discovers this principle of essence-as-activity at work everywhere else in the world-order, too. A forcefully worded claim in the essay "Latium und Hellas, oder Betrachtungen über das classische Alterthum" (Latium and Hellas, or observations on classical antiquity, 1806) testifies to his Romantic tendency to view virtually everything in terms of energy or power rather than substance:

> Nothing living and therefore no form of power at all can be regarded as substance, that either is itself at rest or in which something rests; instead, it is an energy that adheres solely and entirely to the action that it performs in every moment.... No power is fulfilled in that what it has effected up until now.... New things can and must eternally arise. (*GS* 3: 139)

The most important publication of Humboldt's early career, a long treatise on Goethe's poem *Hermann und Dorothea* that is also an analysis of the epic form and of literary representation in general, applies the term "energy" in the context of literary criticism. The words *Kraft, Energie*, and *Wirkung* 'effect' dominate this text, as Humboldt makes the power and impact of the work of art his main theme. *Über Goethes Hermann und Dorothea* (1799) ends by calling for a theory of art that will bring art into conjunction with moral education (Bildung), since this educative effect is badly needed in a time of moral upheaval (Humboldt is writing in Paris during the 1790s). The treatise aims, in other words, at a pragmatic aesthetics. In terms of the relationship between literature and linguistics, it is also worth noting that, in this essay, art does to nature exactly what, in Humboldt's later work, language will do to thought. Just as language relocates thought into the sphere of externality and sound, art relocates nature into the sphere of imagination and aesthetic rules; just as language alters and re-forms thought, art alters and re-creates the natural object (*GS* 2: 126–28). The way art is able to transform nature, finally, is by means of a *Machtspruch* or "powerful utterance" that resembles Herder's *Machtwort* or word of power: "To both, to the ideal and to totality, [the poet] raises himself only in the realm of imagination, only after he has sublimated [aufgehoben] the limited and separate existence of reality, *as if by a word of power*" (*GS* 2: 138; italics added). During the 1790s, when Humboldt expects that he will make his scholarly mark either in literary criticism or in the anthropological-sociological analysis of culture, his work in both these areas is already premised on an understanding of human minds and natural phenomena as powers that exert influence on one another, and that derive their identity from their activity. The breakthrough to a performative linguistics comes when he begins to recognize language as the medium in which this exchange of energies takes place.

HUMBOLDT'S LINGUISTIC TURN

A long letter that Humboldt wrote to Friedrich Schiller in 1800, often identified as the starting-point of his philosophy of language, represents the transition from his theory of the active spirit to a theory of the active word. The letter is still, primarily, a literary-critical text; it constitutes an enthusiastic response to Schiller's *Wallenstein*, which Humboldt has just read. In the first seventeen pages of his critique, he analyzes the genre, the structure, and the characters of the work, then reflects on Schiller's uniqueness in relation to Goethe and Shakespeare, the only other poets he considers comparable to him. Throughout this discussion, the word *Kraft* appears obsessively often. Humboldt refers repeatedly to the power of will, of love, and of ideas; to the dramatic power of Wallenstein and other characters; to Schiller's poetic power and the powers he calls up in his readers and audience; to the power of imagination, a faculty that the German language designates as "image-making power" (Einbildungs*kraft*) in any case. When, in the concluding pages of the letter, Humboldt turns his attention to (as he puts it) the relation in which Schiller stands to language, he carries this discourse of power over into a theory of the word. Schiller, Humboldt claims, uses language not to *display* an object but to *produce* objects insofar as they are objects of thought. But this observation on Schiller's uniqueness soon turns into an insight into the function of language in general:

> Therefore language is—if not absolutely, then at least in sensory terms—the medium by which man simultaneously forms himself and the world, or rather by which he becomes conscious of the fact that he separates a world off from himself [daß er eine Welt von sich abscheidet].... Now it is this which I would like to call the proper power of language—its ability to heighten the drive and the power, constantly—however you wish to

call it—to join more world to itself, or develop it from within itself. (Humboldt and Schiller, *Briefwechsel* 2: 207)

Using the scientific term *abscheiden*, Humboldt likens language to a chemical process by which the speaker separates the self from the world as if precipitating gold from the mixed ore of thought.

As Humboldt begins to analyze the sources of this power, he broaches the issue of temporality that will distinguish his philosophy as a linguistics of *parole* rather than *langue*. The power of language springs from its intrinsically active nature—that is, its existence in the present as constantly evolving discourse rather than in the past as artifact: "The past is past; that which is now acting is only the *power* strengthened by all previous practice and devoted to this activity in this moment" (Das Vergangne ist vergangen, das jetzt Tätige ist nur die durch alle bisherige Übung gestärkte und zu dieser Tätigkeit in diesem Augenblick bestimmte Kraft [*Briefwechsel* 2: 207]). This barely translatable sentence is itself a performance, for Humboldt makes his point not only by describing the power of language but by enacting it through his syntax, by lengthening the clause and thereby the moment (Augenblick), by using deictics to attach the thought insistently to the present moment (zu *dieser* Tätigkeit in *diesem* Augenblick), and by holding back until the end of the sentence the name of the faculty that performs this present activity: *Kraft*. Humboldt's rhetorical manipulation of syntax—which suggests that he is preoccupied not only with the relation in which Schiller stands to language, but with his own relation to it—highlights a final aspect of his linguistic theory as it emerges in this crucial text. The letter marks a major transition in his thought and writing, indeed in his career, from literary criticism to philosophy of language. His ongoing sensitivity to poetic language, though, leads him not only to articulate his linguistic theory for the first time in the context of a commentary on a literary work, but also to direct it explicitly toward the use of language in poetry. Poetry, according to Humboldt, should possess more strength (Stärke) than other artforms because it is the only artistic medium that satisfies the fundamental purpose of language: to understand oneself by distinguishing between—and thereby producing—inner thoughts and external objects. The interdependence of poetry and language marks both of them as "active" (tätig [*Briefwechsel* 2: 209]). But when language is handled expertly, as it is by Schiller, it becomes more than merely active; it becomes "a pure vehicle of power" (ein bloßes Vehikel der Kraft [*Briefwechsel* 2: 210]). It is presumably no accident that Humboldt reaches this conclusion after reading *Wallenstein*, a drama in which characters act on one another with orders, promises, signed oaths of allegiance, and other intersubjective speech acts, while Wallenstein himself manifests a tragic predicament defined by the interrelationship of power, language, choice, and action.

THE HUMBOLDTIAN SPEECH ACT: MIND AND MATERIALITY

A few of the ideas about language and cognition that appear in the letter to Schiller had been formulated years earlier; Humboldt's fragmentary notes "Über Denken und Sprechen" (On thinking and speaking, 1795–96) describe in very similar terms how we use language to articulate "portions of thought" that can be combined in different ways. But it seems to be Humboldt's enthusiastic response to the language of *Wallenstein* that gives him the impetus to develop a full-fledged philosophy of language as an active power that continually modifies the speaker, the hearer, and the world. Strikingly modern, but also typical of the new linguistics of his age, is Humboldt's overwhelming conviction that language is an integral element of cognition: there can be no thought without words. He insists that language is essential to thought, because it is only in the act of articulating perceptions and externalizing concepts of the world through language that the mind can enter into the subject-object relationship that is the basis for rational thought. But the Herder-like encounter of the mind with that which is only designated as an object *through* the encounter is merely the first step in Humboldt's theory of language and cognition. As identified by the individual mind, the word-object is still subjective and even illusory: it requires verification through interaction with the Other. This Other can, in a very pragmatic sense, be another individual; thus the centrality of the dialogic situation, which will be discussed further below. But the Other is also, more generally, the external world, or materiality—even the material element of language itself, as sound or moving air.

"Language," Humboldt declares emphatically, "in the isolated word and in connected discourse, is an *act*, a truly creative *performance of the mind*" (OL 183). When he refers to language as an act, he is first and foremost referring to the moment in which the utterance, by uniting a sound and a concept, gives shape to thought, thus objectifying it and engaging a dialogic process of interaction between the mind and the speech act that has just been produced. Language is thus a synthesis of intellectual activity with vocal force:

> Thought ... is also intrinsically bound to the necessity of entering into a *union* with the verbal sound; thought cannot otherwise achieve clarity,

nor the idea become a concept.... Just as thought, like a lightning-flash or concussion, collects the whole power of ideation [Vorstellungskraft] into a single point, and shuts out everything else, so sound rings out with abrupt sharpness and unity. Just as thought seizes the whole mind, so sound has predominantly a penetrating power [Kraft] that sets every nerve atingle. (*OL* 54–55)

What is striking about Humboldt's diction is the designation of both thought and sound individually as *Kraft*, which is intensified by the comparison of both to lightning—a recurrent Romantic image for instantaneous power, or for a phenomenon whose existence seems to be pure action. As he continues with a more detailed account of how thought binds with sound, Humboldt acknowledges the Kantian principle that the "inner action of the mind" makes intuitions of the world into objects and concepts, but he supplements Kant's system with the conviction that this mental action inevitably takes place in and as language:

Subjective activity fashions an *object* in thought. For no class of presentations [Vorstellungen] can be regarded as a purely receptive contemplation of a thing already present. The activity of the senses must combine synthetically with the inner action of the mind, and from this combination the presentation is ejected, becomes an object *vis-à-vis* the subjective power, and, perceived anew as such, returns back into the latter. But *language* is indispensable for this. For in that the mental striving breaks out through the lips in language, the product of that striving returns back to the speaker's ear. Thus the presentation becomes transformed into real objectivity, without being deprived of subjectivity on that account. Only language can do this; and without this transformation, occurring constantly with the help of language even in silence, into an objectivity that returns to the subject, the act of concept-formation, and with it all true thinking, is impossible. (*OL* 56)

The production of the word is an act that joins the speaker's subjectivity to the world's materiality by providing the mind with a sensible "object" with which it can interact—that is, the objectified verbal utterance itself. Language, a phenomenon that operates midway between the mind and the world and (as thought and sound) partakes of both, also acts on both. As a mental phenomenon, it changes the world in the process of producing a representation of it; as a material phenomenon, it changes the speaking subject by confronting the mind with its Other, a world of objects.

Here, as so often, Humboldt seems to anticipate not only the phenomenological current in twentieth-century philosophy of language as represented by Husserl or Brentano, but also its deconstructionist critique. His emphasis on the otherness and materiality of language, and the way language paradoxically unifies thought by first concretizing the material-spiritual and external-internal differences within it, bears a close resemblance to Derrida's criticism of phenomenology. In *Speech and Phenomena*, Derrida describes how Husserl understands the "auto-affective" hearing of one's own voice as a guarantee of the unity of consciousness and the bond between conscious intention and speech. However, Derrida counters, hearing-oneself-speak can only unify transcendent consciousness with material sound because it first draws this very distinction: "But the unity of sound and voice, which allows the voice to be produced in the world as pure auto-affection, is the sole case to escape the distinction between what is worldly and what is transcendental; by the same token, it makes that distinction possible" (79). Both these viewpoints—a metaphysical commitment and a commitment to the materiality of experience—come together in Humboldt's theory of language as well. While Derrida emphasizes the inevitable distinction between them, though, Humboldt stresses that, as the phenomenon of language shows, the seeming contraries of material and spirit, or "what is worldly and what is transcendental," ultimately have the same origin.

Humboldt characterizes the reciprocal operations of mind and materiality on one another as part of a single act that sometimes carries overtones of divine creation, as when he writes of "the animating breath which the formative power of language instills, in the act of altering the world, into thought" (*OL* 44). Language forms an intermediate and mediating world of its own; in the early 1800s, Humboldt writes of "the sum of all words" as "a world that lies midway between the phenomenal one outside us, and the active one within us" (*GS* 3: 167). After he retreats from public life and his position in the Prussian civil service in 1820, and dedicates himself to the study of an immense range of individual languages, the idea of language as a world and as world-creation develops in two different directions. First, it becomes an image for the independent status of grammatical structure. Suspending external reference, the intermediate world of language evolves its own structural principle, or grammar, that corresponds to the relationship between thoughts in the mind:

> In the same way that language, as the process of making thought sensible, outside of the human mind, opposes to objects a world of single words, of concepts stamped by sounds, so also language creates a new indication of the connections between thoughts, that arises only out of language and belongs only to it, and this indication, understood in the unity of its infinite multiplicity, is the form of grammar. (*GS* 6: 349–50)

Secondly, Humboldt's claim that words create a world of their own is intrinsically related to his concern with the way different languages discover, divide, and shape the world differently, or create different images of reality (*Weltbilder* or *Weltansichten*). Long recognized as one of his most significant contributions to the philosophy of language, this concept clearly has its basis in a belief that words are world-altering, but in itself it leads toward a theory of linguistic relativity rather than a speech-act theory. Performativity is more than a means to an end for Humboldt, however. It appears in his fundamental definition of language as a concept of dynamic interaction between mind and world; but it will show up again in his fully pragmatic theory of discourse in terms of the dynamic interaction of speakers with one another.

SYNTHESIS IN HUMBOLDT AND KANT

A detailed analysis of the kind (or kinds) of performativity Humboldt attributes to language necessitates a return to Kant.[9] For Humboldt, as for Herder and Bernhardi, language is not just the expression, but the actual mode of operation, of the Kantian understanding. "Synthesis," the term Humboldt will adopt for the crucial operation of language, is Kant's term for the key function of the understanding, and it is worth quoting Kant's important definition of synthesis from the *Critique of Pure Reason*:

> But the combination (*conjunctio*) of a manifold in general can never come to us through the senses, and cannot, therefore, be already contained in the pure form of sensible intuition. For it is an act of spontaneity of the faculty of representation; and since this faculty, to distinguish it from sensibility, must be entitled understanding, all combination—be we conscious of it or not, be it a combination of the manifold of intuition, empirical or non-empirical, or of various concepts—is an act of the understanding. To this act the general title 'synthesis' may be assigned, as indicating that we cannot represent to ourselves anything as com-

---

[9]The most extensive study of the relationship between Kant's analytic of the understanding and Humboldt's theory of language is the work of Scharf. Humboldt, in Scharf's view, re-interprets Kant's "transcendental unity of self-consciousness" as the power of language, by demonstrating that the production of an articulated sound, or word, is the means by which a concept arises ("Chomskys Humboldt-Interpretation" 159). While Scharf does not pay particular attention to the dynamic dimension of thought or language, Streitberg, in a more general discussion, notes that Kant's concept of the faculties and Humboldt's concept of language are both potential (rather than actual), and constantly in flux; thus, both are act- and event-oriented rather than being substantial and material (406). Slagle discusses Humboldt's adaptation of Kantian universals and categories to linguistic theory, and Spranger includes the details and dates of Humboldt's reading of Kant.

bined in the object which we have not ourselves previously combined, and that of all representations *combination* is the only one which cannot be given through objects. Being an act of the self-activity of the subject, it cannot be executed save by the subject itself. (*CPR* 151–52/B130)

Making sense of experience involves combining intuitions of it, and combination involves adding something that is not given by sensory perception, but supplied by the mind itself: these are the crucial terms of Kantian synthesis. Humboldt adds one more necessary factor: the mental act of synthesis cannot take place without language, as the medium that combines material and intellect. The unification of intuitions brought about by the understanding, and the unification of sounds brought about by the word, are themselves unified in discourse (Rede): "To the act of understanding that produces the unity of the concept, the unity of the word, as sensory sign, corresponds, and both must accompany one another as closely as possible in thought, through discourse" (*GS* 4: 21). A manuscript note that Humboldt added to this passage explicitly introduces the Kantian term "synthesis," as well as the notion (reminiscent of Bernhardi) that synthesis as a linguistic process involves a translation of "real" being into "ideal" being. The passage climaxes in the "word," described as not merely a material accompaniment or expression of the mental act of synthesis, but as the place where synthesis actually happens:

> In order to transform both into the concept, a new act of the understanding, a synthesis, is necessary, that joins individually perceived things into unity, and transforms the being that is experienced as real into an ideal one [das real empfundene Seyn in ein ideales verwandelt]. The sensory medium for effecting this synthesis—that by which it can easily and effortlessly be repeated in every moment—is the word. (*GS* 4: 21)

Humboldt's most significant definition of synthesis as a performative act of language occurs in *Über die Verschiedenheit des menschlichen Sprachbaues*, where he characterizes utterance as "the act of *spontaneous positing* by bringing-together (synthesis)"—*den Act des selbstthätigen Setzens durch Zusammenfassung (Synthesis)* (*OL* 184/*GS* 7: 213). If the phrase "act of positing" sounds Fichtean, "synthesis," added as a parenthetical clarification, is almost certainly a deliberate allusion to the *Critique of Pure Reason*. "Spontaneous" or "automatic" (selbstthätig) is also a conspicuously Kantian term, which Kant uses to characterize the activity of the understanding as a faculty independent of external stimuli (e.g., "weil [die Synthesis] ein Actus seiner Selbsttätigkeit ist" [*KrV* 135/B130]). Humboldt understands "synthesis," he explains elsewhere, "in the true sense of the word," as a creation of something that was not previously contained in either of the uniting components (*GS* 7: 94). The individual being of both original elements disappears in the new, third element created through their synthesis (*GS* 7: 212). His terminology makes clear that an essentially sexual sense of (pro)creation is at work here, as the model for the synthesis of intellect (*der Geist* or *der Mensch*) and material (*die Welt* or *die Sprache*) that brings forth an articulated concept.[10] But Humboldt also relates the act of synthesis to the aesthetic realm, comparing its profundity and mystery to the perfect marriage of idea with material achieved by an artistic genius (*GS* 7: 95–96).

As the central concept in Humboldt's linguistic theory, synthesis designates a number of related processes in language and in individual languages. Indeed, the capacity for synthesis becomes the criterion that differentiates languages from one another and makes them more or less successful. As Humboldt sets out to trace synthesis in the details of language-use, however, he begins with the caution that it is an *immaterial* aspect of language: neither a substantive element of composition, nor even an "event," but a momentary, indeed evanescent *acting* (keine Beschaffenheit, nicht einmal eigentlich eine Handlung, sondern ein wirkliches, immer augenblicklich vorübergehendes Handeln [*GS* 7: 212]). Therefore, it is impossible to identify any element of the linguistic system positively *as* synthesis; rather, synthesis occurs in the mind of speaker and hearer every time language is actualized in discourse, and it leaves only traces in grammatical form.

Humboldt nevertheless distinguishes three general operations that cast light on the act of synthesis in various languages: "We see it [i.e., the act of spontaneous positing through synthesis] most clearly and manifestly in *sentence-formation*, then in *words derived* by inflection or by affixes, and finally, in general, in all *couplings* of the *concept* to the *sound*" (*OL* 184). The last of these three processes, "*couplings* of the *concept* to the *sound*," comprises the fundamental objectification of thought in words that has already been discussed as the basis of the Humboldtian speech act. For the second process, "*words derived* by inflection or by affixes," Humboldt offers a single, enigmatic example. The act of spontaneous positing through synthesis is embodied in the simple act of joining a root to a suffix that identifies the word as a noun (e.g., "banish-ment"), an act that, through an instantaneous, invisible, almost magical process, evokes the category of substance in the mind as the

---

[10]For an analysis of the sexual metaphoric in Humboldt's theory of language, see Trabant, *Apeliotes* 18–24; *Traditionen Humboldts* 39–43; and "Nachwort" in Humboldt, *Über die Sprache*; also Müller-Sievers, *Epigenesis*.

word is uttered (*GS* 7: 213). The first-mentioned form of synthesis, however—the process of sentence-formation, where spontaneous positing appears "most clearly and manifestly"—is the subject of a lengthier analysis. Although synthesis has no material presence, Humboldt names three elements of the sentence to which it "adheres": the verb (by far the most important of the three), the conjunction, and the relative pronoun (*OL* 185). To the basic synthetic act in which thought and sound come together on the level of the word, Humboldt now adds another level of synthesis, by which two or more concepts come together on the level of the sentence. It is here that the details of his theory of language as a thoroughly performative phenomenon are to be found.

THE MIDPOINT OF LANGUAGE: VERBS

The verb is at once the simplest and the most significant expression of synthesis, and Humboldt refers to it throughout his essays as the "midpoint of language." In one of several lectures he presented before the Berlin Academy during the 1820s, "Ueber das Verbum in den Americanischen Sprachen" (On the verb in the American languages, 1823), he stresses the centrality of the verb in all languages while specifying that its true "verbal nature" lies in "the bringing together of the subject and predicate of the sentence by means of the concept of being" (*ÜS* 82). As Jürgen Trabant comments, in this abbreviated form Humboldt's account of the verb manifests its continuity with traditional formulations such as that of the Port-Royal Grammar of 1660 (*ÜS* 250n). But by shifting the verb to the center of grammatical structure, by applying Kantian terminology, and by focusing on the way verbs link utterances to reality, Humboldt exemplifies the new, pragmatic and phenomenological linguistics of his generation.

Two aspects of the verb need to be considered in presenting Humboldt's concept of utterance as an act that alters the relationship of the speaker to the speech situation. These are—to analyze his phrase "synthetic positing" into its component parts—the act of synthesis and the act of positing. Humboldt alludes to both these functions in dramatic fashion when introducing his analysis of the verb in *Über die Verschiedenheit des menschlichen Sprachbaues*. Since it is the only part of speech that performs the act of synthesis as its proper grammatical function, the verb animates the rest of the linguistic system: "All the other words of the sentence are like dead matter lying there for combination; the verb alone is the centre, containing and disseminating life" (*OL* 185). This living center of language (or, as he also calls it, the "nerve-centre" of all language [*OL* 186]) joins subject and predicate in such a way as to make the sentence itself an expression of linguistic energy:

> Through one and the same synthetic act, it [the verb] conjoins, by *being*, the *predicate* with the *subject*, yet in such a way that the being which passes, with an energetic predicate, into an action, becomes attributed to the subject itself, so that what is *thought* as merely capable of conjunction becomes, in *reality*, a state or process. (*OL* 185)

But the process of synthesizing subject and predicate brings a totally new entity into being. The verb, therefore, also fulfills the "realizing function" that Humboldt elsewhere attributes to language in general, as that which brings thought out of its inner dwelling and into the external world: "The thought, if one may put it so concretely, departs, through the verb, from its inner abode, and steps across into reality" (*OL* 185). If language in general externalizes thought by objectifying it, giving it a material dimension, and making it available for uptake both by a listener and by the speaker, the synthesis brought about by the verb performs a special, intensified "reality function."

Humboldt provides two examples of this whole process, although they remain somewhat obscure until one realizes that the exemplary utterances themselves—"Lightning strikes" and "Mind is immortal"—are not quoted in his text, but need to be supplied by the reader. When we utter or hear these sentences, according to Humboldt,

> We do not just think of the lightning striking: rather, it is the lightning itself that falls. We do not just bring together the mind and the immortal, as capable of conjunction; the mind, rather, is immortal. The thought, if one may put it so concretely, departs, through the verb, from its inner abode, and steps across into reality. (*OL* 185)

The difficult, almost poetic quality of this passage illustrates the functioning of an invisible synthesis. When we say that lightning strikes, Humboldt claims, we are not just forming a logical conjunction between subject ("lightning") and predicate ("strikes")—the sort of mechanical combination of elements that Coleridge would attribute to Fancy. Rather, we are making lightning into something that strikes, or better still, *we are spontaneously positing lightning as that which strikes.*

Although one of Humboldt's examples contains a conjugated verb ("strikes") and the other contains the copula ("is"), he treats both identically. Like his contemporaries, Humboldt accepts from the tradition of universal grammar the analysis of conjugated verbs into adjectival forms plus the copula (i.e., "strikes" derives from "is" + "striking"). Even more dramatic than the verb's ability to synthesize subject and predicate is the fact that "is," whether explicit or else implicit within a conjugated verb, has the ability to create *in reality*, to confer reality on what were internal and not yet fully existing concepts. Humboldt differs here from Bernhardi, who distinguishes between "real existence" and existence as represented or reconstructed in language, and from Coleridge, for whom the "is" of the proposition in itself neither affirms nor denies reality. In Humboldt's work, there is a stronger dedication to the idea that concepts only arise in the first place when they are uttered. He argues repeatedly that a concept only attains existence when externalized and materialized (i.e., made available to the senses) as sound, and its existence is confirmed only when that sound or word returns to the speaker from another person's mouth. Thus, the sentence "Mind is immortal" *creates mind* as an entity that can be thought and responded to. That *is* its reality, a reality it did not have before the utterance took place.

That Humboldt's concept of synthesis involves not just *joining*, but also *positing (or positioning) in reality*, becomes clearer still in several of his writings of the 1820s. The manuscript *Von dem grammatischen Baue der Sprachen* (On the grammatical structure of languages, 1827–29) refers to the verb's "combining, positing power" (zusammenfassende, setzende Kraft [*GS* 6: 362]). In his Academy lecture of 1826, Humboldt explains the interdependence of these two actions more clearly by describing how the verb combines *by* positing—and thereby turns the logical judgment into a sentence:

> Every logical judgment, as an expression of the agreement or non-agreement of two concepts, can be regarded as a mathematical equation. Language clothes this original form of the thought with its own form by synthetically joining the two concepts, and *actually positing* [indem sie ... wirklich setzt] the one as the property of the other by means of the inflected verb, which thereby becomes the midpoint of language. (*GS* 5: 312)

The act of synthesis, in other words, comes to depend on the act of positing. It is only by positing the real existence of a new, third concept (e.g., lightning as that which strikes) that language can join two separate intuitions (lightning, and the action of striking). The fundamental act of positing is a function of the verb-substantive *sein*: "For the connection of the subject with the predicate in the sentence can only proceed through it [i.e., the *verbum substantivum*], through the positing of the connection as existent" (*GS* 6: 370).

This is as far as Humboldt will go in explicating his concept of synthesis, and, as so often in his work, when the going gets rough, hesitations and paradoxes begin to appear. Because the act of synthesis is difficult to grasp, some languages prefer to circumscribe it with other grammatical formulations—and Humboldt himself occasionally retreats to the implication that synthesis in language is only a "stimulating indication" (eine anregende Andeutung [*GS* 6: 361]) of an act that really takes place within the mind. Humboldt's late manuscripts seem to argue that synthesis as a mental concept is an otherwise inexplicable act of spontaneity (ein . . . unerklärlicher Act der Freiheit [*GS* 6: 361]), but it can be represented by external grammatical signs that enact a parallel, verbal act of synthesis. The verbal act, although still invisible and accessible only through traces, can be analyzed somewhat more readily than its mental counterpart. Despite qualifications within his theory, however, Humboldt presents a powerful reinterpretation of Kant's act of synthesis and idealism's act of positing as *verbal* acts, and he extends this concept further than any of his contemporaries into a detailed analysis of the interrelationship between grammatical structures and mental activity.

A brief comparison with one other contemporaneous account of the proposition helps highlight the significance of Humboldt's theory within the early-nineteenth-century context. In the preface to his *Phenomenology of Spirit*, Hegel includes a detailed commentary on the process of understanding the philosophical *Satz*, as he tries to distinguish the conceptual thinking (begreifendes Denken) that is required in the study of philosophy from image-bound or "material" thinking (vorstellendes Denken) on the one hand, and formal argumentation or "ratiocinative" thinking (Räsonieren) on the other. Conceptual thinking involves recognizing *and experiencing* the dialectical movement of the sentence, in which the "self-moving Notion which takes its determinations back into itself" (der sich bewegende und seine Bestimmungen in sich zurücknehmende Begriff) manifests itself "as the *coming-to-be of the object*" (*Phenomenology* 37/ *Werke* 3: 57). In contrast to the usual understanding of a sentence, whereby a static subject is linked to predicates, the speculative judgment or sentence (spekulative Satz) of philosophy enacts a violent, self-reflexive dynamic. Its grammatical subject gets lost as we pass over to the predicate and recognize the latter as substance; brought up short by the unexpected "mass" of the predicate, the intellect experiences a "counter-thrust" by which it is thrown back toward the missing subject and rediscovers it as that *of which* the predicate is the substance. Through this self-reflexive process, what we had taken as an inert, passive subject suddenly becomes dynamic, so that the movement of thought itself becomes the object (nur diese Bewegung selbst wird der Gegenstand [*Werke* 3: 58]). To put it differently, the static, grammatical "subject" gives way to the thinking, human "subject," whose movement of thought forms the crucial act of synthesis on which the sentence depends: "Here, that Subject is replaced by the knowing 'I' itself, which links the Predicates with the Subject holding them" (*Phenomenology* 37).

With Hegel's explication of the speculative sentence in the preface to the *Phenomenology*, the Romantic reinterpretation of the standard proposition as an act, and of the copula as an instrument of becoming rather than a designator of static existence, enters the mainstream philosophical tradition. But it also enters the realm of speculative thought—whereas Humboldt draws his re-interpretation of the proposition out into the intersubjective and pragmatic sphere. Although even Hegel stresses that "explicit expression" (Aussprechen), and not merely an "inward inhibition" (innerliche Hemmung [*Phenomenology* 39/*Werke* 3: 61]), is essential to the conceptual event he describes, his account of verbal action remains focused on the mental activity that words produce in the reader of a philosophical text. His argument relates, moreover, to a specific form of philosophical discourse that stands in contrast to ordinary language. Humboldt, with his account of synthetic positing as the crucial moment in all uses of language whatsoever, universalizes the idea that discourse is a dynamic, simultaneously conceptual and communicative event.

PRAGMATIC ORIENTATIONS: HUMBOLDT, SEARLE, BENVENISTE

The linguistic re-interpretation of the (Kantian) logical judgment, synthesis as a verbal act, the dynamic function of the verb, and the act of "positing in reality": these are the key points that make Humboldt's philosophy significant for the use and understanding of language in the Romantic period. All of them are summed up in the idea that Humboldt revises the analytic sentence of Kantian philosophy, as well as the abstract sentences of eighteenth-century universal grammar, by *situating language in reality, as discourse*. Refusing to regard the proposition as an abstract, objective combination of words, he considers it instead as an utterance produced by an intending subject. His speech act of synthetic positing, if we recall his example of joining a root to a suffix that marks the word as a substantive, is fundamentally an application of linguistic rules—yet it is a notion that brings life to grammatical forms, and grammatical forms to life. Humboldt's analyses of sentences and parts of speech inevitably presuppose a pragmatic context; the synthetic-positing function of the verb, as he describes it, can only be understood in terms of the mental action of the speaker and the corresponding activity generated in the mind of the hearer.

Humboldt's emphasis on a pragmatic context for language brings about extensive resonances between his work and speech-act theory. Austin and Searle, as well as pragmatic linguists like Benveniste, repeat Humboldt's re-interpretation of Kantian philosophy and universal grammar in relation to their own immediate precursors—twentieth-century analytic philosophy of language and a linguistics focused on *langue* rather than *parole*. Searle begins his *Speech Acts* with a set of phenomenologically based questions that are not too far from the ones Romantic theorists like Humboldt and Coleridge are trying to answer: namely, how it is possible for someone to mean something, or to intend the representation of certain objects, or to be understood by a hearer, when uttering certain sounds. His philosophy of language is not merely the taxonomy of illocutionary acts such as promising, ordering, and warning to which it is sometimes reduced by both hostile and sympathetic critics. Instead, the real argument of *Speech Acts* is that every aspect of the relationship of words to the world should be seen as an act, and as part of a theory of action. Thus, like Humboldt, Searle characterizes the act of predication as a basic component of all utterances, and addresses the question of exactly how verbs (particularly the verb "is" in the standard proposition) join two elements to one another. According to Searle,

> To predicate an expression 'P' of an object R is to raise the question of the truth of the predicate expression of the object referred to. Thus, in utterances of each of the sentences, 'Socrates is wise,' 'Is Socrates wise?,' 'Socrates, be wise!' the speaker raises the question of the truth of 'wise' to Socrates. (*Speech Acts* 124)

The effect of this example is to show that the three utterances Searle cites, which perform the different illocutionary acts of asserting, asking, and ordering, all contain the same act of predication: a synthetic act that joins the referent "Socrates" with the predicate expression "is wise." Searle's next example illustrates the significance of these predicative acts: "there is a vast difference between saying of a politician 'Either he is a Fascist or he isn't' and saying of him 'Either he is a Communist or he isn't'" (*Speech Acts* 124), even though neither of these sentences asserts anything but a tautology, and they differ only in the act of predication, or synthesis, that they perform (i.e., joining "politician" with "Fascist" on the one hand, "politician" with "Communist" on the other). Despite the difference between Humboldt's often poetic, and Searle's analytic, diction, both of them are calling attention to the dynamic element within predication, and thereby redefining the proposition as a form of language that acts on reality rather than describing reality.

Humboldt's pragmatically oriented analysis of the proposition finds a more exact echo in the work of Benveniste,[11] who returns a century and a half later to the question of the verb and its relationship to real existence. Benveniste concludes with even greater emphasis than Humboldt that the verb "to be" not only links elements in a sentence to one another, but also performs an "assertive function" that connects the utterance to reality:

> Within the assertive utterance, the verbal function is twofold: there is the cohesive function, which is to organize the elements of the utterance into a complete structure; and there is the assertive function, which consists in endowing the utterance with a predicate of reality.... A finite assertion, precisely because it is an assertion, implies the reference of the utterance to a different order, and this is the order of reality. Added implicitly to the grammatical relationship that unites the members of the utterance is a 'this *is*!' that links the linguistic arrangement to the system of reality. (*Problems* 133)

But it is the analysis of pronouns that forms the most important link between Humboldt and Benveniste—and represents Humboldt's most explicit claim to study language in a revolutionary way. "The utterance containing *I*," Benveniste writes, belongs to the pragmatic level of language,

> which includes, with the signs, those who make use of them. A linguistic text of great length—a scientific treatise, for example—can be imagined in which *I* and *you* would not appear a single time; conversely, it would be difficult to conceive of a short spoken text in which they were not employed. (*Problems* 217–18)

Humboldt draws the same distinction, albeit not between types of text, or between written and spoken language, but between the two perspectives open to the linguistic philosopher. He distinguishes universal grammar, which proceeds from logic and concentrates on cognition or the relation between signifier and signified, from the type of theory that interests him more: one that would take account of the role of a receiver or responder (einem Empfangenden und Zurückwirkenden [*GS* 6: 161]).

---

[11]There are surprisingly few discussions of the remarkable parallels between Humboldt and Benveniste. Baum points out that both of them emphasized the concrete speech act and suggests that this emphasis offers a direction for the future development of linguistics, while Sandor notes that Benveniste's attempt to go beyond Saussure's system-linguistics by developing a "linguistics of the speech act" implies a return to Humboldt.

In a logic-based grammar, first- and second-person pronouns are marginal and only count as stand-ins for the more important parts of the sentence (thus the term *pro*-noun), but once one considers language from the perspective of actual discourse, pronouns become absolutely central. Linguistic historians confirm Humboldt's break with tradition: until the eighteenth century, grammarians tended to consider the pronoun as a handy stylistic device that avoided inelegant repetition of the noun, while Humboldt treats it as a pragmatic and deictic operator (Conte 628; Fava 3).

"*Language lies only in connected discourse*," Humboldt insists (*GS* 6: 147); he often repeats his claim that language must be seen as the totality of all spoken utterances, and that the linguist must study not merely, or even primarily, the linguistic system, but also living speech. Here again, Humboldt is less a unique forerunner of modern linguistics than the best representative of ideas about discourse that were being articulated in similar ways by his contemporaries. Bernhardi agrees that pronouns deserve the special attention of the linguistic philosopher: "pronominal forms are therefore ... representative of language in its entirety, and one can regard them as the highest and most sublimated expressions of human representation" (*Sprachlehre* 1: 264). He also proceeds from pronouns to the pragmatic context of actual speech in which they originate ("*I* and *You* arose through speech, discourse, presence ..." [*Anfangsgründe* 191]), although the context of *parole* is never quite as important for his understanding of grammar as it is for Humboldt. The individual act of speaking is pivotal, however, for Schleiermacher, who was apparently the first to denote it by the term "speech act" (Sprechakt) (89). Schleiermacher is one of the most powerful Romantic representatives of a philosophy of speech or *Rede*; the oral, dialogic situation figures prominently in his work on biblical hermeneutics. In line with his interpretative concerns, he argues that meaning is context-dependent ("everything is in need of closer definition and receives this only in its context" [101]), referring to both the context of the language used by the speaker or writer, and the context of the speaker's or writer's life. With his emphasis on context, Schleiermacher approaches the Wittgensteinian principle that the meaning of a word is its use in the language.

Humboldt's own preference for a linguistics of speech over a logic-based grammar evokes the ambiguity between the propositional *Satz* and the discursive *Satz* (discussed in Chapter 2). In *Von dem grammatischen Baue der Sprachen*, he equates the proposition and the sentence with respect to their connective function: "The logical judgment and the grammatical sentence, through all their formations and deformations, stand on exactly the same footing as far as the joining and dividing of concepts is concerned" (*GS* 6: 346). But logic remains in the realm of the abstract, whereas language takes account of temporality, referentiality, and context. Using dynamic and even violent diction, Humboldt also implies that language adds performative force:

> But logic handles these ideal relations merely on their own terms, in the realm of potential, of absolute being. Language positions them in a particular moment, and represents the subject, as well as the predicate, as active or passive, as seizing to itself or thrusting back. The dead concept of relation [i.e., the copula]—the connective sign of a mathematical equation, as it were—thereby turns into living motion. (*GS* 6: 346)

This moment in which the "dead" proposition becomes animated is also the moment in which the verb is born, and with it the personal pronoun:

> The verb arises, the midpoint and germ of all grammar. Language, moreover, always directs the thought that is apprehended in words toward an Other, who is really, externally present or else thought in the mind. Therein, and in the nature of the verb, which presupposes a person, the pronoun has its origin. Verb and pronoun are therefore the hinges on which the whole of language moves, and when one examines a particular language, one finds that its grammatical particularity lies primarily in the handling of these two parts of speech, while they stand in relation to one another according to the nature of this particularity. (*GS* 6: 346)

What Humboldt distinguishes as the "hinges" of language are the words that modern linguistics calls *deictics*: first- and second-person verb forms and pronouns, along with adverbs of place and time such as "here," "there," "now," "today," "tomorrow." Pointing to and orienting themselves by a present instance of discourse, these words connect the logical-grammatical system of language to the instant of utterance, or logic with reality, and therefore play a central role in theories of performative language—Humboldt's no less than Searle's or Benveniste's.

THE HINGES OF LANGUAGE: PRONOUNS

While Humboldt's theory of pronouns derives directly from his context-based perspective on language, it also exemplifies his reception of German idealism. In a philosophical context colored by the work of Fichte, Humboldt regards cognition as an interaction of I with Not-I—but the pronouns "I" and "you" provide the only way of bringing this interaction into the present time and place of discourse. "You," writes Humboldt, is a Not-I that has been brought into the sphere of mutual influence and communal action (*GS* 6: 26). This characterization of the You also has a Kantian flavor: like Kant, Humboldt distinguishes between a relationship that is passive or determined by external conditions (here, the relationship between "I" and the third-person Other, "he") and one that reveals the autonomy of the human faculties of knowledge, or *Spontaneität der Wahl* (i.e., the I's choice of a You as the person to address): "They [the pronouns "I" and "you"] are really experienced internally, the I in the sense of self, the You in personal choice, whereas in contrast everything that stands under the third person is only perceived, seen, heard, or felt externally" (*GS* 6: 165; repeated at 6: 309).[12]

If the structure of Humboldt's theory of pronouns and dialogue is easily derived from Kantian and idealist philosophy, it is equally easy to align with modern linguistic pragmatics, suggesting that Humboldt actually constitutes an unacknowledged bridge between the two. His account of first- and second-person pronouns illustrates this connection with particular clarity. All language, Humboldt writes, is the expression of fundamental dualities, but the immediate and present one that makes speech possible is the duality of "I" and "you":

> The first thing is naturally the personality of the speaker himself, who stands in continuous and direct contact with nature, and cannot possibly fail, even in language, to set over against the latter the expression of his self. But in the I, the Thou is also given automatically, and by a new opposition there arises the third person, though since the field of the sentient and speaking has now been left behind, this is also extended to the inanimate. (*OL* 95)

One of many parallel statements made by Benveniste comes from the beginning of his 1966 essay "Le langage et l'expérience humaine":

> Each person posits himself in his individuality as an *I* in relation to *you* and *he*. . . . Thus, in every language and at every moment, the one who speaks appropriates the *I*, that *I* which, in the inventory of the forms of the language, is only a lexical given like any other, but which, put into action in discourse, introduces there the presence of the person without whom no language is possible. As soon as the pronoun *I* appears in a speech-act where it evokes—explicitly or not—the pronoun *you* so that together they oppose the *he*, a human experience is established anew and reveals the linguistic instrument that founds it. (3–4)

---

[12]For further analysis of Humboldt's relationship to idealism, see Burkhardt, who interprets Humboldt's orientation toward I-You dialogue as a significant advance over the "transcendental-solipsistic" philosophy of idealism; the latter focuses on the relation of the subject to "objective Not-I's," whereas Humboldt recognizes that the subject orients itself in relation to other subjects ("Dialogbegriff" 152).

Humboldt and Benveniste share a focus on the opposition of I and You, along with the equally significant contrast between I/You and He. The third person, being by definition outside the present instance of discourse, is characterized by both writers as absent and even inanimate, and their concentration on the I/You relationship discloses their orientation toward subjectivity and the present moment of utterance. Yet the above quotations reveal with equal clarity a basic difference between the perspectives of Humboldt and Benveniste on the relative priority of human consciousness and language. For Humboldt, "the first thing is naturally the personality of the speaker," and this is expressed in—indeed, it creates—the mechanism of pronouns in language. Benveniste, conversely, has the I posit itself by appropriating the already-existing mechanisms of language—mechanisms that "found" and "establish" human experience.

The difference, while significant, is not as absolute as it might seem, since both Humboldt and Benveniste make highly ambiguous statements elsewhere about the relative priority of speaker and language. In his essay "Subjectivity in Language," Benveniste argues that subjectivity makes language possible and, simultaneously, that language makes subjectivity possible: "Language is possible only because each speaker sets himself up as a *subject* by referring to himself as *I* in his discourse," and yet "language alone establishes the concept of 'ego' in reality" (*Problems* 224–25). Indeed, the paradox whereby language and subjectivity presuppose one another can itself be traced back from Benveniste to Humboldt. As is evident from the quotation above, Humboldt often privileges the speaking subject—but he also refers to language repeatedly as an "external power," an "independent power," and an independent object that acts on individual speakers as well as on entire cultures (e.g., GS 6: 121, 180, 181). When it is a matter of the relationship between a language and a culture, this double nature of language as both inner human creation and external force can be explained by historicizing the two states and spreading them over a temporal continuum:

> But from speaking there arises language, a stock of words and a system of rules, and it grows, winding its way through the sequence of millennia, into a power independent of the particular speaker, the particular race, the nation, and finally even in a certain way independent of humanity itself. . . . Now the opposite viewpoint appears, according to which language is really a foreign object, and its effect really arose out of something other than that on which it acts. (GS 6: 180)

But the double function of language as *expression of* human consciousness and, simultaneously, *influence on* human consciousness is ultimately embedded in the nature of language, which, as the mediator between subjectivity and objectivity, must partake of both. Language is just as much a force that acts on the individual speaker as a force that acts, historically, on the nation. Since, as Humboldt affirms, "it is a general law of man's existence in the world, that he can project nothing from himself that does not at once become a thing that reacts upon him and conditions his further creation" (OL 214), the word also acts as a constraint against which the soul must strive, lest its "individual nuances" and "capacious inner sensitivity" be imprisoned within the materiality of sound and the generality of meaning (OL 92). Hence the word must sometimes appear as subjective and created, sometimes as objective and independent—and, as in Humboldt's other binary formulations, these contraries are contingent on one another:

> Language is an object, and independent, precisely insofar as it is a subject, and dependent. For nowhere, not even in writing, does it have a permanent dwelling; rather, it must always be produced anew in thought, and consequently must merge completely into the subject; but it belongs to this act of production to make language into an object in just the same way.... (GS 6: 181)

The subject-object dichotomy within the nature of language derives from the basic act of synthetic positing, as words are continually re-created in the mind's encounter with the world—but, precisely because they thereby become objects, they then take on a certain power in relation to the speaker. These polarized perspectives lend Humboldt's theory a remarkable modernity, in that the twentieth-century autonomy of the linguistic medium and the various kinds of difference that language carries within itself are substantially represented in his work. So, however, is a Romantic faith in individual agency, in the unity of the individual mind, and in the unity of all minds, that is for the most part foreign to modern linguistic philosophy.

GRAMMAR AND REFERENCE: HUMBOLDT, HEGEL, DE MAN

In suggesting that the objective nature of language is actually dependent on its subjective nature, and vice versa, Humboldt returns to his characteristic assertion that language somehow exists through the coincidence of contraries. Language can express interiority, he also maintains, precisely because it partakes of materiality, and thus stands for the ultimate identification between spirit and matter or I and Not-I. In his analysis of the pronoun, Humboldt identifies another fundamental ambiguity when he distinguishes between two aspects of discourse: the "grammatical" (i.e., the logical or cognitive relationship between elements in a linguistic structure) and the "material" (i.e., reference to a real-world situation). Although he is willing to regard this, too, as a paradox rather than a dilemma, he intimates that we habitually "attribute" or "foist" (unterschieben) the material aspect of pronouns onto their grammatical function. In part, this happens because we are unable fully to grasp the relationship between language and the real world:

> It [i.e., the pronoun] evidently has, in actual languages, or rather in the way they are understood, a double value: a purely grammatical and a more material one, whereby the latter, due to the inability to understand it absolutely, is attributed to the former in our consciousness. On the one hand, the independent (substantive) pronoun is a true expression of the real [ein wahrer Realausdruck], a true *nomen proprium*, or at least it can be taken as such.... On the other hand, though, it designates nothing but the manner in which self-consciousness opposes itself to that which lies outside of it ... and abstracts from all content. This is its purely grammatical value. (GS 6: 368)

Humboldt has a strategic reason for stressing the "purely grammatical" function of the pronoun, inasmuch as he wants to redefine pronouns—and language itself—as a means of establishing interpersonal relations. He characterizes pronouns, therefore, less as words that stand for specific nouns than as "hypostatized concepts of relation," or "empty" concepts that need to be filled differently in each individual act of utterance:

> *I* is not the individual invested with these particular characteristics, who is found in these particular spatial circumstances, but rather the one who, in this moment, takes up a position opposite another in consciousness, as a subject.... The same holds true for *You* and *He*. (GS 6: 306)

The relational function of pronouns leads Humboldt to theorize, in his 1829 Academy lecture "Ueber die Verwandtschaft der Ortsadverbien mit dem Pronomen in einigen Sprachen" (On the relationship of the adverbs of place to the pronoun in several languages), that certain languages developed their pronouns from designations of the spatial relationship of speakers to one another. But he also recognizes the *temporal* dependence of the I on the moment of discourse—and the paradoxes that this temporal relationship raises. On the one hand, the function of all language is to put thought into objective form; on the other hand, the function of "I" is to introduce the speaker into language as a subject "in this [subjective] moment." The first-person pronoun is thus, by definition, subject and object at once: "It must therefore be an object whose essence consists exclusively in being a subject" (*GS* 6: 163; repeated at 6: 306–7). Benveniste later generalizes this paradox as the "double instance" that arises whenever "I" appears in discourse, because it splits into "the instance of *I* as referent and the instance of discourse containing *I* as the referee" (*Problems* 218). Through Benveniste's influential distinction between *énonciation* and *énoncé*—between the subject who speaks and the subject who is spoken of—Humboldt's paradox of the simultaneously subjective and objective I has become a commonplace of pragmatic linguistics; through adaptations of Benveniste's distinction, particularly by Roland Barthes, it has gained a significant place in literary theory.

Humboldt adds that the pronoun's role in discourse is attended by "great difficulties"—but this is as far as he is willing to pursue the matter. Kant and the idealist philosophers went further in elucidating the problem of the simultaneously subjective and objective, or the infinite and finite, I, and by way of the development of this problematic through Hegel, it also enters into poststructuralist thinking. As Kant recognizes, his own act of founding epistemology on a redefined "I think" raises the problem of how the I can think *itself*:

> How the 'I' that thinks can be distinct from the 'I' that intuits itself (for I can represent still other modes of intuition as at least possible), and yet, as being the same subject, can be identical with the latter; and how, therefore, I can say: 'I, as intelligence and *thinking* subject, know myself as an object that is *thought*, in so far as I am given to myself [as something other or] beyond that [I] which is [given to myself] in intuition, and yet know myself, like other phenomena, only as I appear to myself, not as I am to the understanding'—these are questions that raise no greater nor less difficulty than how I can be an object to myself at all, and, more particularly, an object of intuition and of inner perceptions. (*CPR* 167/B155)

Kant, too, sets the issue aside again in perplexity; but after Fichte's and Schelling's philosophical struggle with the conflict between an infinite and a finite I (well represented by Schelling's early, Fichtean treatise *Vom Ich als Princip der Philosophie*), it is taken up again and given a distinctively verbal inflection by Hegel. In a passage of his *Enzyklopädie der philosophischen Wissenschaften im Grundrisse* (*Encyclopedia*, 1817, 1827, and 1830) that is primarily a critique of Kant's "I think," Hegel appends an exclamation about the paradoxical expression "I," which is both the most specific and the most general of terms:

> when I say 'I,' I *mean* myself *as this one* who excludes all others; but what I say, *I*, is just anyone!—I, who excludes all others from himself.

> Kant availed himself of the clumsy expression, that I *accompany* all my representations, as well as sensations, desires, actions, etc. I is the universal in and of itself, and commonality is also a form of universality, but an external form. (*Werke* 8: 74)

For Hegel, this peculiarity of the I is emblematic of language as a whole, inasmuch as language allows the pure self to assert its universality, but thereby causes the self to disappear or become sublimated into the universal. In his *Phenomenology*, the self announces its pure individuality but simultaneously *re*nounces it to identify with the "abstract universal" or state authority; this "alienation" "takes place solely in *language*, which here appears in its characteristic significance" (*Phenomenology* 308). The process by which language—or, more specifically, speech—sublimates the self within the universal is an extension of the "inner generality" that Hegel discovers in the expression "I":

> It is the power of speech, as that which performs what has to be performed. For it is the *real existence* of the pure self as self; in speech, self-consciousness, *qua independent separate individuality*, comes as such into existence, so that it exists *for others*. . . . The 'I' is this particular 'I'—but equally the *universal* 'I' . . . and its real existence is just this: that as a self-conscious Now, as a real existence, it is *not* a real existence, and through this vanishing it *is* a real existence. This vanishing is thus itself at once its abiding; it is its own knowing of itself, and its knowing itself as a self that has passed over into another self that has been perceived and is universal. (*Phenomenology* 308–9)

Through their role in the dialectical formation of Hegelian *Geist*, the paradoxical, subject-object nature of the I and the corresponding individualizing-universalizing function of speech gain a role in the tradition of Continental philosophy, extending into poststructuralist readings of Romanticism. De Man returns repeatedly to Hegel's analysis of language as an embodiment of the aporia of theory itself—since, in Hegel, "the position of the I, which is the condition for thought, implies its eradication . . . as the undoing, the erasure of any relationship, logical or otherwise, that could be conceived between what the I is and what it says it is" ("Sign and Symbol" 769). This aporia is another iteration of the conflict between grammar and rhetoric, or between the simultaneously cognitive and performative orientation that de Man locates in Romantic texts. He describes the relationship between the grammatical and referential aspects of the pronoun in terms of "subversion": "There can be no text without grammar: the logic of grammar generates texts only in the absence of referential meaning, but every text generates a referent that subverts the grammatical principle to which it owed its constitution"

(*Allegories of Reading* 269). De Man's "grammar" and "referential meaning" are very close to what Humboldt identifies as the "purely grammatical" and the "more material" value of pronouns. Typically, the relationship between these dimensions is an "entirely divergent" one for de Man—indeed, an "impossibility" (*Allegories of Reading* 270)—while Humboldt, also typically, represents it as an ambiguity rather than an aporia, as a remedy that language provides for a cognitive dilemma rather than a dilemma in itself.

In the context of these other formulations of the problematic of the I, Humboldt's enunciation of the difference between logical and pragmatic dimensions of language, especially as they affect the behavior of the first-person pronoun, makes clear that the question of what language does, as well as what it describes, was already there to be asked during the Romantic period. In his linguistic-pragmatic analysis of the question, though, Humboldt opens up a new, dialogic understanding of verbal action. He is generally content to set aside the metaphysical problematic of grammar and reference or universal and individual; true to his dedication to the ideal of "humanity," he is more concerned with the way actual, speaking I's interact in the here and now of discourse. Consequently, he finds Fichte's absolute I alienating "because," as he writes, "it seemed to me to supersede all the real I's and hypostatize a thoroughly chimerical one" (*Wilhelm von Humboldts Briefe* 154–55). The Idealists' philosophy of first principles obliterates an empirical or anthropological understanding of subjectivity that Humboldt finds at least as important. By grounding the relationship of mind and world or I and Not-I in the temporal and interactive medium of language, Humboldt gives subjectivity an *experiential* dimension; no longer purely cognitive or metaphysical, it becomes a function of communication, dialogue, interpersonal experience—ultimately, of history.

Within this interactive, experiential perspective on language, words themselves appear to establish the pragmatic relationships to which they refer. Since the pronoun, like the verb, is an enactor of synthesis, these parts of speech bring about the relationship between speaking subjects, or between subject and object, in the moment when they are used. "The subjects [i.e., the first and second person] determine and alter the relationships from which they derive their existence, in the medium of language, in which thoughts simultaneously attain objective validity," Tilman Borsche observes about Humboldt's theory of language (*Wilhelm von Humboldt* 149). In the process of objectifying existing relationships, the act of utterance modifies them. Rather than Fichte's (and the early Schelling's) absolute I or Hegel's self-sublimating I, Humboldt offers an I that continually re-creates itself as it engages in dialogue with other speakers and with the phenomenal world.

COGNITIVE AND COMMUNICATIVE DIALOGUE

Humboldt's ideas about dialogue exemplify the Romantic tendency to conflate the cognitive and the communicative dimensions of language. While dialogue between speakers forms the basic paradigm for his theory of language, this intersubjective relationship always presupposes other dialogic relationships between speakers and the objective world, and between speakers and language itself.[13] In his 1827 Academy lecture, "Über den Dualis" (On the dual form), Humboldt affirms the importance of one-to-one dialogue as the paradigm for all social uses of language: "All speaking rests on dialogue, in which, even in a group, the speaker always sets the addressees over against himself as a unit" (GS 6: 25). But he also grounds the importance of dialogue in a principle of duality that permeates the natural and social world, touching everything from the bilateral symmetry of the body, to binaries such as male and female, to more abstract oppositions between self and world or between thesis and antithesis (Satz and Gegensatz). This profound dialogism manifests itself not only in the grammatical forms of specific languages, but in the nature of language itself: "There lies in the original nature of language an inalterable duality, and the possibility of speaking itself is conditioned by address and response" (GS 6: 26).

Humboldt regards the dialogic setting as a space of Gegensatz or "opposition," subtended by a spatial metaphor. Language itself allows the speaker to take up a complementary position relative to another subject: "The whole individuality of the speaker is therefore carried over by language into the other, not to repress the latter's own individuality, but in order to fashion from ownness and otherness a new and fruitful contrast [Gegensatz]" (OL 158). In a manuscript variant, Humboldt expands on the significance of the term Gegensatz by adding that "everything in language is at once independence and reciprocity, always resting on the opposition [Gegensatz] of the I and the You of address and response" (GS 7: 179). Containing an etymological allusion to the act of setzen, Gegen-

---

[13]Humboldt's emphasis on the dialogic situation as the basis of linguistic, mental, artistic, and social development raises the possibility of further parallels with twentieth-century theorists from Bakhtin to Levinas. Identifying Humboldt as a forerunner of the "socio-ontological" branch of philosophy, Burkhardt briefly discusses a number of contemporary philosophers who have developed Humboldt's concept of dialogue in different directions, including Feuerbach, Husserl, Heidegger, Sartre, Buber, and Löwith ("Dialogbegriff" 160–61).

satz implies a positing or positioning that is both spatial and philosophical. Humboldt's formulation emphasizes the performative nature of the experience of dialogue: the speech situation puts intersubjective identities in place, but thereby also modifies them, bringing about a synthesis of "ownness and otherness" and fashioning a "new and fruitful" relationship between subjects.

But dialogue is, for Humboldt, also a process of negotiating (with) the phenomenal world. Even when referring to interpersonal communication, he locates the origin of the dialogic principle in individual cognition:

> The word in itself is not an object [Gegenstand]; rather, in contrast to objects, it is something subjective; nevertheless, in the mind of the one who thinks, it is supposed to become an object produced by him and reacting back on him. Between the word and its object there remains such an alienating abyss—the word, when born in the individual alone, so resembles a purely illusory object [Scheinobject]—language cannot be brought to reality by the individual either, but only socially, only in that one daring attempt is made and a new one takes it up. Therefore the word must achieve essence, language must achieve expansion in one who hears and responds. (*GS* 6: 26)

The word, unlike the person addressed (the You as *Gegensatz*), is in itself incapable of taking up a position completely external to the speaker; it is not a *Gegenstand* ("object," but also "that which stands against"). Produced by the individual mind, as if by only one parent, it is first of all a subjective, unreal phenomenon, an illusory object separated by a gulf from its would-be referent. Only by testing it against an Other can its producer hope to receive it back in an actual, legitimate form. Humboldt, in other words, articulates the need for *uptake* on the part of a hearer in a more fundamental and universal sense than speech-act theorists, for whom uptake involves the hearer's recognition of the illocutionary conventions governing an utterance. Humboldt's notion of uptake or response also comprises the hearer's recognition of the speaker's meaning and intended effect, but is in the first instance an acknowledgment of the way the speaker is proposing to objectify the world: "for objectivity is heightened if the self-coined word is echoed from a stranger's mouth" (*OL* 56). This need for uptake may become metaphorical—that is, the speaker may simply proceed *as if* his or her utterance were being confirmed by a hearer, or *imagine* a dialogic context—but it is inevitably present at some level in Humboldt's account of language.

If the origin of dialogue is cognitive, its consequences are sociopolitical. Like Friedrich Schlegel, Johann Jacob Wagner, and other contemporaries, Humboldt credits language with instilling interpersonal feelings like friendship and love; the principle of dialogue in language is responsible for grounding our social ties. In typical Humboldtian fashion, though, the same linguistic principle that brings about social unity also brings about political distinctions. Because all speech, even inner speech, depends on dialogue and thus on identifying someone or something as Other, the mind inevitably carries this principle of separation on into a distinction between those who speak the same way we do and those who speak differently, or natives and foreigners. But the divisive aspect of dialogue is not in competition with the uniting aspect. "Language... unites, *in that* it individuates," Humboldt claims while exploring the reciprocal influence of language and nation on one another (*GS* 6: 125; italics added). Language makes it possible to establish relations between individuals, and nations precisely by concretizing their differences. Again typically, Humboldt identifies distinction itself as the condition of possibility for its opposite, social unity: "This... distinguishing separation is the foundation of all original sociable connection" (*GS* 6: 25).

THE PARADOX OF THE PERFORMATIVE

The structure of thought whereby one element generates its opposite, yet cannot be conceived apart from or prior to its opposite, is to be found throughout Humboldt's work, and throughout the philosophical context in which he is writing. Recurring, usually in the form of a scandal or a crisis, in speech-act theory and poststructuralist thought, this self-reflexive structure suggests an important continuity between Humboldt's theory of language and the modern performative. But Humboldt's analysis of self-reflexive forms and complementary oppositions takes place within a pragmatic and anthropological context, where his concern is to elucidate the relationship among minds, grammars, and cultures as well as possible, even if the phenomenon that joins them—language—is ultimately inscrutable. His motto might be that of the late Wittgenstein: "This is simply what I do" (Wittgenstein 85). And in describing what we do when we speak and write, in terms of the way we thereby generate world for ourselves and for one another, Humboldt offers the potential for turning philosophy of language toward a significant engagement with Romantic literature.

For Humboldt, language inhabits a complex of temporal paradoxes. One needs to study its historical evolution—and yet there is never a time when a language does not exist as an already complete structure within the culture and the minds of the people using it. A language is nothing but the collection of individual speech acts performed by its speakers in ongoing discursive situations—and yet individual speech acts presuppose the background of a complete linguistic system. Dialogic and communal contexts make language possible—and yet these contexts are only formed in the first place by intersubjective speech acts. Language, Humboldt explains in his "Ankündigung einer Schrift über die Vaskische Sprache und Nation" (Announcement of an essay on the Basque language and nation, 1812), originates out of the union that it also founds; and it derives its nature, which *enables* contact with the Other, *from* the Other:

> For language is everywhere a mediator, first between infinite and finite nature, then between one individual and another; simultaneously and through the same act it makes union possible, and originates from it; its whole nature never lies in a single individual, but must always simultaneously be guessed or intuited from the Other; yet it cannot be explained on the basis of both of them either; rather, it is (as that always is wherein true mediation takes place) something unique, incomprehensible, simply *given* in the idea of the union of that which is (for us and our mode of thinking) thoroughly separated, and caught up only within this idea. (GS 3: 296)

Reciprocal influence complicated by a temporal paradox, by which each form of influence seems to presuppose the other: this is, among other things, a version of the hermeneutic circle, a figure of thought best represented by Humboldt's contemporaries Friedrich Ast and Friedrich Schleiermacher. For Schleiermacher, too, this structure of reciprocity underlies a theory of language; Schleiermacher believes (like Humboldt) that each individual speech act presupposes a given language, yet a system of language only develops from acts of speech (78). The part-whole duality of language leads Schleiermacher to develop a double approach to hermeneutics, whereby "psychological interpretation" considers an utterance as the self-expression of the individual, while "grammatical interpretation" conversely emphasizes the influence of the language-system on an individual's utterance, regarding "the individual person only as the location for language and his speech only as that wherein language reveals itself" (79).

But Humboldt more likely inherited this paradox from Kant, for the system of language has the same status in Humboldt's work as the transcendental forms of intuition, space and time, have in Kant's epistemology. On the one hand, transcendental structures (such as space-time or *langue*) are the condition of possibility for thought or speech; on the other hand, they remain empty and perhaps do not even really exist until they are applied in particular acts of representation (for Kant) or acts of utterance (for Humboldt). Another relevant influence is the idealist doctrine of contraries, introduced by Fichte but represented more clearly by Schelling, for whom every element seems to presuppose the existence of its opposite, but at the same time to generate its opposite: transcendental philosophy demands natural philosophy (Naturphilosophie); the self or subject demands world or object; freedom or infinity demands limitation. On the most general level, the concept of positing (Setzen) always involves the concept of opposition (Entgegensetzen) (Schelling 2: 381). The definition of the "original" phenomenon, in each case, is thoroughly implicated in its relation to the "secondary" counterpart.

The reciprocal influence of context and utterance, complicated by a temporal paradox, also haunts poststructuralist and postmodern accounts of the performative. Derrida and Lyotard repeatedly call attention to the way performatives derive their legitimacy from conditions that they themselves found—or, to put it differently, the way performatives derive their ability to act from the fact that they *do* act. The (supposedly pre-existing) conditions that make a performative utterance into an act merge together with the reality that the utterance itself constitutes. Thus, Lyotard writes, it is not the fact that the chairperson of a meeting utters "The meeting is called to order" that causes the meeting to begin; rather, the fact that the utterance "The meeting is called to order" actually does cause the meeting to begin grants the speaker the authority of a chairperson (82). Both Derrida and Lyotard call attention to the "fabulous retroactivity" of declarations, whereby they grant authority to the representatives or signatories on whose authority they also rely (Derrida, "Declarations of Independence" 10; Lyotard 146). If all statements have both performative and constative dimensions, declarations capitalize on this duality by pretending that the situation they aim (performatively) to bring about already (constatively) exists, and thereby seek to conceal the fact that any declaration entails an exercise of power. "One pretends to describe an already-given state of things," Slavoj Žižek writes; "in order to be effective, the 'pure' performative (the speech act which brings about its own propositional content) has to endure an inner split and assume the form of its opposite, of a constative" (97). Performative utterances also involve a collapse of temporality. De Man refers to this temporal sleight-of-hand as "the metalepsis that reverses the temporal pattern of all promissory and legal statements" (*Allegories of Reading* 276), while Shoshana Felman, working within a psychoanalytic frame of reference, shows that promises are "constituted by the act of anticipating the act of concluding" (49). A promise or a law is determined by a future state of affairs, a state that the utterance presumes to be able to name accurately even though it does not yet exist. Like Derrida's declarations, in order to have an effect, these poststructuralist performatives must proceed as if they had *already taken effect*.

This metalepsis or fabulous retroactivity characterizes Humboldt's Romantic performative on fundamental levels. It emerges when he describes the system of language as being generated out of speech acts that are possible only because the system of language already exists, or when he treats pronouns as if they both express existing interpersonal relationships and simultaneously bring those relationships into being. Speech acts, for Humboldt, establish the conditions of their own possibility. Within his frame of reference, a declaration or an act of excommunication would not only posit the political authority of the signatory or the social relationship between speaker and addressee, but would establish the subject-positions of signatory, speaker, and addressee within a world of phenomena in the first place. To put it differently, for Humboldt *all* utterances function analogously to the declaration as Derrida, Lyotard, and de Man describe it: language in general assumes the existence of subjective minds, an objective world, intersubjective relationships, and a grammatical system, even though all these components are negotiated anew in every individual speech act. Thus, a proposition like "Lightning strikes" presupposes the existence of lightning (as material event), and yet the utterance brings lightning into existence (as an objectified concept). Even then, the lightning-that-strikes exists only as an illusory object until this objectification of the world is confirmed by an Other who hears and responds. The utterance superimposes cognitive and communicative moments, and in each case the entity it names somehow exists and does not exist at the time the utterance is made. Every speech act is a daring attempt to give form to self and world. This is even more apparent in the case of first-person utterances such as (to anticipate examples from the dramas of Hölderlin and Kleist) "I am a god" or "I am Amphitryon"—speech acts that express the speaker's preexisting sense of identity, but at the same time posit his identity in a manner that demands a response from the external world.

In Humboldt's phenomenological model of subjectivity and language, every speech act alters the situation of the speaker and the worldview of the hearer, and reacts back on the speaker by acting on the hearer. This is arguably a more consistent, though a less codifiable, description of verbal performativity than, for instance, Searle's, since for Searle the utterance has an effect on hearer and context, but apparently not on the speaker. The source of the speech act is assumed to be an unchanging consciousness, and even the context and hearer are stable enough to be subject to invariant rules. Humboldt's concept of speech, however, involves not only an act of interpersonal communication, but a simultaneous act of individual cognition. The two dimensions are inseparable; I cannot conceptualize the world without testing my conception against an Other in social interaction, nor can I communicate with another without involving that person in my conceptualization. Humboldt's speech act is a totally dynamic intersection of I, You, word, and world, in which each of these terms modifies, defines, and (at the same time) amplifies the others. This synthetic dynamism can help adapt the more analytic twentieth-century formulations of speech-act theory in a way that is particularly appropriate to Romantic literary texts, so as to uncover in them the moments when the speaker's subjectivity is being formed in the act of positing a relationship between I and You, or the speaker's thought shaped by positing a new synthesis of subject and predicate. Humboldt's model of language as acts of synthetic positing emblematizes the speech acts of Romantic writers and their fictional characters, as selves that exist, yet are in the process of becoming, within a world that stands in opposition to them, yet is in the process of being formed.

HUMBOLDT AND ROMANTIC LITERATURE

To stress Humboldt's proximity to twentieth-century developments in philosophy and linguistics, then, is not to deny that he was also representative of the linguistic thought of his time. On the contrary, since he represents par excellence some of the most important ideas in the philosophy of language around 1800—including the inseparability of language and cognition, the role of languages in creating different representations of the world, the active nature of both cognition and utterance, and the importance of dialogue and the individual speech act—his work is immensely significant to an understanding of the context within which Romantic writers were using language. Although much of Humboldt's work, especially his longer manuscripts, remained unpublished during his lifetime, virtually all his important ideas about language and action were made public either in his printed texts or in his presentations before the Berlin Academy during the 1820s. More important than his actual influence on poets and poetry, though, is the way his work makes explicit the performative concepts that were available to all his contemporaries, poets as well as theorists, in the philosophy and linguistics of his time—in the work of Kant, Fichte, Schelling, and Herder, to name only the most important names.

In Humboldt's own work the connection between linguistics and literature is never far to seek. On the contrary, one feature that differentiates the work of Humboldt, Herder, Bernhardi, the Schlegels, and other Romantic philologists markedly from modern linguistics or philosophy of language is their conviction that linguistic study is directly relevant to literature, and even to music or painting. Humboldt's linguistic thought develops directly out of his literary criticism, especially his studies of Schiller's and Goethe's language and its effect on readers or audiences. In his programmatic lecture of 1820 to the Berlin Academy, he builds this orientation toward the study of texts into the discipline of comparative linguistics itself. "The keystone of linguistic study," he writes, is always the actual *use* of language, but especially its "highest and most varied applications" in scientific and artistic discourses (*ÜS* 19).

Humboldt often compares grammatical form to artistic form inasmuch as both provide motivation for the creation of art (*GS* 6: 350); that is, a creative and well-developed grammar can inspire the artist working in that language just as well as an interesting genre or medium can. Grammar is important for literature precisely because it is inherently energetic or dynamic. Like literature, grammar itself expresses the mental power of a people:

> We catch sight of [mental] power only in language, but at the time at which language gained its characteristic form, it must have been present among the people.
>
> For this reason, the genuine grammatical structure can never and nowhere be easily separated from that which we call by a single name, but one that comprehends within itself many different things: literature. Language is always only a medium. The enthusiastic drive that urges toward poetry, philosophy, and science imprints its stamp on language, as its organ. (*GS* 6: 396)

Indications like this locate Humboldt's theory of language at the center of a Romantic view of poetry and philosophy as expressions of energy and power, and encourage, indeed compel, us to read Romantic literature with his concept of performativity in mind.

4

The Performative Coleridge

Samuel Taylor Coleridge encountered Wilhelm von Humboldt in Rome in 1806, when the latter was employed there as Prussian legate to the papal court, and carrying out linguistic research in the Vatican Library in his spare time. In a note to the 1818 edition of *The Friend*, Coleridge recalls reciting Wordsworth's "Immortality" ode for "the illustrious Baron von Humboldt," and adds a respectful appreciation of Humboldt's intellect, judgment, and familiarity with English poetry: "I can only say, that I know few Englishmen, whom I could compare with him in the extensive knowledge and just appreciation of English literature and its various epochs" (F 1: 510n). Neither man records whether they discussed theories of language as well as literature—but it would be both a surprise and a pity if they did not. Coleridge's and Humboldt's philosophies of language coincide on many points, from the historical evolution of language as the self-expression of a people, to the centrality of the verb and of dialogue, to the vital role of language in cognition. They shared similar educational and philosophical influences: both had taken direction in their early philological studies from the innovative Classical scholar Christian Gottlob Heyne in Göttingen, and both were critical readers of Kant. In revising Kantian philosophy to incorporate linguistic and literary principles, both developed important concepts of performativity as a dynamic interrelation among self, word, and world.

Well beyond his encounter with Humboldt, however, Coleridge is the central figure in a study of interrelations between British and German philosophy of language during the Romantic period. Out of his familiarity with both contemporary British linguistics and German transcendental philosophy, out of his critical admiration for thinkers as diverse as Tooke, Godwin, Kant, and Schelling, he developed a theory of language that recognizes the sociopolitical force of utterances but attempts to counterbalance that force with the creative, transcendent, spiritual power of the Word. The evolution of the Romantic performative in his work can be narrativized as a reaction against political rhetoric, followed by an attempt to redeem language by locating its effectiveness in philosophical first principles and in religious belief. During the 1790s, Coleridge's experience of speech acts is predominantly negative, and he denounces the effective but empty words that speakers who possess institutional authority use to manipulate the social order. But in texts like the *Lay Sermons* and *Aids to Reflection*, he confronts these sociopolitical performatives with the more lasting and genuine effectiveness of the language of the Bible. With his development of a theological and philosophical system in the early decades of the nineteenth century, Coleridge's valorization of biblical language grows into a conviction of the centrality of the Word or Logos—conceived of as many things, but among them as a world-creating and world-sustaining performative by means of which we can potentially have access to an immediate and atemporal conception of reality.

Coleridge's revisions to the poem that eventually became "The Destiny of Nations" chronicle the development of what I will call (with conscious anachronism, and polemical intent) his concept of speech acts. When he first drafted it in 1796 under the titles "The Progress of Liberty" and "Visions of the Maid of Orleans," the poem began by denouncing the language of Enlightenment science. Natural philosophers "chain down the winged thought" by constraining nature within a mechanistic philosophy: "themselves they mock/With noisy emptiness of learned phrase" (*CPW* 2: 1025, lines 25–27).[1] But the empty pronouncements of the scientific institution are already counterbalanced by potentially redemptive forms of utterance: God as the "eternal Word" (*CPW* 2: 1025, line 48) and the spiritual voice that calls the poem's heroine, Joan of Arc. Between 1796 and the time the poem was first published in 1817, Coleridge revised the opening verse-paragraphs so as to highlight the power of the poetic voice itself. It now announces its Miltonic intent to "hush all meaner song" and use its spell to call back "man's free and stirring spirit that lies entranced" (1, 11–12). These redemptive speech acts become ever more prominent in later revisions. Paralleling the development of the concept of the Logos in Coleridge's prose, the beginning of the poem gained an extra line between 1817 and 1828. God, who in the first draft was invoked as Father and King, now acquires the epithets "THE WILL, THE WORD, THE BREATH, THE LIVING GOD" (*CPW* 1: 131n). Between 1828 and 1834 Coleridge changed these lines yet once

---

[1]Coleridge's poems are cited from volume 1 of the *Complete Poetical Works* (*CPW*); references are normally given by line number. Some quotations are drawn from earlier versions of the poems as printed in footnotes to the *Complete Poetical Works* or in appendix 1 of volume 2; page references are supplied in these cases.

more, to include the phrase "I am" that became so central to his later philosophy of language and consciousness, and his praise is finally addressed "To the Will Absolute, the One, the Good!/The I AM, the Word, the Life, the Living God!" (5–6).

Yet even in Coleridge's late work, the exact relationship of the Logos to the human discourses of poetry, science, and social interaction remains troubling. If Coleridge's work embodies the desire that the Logos might inform human utterance and render it truly creative, it also admits the possibility that the Logos is itself posited by and in human utterance, that it is a projection of the poet's voice or the philosopher's subjectivity. In various configurations, these coexistent possibilities—that the human word *might* partake of the divine Word, and that the divine Word *must* partake of the human word—characterize Coleridge's repeated confrontation with the question that Searle later identified as the central issue in the philosophy of language: "How do words relate to the world?" (*Speech Acts* 3). Because his preoccupation with the Logos causes him to interpret cognitive processes in terms of language, some of Coleridge's answers to this question unexpectedly anticipate Searle's twentieth-century answers. At the same time, they constitute a background for reading the effect of utterances, the status of verbal constructs, and the dialogic relation of subject and object in Coleridge's own poetry.

THE HOLLOW SPEECH ACTS OF THE 1790S

"I concluded," writes Coleridge in the preface to his *Conciones ad Populum, or Addresses to the People* of 1795, "that this was *not* the 'time to keep silence.'—For Truth should be spoken at all times, but more especially at those times, when to speak Truth is dangerous" (*LPR* 27). As a young intellectual writing and lecturing on political topics during the revolutionary decade, Coleridge regards words as moral and political acts. His poems of the 1790s, besides *being* speech acts with which he is contributing to the public debate about revolution, repression, and liberty, thematize the utterances of politicians, on the one hand, and those of the natural world, on the other. There are voices in the foreground and the background of these texts, so that an opposition arises between the destructive speech acts of statesmen and institutions, and the redemptive utterances of nature, God, or some spirit that connects God and nature with the poet's soul. Both the negative, institutional utterances and the positive, spiritual utterances do things; but the former, while they may have the power to re-organize reality, are exposed as hollow or empty.

This opposition underlies "France: An Ode," a poem that self-consciously advertises itself as a political speech act. When it was first published in the *Morning Post* of 16 April 1798 as a response to French aggression in the Swiss cantons, an editorial headnote underlined the significance of Coleridge's decision to utter his censure in the public press: "What we most admire is the *avowal* of his sentiments, and public censure of the unprincipled and atrocious conduct of France" (*CPW* 1: 243n; italics in original). This first version of the ode bears the title "The Recantation"; it presents itself as a speech act meant to recall and revise earlier texts in which Coleridge bestowed praises or blessings on revolutionary France.[2] The poem's central term—*liberty*—is a word that figures prominently in the age's political documents, above all the French Declaration of 1789 and the American Declaration of Independence. These documents use words like "liberty," "rights," "people," and "nation" performatively, which is to say that they establish new definitions for them while at the same time treating them as independently existing constants that authorize or legitimate the declaration. Coleridge, however, addresses himself *to* "Liberty" in "France: An Ode," implicitly recognizing liberty as an external power beyond the control of his discourse. Throughout the poem, he dissociates liberty from institutional speech acts, from "Priestcraft" and "Blasphemy," asserting that it is apprehensible only by the spirit. The text thus repositions liberty in relation to language, as well as repositioning Coleridge's own discourse in relation to liberty as an independently existing ideal.

The first stanza of "France: An Ode" identifies a natural language of "wild unconquerable sound" in the singing of night-birds and the "solemn music" of woods in the wind, beyond which lies an even more potent divine language in the form of "eternal laws" that the natural elements obey. If the poet cannot create clouds, ocean waves, and woods, he can nevertheless invoke them in roughly the order in which they are created by divine utterance in the Book of Genesis:

> Ye Clouds! that far above me float and pause,
>   Whose pathless march no mortal may controul!
> Ye Ocean-Waves! that, wheresoe'er ye roll,
> Yield homage only to eternal laws!

[2]For an interpretation of this poem, along with "Fears in Solitude" and "Frost at Midnight," as an episode in the war of rhetoric between conservative and radical periodicals during the 1790s, see Magnuson, "The Politics of 'Frost at Midnight.'" A recognition of the performative qualities of the language of the ode, and the political speech acts that Coleridge is denouncing in these poems, adds a further dimension to Magnuson's reading.

>   Ye Woods! that listen to the night-birds singing,
>   Midway the smooth and perilous slope reclined,
>   Save when your own imperious branches swinging,
>   Have made a solemn music of the wind!
>   (1–8)

Calling out the names in an echo of divine *fiat*, the speaker creates a habitable environment for himself while making its elements present to the reader through his exclamatory utterances. He also derives from this habitat an intuition of true liberty, the awareness of which, according to Coleridge's introductory note and again in line 13, is "inspired" by natural objects, so that "Liberty" appears, naturally and impressively, as the concluding word of the stanza: "I have still adored / The spirit of divinest Liberty" (20–21).

The ode distinguishes the "*spirit* of . . . Liberty," evoked by conversation with the elements of nature, from "the *name* / Of Freedom" (87–88), ironically engraved on chains with which the French have bound themselves. Coleridge's contempt for the "name" of freedom, here emphasized by the half-rhyme of "name" and "chain," picks up on other contemporary references to the abuse of inflammatory but empty terms. The "Name of Liberty," Coleridge emphasizes in a note to his "Ode to the Departing Year," was "both the occasion and the pretext of unnumbered crimes and horrors" at the outset of the French Revolution (*CPW* 1: 161n–62n). Edmund Burke comes close to the image of the name as a chain when he calls the word "Protestant" an ironically destructive "charm" or "abracadabra that is hung about the necks of the unhappy" so as to cause disease rather than cure it (*Writings* 9: 647). At issue is not only the image of being burdened with a name, like the Ancient Mariner with his albatross, but also the dehiscence of word from thing. The "charm" to which Burke refers involves a use of words as meaningless yet impressive sounds or inscriptions, as do the two other appearances of the word "name" in "France: An Ode." The final stanza's assertion that liberty will not be limited by "boastful name" (94) is in keeping with the poet's recollection that he "wept at Britain's name" (42) when Britain entered an alliance against France that set her political pose against her essential ethical landscape.

The contrast between the name which is inspired, in that it emerges from an encounter between the human spirit and the spirit of nature, and the hollow name that abstracts from meaning, helps to identify the criteria by which Coleridge characterizes and condemns political uses of performative language. On a level with the abuse of the "name of Freedom" is the rhetoric of the revolutionaries, whose utterances mandate a new political order while violating the sanctity of natural rights. In the second stanza, France's "oath, which smote air, earth, and sea" (23) inverts the proper relationship of nature and language: instead of attending to the voices of nature, as the poet does in stanza 1, the French do violence to nature with their utterances. Their oath foreshadows the "Blasphemy" into which revolutionary discourse will degenerate later in the text (43, 96)—blasphemy involving, as the contemporaneous poem "Fears in Solitude" makes clear, the willful hollowing out of words so as to separate name from entity and meaning from use. But "France: An Ode" offers the poet's converse with nature as a corrective to the misapplied speech acts that brought about the revolution, the ensuing wars, and the invasion of Switzerland. Its concluding stanza dissociates liberty from collective discourse and popular rhetoric: from the "victor's strain," from the praise, prayer, and boastful names in which people try to contain liberty, from priestcraft and blasphemy (91–98). While implying that he himself once sought liberty in these forms of human utterance and power, Coleridge now locates liberty in an unpopulated landscape, representing it not as a word that is heard but a spirit that is felt.

Nevertheless, the ode does not undertake to separate liberty entirely from language, but rather to relocate the language of liberty from a collective to an individual discourse. When it was reprinted in the *Morning Post* in 1802, a prefatory "Argument" described the poem as

> An address to Liberty, in which the Poet expresses his conviction that those feelings and that grand *ideal* of Freedom which the mind attains by its contemplation of its individual nature, and of the sublime surrounding objects . . . do not belong to men, as a society, nor can possibly be either gratified or realised, under any form of human government; but belong to the individual man, so far as he is pure, and inflamed with the love and adoration of God in Nature. (*CPW* 1: 244n)

Rather than being constructed by the performative rhetoric of societal institutions, liberty must be enacted by the poetic utterance of the individual mind. It is ironic, then, that Coleridge's poem is nevertheless presented in the newspaper as public discourse, and his address to liberty repeatedly couched in legalistic terms. The scene of discourse underlying the poem is a courtroom trial, in which the poet is called to account for previous offenses against the spirit of liberty. In the first two stanzas, he asks the natural world to "bear witness" for him (19, 25), in effect to provide him with a character reference; in stanza 4, he petitions liberty to forgive his misinformed words and thoughts. In the middle stanza, which begins and ends with quotations of his former utterances, he formally recalls his own speech acts so that he can, like Shelley's Prometheus, formally recant them. Continuing to use the figural language of legal procedure while ostensibly rejecting the rhetoric of the public sphere, Coleridge may reveal more than he intends about the pervasiveness of sociopolitical speech acts.

The argument of "France: An Ode" belongs in the context of the 1790s debate over natural rights, of which the right to liberty is the prime example. Burke, Paine, Godwin, and Bentham, among others, argued over whether natural rights precede or else depend on the forms of social order, and over whether they are created, confirmed, or restricted by declarations and constitutions. More specifically, Coleridge's ode engages the linguistic aspect of this debate: the question of how terms like "liberty" and "nature" get defined. Bentham (as discussed in Chapter 1) called them fictions of language, while Burke's use of these words in the *Reflections* is in line with the theoretical account he gives of them in his *Philosophical Enquiry into the Origin of Our Ideas of the Sublime and Beautiful* (1757). There, he argues that "compound abstract" words like "virtue," "liberty," or "honor" can be understood without reference to any image or representation, since they acquire their meaning from the way they are habitually used in certain contexts:

> Such words are in reality but mere sounds; but they are sounds, which being used on particular occasions, wherein we receive some good, or suffer some evil, or see others affected with good or evil; or which we hear applied to other interesting things or events; and being applied in such a variety of cases that we know readily by habit to what things they belong, they produce in the mind, whenever they are afterwards mentioned, effects similar to those of their occasions. (165)[3]

Robert Essick's conclusion that, up to the last decade of the eighteenth century, "nature" and "reason" enjoyed the status of terms independent of cultural construction ("William Blake" 199) seems at first to contradict Burke's evident awareness of the constructed nature of abstract

---

[3]For an argument that Burke's identification of the meaning of abstract terms with their use forms part of the "pragmatic turn" in Romantic-period linguistics, see Nerlich and Clarke, *Language, Action, and Context* 98. Turner argues that Burke's description of abstract terms as "unidea'd," as acquiring meaning and power "by custom" rather than through reference to external realities (42), actually makes him more innovative and radical than Paine, at least in terms of his philosophy of language. Also relevant is Blakemore's linguistically oriented reading of Burke and the French Revolution, which leads him to conclude that Burke speaks for many of his contemporaries in lamenting the way the revolution has torn terms (such as "nature," "liberty," "property," or "the people") from their historical context and rendered them empty (*Burke and the Fall of Language* 87–88, 100). Myers, finally, brings speech-act theory to bear on the 1790s struggle for control over meaning, analyzing Coleridge's involvement in the contest for a pragmatic legal definition of the term "fraud" in *The Plot Discovered*.

nouns. But if Essick's claim is correct, then it together with the passage from Burke's *Enquiry* may shed light on Coleridge's semantics in "France: An Ode." "Reason" and especially "nature" are, of course, *not* abstract nouns to eighteenth-century writers, who distinguish them from "liberty" or "honor" on the grounds that they refer to *things*—to a mental faculty and a physical reality, respectively. Nature and reason seem to escape the pragmatic imposition of meaning that Burke exposes. Coleridge's poem, then, seeks to liberate "liberty" from the constructions that have been imposed on it during the French Revolution by relating it back to the "unconstructed" term "nature"—while attempting to demonstrate that the task of defining "liberty" properly belongs not to political parties, but to the individual poetic voice.

"FEARS IN SOLITUDE": THE SERMON IN THE DELL

A companion poem to "France: An Ode," "Fears in Solitude" was also written in the spring of 1798, under the influence of the same political circumstances; an extract from it was published together with the revised version of "France: An Ode" in the *Morning Post* of 14 October 1802, and the two poems appeared together in the pamphlet *Fears in Solitude, &c*, in 1812. Despite its claim to be a discourse of "solitude," this poem, too, exhibits the rhetoric of a public speech act. Coleridge characterizes it in a manuscript note as "a sort of middle thing between Poetry and Oratory" (*CPW* 1: 257n). Like "France: An Ode," it belongs in the dialogic context of the war of words between the liberal and reactionary press; both poems pass judgment on the uses of language in current politics. Demonstrating that "Coleridge responds to verbal acts," Paul Magnuson argues that he exposes and opposes the misuse of public political discourse, and specifically the misrepresentation of his own opinions and writings in the public press: "The truth of language in 'Fears in Solitude' depends on the oath honestly sworn and the clear sense of the reality represented" ("Shaping" 207).

Magnuson identifies the major theme of the poem as the violation of the ninth commandment, which prohibits the swearing of false oaths: "Thou shalt not bear false witness against thy neighbour" (Exodus 20.16). But an even more resonant biblical context for "Fears in Solitude"—a context that draws attention less to the truth-value of language than to its performative nature—can be found in the New Testament's Sermon on the Mount. Jesus supersedes the traditional injunction against false oaths with an injunction against *any* oath: "But I say unto you, Swear not at all. . . . But let your communication be, Yea, yea; Nay,

nay: for whatsoever is more than these cometh of evil" (Matthew 5.34, 37). The evil in oath-taking has to do with the separation of the name by which an oath is sworn from its meaning, so as to render the name a charm or talisman rather than a signifier. Oath-takers are liable to forget that heaven is "God's throne" or that Jerusalem is "the city of the great King" (Matthew 5.34, 35). Surely an aversion to swearing as radical as this lies behind Coleridge's "Fears in Solitude," with its bitter and ironic recapitulations "For all must swear—all and in every place" (73) and "All, all make up one scheme of perjury" (78). The poem's antinomian attitude toward oaths connects it with the public campaigns of some of Coleridge's contemporaries against the laws governing courtroom oaths, including Godwin in *Political Justice*, and Bentham, whose 1813 pamphlet *"Swear Not at All"* takes its title from the Sermon on the Mount.

Throughout the second verse-paragraph of "Fears in Solitude," Coleridge confesses that his own society abuses language, and ends by linking oath-taking and atheism—two conditions in which the name of God risks being emptied of meaning. This entire passage needs to be read in light of the Sermon of the Mount. As Jesus criticizes the heathen who, when they pray, use "vain repetitions" and "think that they shall be heard for their much speaking" (Matthew 5.7), Coleridge denounces his contemporaries as "a vain, speech-mouthing, speech-reporting Guild" (57) by whom the "sweet words / Of Christian promise" are muttered and gabbled o'er (63–72). "Fears in Solitude" calls attention to the actions words perform in society, where they are used as in sorcerers' spells, sorcery being another verbal practice that uses words according to conventional and often nonsensical formulas. The Bible, Coleridge complains, "is made / A superstitious instrument" (70–71), the name of God a "juggler's charm" (80). Although there remains the potential that the Christian Word might "stem destruction" if rightly applied (63–65), language, when appropriated by "Courts, Committees, Institutions, / Associations and Societies" (55–56), becomes constitutive of a misguided political order.

The Sermon on the Mount is itself centrally concerned with performative language, with the way human society is shaped by lawsuits, bills of divorce, oaths, judgments, and public prayers. Jesus seeks to make a society dominated by these speech acts aware of the possibilities of a social order inspired by less restrictive, less institutionalized utterances such as blessings and private devotion. "Fears in Solitude" may even begin to look like an inverted Sermon on the Mount if we consider how the biblical hill is replaced by a dell (an especially meaningful inversion for a poet whose mind runs on domes and caverns), a multitude is replaced by solitude, beatitudes by fears, preaching and blessing by chastising and accusing. The bitterest section of Coleridge's poem, the verse-paragraph in which he denounces the blind warmongering of the British public (86–129), acquires an added irony when read in the context of Jesus's "Blessed are the peacemakers: for they shall be called the children of God" (Matthew 5.9). The only children in Coleridge's passage are children of a wrong-headed society that delights in experiencing war through language, in carrying on a war of words that have been severed from their referents. War is "a thing to talk of" and read about (95), legitimated by "big preamble, holy names,/And adjurations" (101–2), translated smoothly by a "fluent phraseman" into "dainty terms" that are nothing but "mere abstractions, empty sounds" (111–15). The British public understands war as a series of mandates issued by authoritative speakers and expurgated texts published in the papers. But behind the performative power of words about war lies the bloody performance of war, and Coleridge responds with dread (but also implicit veneration) of a divine power that would "make us know/The meaning of our words" (126–27), reuniting word with act and meaning with use.

The significance of performative language in "Fears in Solitude" becomes more complex, though, when the invective of the middle stanzas is put back into the context of the beginning and end of the poem, and the utterance replaced in its dell. This is manifestly a posited poem—located, that is, in a specific natural landscape, but also positioned within a rhetorical frame that highlights the verbal construction of reality. Even in denouncing the things his contemporaries do with words, Coleridge can hardly escape the fact that *his* only medium for creating belief and modifying our apprehension of the world is language. Both the beginning and the end of the poem move in intriguing ways from positing to affirming, or from subjunctive to indicative. The opening lines, which name the dell without asserting anything about it, give way to a curious comparative that readers regard as either incomplete (Kroeber 365) or self-referential (Larkin 12):

> A green and silent spot, amid the hills,
> A small and silent dell! O'er stiller place
> No singing sky-lark ever poised himself.
> (1–3)

By way of three heavily alliterated lines, in which the landscape almost seems to arise out of the incantation of repeated sounds, the poem arrives at the deictic "now," a word that proves significant both here and at the end of the poem:

> The hills are heathy, save that swelling slope,
> Which hath a gay and gorgeous covering on,
> All golden with the never-bloomless furze,
> Which *now* blooms most profusely....
>   (4–7; italics added)

"Now" is the first hint that the poet is describing not just an imagined landscape but one imagined as present, though he has still not asserted its existence. Instead, the preamble moves through two more complex sentences—

> Here he might lie on fern or withered heath,
> While from the singing lark (that sings unseen
> The minstrelsy that solitude loves best),
> And from the sun, and from the breezy air,
> Sweet influences trembled o'er his frame;
> And he, with many feelings, many thoughts,
> Made up a meditative joy, and found
> Religious meanings in the forms of Nature!
> And so, his senses gradually wrapt
> In a half sleep, he dreams of better worlds,
> And dreaming hears thee still, O singing lark,
> That singest like an angel in the clouds!
>   (17–28)

—that meander from the subjunctive ("here he might lie") to a present indicative ("he dreams of better worlds, / And dreaming hears thee still"). Concluding with an apostrophe to the previously evanescent lark, the passage finally identifies the hypothetical "humble man" with the poet himself.

The transmutation of postulate into affirmation occurs again at the end of the poem, most obviously in the transitional exclamation of lines 197 to 202:

>   May my fears,
> My filial fears, be vain! and may the vaunts
> And menace of the vengeful enemy
> Pass like the gust, that roared and died away
> In the distant tree: which heard, and only heard
> In this low dell, bowed not the delicate grass.

The transition takes place by way of a simile that renders the imagined voices ("vaunts / And menace") of the vengeful enemy an actually experienced gust of wind. Figural language allows the poet to move from a subjunctive invocation or prayer—an utterance whose efficacy depends entirely on the performative power of words—to the "reality" of his experience of the natural surroundings. But the very immediacy of the experience, the gust of wind that moves the distant tree yet is "heard, and *only* heard/In *this* low dell," indicates again the privileged positioning of the poem: *this* dell is a fine and private place, limited not only in physical extent, but also by the language that creates it.

The dell may be, as Coleridge stresses, "silent" and thus superficially different from the noisy world of politics, but ultimately it too is constituted by performative language. Like the language of liberty in "France: An Ode," the discourse of the dell cannot remain wholly separate from social discourse. The poem's final verse-paragraph responds to the subjunctive of "May my ... filial fears be vain" by positing an alternative reality, in which the lark and the furze seem a kind of local substitute for the fowl of the air and the lilies of the field that Jesus holds forth in the Sermon on the Mount (Matthew 6.26, 28). Translated into language, they become a promise of divine providence that answers the threats of human political maneuvering. The poem's frame gestures toward a new presence and presentness: "But now," the final verse-paragraph begins, and "now," as at the beginning of the poem, is repeated several times more (203, 207, 221). The final "burst of prospect," which "seems like society" and begins "conversing" with the poet's mind (215–19), is a renewed vision of creation chosen to replace the discourse of society. Yet it is a vision equally constructed by language. The antidote to the abuses of language listed in the middle of the poem is the renewal of an Edenic conversation with nature and society, both imagined as an English landscape painting. Yet even as Coleridge laments the loss of a representative and truthful language, his language, too, assumes the authority to turn postulates into assertions and subjective utterance into general truth.

THE 'LAY SERMONS': POSITING AN IDEAL PERFORMATIVE

Coleridge often quoted from "Fears in Solitude" in later years, using the poem as proof of his patriotic and responsible character. When it was first published in a quarto pamphlet, he had a copy sent to his disapproving brother, the Reverend George Coleridge. He quoted from the poem again in *The Friend* in 1809 (*F* 2: 24–25) and *The Statesman's Manual* in 1816 (*LS* 22), and in a footnote to the second Lay Sermon cited it once more as a witness to his veneration of "my country and its laws" (*LS* 122). In other words, Coleridge asks readers to apprehend the text performatively rather than constatively, as a continuously effective illustration of his own character and that of his antagonists. It becomes a political instrument as much as a document in the history of his poetic career.

The habit of performative rather than constative reading is exactly what Coleridge encourages beginning in his first Lay Sermon of 1816 (better known as *The Statesman's Manual*), particularly when the text to be read is the Bible. Referring again to some of the abuses of language that he denounced in his poems of the 1790s, Coleridge now sets them against a new ideal of effective language that can transcend temporality, if we learn how to respond to it. Early in the tract, Coleridge addresses his chosen audience—the "higher classes"—with an implied reproach for their failure to read the Bible insightfully:

> Would you feel conscious that you had shewn yourselves unequal to your station in society—would you stand degraded in your own eyes; if you betrayed an utter want of information respecting the acts of human sovereigns and legislators? And should you not much rather be both ashamed and afraid to know yourselves inconversant with the acts and constitutions of God, whose law executeth itself, and whose Word is the foundation, the power, and the life of the universe? . . . Do you excuse it as natural curiosity, that you lend a listening ear to the guesses of stategazers, to the dark hints and open revilings of our self-inspired state fortune-tellers, *'the wizards, that peep and mutter'* and forecast, alarmists by trade, and malcontents for their bread? And should you not feel a deeper interest in predictions which are permanent prophecies, because they are at the same time eternal truths? Predictions which in containing the grounds of fulfilment involve the principles of foresight, and teach the science of the future in its perpetual elements? (*LS* 7–8)

In referring to the "acts," "constitutions," and "law" of God, Coleridge at first stresses a certain continuity between the operation of human, political speech acts and divine ones. This analogy is in line with the stated purpose of his text: to demonstrate the relevance of the Bible to statesmanship and urge "an especial study of the Old Testament as teaching the Elements of Political Science" (*LS* 49). But the differences between political speech acts and biblical performatives become increasingly clear. The "guesses" and "dark hints" of politicians and alarmist journalists are parodies of the truly prophetic Word of God, and they miss the intrinsic performative principle that ensures that God's "permanent prophecies" cannot fail. For what Coleridge here calls the "predictions" of Scripture are not prophecies or foretellings at all, in the usual sense: they are "eternal truths" that contain their own fulfilment, words that embody the life and power of the universe.

What unfolds in this passage is a radical ideal of performativity, an ideal that Coleridge came to call Logos. Rather than merely referring to reality, divine speech acts and the language of the Bible constitute reality. Rather than acting *on* objects or *in* the world, the divine word is itself the principle by which objects and the world exist. Rather than reaching proleptically into an uncertain future, like human promises or prophecies, the "eternal" divine performative obviates temporality altogether. Coleridge discovers, in the Logos, the recompense for political speech acts that he ultimately failed to find in poems like "France: An Ode" and "Fears in Solitude." In those texts, he implies that the individual poetic voice might redeem the destructive discourse of society, but his own speech acts turn out to have too much in common with that discourse: they cannot free themselves entirely from the language of societal institutions; they cannot alter reality except by imposing subjective utterance on the world as if it were objective truth. But Coleridge's idea of the Logos obviates these pitfalls by the radical step of thinking away the distinctions of word and object, language and action, present and future. The ideal performativity of the Logos lies in the fact that it renders "the foundation, the power, and the life of the universe" *as* language. To claim that Coleridge here discovers an "ideal" performative is not, of course, to say that he can now obviate the shortcomings of either political or poetic utterance. On the contrary, the point is that the Logos is *only* an ideal that can at best be imitated, but is more likely to be parodied or deformed, by human speech acts. Only through faith—religious faith, but also a kind of faith in grammar—is it invested with meaning. The divine performative figures in Coleridge's system as a posited term by which his linguistic philosophy comes to orient and organize itself.

This emerging ideal acts as a foil for what both Lay Sermons identify as abuses of language and their effects on recent history. *The Statesman's Manual* represents the causes of the French Revolution as a series of misapplied speech acts, from "an assumption of prophetic power" to "the consequent multitude of plans and constitutions" (*LS* 33–34). Drawing on the Old Testament for the elements of political science, Coleridge denounces his power-hungry contemporaries as Isaiah denounced Babylon: "thou hast said in thine heart, I am, and none else beside me" (Isaiah 47.10). Not content with lies, enchantments, and opportunistic constitutions, the instigators of revolution abused the utterance "I am" that is so central to the Bible, to Romantic theories of language, and particularly to Coleridge's own philosophy. In the second Lay Sermon, the words of Isaiah again prove prophetic for the events of the revolutionary era. Coleridge uses Isaiah's characterization of the lying prophet to denounce those who, "in spoken or in printed Addresses, . . .

in periodical Journals or in yet cheaper implements of irritation," plead against the poor, slander the liberals, make false promises, flatter, and even publish articles recommending the curbing of the press (*LS* 147). Summing up, he lists eleven particular crimes by which the false prophet "deviseth wicked devices with lying words" (*LS* 152). All of these are rhetorical moves that separate the use of words from their meaning: making assertions pass for facts; taking facts out of context so as to "enable a man to *convey* falsehood while he *says* truth"; telling only half the story; stating "positions that are true only under particular conditions, to men whose ignorance or fury make them forget that these conditions are not present, or lead them to take for granted that they are"; satire and "jerks of style"; and, finally, meaningless words accompanied by "significant looks and tones" (*LS* 153–54).

While critiquing the speech acts of those invested with societal power, Coleridge tries to teach his readers to recognize true performative language. His use of biblical texts as prescriptions for statesmanship recedes into the background as a more immediate purpose unfolds: to teach proper ways of reading Scripture, history, and texts in general. This aim involves Coleridge in a critique of contemporary systems of education and in ridicule of the new, sensation-seeking reading public, and leads him to the now-famous distinction between symbol and allegory. His account of the symbol in *The Statesman's Manual* is part of a larger theory of biblical language—indeed, part of his theory of the ideally performative Logos. Between a symbolic interpretation of Ezekiel's vision of the divine chariot, and an outline of the difference between symbol and allegory, Coleridge explains the mode of existence of Scripture as the "WORD OF GOD":

> According therefore to our relative position on its banks [i.e., the banks of the stream of time] the Sacred History becomes prophetic, the Sacred Prophecies historical, while the power and substance of both inhere in its Laws, its Promises, and its Comminations. In the Scriptures therefore both Facts and Persons must of necessity have a two-fold significance, a past and a future, a temporary and a perpetual, a particular and a universal application. (*LS* 29–30)

As both "power and substance," both prophecy and history, the Word of God is performative and constative at once. Identifying some of the Bible's explicit speech acts—laws, promises, and comminations or threats—Coleridge's description of the Logos is in sympathy with Austin's conclusion about all language: constative and performative are two sides of the same coin, perspectives on language rather than two separate kinds of utterance.

Coleridge returns to the extraordinary nature of biblical language several times in the *Lay Sermons* and tries to account for it in a number of ways. At the end of *The Statesman's Manual*, he distinguishes between the Bible and other texts, or other forms of knowledge, by asserting that only in the Bible is knowledge coextensive with reality: "The Bible alone contains a Science of *Realities*: and therefore each of its Elements is at the same time a living GERM, in which the Present involves the Future, and in the Finite the Infinite exists potentially" (*LS* 49). To say that the Bible contains a science of realities is not just to assert that it is true, but also that its language relates to reality differently from the way we are used to thinking about language. The language of the Bible is a series of *declarations*, to use Searle's term: it "fits" reality because it causes reality to "fit" its language.[4] In Coleridge's terms, it is "a living GERM, in which the Present involves the Future." Our encounter with this language offers us the potential to understand phenomena in terms of reason, or ideas, or real being, since biblical language suspends our ordinary forms of temporality. It transcends the temporal gap between cause and effect, possible and actual, present and future, the idea and its ground. Only in the Logos—that is, in God and in the biblical Word—do the possible, the real, and the necessary coincide. Thus, Coleridge claims, the Bible "is God everywhere: and all creatures conform to his decrees, the righteous by performance of the law, the disobedient by the sufferance of the penalty" (*LS* 32). Even more emphatically, he characterizes the way the Word brings about the reality it pronounces with the tautological (and, now, Heideggerian-sounding) phrase "the Word speaks": "Ο ΛΟΓΟΣ ΗΦΗ. IPSE DIXIT! So it is: for it is so!" (*LS* 32).

Although Coleridge's theory of the Logos is not as fully developed in the *Lay Sermons* as in other and later works, his theology is well on the way to merging with both his philosophy of mind and his philosophy of language. Reason's "first act of faith," Coleridge writes in *The Statesman's Manual*, corresponds to the word "is" or the representation of being in language:

> *Implicitè*, it is the COPULA—it contains the *possibility*—of every position, to which there exists any correspondence in reality. It is itself,

---

[4] See Searle's taxonomy of illocutionary acts in *Expression and Meaning* (17–19), and his fuller account in *Intentionality* of the "double directions of fit" at work in declarations: "'I now pronounce you man and wife' makes it the case that you are man and wife (world-to-word direction of fit) by way of representing it as being the case that you are man and wife (word-to-world direction of fit)" (171–72). As I have argued in *Creating States* (27), Searle's own attempt to cite the words of God in the Bible as one example of declarations is problematic.

therefore, the realizing principle, the spiritual substratum of the whole complex body of truths. This primal act of faith is enunciated in the word, GOD: a faith not derived from experience, but its ground and source, and without which the fleeting *chaos of facts* would no more form experience, that [sic] the dust of the grave can of itself make a living man. The imperative and oracular form of the inspired Scripture is the form of reason itself in all things purely rational and moral. (*LS* 18)

Reason, as the highest intellectual faculty, and faith, with which reason is interdependent, are both defined according to the forms of language and find their expression in language. The illocutionary force—the "imperative and oracular form"—of biblical language counts for Coleridge as the "form of reason" itself. And reason only becomes a meaningful agent in thought and experience when it performs an act that corresponds to the copula, the basis of logical thought and of the propositional sentence. The "primal act" of faith and reason is specifically represented, then, as a speech act: the assertive proposition (A *is* B), or, alternatively, "the word, GOD."[5]

In identifying the performative quality of biblical language, *The Statesman's Manual* sometimes focuses on the nature of the Word in itself, other times on the role of the reader in responding to the Word. Intriguingly, Coleridge's presentation of the Logos in the *Lay Sermons* suggests that the performativity of Scripture depends to some extent on the reader's hermeneutic involvement with the text. It is one thing to posit an ideal performative in the abstract, but Coleridge also implies that the reader's uptake is needed in order to instantiate its effects, even to give the concept of Logos meaning by bringing it into human experience. He characterizes the New Testament as a series of "promises, that need only a lively trust in them, on our own part, to be the means as well as the pledges of our *eternal* welfare! information that opens out to our knowledge a kingdom that is not of this world, thrones that cannot be shaken, and sceptres that can neither be broken or transferred!" (*LS* 8). *The Statesman's Manual* climaxes in an appeal for active rather than passive reception of Scripture, indeed for a reading that relates the words

---

[5]The passage under discussion here is presumably one of the "scattered hints" to which Wheeler refers in drawing a connection between Coleridge and modern philosophy of language: "There are scattered hints and indications in Coleridge however, of a further elaboration of his conception of Reason, which suggests anticipations of Heidegger's emphasis upon language and being—indeed, which suggests that Reason, when properly understood, is language, and that the emphasis upon language in modern theory is an elaboration of earlier insights in a new terminology" (37).

of the Bible to noumena rather than phenomena, and frees itself from the constraints of space and time. Coleridge objects to a reading of Scripture that, in its negative or "Unitarian" version, would reduce the words of St. Paul to meaning "*only* . . . that a state of retribution after this life had been proved by the fact of Christ's resurrection," or, in its positive or mystifying version, would "believe in St. Paul's *veracity*; and that is enough" (*LS* 45–46). Both these unsatisfactory perspectives regard Scripture as a constative record, though they differ on whether we can or cannot understand its meaning. Coleridge himself advocates an active understanding that brings about a change in individual consciousness. Reading the Bible as a performative text would reactive the power of God's original, world-creating Word: "O what a mine of undiscovered treasures, what a new world of Power and Truth would the Bible promise to our future meditation, if in some gracious moment one solitary text of all its inspired contents should but dawn upon us in the pure untroubled brightness of an IDEA" (*LS* 50).

Coleridge's goal here is to direct attention to the "IDEA" itself, a term by which he refers to the essence of the human spirit, to that which is eternal in it and the world. Ideas are "spoken out everywhere" in the Bible (*LS* 24), but they can also be discovered in other "texts," whether these are verbal or experiential. If the goal of *The Statesman's Manual* is to encourage a reading of Scripture as performative rather than constative, this type of reading can also be applied to human history. Decision-makers fail to realize the applicability of historical situations to their own case because they "read history for the facts instead of reading it for the sake of the general principles, which are to the facts as the root and sap of a tree to its leaves" (*LS* 11). Coleridge is elevating philosophical principles over unessential detail, but the metaphor makes clear that he is also contrasting facticity or constation with the vital force out of which historical fact develops. "History read in the spirit of prophecy," Coleridge calls this mode of understanding in a note to the second Lay Sermon, as he expresses his desire that the facts of history be read by analogy with the inspired Word: "What insight might not our statesmen acquire from the study of the Bible merely as history, if only they had been previously accustomed to study history in the same spirit, as that in which good men read the Bible!" (*LS* 124).

THE LANGUAGE OF ENERGY AND THE
ENERGY OF LANGUAGE

The development of Coleridge's concept of biblical language, as a response to his experience of history and particularly to the political contest for control of language that characterized the 1790s, parallels the development of his theoretical understanding of linguistic issues. Responding to the linguistic philosophy of his contemporaries, he champions a view of words as "energies," "agents," and "living powers"—terms that appear throughout his prose works. An early infatuation with the work of Horne Tooke fostered his interest in tracing words back to their etymological roots, but unlike Tooke, Coleridge could not remain convinced that the roots of all words are either concrete objects or sensory impressions.[6] In a famous letter of 1800 to Godwin, he contends that Tooke's system wants a greater emphasis on the *power* of words—and Coleridge's diction suggests he already half realizes that he, rather than Godwin, is the philosopher who will provide it:

> I wish you to write a book on the power of words, and the processes by which human feelings form affinities with them—in short, I wish you to *philosophize* Horn Tooke's System. . . . In something of this order I would endeavor to destroy the old antithesis of Words & Things, elevating, as it were, words into Things, & living Things too. (*CL* 1: 625–26)

Instead of regarding language as a way of describing the world or communicating information, Coleridge from here on assigns it an absolutely central role in the cognitive process of understanding and experiencing reality—to the point where, in its ideal form, Logos is the principle that creates reality itself.

Like his German contemporaries, Coleridge discerned a particular connection between language and the mental faculty that organizes sensory perceptions into comprehensible unities: the understanding. "In all instances, it is words, names, or, if images, yet images used as words or names, that are the only and exclusive subjects of Understanding," he writes in *Aids to Reflection*; "in no instance do we understand a thing in itself; but only the name to which it is referred" (*AR* 231). Together with Bernhardi, Coleridge believes that the understanding deals exclusively in words, and only "by courtesy of idiom" do we identify words with sensory objects themselves. He relates this distinction to the fundamental duality of *being* and *knowing*. As Logos, language participates even in

---

[6]For Coleridge's relationship to Tooke, see Jackson, McKusick (33–52), and Goodson (*Verbal Imagination* 95–98).

the higher activity of being and the discourse of reason; but words conceived of as human discourse are the essential components of knowing, and instruments of the understanding. In his notebooks, Coleridge defines "knowing" in terms of the logical-grammatical relationship between subject and predicate: "To know any thing for certain is to have a clear insight into the inseparability of the Predicate from the Subject (the Matter from the Form) et vice versâ.—This is a verbal definition: a *real* definition of a thing absolutely *known* is impossible" (*CN* 3: 3588).

Words make it possible to know things because they first of all create "outness"—a term directly related to "utterance," for Coleridge tends to use "utterance" and "outerance" interchangeably. Language brings about the outness without which we could not participate in one another's worlds: "Language & all *symbols* give *outness* to Thoughts/& this the philosophical essence & purpose of Language" (*CN* 1: 1387). But outerance/utterance is again a more universal principle than it may seem, having to do not just with communication but also with cognition. The outness or visible otherness of an object such as a rose, that allows the human mind to relate to it, is also a type of utterance (as will be discussed further in relation to the *Logic*, below). Indeed, Coleridge's later work tends to identify the entire natural world as the outerance of God. A notebook entry of 1822 makes outerance synonymous with the breath of God, which is the Logos: "the Αλη Θεια [Greek 'truth,' which Coleridge suggests is etymologically equivalent to 'breath of God'], or Ruach Elohim [Hebrew 'breath of God'], which a Christian Interpreter would have rendered LOGOS, or *manifested* Intelligence, *Outerance* of the Divine Mind or Will" (*CN* 4: 4870). One of the most encompassing definitions Coleridge provides associates outerance with the universal light that is the first of created things. In a fragment dating from about 1820, he instructs a student:

> You are likewise to keep in mind with regard to the Power, LIGHT, that the word in Gen. I. v. 3. does not <mean> visual Light or solar Light, which was not yet in existence; but that ~~it includes likewise which is no less present in Sound, Odor, and in short in whatever else~~ *goes forth* to *declare*, like a word *spoken*; or remains on the surface (or *out*side) to *distinguish*, like a word *written*; and in both cases, makes the thing outward, and *outers* (now spelt, *utters*) ~~the~~ its nature. <P.S.> Hence the Son of God is called indifferently The Light, that lighteth; and the Word. (*SWF* 2: 850)

This extraordinary passage gives an idea of the scope of Coleridge's ideas about the performative word. It links up with the original paradigm of the Logos, God's creative utterance that brings the universe into being in

Genesis 1; but in this case the first product of the Logos, primal light, is itself identified as a word, or at least analogous to a word. By this analogy the power of the Logos can be conducted, not only into the spoken and written words of human language, but also into the word-like outerances of sound or odor by which the natural world announces its presence to the human mind. The result is a concept of the mind-world relationship that distinctly resembles the dialogic concept of cognition that Friedrich Schlegel outlines in his lectures of 1804–5: "The inner essence and the nature of the plants and animals are as it were the words and language that the distant, reserved You speaks to us" (*KFSA* 12: 338–39).

Other definitions Coleridge provides of words and language pick up the ideas of his German contemporaries, yet integrate these into Coleridge's own constellation of linguistics, philosophy, and theology. In his *Philosophical Lectures* of 1818–19, he echoes the consensus of the new Continental linguistics that words do not merely represent already-formed thoughts, but also participate in the production of thought: "Words are things. They are the great mighty instruments by which thoughts are excited and by which alone they can be <expressed> in a rememberable form" (*Phil.Lect.* 201). He is concerned, however, that the term "instruments" not give the impression that words are always subject to the conscious control of speakers: "words are no passive Tools, but organized Instruments, re-acting on the Power which inspirits them" (*IS* 101–2); "they are *Spirits* and *living Agents* that are seldom misused without avenging themselves" (*CL* 5: 228). While Coleridge is mainly alluding to the likelihood that words will have other meanings and effects than the speaker intends, the autonomy he attributes to language recalls Humboldt's idea that words, once uttered, react back on the speaker's mind and enter into a dialogic relationship with it. Humboldt and Coleridge also share a perspective on language and history. Both describe the way language negotiates between individual minds and the history of a nation, so that history both shapes and is shaped by both individual and collective speech acts. "What a magnificent History of acts of individual minds, sanctioned by the collective Mind of the Country a Language is," Coleridge writes (*L&L* 138), and his *Philosophical Lectures* take up an even more Humboldtian sentiment: "The language of a nation is its character" (*Phil.Lect.* 392, 396).

Coleridge's main difference from Humboldt and other Continental linguistic philosophers lies in the theological perspective he brings to his concept of language. His version of the Romantic performative thus becomes Logos, which is conceived of in various ways: as the second person of the trinity, the antithesis (Christ) of the thesis "I am" (God); as reason, the mental faculty by which humans can achieve access to the infinite; ultimately, as *being* itself. Throughout Coleridge's later writings, this exalted concept of the word coexists with laments over the imprecision with which words are commonly used, and the need to rely on words at all when writing of things that are beyond human expression. Positing an ideal performative does not render Coleridge's own speech acts felicitous; more likely, it sets off their insufficiency. That Coleridge nevertheless appreciated the continuity between the Word and words is suggested in a letter of 1815, where he expatiates on the divine *fiat* in the process of elucidating the proper form of a narrative poem. He adds that he is doing this in order "to shew you the connection between things in themselves comparatively trifling, and things the most important, by their derivation from common sources" (*CL* 4: 546). The "common source" shared by the Logos and human words is the notion of creative energy. On a theological level, Coleridge insists that creation be attributed to the Word, the second person of the Godhead, rather than to the Father, "seeing that no <*true*> energies can be attributed to an Ον αλογον [an entity that is not Logos]; the moment we conceive the divine energy, that moment we co-conceive the Λογος" (*CN* 2: 2445). But the same notebook entry implies that this identity of acts with words also holds true for human language, for the word is "the profoundest and most comprehensive Energy of the *human* Mind" (italics added). A special claim can also be made for the force of poetic language: "The power of Poetry is by a single word to produce that energy in the mind as compels the imagination to produce the picture" (*BL* 2: 128–29). Whether as an aspect of the Godhead, as creators of outness, as autonomous instruments, or as agents of the understanding and the imagination, words do things both in Coleridge's philosophy and in his poetry.

PERFORMATIVE FRAMES: 'AIDS TO REFLECTION'

The concept of an energetic language that plays an integral part in cognition, combined with the capacity for "performative reading" that Coleridge tries to teach in *The Statesman's Manual*, gives his prose works a distinctive pragmatic orientation. Whatever their primary subject matter, these texts are often framed within discourses on the effects of language on hearers or readers. They are structured not unlike the Bible, beginning with a series of *fiat*-like speech acts that construct the mental and discursive world within which the text is to be understood. *The Statesman's Manual* is a sermon on political science contained within a theory of reading that applies, on one level, to the Scriptures, but on another level is surely meant to be instantiated in the act of reading *The Statesman's Manual* itself. The *Logic*, Coleridge's treatise on the syllogism, the role of the understanding, and the Kantian categories, begins with introductory chapters that ground logic in a theory of language, by introducing the verb-substantive as the basis of all language and launching an etymological investigation into the terms "logic" and *logoi* as distinct from the other Greek words for "word," *epos* and *rhema*. *Aids to Reflection* is a study of will and moral action framed within some of Coleridge's most resonant claims for the power of language. In each case, Coleridge makes use of what Kenneth Burke calls a "circumference" (*Grammar of Motives* 77–85) or a "terministic screen" (*Language as Symbolic Action* 44–62)—an introductory declaration that establishes the paradigms of discourse and interpretation for the rest of the text. In each case, too, Coleridge's terministic screen consists of an account of verbal performativity.

In the preface to *Aids to Reflection*, Coleridge lists his objectives in writing a commentary on the work of Archbishop Robert Leighton. Arranging his aims "in the order of their comparative importance," he begins with one that concerns the function of language itself: his goal is "to direct the Reader's attention to the value of the Science of Words, their use and abuse" (*AR* 6–7). He follows this, typically, with a closer investigation of what the word "Words" signifies here. In contrast to Tooke, who was primarily concerned with language as communication when he titled his linguistic treatise Επεα Πτερόεντα '*Winged Words*,' Coleridge prefers the expression "living words" (*AR* 7), which assigns an independent and even organic agency to language. The preface ends with a famous characterization of words as mediators between subject and object or the mind and the thing, that could stand for the Romantic view of performative language: "For if words are not THINGS, they are LIVING POWERS, by which the things of most importance to mankind are actuated, combined, and humanized" (*AR* 10). The belief that words are living powers governs Coleridge's reception of Leighton's words, which he "performs" anew by combining quotations with his own commentary, by actuating them within his own life and times. Both through his terministic screen and through the example of his reading of Leighton, Coleridge demonstrates what it would mean for readers to treat his own text as living language.

The impassioned conclusion to *Aids to Reflection* reveals the significance of this mode of reading for spiritual life. Coleridge returns here to the question of what words do in and to the process of thought, this time invoking the context of natural philosophy. Anticipating criticism he believes will be leveled at him for sounding like a mystic, he first attempts an accurate definition of the term "mystic," then exposes his hypothetical attackers as closet materialists. For a materialist is anyone who regards matter as severed from soul, who cannot see that all *being* is also *action*, and who neglects the role of a intelligent agency—the Logos—in the universe. Coleridge traces the origin of this "Mechanico-corpuscular Philosophy" to Descartes, who offended against the idea of a world created by *fiat* when he reduced bodies to portions of matter in geometric space:

> But in contempt of Common Sense, and in direct opposition to the express declarations of the inspired Historian (Genesis I.), and to the tone and spirit of the Scriptures throughout, Des Cartes propounded it as *truth of fact*: and instead of a World *created* and filled with productive forces by the Almighty Fiat, left a lifeless Machine whirled about by the dust of its own Grinding: as if Death could come from the living Fountain of Life; Nothingness and Phantom from the Plenitude of Reality! the Absoluteness of Creative Will! (AR 400–401)

At issue here is not just the error of Cartesian dualism, but also the status of Descartes's speech acts. Coleridge's particular charge is that Descartes propounded a useful *"Fiction of Science,"* the abstraction and geometric organization of space, as if it were *"truth of fact"* (AR 400). "Holy! Holy! Holy! let me be deemed mad by all men, if such be thy ordinance: but, O! from *such* Madness save and preserve me, my God!" Coleridge responds (AR 401). His exclamatory prayer, by calling attention to the illocutionary force of language as opposed to its constative function, helps dislodge Descartes's claim from the status of objective truth. It makes us realize that even the utterances of philosophers can be read as illocutionary acts rather than truth-bound propositions.

After Kepler and Newton, people realized the shortcomings of Cartesian materialism, which maintains that the universe is regulated by hollow speech acts akin to depersonalized laws and constitutions: "For as a Law without a Lawgiver is a mere abstraction; so a *Law* without an Agent to realize it, a *Constitution* without an abiding Executive, is, in fact, not a Law but *an Idea!*" (AR 402). But in attempting to make sense of this predicament, Enlightenment scientists propounded an equally destructive "truth." "The *Deity itself* was declared to be the real Agent" (AR 403), thus reducing God to an abstract principle or an institution, and undermining the idea of a personal God. The end result of these authoritative speech acts that have been taken for objective truth is not only a misguided science, but a wide-ranging habit of focusing attention on sensory objects, and more specifically on the sensations aroused by objects. Once again, this philosophy manifests itself in linguistic confusion, as a habit "of applying all the words and phrases expressing reality, to the objects of the senses" (*AR* 406). Tooke, with his materialist etymologies, is, one suspects, the primary unnamed antagonist here.

As an antidote, Coleridge submits a paraphrase of Christ's words in John 6.63:

> 'My words,' said Christ, 'are Spirit: and they (*i.e.* the spiritual powers expressed by them) are Truth;'—*i.e. very* Being. (*AR* 407)

The words of Christ are, in Coleridge's terms, utterly tautological. Since Christ *is* Word and Truth, since he is (by identity with the third person of the trinity) Spirit, and (by identity with the first person or "I am") Being itself, all the nouns in the biblical verse and in Coleridge's exegesis—Christ, Spirit, Truth, Being—have the same referent. One is a symbol for all the others. At the same time, Coleridge identifies spoken words with the theological notion of Word by explicitly glossing "words" as "the spiritual powers expressed by them." The Word as Spirit and Truth is equivalent to the words that Christ as a speaker utters in the given passage, which are equivalent to the words we read in the biblical text. The passage compels us to fuse the idea of words read or words spoken—that is, words as *material* marks or sounds—with the idea of a metaphysical Word which is Spirit, Truth, and Being. The line "'My words,' said Christ, 'are Spirit'" could amount to a liar's paradox—*if* spirit and matter were regarded as opposites. But that is Coleridge's point: the spiritual Word acts in and through the sensory word, and through the sensory world. Only the devotees of a mechanico-corpuscular philosophy would reduce Christ's words to sounds or marks, his sentence to simple constation or an unchanging moral principle. Coleridge, on the contrary, calls attention to Christ's speaking as action in the world, as an act that modifies the worldview of his listeners while instantiating Christ's own identity as Word. Moreover, by recontextualizing Christ's words as he cites them, Coleridge participates in their ongoing effectiveness. He performs the quotation by interpreting it as an incarnation of the performative.

Coleridge's defense of a personal deity over a mechanical-materialist philosophy thus issues in a philosophy of language and symbol. The Logos, conceived of as an intelligent and moral God, provides the final refutation of materialist philosophy; conceived of as the language of Scripture, Logos refutes a superficial reading of the Bible for factual truth. Coleridge's identification of matter with spirit through the medium of the word provides a justification for the symbolic language of the gospels, which use familiar sensory objects ("Water, Flesh, Blood, Birth,

Bread") in spiritual senses (*AR* 407). But the word's function as mediator between matter and spirit is not limited to biblical language. Rather, the conclusion of *Aids to Reflection* links up with Coleridge's literary lectures, where he describes language as "a due medium between the thing and the mind" because it partakes of both (*LL* 1: 273). As for Humboldt, so also for Coleridge, the word uniquely joins thought with materiality.

"HYMN BEFORE SUN-RISE": LOCATING THE VOICE OF NATURE

Coleridge's attempt to link the understanding of the physical world with a theory of reading, by way of his philosophy of language, hark back to the traditional figure of the universe as a book in which God's creative purposes are made manifest. In turning this commonplace toward a philosophy of the Word as an ideal performative that can instantiate a moment of atemporal, undifferentiated, spiritual understanding in our encounter with it, Coleridge discovers a kind of recompense for his disenchantment with the speech acts of the sociopolitical world. Yet his poetic treatment of the Book-of-God metaphor—most obviously, in the frequently revised "Hymn before Sun-rise, in the Vale of Chamouni"— exposes the limits and the uncertainty of the Logos as a meaningful vehicle for human cognition and communication with the material world. Coleridge referred to this poem as his "Hymn in the manner of the *Psalms*" (*CL* 2: 864) and cited Milton and Thomson as predecessors (*CL* 4: 974), but his most immediate influence is the German-Danish poet Friederike Brun. "Hymn before Sun-rise" has had the dubious distinction of being the most frequently cited case of plagiarism in Coleridge's poetic canon ever since it was revealed, first by De Quincey, that it is an expanded translation of Brun's twenty-line poem "Chamounix beym Sonnenaufgange," itself an imitation of Klopstock's religious nature poetry. But while Brun's ode needs to be read in the context of her travelogue literature and her expressions of religious feeling in the mode of sensibility, the recontextualization of the poem within Coleridge's canon brings phenomenological concerns, including the role of utterance in establishing the relationship between mind and world, closer to the surface. Moreover, while the first version of the "Hymn" that Coleridge published in the *Morning Post* in 1802 is an expanded but fairly exact translation of Brun's ode, he began almost immediately to revise it in ways that counterpoint the philosophy of language he was simultaneously developing.

In Brun's "Chamounix beym Sonnenaufgange," the encounter between poet and landscape is primarily dialogic. In the first stanza, she contemplates Mont Blanc and responds to it in the mode of the affective sublime; in the next three stanzas, she questions it about its creator; in the final stanza—crucially—the landscape itself answers her:

> Jehovah! Jehovah! Kracht's im berstenden Eis:
> Lawinendonner rollen's die Kluft hinab:
> Jehovah Rauscht's in den hellen Wipfeln,
> Flüstert's an rieselnden Silberbächen.
> (*CPW* 2: 1131)

> (Jehovah! Jehovah! crashes in the bursting ice;
> Avalanche thunders roll it down the ravine;
> Jehovah! rustles in the bright tree-tops,
> It whispers in trickling silvery brooks.)

The breaking ice, the avalanches, the wind, and the brooks all return an answer. In the original 1802 version of his "Hymn," entitled "Chamouny; The Hour before Sunrise," Coleridge incorporates a direct translation of this stanza:

> GOD! GOD! The torrents like a shout of nations,
> Utter! The ice-plain bursts, and answers GOD!
> GOD, sing the meadow-streams with gladsome voice,
> And pine groves with their soft, and soul-like sound,
> The silent snow-mass, loos'ning, thunders GOD!
> (*CPW* 2: 1075; lines 56–60)

But, unlike Brun, Coleridge does not let Mont Blanc have the last word. Instead, he adds his own injunctions, addressed to the rest of the landscape:

> Ye dreadless flow'rs! that fringe th' eternal frost!
> Ye wild goats, bounding by the eagle's nest!
> Ye eagles, playmates of the mountain blast!
> Ye lightnings, the dread arrows of the clouds!
> Ye signs and wonders of the element,
> Utter forth, GOD! and fill the hills with praise!
> (61–66)

As Coleridge revises the poem, any actual response on the part of nature proceeds to disappear, leaving only the echo of the poet's commands. In the version Coleridge sent to George Beaumont in 1803, exactly a year after the *Morning Post* publication, he omitted the lines that translate Brun's last stanza; in other words, he omitted any evidence of the responsive voice of nature. Instead, from now on the constative report of the landscape's utterance gives way to a series of commands to the landscape to pronounce the name of its creator:

> God! *let* the Torrents, like a Shout of Nations,
> *Utter!* Thou Ice-plain, *burst, and answer,* God!
> God! *sing,* ye Meadow-streams with gladsome Voice,
> Ye Pine-groves, with your soft and soul-like Sound!
> And ye too have a Voice, ye Towers of Snow!
> Ye perilous Snow-towers, *fall and thunder,* God!
> (*CL* 2: 521; italics added)

Why this revision? On the one hand, the addition of the word "let," in "let the torrents ... utter," makes the poet's voice imitate God's creative utterance "let there be light." Coleridge's revisions also include a small change to God's own words elsewhere in the poem, making line 48 read "Here *let* the billows stiffen, and have rest" and bringing the language of the "Hymn" a bit closer to still to Genesis and *Paradise Lost*. The note of divine command in the poet's voice is what most modern commentators have responded to, and they tend to read the "Hymn" as free of self-doubt, as a noisy show of confidence in the ability of poetic voice to command the landscape. Thus Reeve Parker writes of the poem's "notorious stridency" (145), Gene Ruoff of its speaker's total freedom from any burden of self-examination and his ability to contain the apparent contradictions of the landscape (195–97), Keith Thomas of "an exuberance and self-confidence that then generate their own egotistical sublime" (99). But—*can* voice command the landscape successfully? Will Chamonix awake when Coleridge calls on it? It may be that his revisions, which obliterate any experience of the landscape's response, need to be read as a rather desperate and poignant reflection on the limitations of poetic voice.

As the "Hymn" develops, Chamounix, and especially Mont Blanc itself, becomes an image for the resistance that voice has to overcome. In all versions of Coleridge's text, the mountain's characteristic attribute is silence: "thou, most awful Form!/Risest from forth thy silent sea of pines,/How silently!" (5–7); "O dread and silent Mount!" (13). While Brun represents the mountain as blindingly bright ("Blendender Gipfel"), in Coleridge's version (set *before,* not *at,* sunrise) it becomes, rather, an emptiness in the "ebon mass" of the sky. In a reversal of figure and ground, it is the surrounding air that appears "substantial," while the mountain peak is a wedge that pierces substance:

> Around thee and above
> Deep is the air and dark, substantial, black,
> An ebon mass: methinks thou piercest it,
> As with a wedge!
> (7–10)

One wonders how this image might be related to the figure of the gap that appears several times in Coleridge's notebooks in 1802, in notations about "gap-tooth'd" faces (*CN* 1: 1084, 1177) or the metaphysical observation "Gap + − = +" (*CN* 1: 1117; i.e., a gap, imagined as a vertical "mark," crossed by a minus sign as a horizontal mark, produces a plus sign; two negatives produce a positive). Most obtrusive is the name "BLANC" itself, all in capitals, which appears in the third line of the poem beginning in the 1809 version (in earlier versions, Coleridge used "Chamouny" as if that were itself the name of the mountain). The apostrophe "O sovran BLANC" is less evocative of the full name "*Mont Blanc*" than it is of a famous passage in book 3 of *Paradise Lost*, where the blind Milton complains that the Book of Nature is for him a "Universal blanc" (*PL* 3: 47–49). In what sense is Mont Blanc (or "Mount Blank"?) there at all, when Coleridge, as Wordsworth exclaimed in 1844, "never was at Chamouni, or near it, in his life" (3: 442), when the mountain that he never saw is imaged as a gap in nature, and when even this "dread and silent" emptiness disappears, giving way to a worship of "the Invisible alone" (13–16)? Filling in the blank is the daunting project of voice and poetry.

"We receive but what we give," Coleridge wrote in "Dejection," a poem published within a month of the "Hymn before Sun-rise";

> And from the soul itself must there be sent
> A sweet and potent voice, of its own birth,
> Of all sweet sounds the life and element!
> (56–58)

That is part of the story told by the evolution of the "Hymn": that Coleridge, unlike Friederike Brun, ultimately cannot portray the landscape as responding to the human subject of its own accord, but only as an echo of what the poet's "busier mind" and "active will" bestows. Yet there is no guarantee that the landscape will return even an echo. "The heavens declare the glory of God. . . . Day unto day uttereth speech," reads the text from Psalm 19 that stands behind both Brun's and Coleridge's poem as a source for the image of a speaking and responsive cosmos. But immediately a qualification, thought to have originated with a cautious scholiast who wanted to forestall pantheistic interpretations that might arise from the image of speaking skies, reminds the reader that "[There is] no speech nor language, [where] their voice is not heard." (The bracketed words are those added by the translators of the Authorized Version in an attempt to rescue both the syntax and the semantics of Psalm 19.3; the Hebrew text simply reads, "No speech nor language; their voice is not heard.") Coleridge's "Hymn" recalls the trope of a speaking cosmos, but also recalls the doubts of the cautious scholiast as it undermines its own expectations about responsive voice. Right up to the end of Coleridge's apparently noisy poem, we actually hear only the poet's directives to the silent mountain:

> Great Hierarch! tell thou the silent sky,
> And tell the stars, and tell yon rising sun
> Earth, with her thousand voices, praises GOD.
> (83–85)

Yet there is only a single voice, speaking for all creation.

With its proliferation of apostrophes—to Mont Blanc, the rest of the landscape, the poet's own soul, his heart, and the "voice of sweet song"—"Hymn before Sun-rise" engages the issues raised by Jonathan Culler in his analysis of the "embarrassing" trope of apostrophe in Romantic literature. "What is really in question" with the use of this trope, according to Culler, "is the power of poetry to make something happen" (62). This is a particularly conspicuous, and convoluted, question in the "Hymn" because the reader's impression that nothing is happening is directly juxtaposed with the impression that something is happening. Nothing happens in the general (but never to be ignored) sense that the text is "only" language; and yet a more specific "nothing" takes place in this poem, in the way the poet's language covers up for the landscape's unresponsive silence. Indeed, the nothing that is the landscape's lack of response is so blatant that it turns into "something"—into the *posited* landscape of Mont Blanc and its *posited* praise of God. If the "Hymn" fails to show the natural world echoing the creative Word, it does highlight the role of the poet in making that word sound. Whatever the poem is, it can be only because the poet's speech act happens; and if this is superficially true of any poem, there is a certain significance, in the context of Coleridge's developing philosophy of language, to a text's calling attention to just that.

COGNITIVE AND VERBAL ACTS IN THE 'LOGIC'

The substitution of a human, poetic voice for the creative Logos that should resound from Mont Blanc challenges Coleridge's philosophical attempts to draw the concept of Logos into a theory of human language and cognition. Like German Romantic thinkers, Coleridge is attracted to the notion of dialogue as the model for the mind's relationship with the world—indeed, as the source of identity itself. This idea finds expression in the manuscript now titled *Logic*, Coleridge's most important—and neglected—study of how words relate to the world, which he planned, wrote, and revised from about 1815 almost until his death in 1834, and which was finally published as part of the *Collected Works* in 1981. An exposition, adaptation, and sometimes straight translation of Kant's *Critique of Pure Reason*, Coleridge's *Logic*, as James McKusick has written, "enacts a 'linguistic turn' on Kant's philosophy" (120).[7] Even more explicitly than the post-Kantian linguists in Germany, Coleridge identifies (Kantian) logic with grammar: "In fact the science of grammar is but logic in its first exemplification or rather its first product, λόγος, discursus, discourse, meaning either, i.e., thoughts in connexion or connected language" (*L&L* 128). In Coleridge's grammatical adaptation of logic, subject and object are identified with nouns, and the act of synthesis with a verb: "In Grammar the Nomen, or Substantive, corresponds to the Subject, Object, or Thing in Logic; and the Verb to the *Act* of the Logicians" (*CN* 4: 4644). His treatise on logical propositions—the *Logic*—is thus also a work on linguistic sentences and universal grammar, which exemplifies his belief that the human understanding can only deal in language.

In his letters, Coleridge referred to the work that is now rather misleadingly titled *Logic* as "my Work on the power and use of *words*" (*L* l), and at one point he gave it the title Επεα ζωντα 'living words.' He conceived of it as a text designed for the use of young men who were preparing themselves for "the pulpit, the bar, the senate, the professor's chair, or ... the public press" (*L* 144)—that is, for professions founded on and perpetuated by powerful, public speech acts. In the second introductory chapter to the *Logic* he immediately establishes the connection between logic, language, and action by way of the "absolute etymon" of the word "logic" itself, or the "particular visual image ... which is at the root of its proper constituent syllable" (*L* 24). This methodology is recognizably inspired by Tooke's theory that all words can be traced back to roots referring to concrete entities. But when Coleridge's analysis of the word "logic" leads him to the original sense of the Greek *lego* as "that of picking up, a taking up a something that had been sought after; hence a choosing, a determining" (*L* 26), the very awkwardness of his syntax reveals the alterations he is introducing into Tooke's philology. Beginning with the word "logic" itself, what Coleridge finds at the root of all language is primarily *action*, and concrete existence only insofar as it is a product of action.

[7]McKusick reads the *Logic* as "radically revisionary" of Kant (119–48). Among other things, he draws attention to the differences between Coleridge's language-centered reading of the First Critique and Herder's attempt to assert the priority of language in his *Metakritik*, a text that Coleridge knew and reviled (132–33).

Indeed, a central principle of the *Logic* is that all things are also, even primarily, acts. "We cannot conceive even the merest *thing*, a stone for instance, as simply and exclusively *being*, as absolutely passive and *actionless*," Coleridge writes, since even a stone, in reflecting light and cohering from many individual particles, manifests an active sense of being (*L* 21). Conversely, lightning is an equally important instance of the conjunction of being and action, for it has existence even though it seems to be purely act: "as little . . . can we conceive or imagine the purest act, a flash of lightning for instance, as *merely* an act, or without an abiding or continuing somewhat, as the inseparable ground, subject, and substance of the action." Using examples from geometry, Coleridge affirms that the geometrical figure that we intuitively take to be the very essence of form or thingness is only the "image or representation" of an "energeia theoretike" or "perceiving energy"—so that a line might be better called an "act of length," or a circle an act of circularity (*L* 73).

The coexistence of action and being is encapsulated and made the basis of all language in Coleridge's foundational idea of the "verb substantive": the "I am," Latin *sum*, or Greek *eimi* that "is the act of being" (*L* 16–17). "I am" represents both an action and the state created by that action; as Coleridge explains elsewhere, "you may take it to mean *an act*—and so it has the power of a Verb—or of a *Thing, Substance, or State*—and then it has the power of a Noun or Substantive" (*SWF* 1: 797). Because all words derive, as Coleridge believes, from the verb substantive, all are hybrids of being and action—"every substantive a verb, and every verb a substantive" (*L* 19). This idea that language originated from a "kernel" representing both a state and an action recurs with great frequency and in several different forms during the Romantic period. The derivation of all words from the verb-substantive "I am" or εἰμι was propounded as a principle of grammar by the Classical philologists William Vincent and J. G. J. Hermann (Perkins, *Coleridge's Philosophy* 27), and, as discussed in Chapter 2, by Bernhardi and even Fichte. Humboldt, too, believed that a "pre-grammatical condition" of indifference between verb and noun is detectable in every language:

> There is in every language a still more or less apparent pre-grammatical condition, from which grammatical development first proceeds. No difference between verb and noun is conceivable here, since each nominal concept can be regarded in terms of being or becoming, thus as a verb, and each verbal concept can be regarded as having become or as the state of becoming, as in the adjective or the substantive. (*GS* 6: 479–80)

In Britain, Alexander Murray, a follower of Horne Tooke's, proposed that all languages originated from nine "proto-words" that "were all both nouns and verbs, and all implied 'power, motion, force'" (Aarsleff, *Study of Language* 83).

In the *Logic*, Coleridge situates his concept of the verb-substantive in the first introductory chapter, thus grounding the entire text in a concept of language as performative (i.e., acting) and constative (i.e., being) at once. The starting point of Coleridge's *Logic*, then, foreshadows the conclusion reached by Austin in his analysis of how everyday utterances relate to the world—namely, that "the dichotomy of performatives and constatives . . . has to be abandoned" (Austin 150), for all utterances both state and perform, and the difference is only one of philosophical perspective.

"What is a fact of all human language is of course a fact of all human consciousness," Coleridge writes in his chapter "On the Logical Acts" (*L* 82), the most important chapter of the *Logic* for establishing the interdependence of cognitive and linguistic acts. He begins by identifying the primary mental act, the condition of possibility for all consciousness, as the Kantian "synthetic unity or the unity of apperception" (*L* 76)—the ability to form a concept by recognizing unity in multeity. Coleridge immediately applies this principle to language, identifying the primary mental act with the basic linguistic act of predication: "above all . . . it is this synthetic unity which first gives meaning and determinate import to the word 'is' in all affirmations" (*L* 76–77). The act of synthetic unity is what allows us to say "the house *is* white" or "Cerberus *is* three-headed." In other words, Coleridge's analysis of the primary mental act explicates *constation* in language (i.e., the statement "the house is white") as the manifestation of a basic cognitive *act*.

Coleridge's diction here implies that the mental act has a certain priority, since it is what "first gives meaning" to the word. This ordering suggests a distinction between him and Humboldt, for whom the word is always already involved in the process of thought. Yet often the question of primacy is undecidable in the *Logic*, for Coleridge inevitably makes his arguments in terms of linguistic examples (affirmative sentences, subjects, predicates, copulas, etc.), in such a way that it is impossible to tell whether he is arguing about the verbal formulations or the logical acts "behind" them—or how these terms could ever be clearly distinguished. The focus of his interest is how propositions—conceived of as *both* mental and verbal acts—relate to the world. In addressing this issue, he invokes a distinction between essence and existence, essence being defined in the *Biographia* as "the principle of *individuation*, the inmost principle of the *possibility*, of any thing, *as* that particular thing," and existence as "the superinduction of *reality*" (*BL* 2: 62). In the *Logic*, Coleridge stresses that the primary mental act that joins a subject with a predicate, thereby creating a *possible* concept, does not yet affirm the *real existence* of the concept. "The understanding is the substantiative power, that by which we give and attribute substance and reality to phenomena," he notes, but immediately goes on to desynonymize the terms "give" and "attribute," as well as "substance" and "reality" (*L* 239). Recognizing a concept's correspondence to reality is a two-stage process, for the understanding has "a twofold character" by which "it gives *and* it attributes substance" (*L* 239; italics added). The first of these stages, the understanding's "essential act," has the performative character of an act of positing: the understanding must "give" a phenomenon substance or *logical essence* before the question of its *real existence* can be entered on at all. Some concepts will only ever have the substance they are given by the mind, for real existence in the world cannot be attributed to them. "It may well be that the subject has no existence but in the mind," as in the case of propositions like "Cerberus is three-headed" (*L* 79). Yet even a three-headed hell-hound, conceived by the mind, is endowed with a certain kind of reality because "the act by which the mind combines the three heads . . . , that is and must be real." Coleridge's epistemological analysis has significant implications for aesthetics and a theory of the imagination; for, as he suggests, if the concepts formed by the primary act of the understanding do not exist in reality, perhaps their mode of existence is that of dreams, or of fiction. Whatever is synthesized by the mind is as real as the mind itself is.

Coleridge arrives at his distinction between different modes of existence by way of a Kantian analysis of the role of the intellectual faculties. But in the context of philosophy of language, his analysis parallels the analysis of the proposition by speech-act theorists a century and a half later. Like Coleridge in the *Logic*, Searle in *Speech Acts* is preoccupied with the kind of act we perform whenever we say a subject "is" something. He characterizes predication as a kind of proto-speech-act, or as a "slice" or dimension of all utterances, and he insists that predicate expressions (e.g., the expression "is red" in "the rose is red") do not refer to elements of reality, because these concepts or expressions exist only in our mode of representation—that is, in language. Although Searle uses a different analytic vocabulary from that of Coleridge, he promotes a similar conclusion about predication: it concerns *essence* (in language) rather than *existence in reality*. Both subject and predicate, according to Searle, are linguistic entities; neither one need exist outside of language (*Speech*

Acts 118). Like Coleridge, Searle characterizes the proposition as a mental and linguistic act of joining, and insists that the superinduction of a commitment to truth is a separate illocutionary act: "a proposition is to be sharply distinguished from an assertion or statement of it" (*Speech Acts* 29).

Both thinkers regard reference to reality as a second, higher-level act. In Coleridge's system, the affirmation of objective reality takes place through the foundational "I am." In its complete (Schellingian) form, "I am I" or "I am myself," this is the proposition that identifies subject ("I") with object ("myself") and unites the ground of existence (the logical principle of identity, or A = A) with the ground of the knowledge of existence (my experiential awareness that I really exist). But beyond the "I am" of the individual speaker or the individual mind, which can only establish certainty to the extent that individual existence is certain, Coleridge sees independent existence as grounded in the eternal "I am," or God:

> If then we elevate our conception to the absolute Self, Spirit, or Mind, the underived and eternal 'I Am,' then and herein we find the principle of being, and of knowledge, of idea, and of reality: the ground of existence, and the ground of the knowledge of that existence, absolutely one and identical.... (*L* 85)

Expressed by means of an utterance, or at least an affirmative statement—"I am because I affirm myself to be" (*L* 85)—existence and identity already have a profoundly verbal dimension in Coleridge's system. In fact, he cites the *grammatical* centrality of the verb-substantive as "the highest possible external evidence" of the "truth" of the title "I Am," as attributed to God in the Old Testament—thus implicitly elevating grammar into a proof of theology (*L* 82).

But in the *Logic* Coleridge goes one step further toward establishing the importance of the speech act for both knowledge and existence:

> The verb (*verbum*), the word is of all possible terms the most expressive of that which it is meant to express, an act, a going forth, a manifestation, a something which is distinguishable from the mind which goes forth in the word, and yet inseparable therefrom; for the mind goes forth in it, and without the mind the word would cease to be a word, it would be a sound, a noise. If we ask ourselves how we know anything—that rose, for example, or the nightingale hidden in yonder tree—the reply will be that the rose (*rosa subjecta*) manifests itself, that it renders itself objective, or the object of our perceptions, by its colour and its odour, and so in the nightingale by its sound. And what are these but the goings from the subject, its words, its verb? The rose blushes, the nightingale sings. (*L* 82)

The "word" or the "verb" of the subject is its fundamental identifying and individuating principle. As in Herder's essay on the origin of language, elements of the natural world impress themselves on human consciousness by uttering a word, and in this act lies the origin of both language and reflective thought. Coleridge emphasizes the way roses or nightingales announce themselves as "speaking" subjects, thereby rendering themselves possible objects of our thought. "I well remember with what delight I made out this idea of Substance while looking at a Rose 9 years ago," he records in a marginal note to Fichte's *Grundlage der gesammten Wissenschaftslehre* (Foundations of the entire Science of Knowledge), illustrating the real significance of such encounters in the development of his own philosophy (*M* 2: 625).

By characterizing roses and nightingales as speaking subjects, Coleridge also lines up with Humboldt, Friedrich Schlegel, and other German Romantic philosophers who considered dialogue the model for reflective thought.[8] The I-Thou relationship becomes an ever more important paradigm in Coleridge's late work. His formulations of it in the "Essay on Faith" (c. 1820) and the *Opus Maximum* manuscript resemble Humboldt's ideas about dialogue in stressing the identity of "Thou" as a freely chosen addressee, equal but logically opposed to the I, and essential to the I's self-consciousness:

> Without a *Thou* there could be no opposite, and of course no distinct or conscious sense of the term *I*. . . . The consciousness expressed in the term *Thou* is only possible by an equation in which *I* is taken as equal to, but yet not the same as *Thou*: and . . . this again is only possible by putting the *I* and *Thou* in opposition to each other, in logical antithesis I mean, as correspondent opposites, as harmonies or correlatives. (*OM* 143–45)

It may seem a major leap from the Romantic ideal of self-expressive subjects in dialogue with one another to the speech-act philosopher's standard definition of speech: "speaking a language is engaging in a (highly complex) rule-governed form of behavior" (Searle, *Speech Acts* 12). Yet Searle, like Coleridge, understands language as the communicative intention of a conscious subject; he can only regard a "noise or mark" as a speech act if he assumes that it "was produced by a being or beings more or less like myself and produced with certain kinds of intentions" (*Speech Acts* 16). Searle would be unlikely to ascribe intentional-

---

[8] The importance of dialogue for Coleridge, who shared with Humboldt the reputation of being a brilliant conversationalist, is a many-faceted subject for discussion. See Degrois for an argument that the self is constituted by dialogism in Coleridge as in modern phenomenology; Macovski (67–101) for a Bakhtinian approach; and Perkins, *Coleridge's Philosophy* 278, for the parallel with Humboldt.

ity to a rose or a nightingale—but this in itself highlights the flexibility of the Romantic conception of utterance. Twentieth-century speech-act philosophers generally assume a conscious, intending, and stable human subject; despite their sophisticated analyses of verbal performativity, including the role of deictics, the interrelation of language and temporality, the pragmatics of the dialogic context, and the dynamics of the speaker's authority, they rarely question the speaker's subjectivity or explore its conditions. This is where Coleridge's work on the active dimension of language might enrich speech-act theory, or at least speech-act readings of Romantic texts: if less analytic, he is nevertheless profoundly concerned with the performative grounding of a subject-position in the first place. His concern with a performative subjectivity is especially relevant to Romantic literature, with its various explorations of human identity, of the mind's relationship with the world, of the status of the speaking subject as well as the status of reality, and of the effectiveness or ineffectiveness of voice.

"FROST AT MIDNIGHT": THE FLUTTERING FILM

To see Coleridge's subject-oriented performative at work in his poetry, we may return to the third poem published together with "France: An Ode" and "Fears in Solitude" in 1798: "Frost at Midnight." As the most successful of his "conversation poems"—and, like all the poetic texts discussed in this chapter, one that Coleridge continued to revise and republish throughout his career—this poem merits a reading in terms of the development of his philosophy of language. In this context, "Frost at Midnight" enacts the moment at which communicative utterance arises from the cognitive encounter between the poet's mind and the tiniest motion of the surrounding world. This originary moment may be seen, in fact, as the condition of possibility for poetry itself, making "Frost at Midnight" a strangely self-reflexive text that enacts the origin of its own discourse.

Idealess and empty at first, the "I" of the poem becomes capable of communicative utterance when his mind seizes on the animated film of ash on a fireplace grate:

> Only that film, which fluttered on the grate,
> Still flutters there, the sole unquiet thing.
> Methinks, its motion in this hush of nature
> Gives it dim sympathies with me who live,
> Making it a companionable form,
> Whose puny flaps and freaks the idling Spirit
> By its own moods interprets, every where

> Echo or mirror seeking of itself,
> And makes a toy of Thought.
>
> (15–23)

Coleridge attributes to the film the same kind of self-expressive act performed by the blushing rose and the singing nightingale in his *Logic*: the fluttering motion is its word, its verb. His struggles with revisions of these lines demonstrate his discomfort with calling the film either "living" or "lifeless." It cannot achieve the status of a conscious mind because, as Coleridge's philosophy constantly affirms, consciousness depends on the ability of the subject to become an object *to itself*. But by manifesting motion, one of the attributes of a subject, the film makes itself into a possible object of the poet's thought. "*Only* that film": because of its verb-like motion, it is the first thing in the text that stands out from the poet's immediate surroundings. Even Coleridge's decision to append to the word "film" a footnote about the custom of referring to this phenomenon as a "stranger," "supposed to portend the arrival of some absent friend," serves to distinguish the word typographically and semantically from the rest of the text and to emphasize the difference that the film makes by its self-expressive motion. As the "sole *un*-quiet thing," it is linguistically marked as different from all the stillness around it; and the homonymic play on "sole" and "soul" makes it seems as if language itself animates the film—granting it the sound of a "soul"—even before the poet begins to think of it consciously as a companion. The outering "word" of the film, the words of the poet, even the phonetic autonomy of language itself conspire to create the conditions for a dialogic encounter, and thus for cognitive engagement.

By becoming both subject and object—becoming a "*stranger*"[9]—the fluttering ash allows the poet to engage in reflective thought, to find an "echo or mirror" of his own spirit. The contiguity of "thing" and "Methinks," in the above quotation, intensifies the idea that thought, especially reflection on the acts of one's own mind ("*me*-thinking"), depends on the stimulus provided by objects. Thinking, for Coleridge, is always transitive—it is always thinking *of* something—since "to think absolutely or indefinitely is impossible for a finite mind at least" (*CL* 4: 885). In Tookean moments, Coleridge propounds an etymological relationship between "think" and "thing":

---

[9] According to Goodson's alternative reading of "Frost at Midnight" in the context of language theory, the *word* "stranger," precisely because it is strange, because it is not a synonym for "grate-film" and thus introduces new possibilities for thought, opens the way to a "recovery of the word as primary agent of imagination" (*Verbal Imagination* 120–27).

> Words as distinguished from mere pulses of Air in the auditory nerve must correspond to Thoughts, and Thoughts is but the verb-substantive Participle Preterite of *Thing* (So in Latin/*Res*, a *thing—reor*, I *think* ... *Res* = thing: res in praesenti = thinking, i.e. *thinging*, or thing out of me = a thing in me.... (*CN* 3: 3587)[10]

"Thinging" is exactly what is going on at this moment in the poem, as the speaker makes a "thing out of me" (the fluttering film) into "a thing in me," or a "thought," and thereby also distinguishes himself as subject from the film as object. Once dialogically engaged in this way, Coleridge's spirit finds another companionable echo in the breath of an infant, his son who sleeps in the cradle beside him. Through the stimulus of the infant's breath (itself "spirit," *spiritus*) the poet can, in the second half of the poem, instantiate a mental dialogue between "I" and "you" for the first time by addressing his son directly.

Coleridge's interaction with the fluttering film and the breathing baby leads to a recasting of the entire world in the mode of prophecy and verbal projection. At the end of the poem, the poet creates, in language, a future for his son. He predicts an existence in which the external world itself is experienced as reflection and utterance, transmuted into an eternal, divine language in dialogue with the human subject:

> But *thou*, my babe! shalt wander like a breeze
> By lakes and sandy shores, beneath the crags
> Of ancient mountain, and beneath the clouds,
> Which image in their bulk both lakes and shores
> And mountain crags: so shalt thou see and hear
> The lovely shapes and sounds intelligible
> Of that eternal language, which thy God
> Utters, who from eternity doth teach
> Himself in all, and all things in himself.
> (54-62)

But the poem's ultimate act of reflection occurs when the prophecy of the baby's future turns back into the poet's present situation. The final verse-paragraph creates a possible world through utterance, suspending a

---

[10]Further references for this etymology and brief discussions of Coleridge's adaptation of Tooke's point are offered by Jackson (85) and McKusick (48-49). McKusick suggests that Coleridge's idea of "thingifying" as "generat[ing] discrete objects by applying linguistic categories to the flux of outward phenomena" represents his solution to the dilemma posed by the unacceptable alternatives of Tookean materialism and Berkeleian idealism. Coleridge's solution is a compromise in the spirit of Kant, but he replaces the Kantian categories with linguistic forms: "language itself offers a solution to this dilemma by suggesting that thoughts and things are somehow interchangeable" (McKusick 51).

vision of nature in the subjunctive mood that hangs on "whether," "or," and "if":

> whether the eave-drops fall
> Heard only in the trances of the blast,
> Or if the secret ministry of frost
> Shall hang them up in silent icicles,
> Quietly shining to the quiet Moon.
> (70–74)

What is crucial here is that these closing lines not only project a vision of the future, but simultaneously transmute the poet's immediate physical surroundings into verbal utterance. The final image of the frost's ministry and the silent icicles echoes the poem's opening line ("The Frost performs its secret ministry") so as to shape the text into a potentially endless spiral. In his letters, Coleridge describes ring-composition as the proper structure of all poetry and associates this structure directly with the *poiesis* or "making" from which poetry takes its name:

> The common end of all *narrative*, nay, of *all*, Poems is to convert a *series* into a *Whole*: to make those events, which in real or imagined History move on in a *strait* Line, assume to our Understandings a *circular* motion—the snake with it's Tail in it's Mouth. Hence indeed the almost flattering and yet appropriate Term, Poesy—i.e. poiēsis = *making*. (*CL* 4: 545)

The particular act of *poiesis* in "Frost at Midnight" depends on performative language. While the beginning of the poem apparently describes the experienced reality of a winter night, its ending rises to a level of meta-discourse in which the same experience is posited in language ("*if* the secret ministry of frost . . ."). That final speech act, moreover, is the result of a progression that originates in the poet's moment of identification with the bit of fluttering ash, a moment enacted in the language of the poem itself. The text, in other words, contains the conditions of its own possibility, because it performs the minimal subject-object interaction—the meeting of the poet's mind and the fluttering film—in which subjectivity, reflective thought, dialogue, and poetic re-creation all begin.

In effect, "Frost at Midnight" is an enactment of Coleridge's linguistically oriented philosophy of consciousness. Subjectivity emerges here in an act of synthesis, by which the mind posits a trace of consciousness in the fluttering film. Like the proposition "Cerberus is three-headed" in the *Logic*, this synthetic act of the understanding is at first unaccompanied by any affirmation of the real existence of that which is imagined. But from the initial encounter with an object in the world, the mind proceeds to a conception of its own unity as the basis for its ability to unify external impressions. It becomes aware that it interprets the external world "by its own moods" and as an "echo or mirror" of itself. This is the ground for the poet's ability to say "I" or "I am," and to enter into an I-Thou relationship with his infant son. The "I am" of the individual mind leads onward to an affirmation of the eternal "I am" "which thy God/Utters, who from eternity doth teach/Himself in all, and all things in himself." Yet the movement toward an increased objectivity, or an awareness of the divine "I am" as the ground of external existence, is counterbalanced by the emergence of an explicitly performative language. The constative utterances of the poem's beginning, that fit words to the external world, give way to performative utterances that fit a future, unrealized, potential world to the poem's words. "Frost at Midnight"—like the Romantic performative whose movement it mirrors—opens onto a phenomenological insight into the way self, word, and world interconstitute one another.

MATHEMATICS, CHRISTIANITY, AND PERFORMATIVITY

I have proposed that Coleridge's theory of language as action develops both out of his own experience of sociopolitical speech acts, and as a response to the same Kantian problematic that led many of his German contemporaries to theorize the importance of language for epistemology and subjectivity. The idea of language as Logos and as outerance that Coleridge develops in this context amounts to a recognition that *all* language is "performative" in respect of its role in establishing the relation between subject and object, or between two subjects, and thus in shaping human consciousness. But it is worth noting, finally, that Coleridge identifies a few special cases in which the fact that words are uttered in certain circumstances changes those circumstances and brings a new situation into being—cases, that is, where language is "performative" in the modern, Austinian sense of the word. Mathematics is one such discourse.[11] The mathematician begins "by making his own terms" in a mode that, were they being made by a philosophical rather than a

[11] The German Romantics also identified mathematical language as mystical, symbolic, and essentially performative, as Fiesel demonstrates with particular reference to Novalis and the painter Philipp Otto Runge. Novalis regards mathematical language as "the realm of ultimate freedom . . . because in it the sign creates the object. . . . Mathematics is a world ex nihilo, the language of the gods—magic—religion" (Fiesel 84).

mathematical writer, would be called "declarations" rather than definitions (*L* 217). These "postulates" assert the writer's "power of productive action" (*L* 218). Like Austin's performatives, the declarations of the mathematician are not subject to the criteria of truth or falsehood: if a mathematician speaks of a cone, then the "cone" is exactly the geometrical figure he or she has conceived of, no matter what the word "cone" may signify elsewhere. In mathematical postulates, Coleridge claims—in what is virtually a textbook definition of performativity—that "the producing act and the product are one and indivisible" (*L* 218).

If the *Logic* assigns a special performative status to the language of mathematics, a self-referential discourse and therefore one with the power to instantiate its own order, it is the language of Christian doctrine that possesses this status in *Aids to Reflection*. Between the preface, with its announcement that words are living powers, and the conclusion, with its demonstration that words are spirit, the entire book portrays Scripture, and the language of religion more generally, as distinct from other discourses. *Aids to Reflection* attributes to Christians the power to use declarative rather than descriptive utterance: "The *Christian* likewise grounds *his* philosophy on assertions; but with the best of all *reasons* for making them—viz. that he *ought* so to do" (*AR* 138). This claim could be read as simple dogmatism; or it could be seen as a belief on Coleridge's part that the language of Christianity operates differently from ordinary, constative language. As the context makes clear, the Christian has the power to state first, then allow the proof of the statement to emerge performatively from the fact that the utterance has been made, understood, experienced. This is a corollary of the fact that the language of Christian revelation relates to reality in a unique way: rather than describing reality, it contains reality—or the promise and prophecy of reality—within itself. "Christianity proves itself, as the Sun is seen by his own light," Coleridge comments in 1823 (*TT* 1: 31); "it is; its evidence is involved in its existence."

Coleridge's account of the language of Christianity in *Aids to Reflection* thus recalls his description of biblical language in *The Statesman's Manual*. In both cases, language has special properties because it transcends the difference between cause and effect, the time lag between promise and fulfilment, and the need to refer to a pre-existing reality. Perhaps it is possible to conclude that, for Coleridge, *the principle of performativity is embodied in the idea of language liberated from normal forms of temporality*. Scripture reflects the perspective of "the Supreme Reason, whose knowledge is creative, and antecedent to the things known" (*LS* 18). The Bible does not refer constatively to past history in the manner of other texts; rather, its language needs to be understood as containing past, present, and future within itself. The language of Christian doctrine does not need to refer to pre-existing proofs, facts, or definitions, since its proof emerges in the act of revelation itself—the act of proclaiming the word and the reader's encounter with the word. In a different but related sense, the language of mathematics is freed from reference to pre-existing objects because it is a direct expression of the creative acts of the mind. What all these forms of language have in common is that they derive from, and are understood by, reason—the mental faculty that can contemplate abstract and eternal ideas. Language in its everyday uses, however, is the vehicle of the understanding, and thus operates within the Kantian transcendental forms of space and time. Words differ—that is, they are separated by spatial or temporal gaps—from their referents or their fulfilment. The question that remains open, for Coleridge and for us as readers of Coleridge, is whether there are distinct modes of language (roughly, the constative language of ordinary discourse and the special performative language of mathematics or religion) or whether the performative dimension of all language could be experienced if we interpret, not according to the forms of the understanding, but according to the form of reason. As either a type of language or a mode of interpretation, the performative maintains the status of a logical construct in Coleridge's system; but as such, it casts its influence over his philosophy of mind, his theory of human experience in the social and natural world, and his use of language in poetic texts.

5

Subjective and Intersubjective Speech Acts in Hölderlin's Work

> Jezt aber tagts! Ich harrt und sah es kommen,
> Und was ich sah, das Heilige sei mein Wort.
> (*StA* 2: 118)

"Now day breaks! I watched and saw it coming,/And what I saw, the holy, let it be my word": the epiphanic moment represented by these lines comes suddenly at the beginning of the third stanza of Friedrich Hölderlin's hymn "Wie wenn am Feiertage..." ("As on a Holiday..."). This fragmentary poem may be read as a series of metaphors for poetic creation—for the synthetic act by which the poet's consciousness converges with nature and language to bring forth "the work of gods and men, the song." Besides being about the genesis of the poetic speech act, though, the text is "performative" in an almost parodic sense. Just as Hölderlin begins to articulate the catastrophic fate that would await the poet if he were to approach the gods unworthily and be rejected by them, his manuscript enacts the catastrophe by breaking off into incoherent notes.

The lines quoted above are the focus of Heidegger's reading of the poem, for he regards the poet's decisive act of naming "the holy" as the act by which the holy, or nature, comes into being:

> Because it is named, and itself even demands naming, the awakening of 'nature' comes in the sound of the poetic word. In the word the being of the thing that is named reveals itself. For the word, in that it names that which has being, divides being from non-being [chaos].
>
> (Weil es aber genannt wird, ja sogar selbst die Nennung fordert, kommt das Erwachen 'der Natur' in den Klang des dichtenden Wortes. Im Wort enthüllt sich das Wesen des Genannten. Denn das Wort scheidet, indem es das Wesenhafte nennt, das Wesen vom Unwesen.) (58)

The deictic "now" with which Hölderlin's line begins is, for Heidegger, a conclusive indication that the advent of the holy happens in the utterance itself, since "the 'now' clearly names the moment in which Hölderlin himself says 'Now day breaks!'" (Das 'Jezt' nennt ja doch eindeutig den Zeitpunkt, in dem Hölderlin selbst sagt: 'Jezt aber tagts!' [75]). But de Man, in an early review of Heidegger's exegeses of Hölderlin, challenges the philosopher's enthusiastic reading of these lines, arguing instead that they call into question the entire possibility of naming being: "[Hölderlin] does not say: das Heilige *ist* mein Wort. The subjunctive is here really an optative; it indicates prayer, it marks desire, and these lines state the eternal poetic intention, but immediately state also that it can be no more than intention" (*Blindness and Insight* 258). For de Man, the event that occurs in these lines is not the coming-into-being of the holy, but the split between immediate being and a mediating language, or the articulation of the difference between absolute being and the "non-simple form" of being that is the only one available to human language (*Blindness and Insight* 259).

Reading the lines in the context of contemporary and Romantic philosophies of language extends the range of interpretive possibilities. According to the speech-act theory of Austin and Searle, Hölderlin's phrase "let the holy be my word" is a declaration, an explicit performative that fits words to the world at the same time that it transforms reality so as to fit the world to the words. Questions would arise, within the bounds of this theory, about the source of the speaker's authority and the conditions necessary to the success of his declaration. According to the rules of language, where Searle in particular seeks his criteria for the definition of illocutionary acts, the utterance institutes a new state of affairs for the speaking subject (in which "the holy" = "my word"). But in intersubjective terms, or in terms of the social conventions that Austin initially stresses and Searle also brings to bear when defining declarations, speech-act theory exposes the fallibility of Hölderlin's lines: the poet simply lacks any apparent authority to issue such a declaration, and any indication of uptake or acknowledgment by a hearer or audience is conspicuously absent.

Benveniste's work provides an answer of sorts to the question of authority, inasmuch as it would call attention to the way these lines themselves create the speaker's subjectivity and ground his discourse in his ability to articulate himself—for the first time in the poem—as "I." In attempting to make Austin's definition of the performative more rigorous, Benveniste considers the relationship between authority and action that obtains in performative utterances. Authority often involves sociopolitical power, but it also depends on the speaker's unique right to make his or her own commitments, pledges, or promises: "acts of authority are first and always utterances made by those to whom the right to utter them belongs" (*Problems* 236). This subject-centered notion of authority as ultimate responsibility for one's own acts, which is interwoven with Benveniste's belief that subjectivity itself depends on the ability to place oneself in language as "I" (*Problems* 224), *might* validate Hölderlin's translation of "what *I* saw" into "*my* word." Since the speaker is responsible for defining the position of the self by articulating it in language, he is also responsible for declarations that orient themselves by the position of the I and involve its perceptions and commitments.

But "let the holy be my word" is also a rather exact description and (at the same time) demonstration of a Humboldtian speech act. The indeterminate "it" that approaches from some place external to the speaker is objectified by his utterance as "the holy." It is brought into relation with the speaking subject *by* his word—that is, because language itself bestows on "the holy" the status of an object—and simultaneously designated *as* his word. The act of making the holy (and "the holy") into a word, an act that the utterance both names and performs, modifies, in turn, the poet's subjectivity. Among other things, it allows him to identify himself with the community of holy poets who have thus far only been named in the third person, but for whom he henceforth speaks in the first person plural.

Like the speech act as Humboldt describes it, Hölderlin's line captures an ambiguity in the relationship between the subject and language. On one hand, the poet's claim is grounded in human consciousness, sensory perception, and past experience. In this sense, it might be (clumsily) paraphrased, "I have seen the holy, and I shall henceforth represent what I saw by my word"—a paraphrase that assigns language a basically referential or constative role. But it is also possible that experience is being subordinated to the performative power of language, as if to say, "(I posit that) my word, which hereby comes into existence, shall be the holy and shall substitute for what (I say) I have seen." Is the holy (or at least an objectified version of it) *embodied in* the poet's word, or does the word itself, in the form of Hölderlin's poem and of this specific performative utterance, *generate* the holy? The speech act engages a reciprocal relationship between speaking subject and articulated object, between I and Other, and between language and reality, and engages as well the questions raised and left unanswered by Romantic theorists about the relative priority of consciousness and language.

All of this is encapsulated in an image of dawn, and as the stanza continues the coming of daylight merges with two further images of origin:

> Now day breaks! I watched and saw it coming,
> And what I saw, the holy, let it be my word.
> For she, she herself, who is older than the ages
> And higher than the gods of Orient and Occident,
> Nature has now awoken amid the clang of arms,
> And from high Aether down to the low abyss,
> According to fixed law, begotten, as in the past, on
>   holy Chaos,
> Delight, the all-creative,
> Delights in self-renewal.
>
> (*Poems* 373 [slightly altered])
>
> (Jezt aber tagts! Ich harrt und sah es kommen,
> Und was ich sah, das Heilige sei mein Wort.
> Denn sie, sie selbst, die älter denn die Zeiten
> Und über die Götter des Abends und Orients ist,
> Die Natur ist jezt mit Waffenklang erwacht,
> Und hoch vom Aether bis zum Abgrund nieder
> Nach vestem Geseze, wie einst, aus heiligem
>   Chaos gezeugt,
> Fühlt neu die Begeisterung sich,
> Die Allerschaffende wieder.)
>
> (*StA* 2: 118)

The stanza allows for a historical reading, according to which the dawn that Hölderlin heralds would be not only the dawn of a new century (the poem was written in 1800), but also the dawn of a new world-order announced by the "clang of arms" of the French Revolution or the Napoleonic wars.[1] But this historical moment is figured in terms of the original creation of the world, and therefore also in terms of creation by the word. Hölderlin evokes a Hesiodic myth of creation in which a god-filled nature arises from chaos "according to fixed law," and the conjunction of light, word, and creation cannot help but recall the biblical Genesis as well. In the rest of the poem, the image of a sudden advent of light coalesces into the same image that Humboldt uses as an example of synthetic positing in language, and Coleridge as an instance of action coinciding with existence: the image of lightning. It is Hölderlin's central symbol in this text for that which descends from heaven to summon the poet—inspiration, Zeus's thunderbolt, deified nature, the holy word.

In their openness to Romantic and contemporary formulations of performativity, the lines from "Wie wenn am Feiertage..." can stand as an emblem for one aspect of Hölderlin's writing that is to be examined in

---

[1] Kirchner proposes, for instance, that the stanza contains an allusion to the decisive victory of Napoleon—who held an enduring fascination for Hölderlin—at Marengo in June 1800 ("Hölderlins Entwurf" 66).

this chapter. At issue here is the paradoxical way utterance is generated by subjectivity, at the same time that subjectivity is generated by utterance—so that the identity of the speaker and the effect of speech somehow depend on one another. But this aspect of Hölderlin's poetry is complemented by an awareness of what words do in an *intersubjective* sphere, or how they determine and alter relationships between speakers. At one extreme, Hölderlin examines the way institutional utterances, such as the vow to a secret brotherhood or excommunication from a society, impose themselves on personal relationships; but, typically for a Romantic thinker, his sense of the effects of words in social contexts is rooted in a phenomenological understanding of the way language constructs relationships between mind and world in the first place.

I will examine these interrelationships of cognition and communication in the language of several works of Hölderlin's "maturity"—that is, the intensely productive decade preceding his institutionalization in 1806. Performative principles can, to begin with, generate a new reading of Hölderlin's novel *Hyperion, oder der Eremit in Griechenland* (Hyperion, or the hermit in Greece) as the tragedy of a protagonist caught between ineffective words on the one hand, and overly rigid social speech acts on the other, who therefore fails to fulfil his own capacity for felicitous utterance. *Der Tod des Empedokles* (The death of Empedokles)— which, as a drama, intrinsically foregrounds verbal action—illustrates how subjective and intersubjective dimensions of utterance overlap and conflict in the confrontation between the philosopher Empedokles and the community of Agrigentum. As analogues for the poet, both Hyperion and Empedokles represent him as a speaking subject in a social context, but one whose speech acts never quite bring subjective and intersubjective worlds into alignment. The model of the poet as a subject speaking to specific addressees then needs to be carried over into a reading of Hölderlin's poetry, which, like the linguistic philosophy of his contemporaries Humboldt, Herder, Schleiermacher, and Coleridge, is constructed on dialogic principles. Tracing the development of these principles shows that intersubjective scenes of discourse are crucial to the reading of his major hymns, for their illocutionary force forms a vital part of their vision of a new discursive community.

'HYPERION': THE FAILURE
OF PERFORMATIVE UTTERANCE

Hölderlin's epistolary novel, published in two parts in 1797 and 1799, appears at first to deny the power of language altogether. Its first-person narrator, the young Greek Hyperion, repeatedly laments the failure of his own words to have an effect, and indeed the futility of language in general; these failures of the word are embedded in the other failures he experiences, as he loses, in turn, his mentor, his father, his beloved, and his best friend. The story, which Hyperion relates in a series of letters to his German friend Bellarmin, begins with Hyperion's idyllic upbringing with his mentor Adamas. This episode ends in grief when Adamas departs for the depths of Asia. Hyperion himself moves to Smyrna and begins a close friendship with the revolutionary fighter Alabanda, which also ends unhappily when the two quarrel and part. He then takes up an invitation to visit the island of Kalaurea, where he meets Diotima; the two fall deeply in love and become engaged. Driven to try to aid his people, Hyperion rejoins Alabanda and takes up arms in the war against the Turks, but undergoes a spiritual crisis when he is disillusioned by the reality of human behavior in battle. Diotima, left behind on her island, sickens and dies; Alabanda, revealing that for Hyperion's sake he has broken his oath to a secret society, departs, presumably to be killed for his treachery. At the end of the second part of the novel, Hyperion undertakes a journey to Germany but is immediately disillusioned by the soulless behavior of its people, and finds his only remaining consolation in an experience of nature in the springtime.

The majority of references to speech in the novel are skeptical ones.[2] Hyperion deplores the impotence of language and only rarely acknowledges any aspect of its power. "I would like to be able to speak," he laments (StA 3: 50), but "words, like snowflakes, are useless, and only

[2] Important secondary texts for the following discussion are Haberer's studies of speech and discourse in Hölderlin, particularly *Sprechen, Schweigen, Schauen. Rede und Blick in Hölderlins "Der Tod des Empedokles" und "Hyperion"* (which also provides a comprehensive review of Hölderlin scholarship as it concerns the topics of language and discourse). Haberer demonstrates that Hyperion does not simply condemn "speaking" in favor of "not speaking" (schweigen), as is sometimes assumed; rather, the narrator alternates between an "almost childish faith in the power of the word" and a rejection of it (*Sprechen, Schweigen, Schauen* 255). Other characters, too, have both positive and negative experiences of speech: Diotima begins as the silent one (die Schweigende) but becomes an enthusiastic speaker as she approaches her death, while Alabanda develops in the opposite direction. Haberer aims to place new emphasis on the social context of discourse in Hölderlin's drama and his novel, but she relies primarily on traditions of myth, ritual, and superstition to define verbal acts, and consequently focuses on the magical power of the word (Sprachmagie) rather than the illocutionary force that words acquire within specific discursive contexts. My reading agrees with Haberer's in many respects, but differs in setting *Hyperion* and *Der Tod des Empedokles* in the context of speech-act theory and Romantic philosophy of language.

cloud the air" (*StA* 3: 95); "language is a great superfluity" (*StA* 3: 118).[3] But the first-person narrative form allows us, and indeed requires us, to contextualize these deprecations of language that appear in Hyperion's letters by relating them to his experience and development. Hyperion may be regarded as a protagonist who senses that it lies within his reach to harness the efficacy of language, but whose tragedy is precisely that he fails to take up the role of one whose words are effective in changing his world. He might have become, we learn, a teacher or a poet; this is the role that Diotima represents to him in the central scene of the novel, when they discuss their future and the future of Greece during a visit to the pre-eminent site of Greece's past, the Acropolis. At that moment Hyperion declares, using explicit performatives, his readiness to take up the role of a public speaker. But this mission requires a form of language that combines the power of individual creativity with the validating response of a community; and, although the novel seems to offer examples of such hybrid speech acts, Hyperion fails to place his faith in them. The second volume records his attempts to channel his energy toward violent physical action rather than verbal action, and chronicles the losses that result. However, the unexpected mitigation of Hyperion's crisis in the last letter represents a semi-recovery of the performative, as his final utterance points to the way language might restore dialogic relationships between self and Other.

The type of language to which Hyperion does accord world-altering power is the magical word, conceived of either as a magic formula or as a mystical act of naming. Under certain circumstances Hyperion is able to participate in epiphanic scenes of naming, or else to discover a soul-changing experience in expressive, creative, individual utterance. The possibility of such a word first arises in the context of Hyperion's conversations with Adamas, to whom Hyperion is alluding when he describes the regenerative and educative power of a "valiant man's" word:

> A friendly word from the heart of a valiant man, a smile in which the consuming glory of the spirit lies concealed, is little and much, like a magical password that conceals death and life in its simple syllable; it is like spiritual water that springs from the depths of the mountains, and conveys to us the secret strength of the earth in its crystal droplet. (*StA* 3: 12)

[3]Haberer calls attention to the important distinctions between these negative allusions to speech, differentiating between unwillingness to speak, inability to speak, and prohibitions against speaking (*Sprechen, Schweigen, Schauen* 196–203 and 265–70).

But this early characterization of the word as restorative water is undercut by later passages that figure the word negatively in terms of other natural elements: as snowflakes that cloud the air (*StA* 3: 95), as fire that flares up and is gone (*StA* 3: 159), or as something that only the winds hear (*StA* 3: 151). The problem with the magical word, and with the spiritual language that Adamas's teaching seems to represent, is that there is no guarantee for its effectiveness. As soon as Hyperion leaves his study of nature and ancient culture with Adamas, and enters the arena of political action with his friend Alabanda, the magical word has to be rejected, as if it required an uptake that it will not find among a hostile public. With Alabanda Hyperion discusses grandiose plans for the future, but not, he assures Bellarmin, as if they think to bring them about through magical formulas—"not as if we had, in an unmanly way, created our world as with a magic word, and, like inexperienced children, not counted on any resistance; Alabanda was too sensible and too valiant for that" (*StA* 3: 27). The rejection of the magical performative is quite precise. Characterized in the context of Adamas's instruction as the word spoken by a *tapfern Mann* or "valiant man," it is now abandoned as unmanly and childish, and Alabanda is too *tapfer* to use it. Later, Hyperion berates himself for relying on words that are unable to achieve what Alabanda achieves through pure action: "you want to make do with words, and with magic formulas you conjure the world?" (*StA* 3: 95). Hyperion's rejection of magical words, and the spiritual language of his philosophical mentor, is a first indication of his inability to conceive of an effective role for speech acts in the sociopolitical world.

An alternative model for performative utterance, which has a more intrinsic social dimension, is the act of naming as a recognition of the Other and the establishment of a relationship with him or her. Brigitte Haberer shows how Hyperion's relationship with Diotima comes about in and as a few crucial acts of naming, of which the most important is the climactic scene where they declare their love for one another (*Sprechen, Schweigen, Schauen* 203–11). This declaration apparently consists solely of uttering one another's names, since no other conversation is possible:

> O, my Hyperion! a voice now called to me; I leapt to add, "my Diotima, O my Diotima!" Beyond this I had no word and no breath, no consciousness....
> Here there is a gap in my existence. I died, and as I awoke, I lay on the heavenly maiden's breast. (*StA* 3: 72)

Naming and utterance are implicated here in existence (Daseyn) itself. Recognizing the existence of the Other by uttering her name causes a figurative death, but this is followed by restoration to a fuller life. In key scenes of the novel, as Haberer notes, alterity and existence are brought together by an emphatic utterance of the phrase *du bist* 'you are' (*Sprechen, Schweigen, Schauen* 207–11). Diotima recalls this same moment of mutual naming in her letter to Hyperion as a scene of discourse in which both partners desperately seek affirmation of the existence of the You: "bist dus? bist du es wirklich?" (*StA* 3: 110). Exactly the same formula marks the reunion of Hyperion with Alabanda, as the latter, unable to distinguish Hyperion in the dusk but recognizing his voice, calls out, "bist du's?" (*StA* 3: 106).

Both Hyperion and Diotima echo these utterances in relation to elements of nature, calling them by name and addressing them as *du*—thereby using, as Humboldt would say, the freedom of the mind to select an element of the world, invest it with a subjectivity like the mind's own, and set it over against the mind in a scene of co-operative exchange (*GS* 6: 26). But this mode of conversation has positive and negative enactments. During the happy days of their betrothal, Diotima, like Milton's Eve in *Paradise Lost*, uses her intimate relationship with nature to give new and better names to the flowers in her garden: "She named them all by name, and out of love for them created new, more beautiful names, and she knew exactly the merriest time of each one's life" (*StA* 3: 56). Diotima and Hyperion together use the metaphorical language of poets to rename earth and heaven for themselves: "We called the earth one of the flowers of heaven, and called heaven the infinite garden of life" (*StA* 3: 54). But Hyperion also characterizes his grief and loss precisely as an inability to address nature as *du*, and as an passive echoing of its conventional names: "Now I no longer said to the flower, you are my sister! and to the springs, we are of one race! Now I gave each thing its name loyally, like an echo" (*StA* 3: 42). Hyperion's reference here to the elements of nature as things that keep their names marks his lapse into thinking of nature in a third-person mode, as the object conceived of as absent from the scene of discourse.

But the act of creative naming still provides no reliable basis for a performative that will function in a social context beyond one-to-one dialogue. Instead, as a sharp contrast to the intimacy of his relationship with Diotima, Hyperion experiences the alienation brought about by institutionalized speech acts that relate human beings to one another in rigid, unfeeling ways. Alabanda's oath to the *Bund der Nemesis* or "Nemesis Band" may be described as the paradigm of a destructive, institutionalized speech act; he relates how he made over his "blood and soul" to the *Bund* in a "solemn" or "ceremonial" (feierlich) procedure (*StA* 3: 139). The oath is, in its essence, a proleptic and convention-bound performative, in which the oath-swearer commits him- or herself with respect to future behavior by the utterance of a set form of words; the oath to a secret brotherhood, which reinforces linguistic conventions with rituals and prohibitions, is even more so. In *Hyperion*, the rigid conventionality of this speech act is specifically opposed to feeling, passionate friendship, and the freedom to choose with whom one will converse. "For the sake of my loved one I broke my vow," Alabanda relates, narrating how his love for Hyperion left him no choice but to break with his society brothers (*StA* 3: 139). If the words of Adamas, and Diotima's acts of naming, are motivated by love and spiritual autonomy—but apparently have no basis for effectiveness in a wider social context—Alabanda's oath is caught in the opposite bind. It is *overly* effective in shaping the social order, to the extent that its power cannot be suspended. Alabanda departs from Hyperion to return to the *Bund* in the expectation of being killed for his treachery; his oath disallows behavior based on sentiment and freedom.

Two events in Hyperion's story do, however, provide a model for utterance that combines individual creativity with convention, and brings subjective identity into harmony with intersubjective relations. The climax of Hyperion's experience with Adamas occurs when the two climb Mount Cynthus on Delos, the site of an ancient festival in honor of the sun-god, and Adamas symbolically dedicates his pupil to the rising sun:

> Now he arose in his eternal youth, the ancient sun-god; contented and effortless, as always, the immortal Titan with his own thousand joys soared upwards, and smiled down on his desolate land, on his temples and his pillars which fate had thrown down before him like withered rose petals that a child thoughtlessly tore from the bush in passing, and scattered on the ground.
>
> Be like him! Adamas called to me; seizing me by the hand, he held it toward the god, and it seemed to me that the morning breezes carried us off with them and brought us into the train of the holy being, who now mounted to the summit of heaven, benevolent and great, and filled the world and us wonderfully with his power and his spirit. (*StA* 3: 15–16)

Since the unnamed sun-god is, in fact, the god Hyperion, Adamas's exhortation to his pupil to "Be like him!," accompanied by a ceremonial raising of the hand toward the sun, constitutes a kind of baptism. As such, it combines semi-conventional and completely private elements. "Conventional" are the authority Adamas exercises as Hyperion's elder and mentor, the setting of the episode in a ritually significant location (i.e., on a mountaintop, and at the site of a traditional festival), and the use of an explicit performative, "Be like him"—which could, in this context, be either a command or an identity-altering declaration. Yet the words spoken by Adamas do not correspond to any prescribed formula, nor does he hold any official position that would authorize him to perform a ritual of baptism. Rather, his motivation for teaching Hyperion and for performing the symbolic baptism is love and spontaneous choice.

The immediate effect of Adamas's utterance is spectacular: Hyperion experiences an ecstatic exhilaration, as if he were in fact being drawn through the heavens with the god whose name he bears. Even in retrospect, he can be inspired by Adamas's words to reflect on the god-like potential of the human soul. Yet as he recounts the experience to Bellarmin, Hyperion also locates it in a context of grief and loss. The next words of Adamas that he recalls are "you will be lonely," for at this moment Adamas announces his intended departure (*StA* 3: 16). Even the possibility of recollecting the enthusiastic experience is threatened by the burdensome present, that counters the memory of Adamas's performative utterance with an unspecified curse: "Alas! not even a lovely dream can thrive under the curse that weighs down on us" (*StA* 3: 15).

Hyperion's quasi-baptism at the beginning of the first volume has a counterpart at the beginning of the second volume: the formal betrothal or quasi-marriage he and Diotima celebrate on the evening before Hyperion's departure for battle. This is the other relationship the novel refers to as a "Bund" (*StA* 3: 100), which suggests that it also needs to be seen as a redemptive counterpart to the *Bund der Nemesis* and Alabanda's oath. Hyperion asks Diotima's mother to bless and sanctify their union, with their assembled friends as witnesses, in anticipation of their official marriage when he returns. The couple proceeds to kneel before her mother and each of them utters a kind of marriage vow—addressed neither to the other nor to God, but to nature:

> Long, O nature, I called out, has our life been one with you; and youthful as heaven, like you and all your gods, is our own world, through love.
> We strolled in your groves, Diotima continued, and were like you; we sat by your springs, and were like you; we went there over the hills, with your children, the stars—like you. (*StA* 3: 101)

Following these testimonials, which are formulaic in rhetorical structure yet spontaneous in sentiment, Diotima's mother and the assembled companions are called on to witness that their love is "holy and eternal" like nature itself:

> I am a witness, said her mother.
> We are witnesses, called the others. (*StA* 3: 101)

The scene—which imitates a marriage ceremony, but uses non-conventional formulas and relies on an authority that is not derived from any state or religious institution—matches quite exactly one of the possible "misfires" Austin describes for the speech act of marrying. A "misapplication" of the performative occurs when it is a non-ordained mother, and not a priest, who is conducting the ceremony (Austin 15–16). Clearly it is not the invalidity of these utterances that is being highlighted in *Hyperion*, though, but rather the meaningfulness they acquire precisely from the fact that the conventions are being deformed. Diotima's mother is invested with the power to bless the couple's union, and the friends to witness it, by the love and trust that subsist among them. Here the freedom that is missing from Alabanda's institutionalized vow extends to a freedom to choose and re-form social conventions. The ceremony that results is a hybrid of public, institutional forms (the vow, the act of witnessing) and the I-You dialogue with nature that the novel values, but otherwise locates outside a social context. The quasi-marriage of Hyperion and Diotima also represents a marriage of two types of performative: the social and the subjective speech act.

But the betrothal scene has a tragic coda, in which one further utterance affirms the link between speech and being, and demonstrates that the performative can at least figuratively kill:

> Now there were no words left for us. I felt my heart at its limit; I felt ready for the parting. I will leave now, dear friends, I said—and life fled from all their faces. Diotima stood there like a marble statue, and I could feel her hand die in mine. I had killed everything around me, I was alone and dizzy in the face of the limitless stillness, where my brimming life no longer found anything to hold on to. (*StA* 3: 101)

A moment after Diotima's mother has pronounced their love eternal, Hyperion's utterance "I will leave now" re-introduces temporality with the deictic "now," re-introduces the autonomy of the I after it has supposedly been dissolved within the I-You-We relationship of the lovers and nature—and it kills all around it. In contrast to the active uptake that the lovers' vows found among their assembled friends, Hyperion's word meets with silence. His utterance is clearly effective, but the effect is mortal: if the betrothal scene is, to complicate Austin, a *felicitous misfire*, then Hyperion's utterance finds its mark. His reassertion of an independent subjectivity already counts as a kind of departure from the union, and the utterance figuratively kills Diotima just as his actual departure will lead to her actual death. It is, according to Hölderlin's use of the term in the annotations to his translation of *Antigone*, a *tödtlichfaktisches Wort*—a fatally factual word (*StA* 5: 269–70).

The baptism scene and, even more, the betrothal scene, suggest models for speech acts that locate the self in the world, relating it to others and to nature in an act of spontaneous choice, yet also take account of mechanisms of verbal interaction within a community. But the potential of this type of performative is called into question at the midpoint of the novel, in the scene that is critical for Hyperion's development. At the end of the first volume, he, Diotima, and some of their companions visit the Acropolis, where Hyperion is moved to make a long speech on the Greek past, on art, philosophy, reason, love, and the ideal of *hen diapheron eauto* ("the one differentiated within itself") as the basis for spiritual and social order. Joining the intellectual debate, Diotima raises it to a meta-level by making Hyperion's discourse itself the subject of her arguments. She urges him to give his people what he has to give—his intellect, his words—and predicts that he will become "an educator of our people" and "a great man." Hyperion is inspired by his own rhetoric and hers to proclaim—in the spirit of other Romantic revolutionary declarations such as Blake's "Empire shall be no more!"—the inauguration of a new world-order:

> Let it be different from the ground up! Let the new world spring up from the roots of humanity! Let a new deity reign over them, a new future open up before them.
> In the workshop, in the houses, in the assemblies, in the temples, let it be different everywhere! (*StA* 3: 89)

This speech act is a pivotal point for the forces that determine Hyperion's fate and that of his people. If these declarations are to be effective, they must secure the uptake not only of Diotima and his other friends (who have, ironically and ominously, left the couple alone, preferring to converse with two British antiquarians), but also of the Greek people in general. Yet the people must first be brought to the point where they can conceptualize a new world-order in harmony with nature and culture, which can only happen through the instruction that Hyperion, as educator, would provide. If the people legitimate his proclamation of a new order, he will be their educator and a great man; if he educates them successfully, they will legitimate his proclamation of a new order. This is the paradox of the performative, always particularly acute in the language of Romanticism, where speech acts create the conditions of their own possibility.

The inability to accept the challenge posed by this paradox is Hyperion's tragedy. No sooner has he uttered his declaration than he begins to doubt its legitimacy. When Diotima tells him he will have to spend three to four years traveling and studying before he can take up his vocation, he is no less eager, yet he already begins to read this delay in the fulfilment of his declaration as a fatal dehiscence of word from deed and decision from action: "Can there be contentment between the resolution and the act?" Diotima must reassure him that he is the kind of speaker whose words *are* acts: "It is the repose of the hero, said Diotima; there are resolutions that, like the words of the gods, are command and fulfilment at once—and such is yours" (*StA* 3: 89).

But Hyperion, doubting, chooses to subordinate language to immediate, physical, and violent action, by rejoining Alabanda and leaguing himself with the Russians in their battle against the Turks. He attempts to transpose his declaration of a new world-order into the context of armed rebellion, insisting to Alabanda, "everything must be rejuvenated, it must be different from the ground up" (*StA* 3: 111). The altered form of this utterance is revealing: no longer a declaration ("Let it be different from the ground up!"), it is now a statement ("It must be different from the ground up") used in a frenzied exhortation to action, but already with an anticipation of despair. The context Hyperion has chosen, in which words are used to command and to rouse to rebellion, is not on par with his declaration of a new world to an enlightened community, his baptism by Adamas, or his vows to Diotima and nature—profounder and more complex performatives that invoke the very spirit of speaker and addressee and seek to alter their conceptual horizon. Abandoning the mission to which he had committed himself while with Diotima, he figures his earlier utterances as a now broken promise: "Alas! I promised you Greece, and now you receive only a lament for it" (*StA* 3: 118).

Two redemptive moments remain. The first lies in the form of the novel itself, and the implications, analyzed by Lawrence Ryan and Friedbert Aspetsberger, of Hyperion's recollecting his experience and repeating it in language from a standpoint at the end of the process of development that he is describing. In the first paragraphs of the novel Hölderlin laments his original decision in favor of physical action: "Oh, had I never acted! how much richer would I be in hope!" (*StA* 3: 8). But in writing the letters to Bellarmin he finally does substitute a linguistic engagement with experience for material intervention. "Language is [Hyperion's] link to Bellarmin and to the transformation of the world into a better future," Aspetsberger writes, stressing the reflective and communicative function of language in Hyperion's letters—although he adds that the letters thereby also expose the inability of language to express immediate experience (158–60). Haberer summarizes the significance of the novel's epistolary and recollective form for a discourse-centered reading: "Only *as* language do the experiences of the past, which have after all led to the linguistic competence that becomes evident in the writing of the letters, gain their meaning for the formation of identity" ("Zwischen Sprachmagie und Schweigen" 133).

The second redemptive moment occurs in the enigmatic ending of the novel. Hyperion ends his letters still denouncing the "empty words" of society in general (StA 3: 159). But in the same breath he ironically reaffirms the role of language in performing identity and bringing at least private, intersubjective relationships into being. Hyperion relates how, surrounded by the charms of nature on a spring day, he finds his way once again to a dialogic recognition of the Other. Echoing the forms of speech that, in this novel, characterize intimate conversation, Hyperion once again addresses the sun and the breezes as "you" and calls them his brothers, then gives voice to his intense desire for Diotima: "Diotima, I called, where are you, oh where are you?" (StA 3: 158). Against all expectation, his question is answered; he seems to hear the dead Diotima's voice in the natural surroundings, a "dear word from a sacred mouth" (StA 3: 159).

Hyperion's response to this experience, a passage of lyrical prose with which the novel ends, confirms the impression that his utterance itself is here re-establishing relationships and even calling Diotima back into existence:

> We too, we too are not parted, Diotima, and the tears shed over you do not comprehend it. We are living tones, we harmonize in your melodious sound, O Nature! who may tear that asunder? who may part the lovers?
>
> O soul! soul! loveliness of the world! you indestructible one! you delightful one! with your eternal youth! *you are*; what then is death and all the woe of humankind?
>
> (Auch wir, auch wir sind nicht geschieden, Diotima, und die Thränen um dich verstehen es nicht. Lebendige Töne sind wir, stimmen zusammen in deinem Wohllaut, Natur! wer reißt den? wer mag die Liebenden scheiden?—
>
> O Seele! Seele! Schönheit der Welt! du unzerstörbare! du entzükende! mit deiner ewigen Jugend! *du bist*; was ist denn der Tod und alles Wehe der Menschen?) (StA 3: 159; italics added)

These dramatic apostrophes reaffirm the illocutionary effect of the vows that Hyperion and Diotima exchanged with each other and with nature; despite the death of Diotima and his own grief, Hyperion affirms that the union of lover, beloved, and nature is undissolved. But beyond alluding to this unity, Hyperion performs it. Describing the united entities as voices in harmony with one another, Hyperion loses his voice in theirs, so that the referential structure of his language begins to dissolve. Who or what is the referent of *du unzerstörbare* 'you indestructible one' and *du entzükende* 'you delightful one'? "Soul" and "loveliness of the world" are both possible antecedents, but the ultimate referent could equally well be nature or Diotima. The ambiguity is especially marked in German, since the feminine epithets imply a feminine referent, which could be any of *Seele, Schönheit, Natur,* or *Diotima*: suddenly these terms are spiritually as well as grammatically indistinguishable. To this no-longer-differentiated addressee Hyperion addresses the words that resonate with his previous, intimate exchanges with Diotima, Alabanda, and elements of nature: *du bist*. More than a recognition of the Other, this is a recognition that the self is merged with the Other; and the ability to declare "you are" in this absolute way[4] marks the recovery of some sense of self beyond loss and disillusion. If Hyperion fails to discover a socially or politically effective form of expression, he at least ends by reaffirming, more strongly than before, the role of language in placing the self phenomenologically and dialogically in the world.

Only through creative utterance arising from individual will, one might conclude from a reading of Hölderlin's novel, can private feeling and intellect modify the otherwise rigid and even tyrannical forms of social life; but individual utterance always runs the risk of misfiring. Even the privileged performatives in the novel—the symbolic baptism, the exchange of vows, and the declaration at the Acropolis—are immediately followed by departure and loss, as if to indicate their ultimate failure to establish a stable discursive community. Innovative speech acts require the uptake of addressees, but must themselves establish the conditions under which that uptake can be given, or the conditions within which they count as meaningful social actions. Hyperion's tragedy is that he cannot risk, trust, negotiate, or perhaps even understand his own capacity for performative utterance, and is trapped in or discouraged by its paradoxes. Such a reading ascribes to Hyperion himself most of the responsibility for his own misfortune—mitigated, perhaps, by the fact that the paradoxes that baffle him are real and persistent properties of expressive utterance in a political world.

[4] Hamlin comments, in the course of a detailed reading of the final pages of *Hyperion*: "Where else does Hölderlin use such an absolute sense of the verb 'to be'? It appears to affirm an existential condition beyond all human limits, beyond all mortal time" (*Hermeneutics of Form* 155).

'DER TOD DES EMPEDOKLES': UTTERANCE,
UPTAKE, AND IDENTITY

In contrast to *Hyperion*, a number of obvious and general reasons could be offered for regarding Hölderlin's uncompleted drama, which exists in several drafts dating from the late 1790s, as a play of speech acts. The word "word" appears in it with obsessive frequency, often because characters are explicitly pondering the effects of language on others or on themselves. The drama contains remarkably little action, and the main "events" that do occur are either verbal utterances or responses to utterances. One crucial speech act takes place before the text begins: the philosopher Empedokles has apparently committed an act of blasphemy in declaring himself equal to the gods. This causes Hermokrates, priest of the town of Agrigentum, to curse Empedokles by banning him from communication with any of the townspeople. The curse brings about the only real movement in the drama, Empedokles' wandering from Agrigentum to Mount Etna, but it also generates other responses in the form of further speech acts. Empedokles' young disciple Pausanias immediately pronounces a blessing on his master in an attempt to mitigate the priest's curse, while Empedokles himself angrily pronounces a counter-curse on the townspeople. At the end of the drama, once a delegation of citizens has come to ask forgiveness of Empedokles and bring him back to the town, the curses of both Hermokrates and Empedokles are annulled by Empedokles' blessing on the people, just before he departs from them again to seek reconciliation with nature and the gods by a suicidal leap into the volcano of Etna.

Not only does *Der Tod des Empedokles* operate primarily through verbal action, but it thematizes the issue of when and how speech acts become effective. The characters need to address these questions because the drama presents a situation in which subjective and intersubjective contexts for performative utterance collide. *Der Tod des Empedokles* shows how speech acts operate within a system of societal conventions and structures of authority, but also how expressions of individual will and creativity can cut across and deform those structures. By setting extremely individualistic, expressive, or phenomenological utterances against extremely conventional, institutional, or socially authoritative ones, the drama challenges us to consider the role of discourse in generating both subjective identity and the intersubjective sphere.

These two frames of reference, the subjective and the public, coalesce around Empedokles' initial, self-deifying pronouncement. Although it resonates throughout the drama, the reader never encounters this utterance directly. Rather, it is alluded to at length in a dialogue between the priest Hermokrates and Kritias, the political ruler or Archon of Agrigentum, and it is recalled (although carefully not repeated) in Empedokles' own monologues and his dialogues with Pausanias. Hermokrates claims twice that Empedokles called himself a god, and stresses that this utterance occurred in a public context:

> HERMOKRATES. For the gods have taken his strength from him, since the day that the intoxicated man called himself a god before all the people.
>
> > (Denn es haben
> > Die Götter seine Kraft von ihm genommen,
> > Seit jenem Tage, da der trunkne Mann
> > Vor allem Volk sich einen Gott genannt.)
> > (185-88)[5]
>
> HERMOKRATES. Madman! did you imagine that they would rejoice with you, when you recently called yourself a god before them?
>
> > (Verruchter! wähntest du,
> > Sie müßtens nachfrohlokken, da du jüngst
> > Vor ihnen einen Gott dich selbst genannt?)
> > (614-16)

Hermokrates, whose own power as a priest depends on sociopolitical institutions and their discursive conventions, necessarily associates the transgressive aspect of Empedokles' words with their function as a public utterance.[6] Indeed, he cannot interpret Empedokles' speech act otherwise than as an attempted play for political power:

> HERMOKRATES. Then you would have ruled in Agrigentum, a sole, allpowerful tyrant, and yours, yours alone would have been the good people and this lovely land.
>
> > (Dann hättest du geherrscht in Agrigent,
> > Ein einziger allmächtiger Tyrann
> > Und dein gewesen wäre, dein allein
> > Das gute Volk und dieses schöne Land.)
> > (617-20)

---

[5]Unless otherwise identified, quotations from *Der Tod des Empedokles* are drawn from the "Erste Fassung" as printed in volume 4 of *StA*, and are identified by line number. Variants in the second draft that have a significant bearing on the points under discussion are taken account of in the notes.

[6]In the second draft of the drama, which Haberer analyzes in detail, Hermokrates accuses Empedokles of a different transgression, for which the public context is still more of a determining factor: he intimates that Empedokles has betrayed holy secrets to the lay people (Haberer, *Sprechen, Schweigen, Schauen* 73-81).

But in performing his self-deifying declaration, according to Hermokrates, Empedokles misread the conventions. His proclamation of himself as god, or as tyrant, does not win uptake from the people: they maintain only a shocked silence (Sie schwiegen nur; erschroken standen sie [621]). As the priest sees it, Empedokles' attempt to overturn the existing power structure is doomed because he underestimates the tenacity of the rules about permitted and forbidden speech. Empedokles' shocking declaration does not leave a dent in the discursive conventions, even if, as both Hermokrates and Kritias admit elsewhere, he has succeeded in overturning other legal and social conventions in Agrigentum:

> KRITIAS. The people are drunk, as he himself is. They listen to no law, no urgency and no judge; traditions are, like peaceful shores, inundated by unfathomable torrents.
>
>> (Das Volk ist trunken, wie er selber ist.
>> Sie hören kein Gesez, und keine Noth
>> Und keinen Richter; die Gebräuche sind
>> Von unverständlichem Gebrause gleich
>> Den friedlichen Gestaden überschwemmt.)
>> (189–93)
>
> HERMOKRATES. Law, and art, and custom, and holy legends, and whatever came to maturity in good time before him—that he stirs up, and he cannot bear to have joy and peace among the living.
>
>> (Gesez und Kunst und Sitt und heilge Sage
>> Und was vor ihm in guter Zeit gereift
>> Das stört er auf und Lust und Frieden kann
>> Er nimmer dulden bei den Lebenden.)
>> (231–34)

Empedokles himself confirms that he once claimed to be a god, or mightier than the gods: "I alone was God, and proclaimed it in brazen pride" (ich allein/War Gott, und sprachs im frechen Stolz heraus [482–83]). But he places the utterance in a subjective context. As far as he is concerned, the transgression was not political but spiritual, since through his utterance he shattered the unity between himself and a deified nature. Yet the accounts of Empedokles and Hermokrates agree on one point: that semantically, and in all likelihood grammatically, Empedokles' transgressive words were an "I am" utterance: "I am a god," he presumably said, or "I am equal to the gods." This formulation resonates not only with the "I am" utterances of Yahweh in the Hebrew and Jesus in the Christian Scriptures, but also with Hölderlin's philosophical context and Romantic philosophy of language. Empedokles sets himself up as something like a Fichtean absolute I, or the expanded individual ego as which the Romantics often understood the Fichtean I.[7] His utterance symbolically places him in the position of a first principle to which all other entities are related as objects, their existence dependent on his act of self-positing—which may be a way of interpreting Hermokrates' statement that Empedokles claimed the gods came into existence through his word (225). The fact that this act of self-positing is represented as a specific utterance fits with the new emphasis placed on speech acts by Romantic linguists like Humboldt, who claim that subject-positions are created by acts of utterance, since the use of pronouns determines and alters the relationship between speaker and world.

By contrast, Empedokles represents his former state of unity with nature and the gods in terms of an act of *Erkenntnis* or recognition in which he addressed natural objects, such as the light of heaven, as "you": "Then I knew you, then I called out: you live" (Da kannt' ich dich, da rief ich es: du lebst [384]). For Humboldt, and for first-generation Romantics like Friedrich Schlegel and Novalis, addressing nature as You involves bringing it into the sphere of co-operative exchange by recognizing it as another subject equal to and co-original with oneself. But in calling himself a god, Empedokles recalls in his opening monologue, he "thought [only] of himself" (dachtst du/An dich [339–40]). The self-reflexive act that Fichtean philosophy sees as the birth of existence and knowledge here represents the death of Empedokles' *Erkenntnis* and oneness with nature. Pausanias, overhearing Empedokles' self-recriminations without distinguishing the words, remarks on the "unfamiliar deathly tone" (der fremde Todeston [365]) that now colors his speech. In terms of the sequence of speech acts in the drama, whereby Empedokles' self-deification calls forth Hermokrates' curse and the chain of responses that culminates in Empedokles' resolution to commit suicide, the original self-deifying utterance is another *tödtlichfaktisches* or "fatally factual" word: it not only represents the death of Empedokles' spiritual unity, but triggers his actual death.

Empedokles' "I am" utterance, then, has the illocutionary effect of altering his position in relation to nature, and the perlocutionary effect of making him feel spiritually alienated from his gods. And, even if the point of the self-deifying utterance was to set Empedokles apart from the intersubjective sphere in which ordinary humans interact with one another, it has further ramifications in precisely that sphere. In the context of the conventions for public discourse, Empedokles' illocution counts

---

[7]For a detailed account of Hölderlin's response to Fichte, especially in relation to the proposition "I am I," see Henrich 485–515.

as an act of blasphemy. As such, it incurs the perlocutionary effect of angering Hermokrates and the citizens of Agrigentum. Because the effect of the utterance is to bifurcate Empedokles' spiritual and social identity, and because it sets him in a new, distanced relation to nature as a world of objects, one might say (invoking Habermasian terms) that Empedokles' speech act *opens up the division between subjective, intersubjective, and objective spheres*. It is, in this sense, a truly originary utterance that is appropriately never voiced in the drama itself, but is present only in the responses, paraphrases, and allusions it elicits.

Positing that Empedokles' utterance had this form and this effect makes the question of identity, and how it is shaped by language, central to the drama. Empedokles' subjective identity and his social identity are altered by the act of declaring publicly "I am [a god]," and the question of who he is—or, rather, who he was and who he has now become—is repeatedly posed by Empedokles himself and by his interlocutors. In his first dialogue with Pausanias, he recollects his former existence as a "Glüklicher" (409), the blessed intimate of nature and the gods, but immediately questions, "Am I still as I was?" (Bin ich es noch? [416]), and then laments, "I am no longer" (ich bin/Es nimmer [428–29]), even as Pausanias tries in vain to reassure him, "You are that still, as sure as you ever were" (Du bist es noch, so wahr du es gewesen [430]). Hermokrates, preparing to pronounce his curse on Empedokles, challenges him to repeat his self-deifying claim before the people once more, by urging them to ask him who he is (Ihr möget nur/Ihn selber fragen, wer er sei [546–47]).

Once Empedokles' attempted self-deification opens up a gap between the way he sees himself (as an alienated sensibility) and the way the public sees him (as a blasphemer), his subjective and intersubjective identities develop separately over the course of the drama. Hermokrates, the champion of sociopolitical roles and institutional speech acts, tries to impose on Empedokles a purely intersubjective identity by altering the way others see him. He appears to succeed in doing so, as Empedokles, driven out of the city, is identified even by a peasant in the mountainous wilderness as the one marked by a priestly curse: "I know you. Beware! That is the cursed one of Agrigentum" (Ich kenn euch. Wehe! das ist der Verfluchte/Von Agrigent [1136–37]). The ability of utterances to alter public identity is a function of the uptake they elicit from an audience—and uptake, or the question of how utterances acquire validity in an interpersonal context, is one of the central issues in *Der Tod des Empedokles*. A key phrase in the drama is *der Sinn des Volk*—the mind of the people, the collective will, or even public opinion. It is the object on which public speech acts work, but also the *means by which* they work, and the drama contains a number of discussions about how the mind of the people determines the effectiveness of speech.

Since Hermokrates' sociopolitical authority can—as the drama vividly demonstrates—be revoked if the public refuses its consent, he shows the liveliest concern for the *Sinn des Volk*. His first dialogue with Kritias reveals their shared interest in the question of whose words, Hermokrates' or Empedokles', will win uptake from the public. Kritias poses, almost formulaically, three questions to test the possibility that the curse Hermokrates plans to pronounce on Empedokles will misfire:

> KRITIAS. But if the bold man should master the weak populace—don't you fear for me and for yourself and for your gods?
> HERMOKRATES. The priest's word will break the bold spirit.
> KRITIAS. And, when the one they have loved for so long suffers shamefully under the holy curse, will they really drive him out of his gardens, where he likes to live, and out of his native city?
> HERMOKRATES. Who may tolerate in the land the mortal whom the well-deserved curse has marked?
> KRITIAS. But if you yourself appear as a slanderer before those who revere him as a god?
> HERMOKRATES. Their frenzy will alter, once they again lay eyes on the one who they imagine has already departed to the heights of divinity!
>
> > (KRITIAS. Doch wenn des schwachen Volks
> > Der Kühne sich bemeistert, fürchtest du
> > Für mich und dich und deine Götter nicht?
> > HERMOKRATES. Das Wort des Priesters bricht
> > den kühnen Sinn.
> > KRITIAS. Und werden sie den Langgeliebten dann
> > Wenn schmählich er vom heilgen Fluche leidet,
> > Aus seinen Gärten, wo er gerne lebt,
> > Und aus der heimatlichen Stadt vertreiben?
> > HERMOKRATES. Wer darf den Sterblichen im
> > Lande dulden,
> > Den so der wohlverdiente Fluch gezeichnet?
> > KRITIAS. Doch wenn du wie ein Lästerer erscheinst
> > Vor denen, die als einen Gott ihn achten?
> > HERMOKRATES. Der Taumel wird sich ändern,
> > wenn sie erst
> > Mit Augen wieder sehen den sie jezt schon
> > Entschwunden in die Götterhöhe wähnen!)
> >   (252–66)

Despite Hermokrates' apparent confidence in the power of priestly authority to overcome the "bold sense" that Empedokles' words have instilled in the people, his behavior betrays uneasiness. He reveals, in fact, that he has already pre-tested the effectiveness of his public pronouncements, by promising the citizens a day earlier that he would bring them to Empedokles, and ordering them to stay at home until then:

> HERMOKRATES. So I told them that today I would lead them to him; in the meantime, everyone should quietly stay in his own house. That is why I asked you to come out with me, so that we could see if they listened to me. You see, there is no one here. Come along then.
>
>> (Drauf sagt' ich ihnen, daß ich heute sie
>> Zu ihm geleiten wollt'; indessen soll
>> In seinem Hauße jeder ruhig weilen.
>> Und darum bat ich dich, mit mir heraus
>> Zu kommen, daß wir sähen, ob sie mir
>> Gehorcht. Du findest keinen hier. Nun komm.)
>> (271–76)

The townspeople stayed indoors at Hermokrates' command; the test has worked. But the scene in which Hermokrates curses Empedokles still dramatizes a struggle over the *Sinn des Volk*, and thereby exposes the operation of intersubjective speech acts. The Agrigentians react to the first utterances of both Hermokrates and Empedokles with incomprehension and indecision:

> A CITIZEN. What was it he said there?
>
>> (Was hat er da gesagt?) (513)
>
> FIRST CITIZEN. What it is, Hermokrates—why does the man speak those curious words?
>
>> (Was ist es denn, Hermokrates, warum
>> Der Mann die wunderlichen Worte spricht?)
>> (558–59)

But the second of these questions, wherein one of the citizens specifically asks *Hermokrates* for an interpretation of Empedokles' words, already indicates in whom the questioners will place their confidence. Their consent is forthcoming after Hermokrates' next utterance, in the form of an unusually explicit statement of uptake: "We readily believe you" (Wir glauben dir es wohl [565]). Hermokrates tests the will of the people yet once more before proceeding, by insinuating that Empedokles and Pausanias might in fact be allowed to get away with ignoring the conventions of public discourse, if they have won over the townspeople: "He who has won the people to himself may say whatever he likes" (Wer sich das Volk gewonnen, redet, was / Er will [585–86]). But the response is an even clearer declaration of solidarity from three of the citizens:

THIRD CITIZEN. Fellow citizens! I want nothing more to do with these two.
FIRST CITIZEN. Say, how came it that this one made fools of us?
SECOND CITIZEN. They have to go, the disciple and the master.

(DRITTER AGRIGENTINER. Ihr Bürger! ich
    mag nichts mit diesen Zween
    Ins künftige zu schaffen haben.
ERSTER AGRIGENTINER.   Sagt,
    Wie kam es denn, daß dieser uns bethört?
ZWEITER AGRIGENTINER. Sie müssen fort,
    der Jünger und der Meister.) (592–95)

Having found the opportune moment—"Now it is time!" (596)—Hermokrates now proceeds with his formal denunciation and excommunication of Empedokles. But he has been anticipated by the townspeople, who, in the lines cited above, assent to the banishment of Empedokles and Pausanias *before* Hermokrates has actually pronounced the curse. Moreover, in his remorse for the sin of blaspheming the gods, Empedokles testifies that he is already abandoned and alone, "like one who has been banished" (wie ein Ausgestoßener [424]); he even offers to pronounce a curse on himself. When the priest's curse finally comes, it is, in at least two senses, a *citation*. As an institutional speech act, it cites a recognized formula for excommunication; beyond this, his words have been anticipated by his audience, including both the townspeople and Empedokles himself. The formal act of banishing takes effect because it has somehow already taken effect. By presenting this, the most explicit public speech act in the drama, as an echo of earlier speech acts, Hölderlin assigns political performatives a secondary or belated status, implying that they merely confirm what subjective utterances have already achieved.

The citational quality of Hermokrates' curse also points to something inherently self-referential in the act of banishing. In forbidding all forms of communication between Empedokles and the citizens of Agrigentum, the curse cuts Empedokles off from the conventions that would give his own utterances intersubjective validity. Hermokrates explicitly forbids the people to give assent to even one of Empedokles' words, or to perform even the most basic speech act of greeting:

HERMOKRATES. And woe betide, from now on, whoever receives a
    word of yours amicably into his soul, whoever greets you and offers
    his hand to you....

    (Und wehe dem, von nun an, wer ein Wort
    Von dir in seine Seele freundlich nimmt,

> Wer dich begrüßt, und seine Hand dir beut....)
> (644–46)

But Empedokles has already forfeited the uptake of the citizens—as they show by explicitly giving their assent to Hermokrates' words instead. Empedokles is vulnerable to being shut out from discursive conventions because he is *already* shut out from discursive conventions, and therefore cannot appeal, as the priest can, to the *Sinn des Volk*. The speech act of excommunication, at least in the form in which Hermokrates performs it, has a special relevance for the issue of whether and how a speaker's utterances achieve intersubjective validity, since excommunication is itself the condition of being unable to "speak" within a discursive community. Perhaps this explains why it is the most explicit and detailed performative utterance in *Der Tod des Empedokles*, and forms a kind of counterpart to the central speech act in *Hyperion*—Hyperion's declaration of a new world, that seeks to bring this world into existence, yet will only find uptake if a new, enlightened public already exists.

Hermokrates' speech act, then, effectively gives a public name to the alienated condition in which Empedokles finds himself throughout the first part of the drama.[8] The priest's performative utterance is thereby relegated to the sociopolitical level—and the counter-example of Empedokles' utterances suggests that words perform their most profound acts elsewhere than in a political context. Although he does not have authority to challenge Hermokrates' curse on its own level, Empedokles responds with a counter-curse that invokes an entirely different use of language. Whereas Hermokrates annulled the *social* identity of Empedokles, Empedokles' curse annuls even the *material* existence of its addressees:

> EMPEDOKLES. Ha! May ruin strike you, you nameless ones! Die a slow death, and the priest's raven-song go with you! And since wolves gather there where corpses are, so may there come one for you too; let him sate himself on your blood, let him purify Sicily of you. May the land wither, where once the purple grape gladly grew for a better people, and golden fruits in the dark glade, and choice grain—and one day the stranger will ask, when he treads on the rubble of your temples, if the city once stood here.
>
> (ha geht
> Nun immerhin zu Grund, ihr Nahmenlosen!

---

[8] Kommerell offers a similar but still more universalizing interpretation of the curse, when he suggests that Hermokrates in effect stands for the reality of life in an alienating and conflict-filled society. His curse, then, "is nothing other than the condition of communal life itself, which fulfils itself in an excess of divisions" (269–70).

Sterbt langsamen Tods, und euch geleite
Der Priesters Rabengesang! und weil sich Wölfe
Versammeln da, wo Leichname sind, so finde sich
Dann einer auch für euch; der sättige
Von eurem Blute sich, der reinige
Sicilien von euch; es stehe dürr
Das Land, wo sonst die Purpurtraube gern
Dem bessern Volke wuchs und goldne Frucht
Im dunkeln Hain, und edles Korn, und fragen
Wird einst der Fremde, wenn er auf den Schutt
Von euern Tempeln tritt, ob da die Stadt
Gestanden?)
(748–61)

As curse counters curse, Empedokles' preoccupation with essential identity counters Hermokrates' preoccupation with public identity. Setting the Agrigentians over against himself as "you," Empedokles causes this you to disappear over the course of his speech until only an anonymous "he" (the stranger who wanders by) is left. His curse, with its echoes of the voice of the exiled Hebrew prophet, rejects sociopolitical conventions in favor of an alternative source of authority.

What is this alternative authority? Throughout the drama, characters testify to the identity-altering and even reality-altering effect of Empedokles' words. Kritias's daughter Panthea recalls the "spirit in his speech" (der/Geist in seinem Wort [66–67]), and Empedokles refers to himself as one through whom the spirit spoke (durch wen der Geist geredet [1748]). Pausanias recalls how a word from Empedokles, spoken in a sacred moment, changed his life (445–49).[9] Especially in one-to-one dialogue, Empedokles shows an extraordinary ability to induce agreement in his interlocutors. Even after the excommunication has been pronounced, Kritias listens and agrees to Empedokles' request that he take Panthea away; Kritias and the Agrigentians later agree to leave him on Mount Etna, even though they desire to bring him back to Agrigentum. Pausanias explicitly describes the way Empedokles' words compel him, in despite of his own will, to obey:

PAUSANIAS. Your word masters me wonderfully, I must give way to you, must obey you—I want it and want it not.

[9]Intensifying these allusions, the second draft of the drama ends with Panthea's report that the citizens who sought out Empedokles on Mount Etna, and experienced his final exhortation and blessing, descended from the encounter with their faces glowing from the effect of his words, just as Moses' face shone when he descended the mountain after receiving the Ten Commandments from God: "And their faces shone even in their sorrow, from the word he spoke" (Und ihnen glänzt' im Laide das Angesicht/Vom Worte, das er gesprochen [711–12]).

> (Mich meistert wunderbar dein Wort, ich muß
> Dir weichen, muß gehorchen, wills und will
> Es nicht.)
>
> (1908–10)

As he describes this situation once more to Panthea and her friend Delia, Pausanias emphasizes that the words of Empedokles work differently from the normal process of persuasion. Although they overpower, they evoke liberty rather than submission in the listener:

> PAUSANIAS. He reaches into my soul, when he answers and tells me his will. . . . It is not vain persuasion, believe me, when he takes hold of one's life . . . but when the decisive word came from his lips, then it was as if a heaven of joy reverberated in him and me, and without a word of protest it took hold of me, yet I only felt more free.
>
> > (Er greift in meine Seele, wenn er mir
> > Antwortet, was sein Will' ist
> > . . . .
> >   Es ist
> > Nicht eitel Überrredung, glaub es mir,
> > Wenn er des Lebens sich bemächtiget
> > . . . .
> >   doch wenn das Wort
> > Entscheidend ihm von seinen Lippen kam;
> > Dann wars, als tönt' ein Freudenhimmel wieder
> > In ihm und mir und ohne Widerred'
> > Ergriff es mich, doch fühlt ich nur mich freier.)
>
> (2006–23)

Empedokles' words of power literally change the hearer's mind. While acknowledging the subjectivity and freedom of the listener, they apparently communicate a superior consciousness that works its way into the listener's own cognitive process to bring about a revolution in understanding.

Hermokrates, by contrast, persuades by attempting to negotiate the conventions of intersubjective discourse. *Der Tod des Empedokles* exposes the dangers of Hermokrates' approach, inasmuch as the uptake that was granted him can be—and is—rescinded again. In the final scenes of the drama, Hermokrates and the Agrigentians seek out Empedokles and Pausanias on Mount Etna in order to retract the curse and beg them to return to the city. At this point, Hermokrates' utterances abruptly begin to fail of their expected uptake; his attempt to mollify Empedokles by reporting that the citizens have forgiven him elicits abuse rather than thanks. "This is how you thank us?" Hermokrates asks, incredulously, seeing his illocution fail (1327). The uptake he had counted on from the citizens also vanishes, as they assent instead to Pausanias's threat to take revenge on Hermokrates for the curse. One of the Agrigentians explicitly describes how Hermokrates, before and during the banishment scene, manipulated the public's *Sinn*:

> SECOND CITIZEN. Do you still dare move your lips? you, you made us evil; you blathered all our sense away, you stole the demigod's love from us! He is no longer what he was.
>
> > (Regst du noch die Zunge? du,
> > Du hast uns schlecht gemacht; hast allen Sinn
> > Uns weggeschwatzt; hast uns des Halbgotts Liebe
> > Gestohlen, du! er ists nicht mehr.)
> > (1397–1400)

Hermokrates' use of language is rooted in sociopolitical authority, which in turn is a function of the particular "marketplace" in which he finds himself. Indeed, the role of Hermokrates prefigures the account of the performative given by the sociologist Pierre Bourdieu, for whom the language and authority of the priest are a key example of the way all social authority derives from "the mystery of ministry . . . which constitutes the legitimate representative as an agent capable of acting on the social world through words" (75). Contra Austin, Bourdieu argues that the principle of performativity is not to be found within linguistic structure, but "comes to language from outside," from the societal power structure that endows certain speakers with authority (109). But this authority, as Hermokrates' situation now illustrates, depends on the "complicity" of listeners, indeed on a failure of awareness on their part, that allows them to be duped into according the speaker performative power. "Misrecognition," Bourdieu concludes, "is the basis of all authority" (113). The citizens of Agrigentum now seem to come to the same realization; reacting against their own complicity in Hermokrates' curse, they expose the foundation of the priestly authority in the dynamics of the relationship between the social group and its designated agent.

When this happens, Hermokrates himself, despite his careful analysis of the *Sinn des Volk*, cannot control and does not understand the effect of his words. "Do you know what you have done?" Empedokles asks him (1333), as does one of the citizens (1423); the only response Hermokrates is able to offer is "I don't understand his ravings at all" (Den Rasenden begreif ich freilich nicht [1358]). Having successfully, if temporarily, altered the relation of Empedokles to the people, Hermokrates has simultaneously altered his own relation to them. Uttering the curse marks him in the eyes of the citizens as the public and verbal antagonist of Empedokles, and they now accuse him of calling up Empedokles' counter-curse (1407–9). Moreover, in terms of the logical sequence of speech acts in the drama, Hermokrates' act of banishment is the catalyst that motivates Empedokles to issue his parting speech to the Agrigentians on Mount Etna—a speech in which he changes his curse into a blessing, but also urges a full reformation of the social and political order. Once Empedokles has been shut out of the discursive conventions that constitute society, he can reflect on them and decree their transformation. Just as Empedokles' original act of self-deification had the opposite effect of what was intended, so Hermokrates' curse, in trying to uphold and confirm the conventions of sociopolitical discourse, ultimately generates the potential to overturn them.

The drama brings its participants to the point of a revolution in the relationship between utterance and identity. After reconciling with Empedokles but before experiencing his call for a new world-order, the citizens try to implicate him in the existing political conventions by offering to make him king. His response that "This is no longer the age of kings" (Diß ist die Zeit der Könige nicht mehr [1449]) meets with complete incomprehension on their part. Neither accepting nor declining their offer, Empedokles voids the offer itself by declaring that "king" is no longer a valid term in the discursive, or political, order. Unable to situate themselves and him in terms of the conventions familiar to them, the townspeople respond by questioning Empedokles' identity on the most basic level: "Who are you, man?" (Wer bist du, Mann? [1450]). The same question reappears shortly after in the context of one-to-one dialogue between Empedokles and Pausanias:

EMPEDOKLES. For what do you take me?
PAUSANIAS. O son of Urania! how can you ask that?

(EMPEDOKLES.   Wofür
     Erkennst du mich?
PAUSANIAS.   O Sohn Uraniens!
     Wie kannst du fragen?)
                                        (1846–48)

In this instance the dialogue eludes discursive conventions in a different way and on a different level, for the reader perceives an echo of the dialogue between Jesus and his disciples in the gospels, in which Jesus asks "whom say ye that I am?" and Peter confesses that he believes Jesus to be "the Christ, the Son of the living God" (Matthew 16.15–16). The allusion, unavailable to the speakers themselves, ironically implies some kind of fulfilment of Empedokles' claim to be a god, albeit on a level he can neither intend nor experience.

Instead, the restitution that Empedokles does experience in respect of his original transgression occurs in his final words. Addressed to "Jupiter the Liberator," this ecstatic utterance anticipates the reunion with the divine that Empedokles now expects to find only in death. The contemplation of non-being inspires him to a remarkable declaration of being:

> EMPEDOKLES. I am astonished, as if I began only now to live, for everything is otherwise, and only now *am I, am*—
>
> > (staunen muß ich noch, als fieng
> > Ich erst zu leben an, denn all ists anders,
> > Und jezt erst *bin ich, bin*—)
> > (1919–21; italics added)

These words constitute the *Aufhebung* of Empedokles' original transgressive speech act. While his first "I am" utterance is only paraphrased in the drama, this one is presented (its presentness intensified by the deictic "only now"); while the former represented the death of unity, the latter announces reunion and rebirth; while the former claimed for Empedokles the status of an immortal, the latter rejoices in mortality. But the utterances are parallel in their focus on subjectivity and on the effort of articulating being in language—achieved here by the formulation "bin ich, bin" that literally contains the I within being.

The crucial difference between the assertions "I am [a god]" and "only now am I, am" is that the second is spoken in a context in which Empedokles is not thinking of himself, but intensely aware of the presence of the Other—of "you." In his final speech, Empedokles declares "I am" in a context where "everything is otherwise." He addresses Jupiter, nature, his own heart, his eye, and even his own self as an immediately present You, and ends with an apostrophe to the rainbow: "*as you are*, so is my joy" (*wie du bist*, so ist meine Freude [1942; italics added]). The last words spoken by Empedokles echo Hyperion's last words ("du unzerstörbare! du entzükende! mit deiner ewigen Jugend! *du bist*" [StA 3: 159]), and embody the spirit of Hölderlin's philosophical writings when they suggest that a true act of self-identification involves recognizing oneself in the Other. "How then is self-consciousness possible?" Hölderlin asks in the fragment "Urtheil und Seyn" (Judgment and being): "Through setting myself over against myself, separating myself from myself, but, notwithstanding this separation, recognizing myself in the opposite as the same" (StA 4: 217). According to the radically dialogical concept of identity that runs through Hölderlin's work, as through the phenomenological linguistic theory of Humboldt and Coleridge, acknowledging the existence of the You represents a more open and receptive, yet a truer and more stable way of saying "I am."

If Empedokles' original act of self-deification set him apart from others and distanced him from the natural world, his final speech act represents the achievement of another concept of identity, that understands the self as existing only within otherness. *Der Tod des Empedokles* achieves a certain fulfilment on this level of verbal action—always subject, however, to the dark irony that Empedokles is about to kill himself. Nevertheless, the drama implies that its protagonist's expressive, phenomenological speech acts work even within the sociopolitical sphere, deforming its conventions and promising to transform it even after his death. The speech acts of Hermokrates, on the other hand, are represented as manipulative, for they exploit discursive conventions so as to impose on the minds and the identities of others; derivative, because they cite conventional formulas and perhaps only enact on a political level what is already the case on a deeper, spiritual level; and temporary in their effect, because they can always be superseded by later, more effective speech acts. Although the drama hinges on the fatal consequences of Empedokles' utterance, it is ultimately his language that continues to be valorized as a performative discourse that relies on individual cognition, on essential being rather than social identity, and on an intimate relationship between two consciousnesses.

THE DIALOGIC HÖLDERLIN

Not only in *Hyperion* and *Der Tod des Empedokles*, but also throughout his poetry, Hölderlin is deeply concerned with what language does in an interpersonal context. A reading of the illocutionary forces in his poetry suggests, therefore, that the traditional image of Hölderlin as an isolated visionary whose enigmatic language and enthusiastic sensibility set him apart from his contemporaries, even before he was cut off from them entirely by mental illness, needs to be supplemented by the awareness of a *social*, or at least a *dialogic*, Hölderlin. Some recent studies of his language and his historical context point in this direction. Among other features of Hölderlin's style, such as his use of Swabian dialect and oral idiom, Gerhard Kurz calls attention to the rhetorical, oratorical, and pragmatic dimensions of his poetry. Kurz claims that the exposition of a scene of discourse is a standard feature of Hölderlin's poems, and he lists the speech acts and modes of utterance that typically occur in them (34–35). Extrapolating from Hölderlin's frequent use of dialogic tropes such as apostrophes and dedications, Kurz proposes that his poetry is informed by the belief that both language and individual identity develop through dialogue. Although Kurz does not identify it as such, the general principle he discovers in Hölderlin's poetry is in fact an entirely Humboldtian philosophy of language: "In order to *be* at all, the individual must come out of himself, relate himself to and turn towards another, communicate himself. . . . Speaking and understanding presupposes a common language and forms a new one" (Kurz 35).

With reference to the historical and literary-historical context, William Scott McLean argues that in his mature work Hölderlin tried to develop a poetics of the intersubjective sphere, where value lies not in isolated individual identity, but in the individual's implication in a field of relationships to others and to the natural world. McLean claims that this intersubjective impulse runs counter to the prevailing late-eighteenth-century ideology of individualism as exemplified by the vogue of pietism in religion and sentimental novels among the reading public, and he locates it mainly in *Hyperion*, in Hölderlin's fragmentary essays on poetic theory, and in the late, unfinished poetic drafts. But a study of illocutionary acts in Hölderlin's poetry suggests that McLean's argument about the intersubjectivity of his later work is more limited than it needs to be. An intersubjective impulse actually marks the whole of his poetic career, emerging in the dialogic structures and the explicit scenes of discourse that characterize even his earliest poems. The real limiting factor in the definition of a social Hölderlin, by contrast, is the degree of success that his dialogic gestures achieve. How many of his poetic texts can be characterized as actual experiences of dialogue—or even as successfully imagined exchanges of thought and feeling between two consciousnesses—and how many manifest, rather, the *desire* for productive exchange with an Other? It is because of this persistent uncertainty that Hölderlin's poetry is aptly read under the aspect of the Romantic performative. Hölderlin's dialogic speech acts create the conditions of their own possibility, inasmuch as they *posit* the existence of an addressee even as they perform the discourse that takes place between poet and addressee. In the linguistic theory of Humboldt or Bernhardi, language creates the subject-positions I and You; in Hölderlin's poetry, this principle reappears as an implication that the dialogic partner is always only a verbal construct. His vocatives and dedications, his pronouns and deictics, and his explicit references to the things we do with words, suggest (and underscore) the possibility that language may *found* the intersubjective context even as it purports to *ground* itself in a pragmatic situation.

The very frequent use of dedications in Hölderlin's early poetry, either contained in titles or immediately following the title, is a first sign of the importance he attaches to scenes of discourse. Titles like "An

Stella" (To Stella), "An die Ehre" (To Honor), "Hymne an die Unsterblichkeit" (Hymn to Immortality), "Melodie: An Lyda" (A melody: to Lyda), "Hymne an die Muse" (Hymn to the Muse), or "Hymne an die Freundschaft: An Neuffer und Magenau" (Hymn to Friendship: to Neuffer and Magenau) do not simply illustrate an acquiescence in eighteenth-century poetic convention or a habitual use of the mannerisms of the ode. Rather, they establish a situation for dialogic address that is always taken seriously in the poem itself. Virtually all of Hölderlin's poems, whatever the form of the title, assume a scene of discourse in which the poet as I addresses a human or divine figure, or an element of nature, as You. Most of them also have a conspicuous performative dimension, in that they direct some illocutionary force, such as praise or exhortation, toward the figure named in the title—and the texts themselves constitute those acts of praise or exhortation.

The pronounced dialogical appeal of Hölderlin's poetic language is the subject of a third critical study, Rolf Zuberbühler's book on Hölderlin's dedicatory poetry.[10] Zuberbühler notes that the drive to address a *du* is an inner necessity that shapes all of Hölderlin's writing, and he interprets this characteristic in primarily psychological terms. Hölderlin's dedicatory poems typically begin in a condition of loneliness, out of which the poet rescues himself by calling to a friend or friends to come "into the open," to a place where discourse about the life of the spirit becomes possible. The poet lapses back into loneliness at the end, although a final address to the friend often provides the means by which the poem's vision can be held fast, and prevents a fall into despair (Zuberbühler 19–20).

This analysis focuses on the spiritual and emotional source of Hölderlin's dedicatory poetry, but the address to an Other should also be read as a performative gesture. Like Hyperion's urgent cry "where are you, oh where are you," Hölderlin's dedicatory addresses voice the desire for the Other even as, through the act of utterance itself, they open up space for a potential response. As at the ambiguous ending of *Hyperion*, though ("*it seemed to me* that I heard Diotima's voice . . ."), the status of the re-

---

[10]Zuberbühler's book *Die Sprache des Herzens* (1982) represents the first systematic, literary-critical study of Hölderlin's address to a You, a characteristic of his poetry that earlier commentators often remarked on in passing. In a linguistic analysis of the last poem Hölderlin wrote before his death in 1843, for instance, Jakobson and Lübbe-Grothues discuss the "disturbed dialogic competence" occasioned by his mental illness (79). They contrast this condition with the importance of dialogue for the young Hölderlin by citing Nussbächer's 1971 comment on the dialogic origin of Hölderlin's poetry: "His dialogic nature sought out conversation, and out of the conversation with a 'you' his song arose" (Jakobson and Lübbe-Grothues 64).

sponse remains in question; there is always the possibility that nothing is called forth by the poet's utterance except an echo of that utterance in empty space. This situation characterizes several of Hölderlin's earlier hymns addressed to abstract entities—a form that, while typical for late-eighteenth-century lyric, sets up an important model for the dialogic situation in Hölderlin's major poetry. In "Hymne an die Unsterblichkeit," the Spirit of Immortality counters thoughtless worldly activity, and the temptation to doubt the existence of an afterlife, with speech acts that she directs to the attentive listener. In accordance with her divine commands, the free soul overcomes all baser passions and is inspired to swear allegiance to the fatherland, thereby gaining the reward of being blessed by Immortality (*StA* 1: 118–19). The sub-text of the poem is that Immortality, whose existence is unverifiable by the standards of earthly life, can *only* influence worldly action if the soul communicates with her in what is figured as a language of commands, blessings, and praise. Tracing the speaker's doubts of and renewed faith in the existence of Immortality, the poem affirms the necessity of the soul's uptake of her speech acts. The poet offers this uptake at the turning point of the poem by his emphatic affirmation of Immortality's existence: "No, Immortality, you are, you are!" (Nein, Unsterblichkeit, du bist, du bist! [*StA* 1: 117]).

"Hymne an die Unsterblichkeit" is representative of several of the hymns Hölderlin wrote during his years as a student in Tübingen, in the way the abstract entity evoked in the title gains whatever reality she has through a dialogic exchange with the poet. "Hymne an die Schönheit" (Hymn to Beauty) and the two poems titled "Hymne an die Freiheit" (Hymn to Liberty) work in comparable ways. Even when, as in these poems, Hölderlin addresses a deity or an abstraction rather than another human being, the context is one of ordinary dialogue and familiar speech acts—and the *response* of a dialogic partner carries particular weight. This emphasis on the hearing of speech acts and the acknowledgment of their illocutionary force fits with the conditions for discourse as described by Searle and Habermas, who stress that uptake is necessary in order for an utterance to count as a social act. But Hölderlin's poetry also suggests that uptake confers a certain bond to reality that subjective utterances would not otherwise have. In this sense, it engages Humboldt's theory that communication is necessary to cognition, because cognitive acts are only validated when the words of one speaker are acknowledged and accepted by another: "Therefore the word must achieve essence, language must achieve expansion in one who hears and responds" (*GS* 6: 26).

"GERMANIEN": UPTAKE?

Against the background of the early hymns to Immortality, Beauty, and Liberty, in which the utterances of these deities are framed by the poet's affirmative response and his exhortation to his contemporaries to respond, the poem "Germanien" presents an open-ended speech act. The dialogic structure of the earlier hymns now takes on new dimensions, and implicates the reader in a different way. "Germanien" is figured as a place and a culture characterized by speech, in contrast to the world of antiquity, which is associated here with sight or vision. The ancient world is a place where "images of gods" "appeared," where their "beautiful face" can be "seen," the Orient a landscape on which one can look out (Daß schauen mag bis in den Orient/Der Mann [StA 2: 150]). The poet's German homeland, however, is a land where the waters lament together with the human heart, a place that is full of promises (Verheißungen) and threats (drohend auch), where both images and utterances rain down from the aether:

> But down from Aether falls
> The faithful image, and words of gods rain down
> Innumerable from it, and the innermost grove resounds.
> *(Poems 403)*
>
> (Vom Aether aber fällt
> Das treue Bild und Göttersprüche reegnen
> Unzählbare von ihm, und es tönt im innersten Haine.)
> *(StA 2: 150)*

The imagery of the first three stanzas is meteorological on one level, the azure skies of Greece being contrasted with the darker, more variable conditions of northern Europe. But the difference between clear and uncertain heavens symbolizes the difference between the direct relationship of gods and humans in the ancient world and their modern relationship, marked by mediation and the consequent need for interpretation. Above all, the relationship between the heavenly and the earthly now involves discourse rather than vision or physical experience. Once he has flown from the Orient to Germany, Zeus's eagle no longer carries off his earthly prey as he once did Ganymede, but instead *speaks to* the maiden Germania.

More complex than a direct annunciation to Germania—although the Annunciation is another paradigmatic scene of discourse that lies behind this poem—the eagle's interaction with her is a play of recognition, secrecy, and revelation. The eagle, sent as a messenger to Germania, recognizes her at once, but recognizes also that she does not know herself.

His words to her are therefore predicated on a secret mini-dialogue that he first has within himself, in which he resolves to speak an "other" word in order to test her: "you the unbreakable/A different word must try" (Dich, unzerbrechliche, muß/Ein ander Wort erprüfen). Evidently, the eagle resolves to utter something other than a simple declaration of Germania's destiny—to utter a word that will compel her to *perform* her destiny in and through her response to him.

His address to her begins with the resonant recognition of the Other that recalls similar utterances in *Hyperion* and *Der Tod des Empedokles*: "You are it" or "It is you" (Du bist es). At the end of his speech (and of the poem), he closes the circle of recognition by pronouncing her name: "Germania." But between these two affirmations of identity the eagle utters injunctions that demand a response:

> O drink the morning breezes
> Until you are opened up
> And name what you see before you;
> No longer now the unspoken
> May remain a mystery
> Though long it has been veiled
> . . . .
> Once only, daughter of holy Earth,
> Pronounce your Mother's name.
> (*Poems* 405–7)

> (O trinke Morgenlüfte,
> Biß daß du offen bist,
> Und nenne, was vor Augen dir ist,
> Nicht länger darf Geheimniß mehr
> Das Ungesprochene bleiben,
> Nachdem es lange verhüllt ist
> . . . .
> O nenne Tochter du der heiligen Erd'
> Einmal die Mutter.)
> (*StA* 2: 151–52)

The eagle enjoins Germania to *speak*—and the distinctive tension of this text lies in the fact that Germania does *not* speak, or rather that she does not speak yet. Against the background of Hölderlin's early hymns, where a deity's address to the poet is typically met with explicit uptake, the silence at the end of "Germanien" is pregnant. It underscores the performativity of the eagle's utterance—not only in terms of its conventional illocutionary forces (i.e., commanding, exhorting, informing), but also in terms of the self-reflexive, Romantic speech act. His address to Germania aims to make her into what he predicts she will become—that is, into one who speaks, one who responds with appropriate uptake to divine summons. Germania's appropriate response would be to validate his act of naming her by recognizing and naming the beings to which she is related: "name what you see before you"; "Once only, daughter of holy Earth,/Pronounce your Mother's name." The eagle characterizes naming as an effectual act that revives ancient divinity: "at their name/Divine things past ring out from time immemorial" (bei dem Nahmen derselben/Tönt auf aus alter Zeit Vergangengöttliches wieder). But the success of the act of naming that is taking place in his speech itself remains an open question: it depends on Germania's willingness to recognize the eagle's utterance *as* an act of creative naming *by* acceding to the name and identity that he proposes to her.

The eagle reveals why Germania should trust herself to respond, disclosing that he visited her once before, and left her the gift of speech while she slept:

                    Yet I did not misjudge you
      And secretly, while you dreamed, at noon,
      Departing I left a token of friendship,
      The flower of the mouth behind, and lonely you spoke.
                             (*Poems* 405)

                (Ich miskannte dich nicht,
      Und heimlich, da du träumtest, ließ ich
      Am Mittag scheidend dir ein Freundeszeichen,
      Die Blume des Mundes zurük und du redetest einsam.)
                                (*StA* 2: 151)

Uncovering his own secret, the eagle also urges Germania to name "the unspoken" and bring it into the light:

      And name what you see before you;
      No longer now the unspoken
      May remain a mystery
      Though long it has been veiled....
                (*Poems* 405)

      (Und nenne, was vor Augen dir ist,
      Nicht länger darf Geheimniß mehr
      Das Ungesprochene bleiben,
      Nachdem es lange verhüllt ist....)
                (*StA* 2: 151)

In terms of his own utterance as well as Germania's, the eagle-messenger calls attention to the right moment for speech. The final lines of the poem give the "right moment" the connotations of an appropriate public occasion, as the eagle presents Germania to herself in the role of a priestess who addresses kings and nations:

> Amid your holidays,
> Germania, where you are priestess and
> Defenceless proffer all round
> Advice to the kings and the peoples.
>
> *(Poems* 407)
>
> (Bei deinen Feiertagen
> Germania, wo du Priesterin bist
> Und wehrlos Rath giebst rings
> Den Königen und den Völkern.)
>
> *(StA* 2: 152)

By his pronouncement, the eagle authorizes Germania to take on the role of a public speaker—or at least makes this role available to her if she assents to it. The poem thus consists of a *mise en abîme* of speech situations: the poet's address to nature and the gods in the first two stanzas opens onto an incomplete dialogue between Zeus's eagle and Germania, which ends by projecting Germania into a scene of public discourse where she might address the nations. All these situations are constructed around phenomenological and epistemological crises: recognition of the self, the Other, and the relation between them; appropriate degrees of knowledge on the part of speaker and addressee; and the discovery of the felicitous moment for speaking and naming.

Most importantly, though, the central scene of discourse between the eagle and Germania casts the reader in a special performative role. For the dialogic situation in this text seems, at first sight, to be reversed, compared to Hölderlin's early hymns: the semi-divine female, Germania, is not the one who speaks (as do Liberty, Beauty, or Immortality), but the one who is spoken to. The role reversal is explained by the identification of the semi-divine priestess Germania with the nation ("Germanien") to which the poet and reader both belong. The text implies a gradual consolidation of identities: it begins with an address from the poet as I to a plural You (representing first the "waters of home" and then the "departed gods"); the I is subsumed (at line 30) into a We that includes his audience; and the We is subsumed, in turn, into the character Germania, the recipient of the eagle's summons. But Germania's response is left unspoken. The text thus sets up a performative situation in which both poet and reader are implicated; for the uptake required is *our* uptake, the word that the eagle utters to "try" Germania is trying *us.*

By involving poet and reader in its scene of address and potential response, "Germanien" casts light on the tensions within the Romantic performative, and on the relation between Romantic performative and poetic text. The eagle's address to Germania is a self-reflexive speech act that engages the central concerns of Romantic linguistics, with its positing of an I and a You and its focus on the way the identity of the You might be realized. But his prediction of Germania's future, breaking off without comment from either Germania or the poet, remains suspended in some indeterminate relation to actuality. Only if Germania is the kind of speaker the eagle postulates will she validate his utterance by granting it uptake; yet it is the very act of responding with kairotic recognition that will make her into the speaker he postulates. The hermeneutic paradox of the Romantic performative makes itself felt—and because the figure of Germania coincides with the reading audience, it is possible to extend this paradox to the status of the poetic text in general. All poetry, like the speech of the eagle, on some level requires validation by a reader, especially if the poetic text is engaged in positioning the reader within a conceptual moment or a historical space. As in "Germanien," such validation would involve a combination of perception (reading or hearing the text in the first place), interpretation (assigning some kind of meaning to it), and instantiation (placing oneself in relation to it, for instance by choosing to identify or not to identify with Germania). A text that presents itself as an open-ended dialogue, or an illocutionary act in need of uptake, implies that the Romantic performative could be mapped onto the Romantic lyric: both are acts of positing, and whatever reality or legitimation they attain depends on another subject's willingness to acknowledge the act they are performing.

"FRIEDENSFEIER": THE SOCIAL HÖLDERLIN

To relate Germania's response, which bears on the political role the eagle foresees for her, to the reader's imaginative response, is to raise again the difficult question of the relation between social and cognitive speech acts. What role, if any, do poetic utterances have in a sociopolitical setting, and does the function of language in forging relationships between subject and world, as Romantic theorists describe it, have anything to do with its function in forging community between subjects? These questions arise throughout Hölderlin's late hymns—texts that almost always set their imaginative transformations of the world in the context of one-to-one dialogue, and sometimes also in the wider context of a community joined by language.

The festival, as a celebration of community among human beings as well as between humans and gods, is a recurrent theme of the late hymns. A model for these communal events is certainly to be found in the Greek festivals that formed the context for performances of the poetry of Pindar or the tragedians, texts that Hölderlin both translated and imitated, or in the festival of the sun-god as commemorated briefly in *Hyperion*. As Mona Ozouf notes, these classical festivals also provided inspiration and symbolism for the major public celebrations taking place in Hölderlin's own day: the revolutionary festivals of 1790s France (5, 273–75). "Friedensfeier" ("Celebration of Peace"), the most important of Hölderlin's festival poems, maintains a particular connection to the events of post-revolutionary France; by the poet's own account, it was occasioned by the Peace of Lunéville, declared in February 1801, in which he invested his hopes for a new age of freedom. Karlheinz Stierle places the poem in a direct relationship to historical circumstances by interpreting it in the context of the French revolutionary festivals, which are themselves allegorical representations or performances of concepts embodied in privileged words, such as *liberté, égalité,* and *fraternité* (489).

"Friedensfeier," which was not rediscovered in its final form until 1954, exists in several draft versions that the Stuttgart edition of Hölderlin's works prints under the title "Versöhnender der du nimmergeglaubt ..." (Conciliator, you that no longer believed in ...). The theme that emerges more and more strongly in the course of Hölderlin's revisions is that of the god-man, the deity who visits the poet's festival in the shape of a mortal and a friend. If the poem is an idiosyncratic rendering of the Incarnation, then the modulation between divine and human extends into the frequent but fragmentary scenes of discourse that it presents. In its gnomic allusions to different forms of speech, "Friedensfeier" implies a movement away from divine utterance, and toward human discourse, that has general relevance for Hölderlin's mature poetry. But the allusions to different discursive contexts continually raise the question of the context in which the poem's own illocutionary acts are to be understood. "Friedensfeier" focuses attention on whether *poetic* or *fictional* speech acts—taking both those terms in their etymological sense of image-making and world-creating—inaugurate, imitate, or indeed stand in any relation at all to the speech acts that bind together a discursive community.

To attempt to bring together the cognitive dimension of Hölderlin's poetic language, and his concern for communication as the basis for community, is to locate his work somewhere between the classic, philosophizing interpretation of Wolfgang Binder and the more recent, more historicizing ones of Rainer Nägele and Karlheinz Stierle. Binder's emphasis on creative (stiftendes) naming, and on the way Hölderlin's language founds the real by revealing a spiritual order behind material reality, is reminiscent of Heidegger's reading of Hölderlin. But Binder gives a cognitive, even dialogical turn to the Heideggerian idea of the quasi-mystical autonomy of language by relating Hölderlin's texts to Kantian and idealist epistemology, as well as to a tradition of linguistic philosophy deriving from Herder and Hamann. It is in this context that he describes the nature of Hölderlin's poetic language in the 1955–56 essay "Sprache und Wirklichkeit in Hölderlins Dichtung" (Language and reality in Hölderlin's poetry):

> Thus his poetry intends [intendiert] objects only in such a way that it simultaneously makes these into events in the process of speaking and hearing. Its form is no static aesthetic configuration, but rather the epitome of that in which what is meant in the poem happens as an act and becomes reality. (36)

If Binder draws out the phenomenological aspect of performativity, by which Hölderlin's utterance instantiates and constantly re-activates the encounter between self and world, Nägele places Hölderlinian utterance and subjectivity in the context of a historical hermeneutics. Writing a generation after Binder, on the poem "Brod und Wein" (Bread and wine) but also with reference to "Friedensfeier," Nägele describes Hölderlin's use of language as part of a historical project, shared by his contemporaries Schiller, Novalis, and above all Hegel, to re-activate the "dead letter" represented by the institutional language of church and state and ground a new public sphere in "utopian intersubjectivity" (33). A specific response to the experience of the French Revolution, this new intersubjectivity is conceived as incorporating the experience of love and friendship; ironically, however, it also resembles a restricted, cult-like congregation of specially chosen individuals. Stierle, finally, places "Friedensfeier" specifically in the context of "festival literature," the poems and hymns written for the French revolutionary festivals—of which the largest one, held 3 November 1801, was the festival of peace (489–90). Yet rather than celebrating an already achieved, historical peace, Hölderlin's hymn projects the historical I as a poetic I and "phenomenalizes" or brings to consciousness the concept of peace itself: "Hölderlin's poem is not the celebration of a peace, but, as it were, the poetic celebration of the concept of peace itself. In this sense the celebration of peace becomes a phenomenolization of its concept" (516).

Nägele's and Stierle's essays address the difficulties of reconciling text-based interpretation with history, and the tension is compounded by setting Binder's formal, phenomenological approach alongside their historically informed ones. Against this background, we may formulate the confrontation between poetic-subjective and social-intersubjective contexts differently again. How, the question would be, does "Friedensfeier" fit within a *linguistic*-historical context—that of the pragmatic and dialogic understanding of language which arose in the decades after the French Revolution? And how, if at all, does the dialogic exchange between text and reader contribute to the vision of discursive communities offered within the text—a discursive order that it seeks, performatively, to inaugurate? Under what conditions could the text possibly be said to found the kind of discourse whose founding it describes?

The ideal of social discourse among equals, sustained by the exchange of familiar speech acts, becomes progressively more prominent in successive drafts of "Friedensfeier." The first two drafts still allude to an older, more mysterious, more powerful, yet somehow alienating type of utterance:

> Far off, but awe-inspiring, droned the community's singing
> Where like a holy wine, the more mysterious responses,
> Aged now but once more mighty, grown up
> In summer from the thunderstorms of God,
> Could yet allay my cares
> And doubts, but never I knew what was happening to me. . . .
> *(Poems* 423)

> (Fern rauschte der Gemeinde schauerlicher Gesang,
> Wo heiligem Wein gleich, die geheimeren Sprüche
> Gealtert aber gewaltiger einst, aus Gottes
> Gewittern im Sommer gewachsen,
> Die Sorgen doch mir stillten
> Und die Zweifel aber nimmer wußt ich, wie mir geschah. . . .)
> *(StA* 2: 130; also 133)

Replacing this "terrible song" (schauerlicher Gesang) with a festival to which he invites the divine youth, a god in the form of a friend, the poet inaugurates a new form of intersubjective discourse. Early versions of the poem characterize this discourse in terms of the simple speech acts of greeting and thanking. "Göttlicher sei/Am Abend deiner Tage gegrüßet," the first draft concludes: "divine one, let/Us greet you at the Evening of your days" *(StA* 2: 132/*Poems* 431). From the mysterious and awe-inspiring song of the ancients, the poem moves toward the act of greeting, the most basic and conventional of the speech acts that ground a social order. In both of the first two versions, the new order of social discourse is also symbolized by the conventional return of thanks for a favor, a convention the poet imagines as being extended to heavenly gifts once these gifts can be recognized as having something divine *and* something human about them:

> And human beneficence is followed by thanks,
> But god-sent gifts for years at first
> By suffering and confusion,
> Till property is established and earned
> And his a person may also call them then
> The humanly divine.
> *(Poems* 429; altered to translate the second draft)

> (Und menschlicher Wohlthat folget der Dank
> Auf göttliche Gaabe aber jahrlang
> Die Mühn erst und das Irrsaal,
> Bis Eigentum geworden ist und verdient
> Und sein sie darf der Mensch dann auch
> Die menschlich göttliche nennen.)
> *(StA* 2: 135)

In another early draft, God's decision to take on the burden and the fate of mortals brings about a state where there is "one language among the living" (Daß . . . eine Sprache unter Lebenden/sei [*StA* 2: 137]).

The final version of "Friedensfeier" takes this idea of a communal language one step further, describing the day of the festival as an occasion of intimate conversation and choral song—Hölderlin's recurrent image for the ideal form of human expression:

> But where in hymns hospitably conjoined
> And present in choirs, a holy number,
> The blessèd in every way
> Meet and forgather, and their best-beloved,
> To whom they are attached, is not missing; for that is why
> You to the banquet now prepared I called,
> The unforgettable, you, at the Evening of Time,
> O youth, called you to the prince of the feast-day; nor shall
> Our nation ever lie down to sleep until
> All you that were prophesied,
> Every one of you Immortals,
> To tell us about your Heaven
> Are here with us in our house.
> *(Poems* 441)

> (Wo aber bei Gesang gastfreundlich untereinander
> In Chören gegenwärtig, eine heilige Zahl
> Die Seeligen in jeglicher Weise
> Beisammen sind, und ihr Geliebtestes auch
> An dem sie hängen, nicht fehlt; denn darum rief ich
> Zum Gastmahl, das bereitet ist,

> Dich, Unvergeßlicher, dich, zum Abend der Zeit,
> O Jüngling, dich zum Fürsten des Festes; und eher legt
> Sich schlafen unser Geschlecht nicht,
> Bis ihr Verheißenen all,
> All ihr Unsterblichen, uns
> Von eurem Himmel zu sagen,
> Da seid in unserem Haußé.)
>
> (StA 3: 536)

Dialogues of several kinds cross in this stanza: the singing, described as the activity of multiple choirs; the thrice-repeated address to the holy guest as "you" (dich); and the image of an intimate conversational round of mortals and immortals, expressed in lines that themselves have an antiphonal ring through the alternation of "we" and "you" ("our nation"—"all you that were prophesied"; "you Immortals"—"tell us"; "your Heaven"—"our house").

The antiphonal quality of the verses suggests that more than prophecy is going on here—or else that the prophecy strives to be self-fulfilling. All the versions of "Friedensfeier" seem to point toward a new paradigm for the creative word, variously characterized as intersubjective, pluralist, or non-exclusive—as egalitarian exchange for which greeting or thanking provide the model, or as conversation over a hospitable meal. But, just as the festivals of the French Republic centered on the performance of public speech acts that would consolidate a new social order, this textual festival performs speech acts that strive to *enact* rather than describe a new sense of community.

In what sense could it be valid to say that the language of the poem itself participates in the instantiation of a new discursive order? This perspective on the text inevitably broaches the problematic relationship between the role of utterance in a societal context and the role of utterance in a lyric poem. Like Romantic language theorists, Hölderlin brings these forms of language together by striving to give a cognitive basis to communicative discourse. The lines that have become the most famous passage of "Friedensfeier" proclaim that God and mortals experience one another through language, as an equalizing "law of love" governs their relationship:

> For once, however, even a God may choose
> Mere daily tasks, like mortals, and share all manner of fate.
> This is a law of fate, that each shall know all others,
> That when the silence returns there shall be a language too.
> Yet where the Spirit is active, we too will stir and debate
> What course might be the best. So now it seems best to me
> If now the Master completes his image and, finished,

    Himself transfigured by it, steps out of his workshop,
    The quiet God of Time, and only the law of love,
    That gently resolves all difference, prevails from here up to Heaven.
       Much, from the morning onwards,
    Since we have been a discourse and have heard from one another,
    Has human kind learnt; but soon we shall be song.
                                              (Poems 439)
    (Einmal mag aber ein Gott auch Tagewerk erwählen,
    Gleich Sterblichen und theilen alles Schiksaal.
    Schiksaalgesez ist diß, daß Alle sich erfahren,
    Daß, wenn die Stille kehrt, auch eine Sprache sei.
    Wo aber wirkt der Geist, sind wir auch mit, und streiten,
    Was wohl das Beste sei. So dünkt mir jezt das Beste,
    Wenn nun vollendet sein Bild und fertig ist der Meister,
    Und selbst verklärt davon aus seiner Werkstatt tritt,
    Der stille Gott der Zeit und nur der Liebe Gesez,
    Das schönausgleichende gilt von hier an bis zum Himmel.
       Viel hat von Morgen an,
    Seit ein Gespräch wir sind und hören voneinander,
    Erfahren der Mensch; bald sind wir aber Gesang.)
                                              (StA 3: 535–36)

Much has been written about these last lines in terms of Hölderlin's characterization of human relationships in history as "discourse," a term that he opposes to "song" as a future ideal. But what also needs to be considered is his use of a declarative mode of figural language: that is, his act of presenting us with the propositions "we have been a discourse" and "we shall be song," and requiring us to incorporate them into some model of reality. This type of cognitive challenge occurs, of course, throughout the poem and throughout Hölderlin's late hymns, but acquires a self-reflexive dimension in this case, as the poet *uses* discourse (or song?) to define human beings *as* discourse and song.

The strangeness of Hölderlin's diction encourages a performative reading, within which the verb "to be"—the fundamental verb that caused so much consternation for Romantic philosophers of language—really does need to be understood in terms of both being and action. Hölderlin's line "Seit ein Gespräch wir sind" offers one of many possible examples where a reading of his poetic language is enriched by Coleridge's idea of the verb-substantive or by Humboldt's theory of synthesis—according to which, as Humboldt writes, a predicative utterance such as "mind is immortal" works by compelling us to think "mind" and "immortal" together in such a way that a new entity, immortal mind, actually comes into being through the speech act (OL 185). This is as apt a description as any of the way Hölderlin's language works. "Since we have been a discourse" brings together the concepts "we" and "discourse" in such a way as to *create us as discourse*; "we shall be song" brings together "we" and "song" so as to *make us into song*. Since the relationship of language and reality was being re-thought by linguistic philosophers as well as poets in the post-Kantian generation, the re-evaluation of "being" and the verb "to be" by Romantic linguists might find some immediate applications in considering the connotations and the performative force with which a poet like Hölderlin uses this verb. What would it mean to a line like "Since we have been a discourse" that Humboldt was beginning to analyze the way "to be" posits a new synthesis between subject and predicate in the moment the words are uttered? Or that Bernhardi had recently determined that in using the verb "to be," language substitutes "ideal" being for "real" being, but that poetry is the one context in which ideal and real being coincide? Utterances like Hölderlin's may need to be heard in a new performative register, if we realize that post-Kantian linguists were altering (quite literally) the way things *are*.

For Hölderlin's "Friedensfeier," such a reading assumes that the poet's vision of a new discursive community radically implicates whatever ability his own language has to construct new relations between mind and world. Not only can his language, particularly his verbs, be read as performative rather than constative, but perhaps the propositional statements in his poetry need to be experienced as illocutionary acts that await uptake from a dialogic partner. To put it differently, perhaps the vision of social discourse and ideal community in "Friedensfeier" ultimately depends on a felicitous conversational relationship between poet and reader, in which the reader will acknowledge and accept as reality the poet's claims that humanity is discourse and that the festival has begun. This displacement of the poem out of a historical context and into a hermeneutic and cognitive one is encouraged, not only by Hölderlin's use of declarative utterance, but by the specific dialogic situation into which he sets the final version of the poem. His headnote urges the reader to tolerate his strange language, as a first step to comprehending it:

> All I ask is that the reader be kindly disposed towards these pages. In that case he will certainly not find them incomprehensible, far less objectionable. But if, nonetheless, some should think such a language too unconventional, I must confess to them: I cannot help it. On a fine day—they should consider—almost every mode of song makes itself heard; and Nature, whence it originates, also receives it again.

The author intends to offer the public an entire collection of such pieces, and this one should be regarded as a kind of sample. (*Poems* 433)

(Ich bitte dieses Blatt nur gutmüthig zu lesen. So wird es sicher nicht unfaßlich, noch weniger anstößig seyn. Sollten aber dennoch einige eine solche Sprache zu wenig konventionell finden, so muß ich ihnen gestehen: ich kann nicht anders. An einem schönen Tage läßt sich ja fast jede Sangart hören, und die Natur, wovon es her ist, nimmts auch wieder.

Der Verfasser gedenkt dem Publikum eine ganze Sammlung von dergleichen Blättern vorzulegen, und dieses soll irgend eine Probe seyn davon.) (StA 3: 532)

This direction to the reader places the poem in a linguistic-pragmatic context, shaped, as is typical of the Romantic performative, by both the cognitive and the communicative dimension of language. Humboldt brings these two aspects together even more directly than Hölderlin when he describes the way the world-constituting function of language is interwoven with its dialogic function, so that the speaker's word only gains substance through the acknowledgment of a responsive hearer: "the word, when born in the individual alone, so resembles a purely illusory object—language cannot be brought to reality by the individual either, but only socially, only in that one daring attempt is made and a new one takes it up" (*GS* 6: 26). The poem's deictics ("*since* we have been" and "*soon* we shall be"), and the juxtapositions of noun and predicate that require acts of synthesis from the reader, locate "Friedensfeier" in the same hermeneutic space as "Germanien," as a text awaiting the potential but by no means certain uptake that a reader might bestow.

"PATMOS" AND THE APOSTROPHIC CODA

Second-person address in Hölderlin's poetry, whether it be the address of Zeus's eagle to Germania or that of Hölderlin to his reader in the headnote to "Friedensfeier," gives his texts a pragmatic turn. Their language needs, in consequence, to be read not only for what it says but for what it does—and, crucially, for the way meaning and performance depend on one another. This interdependence also shows up in many of the poems that are dedicated to specific addressees, in which the "pragmatic turn" from a third-person narrative to I-You address typically happens in the second half of the text. Several of Hölderlin's poems of the mid-1790s set up this pattern, and in his odes and major hymns it becomes almost a convention. The turn to second-person address in the final stanzas of poems like "Gesang des Deutschen" (The German's song), "Der Main" (The River Main), and "Der Rhein" (The Rhine) is often rhetorically dramatic, and, as in "Gesang des Deutschen," may be signaled by an explicit formula of greeting: "What's best in you I'll greet, then, my fatherland,/With names all new.... Urania, let me greet you" (Nun! sei gegrüßt in deinem Adel, mein Vaterland,/Mit neuem Nahmen.... Urania, sei gegrüßt mir!) (*Poems* 613/*StA* 2: 4).

But in Hölderlin's late hymns, especially when they thematize the creation of some kind of discursive community, the relation between the poem's apostrophic structure and its meaning becomes more complex. "Patmos" is the best example of such an interaction of constative meaning with performative force, whereby the dialogic address at the end both depends on and actualizes the relationships that the language of the poem has set up. Like the poems mentioned above, "Patmos" contains a narrative section that turns, in the last two stanzas, toward an I-You address. More specifically, the core of the poem is a third-person narrative about the experience of the apostles during the final days of Christ's life and the first days of his absence, which is contained within another third-person narrative about the arrival of John, the seer of Revelation (whom Hölderlin considers identical with the apostle John), on the island of Patmos. Both these narratives are framed within a first-person account of the poet's prayer for visionary power, his address to the dedicatee of the poem, and his pronouncement on the task of German poetry. Each layer of narrative informs the one that frames it: John's experience of intimate friendship with Jesus shapes his later existence on Patmos, and the experience of John on Patmos shapes Hölderlin's self-conception as visionary poet. John's central experience of the divine, finally, is presented as one of communion and conversation—perhaps not unlike the experience of intimacy between Hölderlin, his friend Isaak von Sinclair, and their patron, Landgrave Friedrich Ludwig of Hessen-Homburg, to which Hölderlin was responding in the writing of the poem.

"Patmos" is dedicated and was presented to the Landgrave of Homburg, a pious man who had shown kindness and condescension toward Hölderlin at their meeting in Regensburg in the autumn of 1802, and had expressed the wish that a contemporary poet would defend biblical revelation against modern liberal interpretations of the Bible. In the fair copy of the poem that Hölderlin prepared for the Landgrave in January 1803, a dedication to him appears directly beneath the title "Patmos." But Hölderlin actually addresses the Landgrave only in the penultimate stanza, where he suddenly apostrophizes a "you" who is loved by the gods and respects their will. This turn to direct address is prepared for in a passage that shifts attention to the interpretation of the Word, and that may be read as an epiphany of verbal performance:

>   For when heavenly triumph goes higher
>   The jubilant son of the Highest
>   Is called like the sun by the strong,
>   A secret token, and here is the wand
>   Of song, signalling downward,
>   For nothing is common. The dead
>   He reawakens whom coarseness has not
>   Made captive yet. But many timid eyes
>   Are waiting to see the light.
>   They are reluctant to flower
>   Beneath the searing beam, though it is
>   The golden bridle that curbs their courage.
>   But when, as if
>   By swelling eyebrows made
>   Oblivious of the world
>   A quietly shining strength falls from holy scripture,
>   Rejoicing in grace, they
>   May practise upon the quiet gaze.
>   (*Poems* 473–75)
>
>   (Wenn nemlich höher gehet himmlischer
>   Triumphgang, wird genennet, der Sonne gleich
>   Von Starken der frohlokende Sohn des Höchsten,
>   Ein Loosungszeichen, und hier ist der Stab
>   Des Gesanges, niederwinkend,
>   Denn nichts ist gemein. Die Todten weket
>   Er auf, die noch gefangen nicht
>   Vom Rohen sind. Es warten aber
>   Der scheuen Augen viele
>   Zu schauen das Licht. Nicht wollen
>   Am scharfen Strale sie blühn,
>   Wiewohl den Muth der goldene Zaum hält.
>   Wenn aber, als
>   Von schwellenden Augenbrauen
>   Der Welt vergessen
>   Stillleuchtende Kraft aus heiliger Schrift fällt, mögen
>   Der Gnade sich freuend, sie
>   Am stillen Blike sich üben.)
>   (*StA* 2: 170–71)

"Hier ist der Stab/Des Gesanges"—"here is the staff of song"—the poet proclaims, in the lines that are often read as the climax of the poem but about which there is little critical consensus. The staff or wand has been identified as the baton of a conductor leading a choir of the heavenly host at the apocalyptic marriage of Christ and the Church, but also as the *rhabdos* of the Homeric bard, the *thyrsus* of the Dionysiac worshiper, the Roman *lituus* or augur's rod, and the staff of Hermes, with which, as both Homer and Virgil relate, he charms the waking and wakes the dead. In the context of a poem entitled "Patmos," however, the *Stab* also suggests an allusion to the "measuring rod" of Revelation 11.1 and 21.15.[11] Both these verses relate to a scene of triumph like the one Hölderlin describes, in which the Son of God returns and Jerusalem is restored as the visionary city in which everything is holy—or, as Hölderlin puts it, nothing is common (nichts ist gemein). As the seer John reports in Revelation 11.1, an angel produces a measuring rod and requires him to measure the holy city. The *Stab* in Hölderlin's "Patmos," though, appears inexplicably, as if produced by language itself, so that the announcement "*hier* ist der Stab" with its unmotivated deictic constitutes the moment of most intense presence and presentness in the poem. The *Stab* has no clear referent; we construct this staff out of the discursive context, instead of constructing the context out of our knowledge of what a measuring rod is, as the reader of Revelation is able to do. "Here" in the first line of stanza 13 corresponds to "now" in the first line of the following stanza, as if to locate the reader in a performative moment when the poem is no longer describing or referring to an event, but enacting one. This event is figured as apocalyptic, but it might also be read in terms of the pragmatic context in which the poem belongs. Foreshadowing the poet's imminent apostrophe to his addressee, the utterance "hier ist der Stab/Des Gesanges" seems to effect the presentation of the poem itself; we imagine Hölderlin handing it to the Landgrave as his own "staff of song."

The scene of dialogue and exchange between John and an angel on Patmos, as narrated in Chapters 10 and 11 of Revelation, provides a background against which to read the communicative action that takes place at the end of "Patmos." In the biblical scene, the angel hands John a book, directing him to eat it, and a staff, directing him to use it in measuring the temple of God. The book and the staff are linguistically joined in "Patmos," the *Stab* of stanza 13 foreshadowing the *Buchstab* ("letter of the alphabet," but literally "book-staff") in the final lines of the poem:

> but what the Father
> Who reigns over all loves most
> Is that the solid letter

[11]The rod is a *Rohr* 'reed' in Luther's Bible, but a *Meßstab* 'measuring rod' in other German translations. The relationship of "Patmos" to Revelation is by no means straightforward; as Hamlin has noted, while the poem contains numerous echoes of the New Testament, especially the Gospel of John, the Book of Revelation is surprisingly—perhaps conspicuously—avoided ("Task of Interpretation" 14). But even oblique allusions to Revelation, like the one proposed here, radically revise the concept of vision and the visionary.

> Be given scrupulous care, and the existing
> Be well interpreted. This German song observes.
> *(Poems 477)*
>
> (der Vater aber liebt,
> Der über allen waltet,
> Am meisten, daß gepfleget werde
> Der veste Buchstab, und bestehendes gut
> Gedeutet. Dem folgt deutscher Gesang.)
> *(StA 2: 172)*

One wonders if the staff in the form of a book, as it appears in the second-last line of "Patmos," is the historical trace or objective reality of the staff of song. The *Stab* appears in an epiphanic moment of presence and performance; the *Buchstab* appears as a fixed record of that moment which is given us to interpret.

Between the epiphanic moment when the Son of the Highest descends, and the final affirmation of the "solid letter," there is an apostrophe to the Landgrave of Homburg. Hölderlin's initial dedication of the poem to him finally comes to the fore in the penultimate stanza, where he locates himself in relation to the Landgrave as one who is also loved by the gods and respects their will:

> And if the Heavenly now
> Love me as I believe,
> How much more you
> They surely love,
> For one thing I know:
> The eternal Father's will
> Means much to you.
> *(Poems 475)*
>
> (Und wenn die Himmlischen jezt
> So, wie ich glaube, mich lieben
> Wie viel mehr Dich,
> Denn Eines weiß ich,
> Daß nemlich der Wille
> Des ewigen Vaters viel
> Dir gilt.)
> *(StA 2: 171)*

It is apparent from Hölderlin's drafts that this penultimate stanza was actually the first one to be written. Even before Hölderlin's first meeting with the Landgrave, as Werner Kirchner shows, this passage connecting an "I" to a "you" had been composed and was waiting to be incorporated into a poem ("Hölderlins Patmos-Hymne" 64). Conversely, "Patmos" was first composed as a poem awaiting an addressee: in the first full draft, a space was left beneath the title for a dedication that was not yet there. From the beginning, Hölderlin writes in full consciousness of a relation between subject and addressee—but it is a relation that exists *in his language* before it corresponds to a historical person and an actual experience. In the context of the completed poem, the second-person address comes in only at the end and depends explicitly on the loving relationship between the poet and God that has been negotiated within the text (*"wenn* die Himmlischen jezt . . . mich lieben . . .").[12] In other words, Hölderlin's addressee appears as a *product* of the hermeneutic experience that "Patmos" enacts—and the poet's own identity is formed in the act of placing himself in relation to this newly generated addressee. His very name—*Johann Christian Friedrich* Hölderlin—bears the traces of all those with whom he stands in relation: the two beings he addresses in the poem (God/Christ and the Landgrave Friedrich) and the object of his interpretation (John/Johannes, the disciple and seer).

The vision that "Patmos" offers, then, is first of all one that assigns language a performative role in creating objects—like a "staff of song"— on which the mind can fasten. With the translation of the *Stab* into a *Buchstab*, the object that demands response becomes a verbal text itself. Both these relations—mind/object and mind/text—engage Humboldt's theory of cognition as a linguistic act, whereby the speaker enters into a responsive relationship with the mental object his or her utterance creates. Like Humboldt, Hölderlin interweaves cognitive, object-creating speech acts with the communicative appeal to an addressee. The experience represented by the final stanzas of "Patmos," which bring together the appearance of the "Son of the Highest" and the "staff of song" with an address to the Landgrave, thus has distinctive effects in each of the objective, intersubjective, and subjective spheres. Its products are a created object, the solid letter of Scripture; an intersubjective relationship between the Landgrave and Hölderlin, by virtue of which they eventually come to occupy the social roles of patron and grateful poet; and an altered self-consciousness on the part of the poet himself. The self-conscious or subjective aspect of the experience is signaled by the fact that the poet subsequently adopts a first-person *plural* perspective—"*We* have served Mother Earth . . ."—*Wir* haben gedienet der Mutter Erd' . . .—that implies his new identification with a community of interpreters.

[12]Shaffer also draws attention to the fact that "the intimacy of 'Ich' and 'Dich' is established through the gods' love for them," in order to point out the precarious status of relationships in "Patmos": the intimate personal relationship of I and You is the strongest bond the poem offers, yet even this relationship depends on the uncertain presence of unfathomable gods (178–79).

The modulation from I to We at the end of "Patmos" brings us back to where this chapter began, for this is the same pattern that appeared in "Wie wenn am Feiertage...": after the performative moment marked by the utterance "let the holy be my word," the speaker begins to identify himself with a community of poets. The complexities of verbal action in both these texts result in large measure from the fact that Hölderlin's speech acts take place in both a subjective and an intersubjective sphere; they are both cognitive and social; or, put yet another way, they relate mind to object as well as relating the self to other selves. Hölderlin's texts represent a series of sometimes visionary, sometimes resigned expressions of the desire that the poet's cognitive speech acts might also provide the basis for social discourse. The utterances of his Empedokles do prevail over the purely sociopolitical performatives of Hermokrates, and Empedokles eventually discovers a dialogic form of utterance through which to relate himself to his environment—but all at the cost of renouncing physical life. For Hyperion, too, the discovery of forms of language through which he can converse with the natural world, with Bellarmin, and with the spirit of Diotima are a problematic compensation for the loss of his actual network of social relationships. Hölderlin's hymns locate the poet-figure in yet other speech situations, and suggest potential connections between the ideal creativity of the poetic word and the community-building power of intersubjective discourse. His language persistently reaches out to at least one dialogic partner—until the very reiteration of his address to the Other underscores the fact that there is *only* address, and a response remains in suspense. The speech acts of Hölderlin's poetry seem to await uptake, either from a specific addressee who shares the conditions of Hölderlin's historical moment, or from the more anonymous reader within a less determinate history. In a pragmatic context, his texts occupy the mode of the not-yet-realized; with their dialogic appeal, they highlight the reader's role in completing the performative gesture of the poetic speech act.

6

Kleist and the Fragile Performative Order of the World

One of Heinrich von Kleist's anecdotes, written in 1810 and entitled "Der Griffel Gottes" (The stylus of God), concerns a wicked Polish countess who tries in vain to buy herself a blessed afterlife by endowing a monastery. Instead, divine judgment descends on her costly monument:

> On the next day lightning struck the grave marker, melting the bronze, and left nothing standing except for a number of letters, that, read together, spelled out: *she is judged!*—The incident (the scribes may explain it) is well founded; the grave marker still exists, and there are men living in this city who have seen it, complete with the above-mentioned inscription. (*SWB* 2: 263)

As it so often does for Hölderlin, lightning here represents the utterance of God. But it is not, as in Hölderlin (or, for that matter, Humboldt or Coleridge), a mere metaphor for language; rather, divine lightning actually produces language, forming letters of molten bronze in a process that can be accounted for neither in terms of nature nor of culture. Although the end of the anecdote offers the possibility of eye-witness testimony, an explanation of the incident is, with palpable irony, left up to "scribes" or "scholars of writing" (die Schriftgelehrten). Above all, the source of the inscription and the authority behind it remain open questions; the title may suggest that the lightning bolt be identified as God's stylus, but why should we trust the title? There is, at least, a certain visual connection between a long, pointed lightning bolt and a writing-instrument, which may be why the text does not suggest a complete absence of intentionality, as might be the case with a poem found inscribed in the sand after a wave had retreated (to cite an image featured in 1980s debates over intentionality and interpretation [Knapp and Michaels 727–29]). Rather than an absence of authority, the problem in Kleist's text is that there are too many possible authorities whose acts of writing and interpretation impose themselves on one another: the invisible narrator of the story, the putative eye-witnesses, the scribes who are called on to interpret the inscription, God or the lightning, and the countess herself—whose German title, *Gräfin*, is suspiciously cognate with Greek *graphein* 'to write.'

The question of authority is all the more vexing in Kleist because crucial utterances in his fiction and drama tend to be written rather than oral—and thus open to a poststructuralist reading, according to which written texts are intrinsically alienated from both an authorizing source and an uptaking reader. Kleist's anecdote of the Polish countess epitomizes the problems generated by speech acts in his works, from the difficulty of interpreting written performatives, to the disruption caused by an intrusion of the supernatural into human language, to the unsettling interference of verbal structures with physical experience (and vice versa). It also exemplifies a recurring parallel between the speech act in the text—the mysterious inscription on the gravestone—and the text itself as a speech act, a mysterious inscription on the page.

The need for interpretation, and the absence of any guarantee of truth, are exactly the conditions that characterize Kleist's response to Kant. As he testifies most famously in letters written during the spring of 1801, Kleist's encounter with "the newer, so-called Kantian philosophy" convinced him that the human understanding cannot have access to truth about the world as it is, for "we cannot decide if that which we call truth truly is truth, or if it only seems so to us" (*SWB* 2: 634). Since truth and spiritual education (Bildung) had been Kleist's sacred ideals since childhood, this realization casts him into a state of aimlessness and despair, in which his only remaining thought is "my only, my highest goal has fallen." Although generations of scholars have probed the sources of Kleist's "Kant crisis" as a crisis of perception, epistemology, and moral judgment, only occasionally have critics noted that this experience is also a crisis of language. In a footnote to a detailed reading of Kleist's drama *Die Familie Schroffenstein* as a "tragedy of the speaking individual" or a "tragedy of language," Hinrich C. Seeba laments that "the overvalued Kant crisis has repeatedly obscured the view of the primarily linguistic character of his crisis of consciousness" (122–23). John H. Smith, setting traditional interpretations of Kleist's response to Kant in the context of a dialogic reading of Kleist's prose, proposes a more positive interpretation of the nexus formed by Kleist, Kant, and language. In Smith's view, Kleist's negative response to the epistemology of the Critiques is counterbalanced by the more positive insight that he gained from Kant's *Metaphysics of Morals*, specifically from the idea that dialogic method does offer a path to the recognition of the moral law. Accordingly, in Kleist's essays and novellas knowledge always needs to be elicited through dialogue, even though the language of social discourse is always inadequate and communication is always disturbed.

Following on readings like these, I would propose that Kleist's theory of language—its potential, its limitations, its inevitability, and its uncontrollable effects—is vital to his theory of knowledge. Indeed, Kleist's response to Kant parallels that of contemporaries like Hölderlin, Humboldt, or Bernhardi insofar as they all theorize the latent role of language in Kantian (and Fichtean) philosophy. But in Kleist's work problems of cognition blend with problems of social and political discourse. As a onetime student of law and political science at the Universities of Frankfurt/Oder and Königsberg, and the failed aspirant to a position in the Prussian civil service, Kleist is obsessed with the operation of legal and institutional, as well as individual, utterances. Thus, his work may be brought into relation not only with post-Kantian linguistic philosophers, but also with the more politically oriented philosophers of the same generation in Britain, particularly Bentham and Godwin.

The world represented in Kleist's texts typically features a specialized and obtrusive verbal code that not only regulates, but *constitutes* the reality that characters experience. Kleist's dramas, especially, locate the origin of this social code in explicit performative utterances such as oaths or formal declarations. Individual characters confirm these originary performatives with their own utterances, even as they struggle against the constraints that the dominant code imposes on their behavior and identity. The speech acts of Ottokar Schroffenstein, Penthesilea, and Prince Friedrich of Homburg affirm the social order, yet also—sometimes even simultaneously—challenge that order. Although the legal and ethical conflict between these individuals and the universal law is a familiar theme in Kleist scholarship, the conflict also needs to be set in a linguistic context. The dilemma of Kleist's characters foreshadows poststructuralist analyses of the performative, including the de Manian tension between (universalizing) grammar and (individualizing) rhetoric; the Derridean speech act, defined by its possibility of failure; and the condition that Shoshana Felman has called "the scandal of the speaking body." *Le scandal du corps parlant*, the original French title of the book by Felman translated into English as *The Literary Speech Act*, is a phrase that nicely captures the irresolvable conflict encountered everywhere in Kleist's work between the immediacy of physical experience and the reflective structure of language.

As argued elsewhere in this book, these modern formulations are anticipated by the pragmatic orientation of linguistic philosophy around

1800, and the speech acts in Kleist's texts emphasize precisely these connections. Although Kleist never directly enters into dialogue with the linguistic thinkers of his age, some of his work does introduce an explicit linguistic-pragmatic perspective. *Amphitryon* complicates the conflict of individual utterance with social discourse by depicting a performative relationship between what one says and what one is: the drama juxtaposes its protagonist's essential or permanent identity with identity that is established by an utterance of the form "I am [Amphitryon]," and explores the extent to which personal identity may even be dependent on the public's acknowledgment of such a declaration. Kleist's one, brief essay on philosophy of language, "Über die allmähliche Verfertigung der Gedanken beim Reden" (On the gradual completion of thoughts while speaking), focuses on the relationship of cognition and language, bringing to this Romantic issue a new concern with the body and physical experience. Verbal codes, as the dramas demonstrate, regulate individual behavior and translate the brute facts of the physical world into public, institutional facts; yet Kleist's essay on thought and language also argues that bodily experience helps shape verbal utterance in the first place. The result—manifested in novellas like *Michael Kohlhaas* and "Der Zweikampf"—is an interinvolvement of the most elemental physical experiences with contracts, laws, petitions, declarations, edicts, oaths, and judicial sentences. Psychologically and even epistemologically, Kleist's characters are compelled to experience reality as, and through, a dense and bizarre network of subjective and intersubjective speech acts. Kleist's dramas and novellas imply that a social order founded on performative utterances is essential—and yet that the performative order of the world is poignantly fragile, because of its basic incommensurability with physical experience as well as its inability to accommodate a transcendent or supernatural dimension.

THE CONSTITUTIONS OF THE SCHROFFENSTEINS, THE AMAZONS, AND THE PRUSSIANS

Kleist's version of the Romantic performative, as an utterance that alters the speaker's position within his or her environment, encapsulates the struggle for identity that characterizes many of his plays. These identity-shaping performatives take place against the background of societies in which authoritative utterances generate universal codes of behavior, such as the Amazon code in *Penthesilea* or the Prussian military statutes in *Prinz Friedrich von Homburg*. Kleist's early drama *Die Familie Schroffenstein* (The Schroffenstein family) provides the most vivid example of a social order constructed by performative utterance,[1] for it begins with a scene in which Rupert, Count Schroffenstein, swears, and makes his household swear, an oath of vengeance against the household of Sylvester, head of the other branch of the house of Schroffenstein, whom Rupert deems responsible for the murder of his nine-year-old son. After swearing on the sacred host at the boy's funeral mass, Rupert instructs his remaining son Ottokar to take a precise and relentless oath:

> RUPERT. I swear on the host, vengeance! vengeance
> Against the house of Sylvester, Count Schroffenstein.
> *He takes communion.*
> It's your turn now, my son.
> OTTOKAR. My heart
> Bears your curse to God as if on wings.
> I swear vengeance, just like you.
> RUPERT. The name,
> My son, name the name.
> OTTOKAR. Vengeance I swear
> Against Sylvester Schroffenstein!
> RUPERT. Make no mistake.
> An oath like ours comes to the ear of god
> And he arms each word with lightning bolts.
> So weigh them carefully. Say not
> 'Sylvester,' but say 'all his house';
> That will be safer.
> OTTOKAR. Vengeance, I swear, vengeance
> Against Sylvester's murderous house.
> *He takes communion.*
>
> (RUPERT. Ich schwöre Rache! Rache! auf die Hostie,
> Dem Haus Sylvesters, Grafen Schroffenstein.
> *Er empfängt das Abendmahl.*
> Die Reihe ist an dir, mein Sohn.
> OTTOKAR. Mein Herz
> Trägt wie mit Schwingen deinen Fluch zu Gott.
> Ich schwöre Rache, so wie du.

---

[1] Seeba offers an important reading of this drama as a "tragedy of language," in which the final scene, where the head of each of the Schroffenstein houses inadvertently kills his own child, is the ironic fulfilment of the curse with which the play began, a speech act that "involuntarily draws in the cursor himself" (131). Especially significant is Seeba's claim that Kleist manifests his skepticism about language by exposing a dilemma inherent in language itself, whereby it forces our consciousness of reality into restrictive structures: "Like Pandora's box, language contains the doom of the world, the poison of suspicion, that already possesses a judgment before it judges. Language is that striving after definiteness, with which people of prejudgment fix ambiguous reality into their polarized scheme of consciousness" (141).

> RUPERT.   Den Namen,
>   Mein Sohn, den Namen nenne.
> OTTOKAR.   Rache schwör ich,
>   Sylvestern Schroffenstein!
> RUPERT.   Nein irre nicht.
>   Ein Fluch, wie unsrer, kömmt vor Gottes Ohr
>   Und jedes Wort bewaffnet er mit Blitzen.
>   Drum wäge sie gewissenhaft.—Sprich nicht
>   Sylvester, sprich sein ganzes Haus, so hast
>   Dus sichrer.
> OTTOKAR.   Rache! schwör ich, Rache!
>   Dem Mörderhaus Sylvesters.
>   *Er empfängt das Abendmahl.)*
>   (23–35 / *SWB* 1: 52)

Against the background of this initial, formal utterance, the details of the crisis in the Schroffenstein clan quickly unfold as a series of further speech acts. A clergyman explains, for the benefit of the audience as well as the younger generation of Schroffensteins, that the feud between the two houses had its origin in a testamentary contract (Erbvertrag) that set the two families at odds over the entire Schroffenstein estate. Ultimately, this world-order owes its organization to a performative document, which scholars have interpreted as an allusion to the covenant God makes with fallen humanity in the Garden of Eden, but also as a critique of the Enlightenment tradition of social contract stemming from Hobbes (Seeba 143, Stammen 72–73). The drama depicts Ottokar's doomed attempt to transform the feudal order imposed on the Schroffenstein clan by an ancient testamentary contract and confirmed by recent oaths—his own included—of vengeance or allegiance. As lover of his enemy's daughter Agnes, as would-be reconciler of the two houses, and even as a kind of detective who discovers the truth behind his brother's death, Ottokar strives to change the constitution of his social world while establishing an alternative identity for himself within it.

The ironic situation whereby Ottokar challenges the performative order that he himself confirmed with his initial oath finds an echo in Kleist's other dramas. The society of the Amazons in *Penthesilea* lies somewhere between the feudal order of *Die Familie Schroffenstein*, where the speech acts that determine relationships and behavior are formal, individual oaths and contracts, and the conventions of (supposedly) historical political jurisdictions, like the Prussian state in *Prinz Friedrich von Homburg*. The parameters of this world-order are laid out in the crucial fifteenth scene of the play, where the Amazon Queen Penthesilea and the Greek hero Achilles confess their mutual attraction in a conversation heavy with issues of identity, with questions of the form "who are you" (wer bist du), affirmations of the form "it is I" (ich bins), and acts of naming. But Penthesilea's and Achilles' declarations to one another are already fraught with conflict, since their exchange has as much to do with who *belongs to* whom as about who one *is*. It becomes clear that, for Penthesilea, negotiating a relationship with Achilles will involve a transgression of the societal code that she is sworn to uphold—and yet she grounds her representation of herself in precisely that code. As she explains to Achilles, her Amazon society was brought into existence by the founding speech acts of an assembly of women, who, having killed their foreign masters, resolved to establish an independent female state:

> PENTHESILEA. And then they held a council
> where it was decreed as follows: Women
> capable of acting so heroically
> needs must be unfettered as the wind
> that blows across the open steppes and shall submit
> to men no longer. Let a state, a women's one,
> complete in all respects, be instituted
> where men's boastful, overbearing voices
> shall never be allowed to clamor noisily
> again, a state which gives itself its own
> laws, worthily, obeys itself, defends
> itself, and Tanaïs shall be its Queen.
>
> (*Five Plays* 227)
>
> (Und dies jetzt ward im Rat des Volks beschlossen:
> Frei, wie der Wind auf offnem Blachfeld, sind
> Die Fraun, die solche Heldentat vollbracht,
> Und dem Geschlecht der Männer nicht mehr
>   dienstbar.
> Ein Staat, ein mündiger, sei aufgestellt,
> Ein Frauenstaat, den fürder keine andre
> Herrschsüchtge Männerstimme mehr durchtrotzt,
> Der das Gesetz sich würdig selber gebe,
> Sich selbst gehorche, selber auch beschütze:
> Und Tanaïs sei seine Königin.)
>
> (1953–62/*SWB* 1: 388–89)

The question of authority that plagues all initiatory speech acts arises at once, when a voice in the crowd questions the validity of these resolutions by pointing out that a state of women will hardly be able to maintain itself against its warlike neighbors. At this, Queen Tanaïs pauses for a moment to test the uptake the objection receives: "The Queen did nothing/for a moment, waiting silently to see/what fate these words would have" (Die Königin stand einen Augenblick,/Und harrte still auf solcher Rede Glück [1983–84/*Five Plays* 228/*SWB* 1: 389]). Then, as the assembly responds with a "craven ripple spreading all around," she tears off her own right breast, baptizes the women with her blood as "Amazons" or "Breastless Ones," and institutes a semi-political, semi-cultic code of behavior to ensure both the defense and the procreation of her people. The acts that found the Amazon state, in other words, involve violence interpreted and realized in performative utterance: the slaughter of the men culminates in the public declaration of a female state; Tanaïs's self-mutilation, which makes the separate state into a separate race by establishing a physical difference that will henceforth mark its inhabitants, also counts as a formal act of baptism by which the people is given its name. From the originary scene that Penthesilea relates there derives a semiotic code that binds together physical and verbal performance and governs the behavior of all the Amazons, while it constitutes them as "Amazons" in the first place.

Although the ostensible battle in *Penthesilea* is between the Amazons and the Greeks, the real focus of the drama is the internal battle within Penthesilea—a battle between the code of behavior she is sworn to uphold, because it constitutes her identity and that of her people, and the emotional experience that conflicts with it. Even before she meets Achilles, she fails to act entirely according to the laws of her people; her love for her mother causes her to obey her mother's dying words, when she counsels Penthesilea to seek out the hero Achilles for herself, instead of allowing the war-god Mars and the fortunes of battle to determine her victim for her. But the critical point on which experience conflicts with law is the Amazon prohibition against mating with any man except the one an Amazon has conquered in battle. Like Ottokar when he swears vengeance against Sylvester's household, Penthesilea actually intensifies the force of the code that governs her identity by pronouncing a curse on herself, were she to break this fundamental article:

> PENTHESILEA. A curse on me if ever I endure
> such shame! A curse on me if ever I
> accept a man I haven't won in worthy
> fashion, with my sword!
> (*Five Plays* 215)

> (Fluch mir, wenn ich die Schmach erlebte, Freundin!
> Fluch mir, empfing ich jemals einen Mann,
> Den mir das Schwert nicht würdig zugeführt.)
> (1579–81/*SWB* 1: 376)

What Penthesilea does not know is that Achilles has made a vow of his own, swearing not to rejoin his companions until he has conquered and bedded the Amazon queen:

> ACHILLES. I'll never turn my chariot
> back to camp and friends, or even look at
> Pergamon again, till she's my bride
> and with her forehead wreathed in deadly wounds
> parades beside me through the streets of Troy,
> feet first!
>
> (*Five Plays* 179)
>
> (den Wagen dort
> Nicht ehr zu meinen Freunden will ich lenken,
> Ich schwörs, und Pergamos nicht wiedersehn,
> Als bis ich sie zu meiner Braut gemacht,
> Und sie, die Stirn bekränzt mit Todeswunden,
> Kann durch die Straßen häuptlings mit mir
> schleifen.)
>
> (610–15 / *SWB* 1: 342)

These conflicting speeches set up a situation in which Achilles effectively excommunicates himself from the Greeks until he conquers and weds Penthesilea, but she excommunicates herself from the Amazons if she weds him without herself being the conqueror. One of them will forfeit his or her superiority (or even life) if they meet in battle, but at least one of them will forfeit his or her social identity in any case, because their declarations define a situation that is inconsistent with their simultaneous existence as an Amazon and a Greek.

The opposed vows of Penthesilea and Achilles ensure that, although their encounter is a physical battle and, at the end, one of inhuman violence, its outcome will also be curiously determined by speech acts. Achilles is able to conquer Penthesilea because her own command to her troops not to harm him (made because she has, in defiance of the Amazon code, chosen him for herself) allows him to break through her guard and reach her. Their long interview in the fifteenth scene is possible only because Achilles has promised Penthesilea's companion Prothoe that he will delay telling the queen that *he* has conquered *her*, and not she him, so that she can continue for a while under the delusion that he is her prisoner and hence her lawful mate. Once Achilles does reveal the truth, Penthesilea desperately tries to deny it in the seventeenth and eighteenth scenes by ordering him to follow her to Diana's temple at Themiscyra, even as he is giving his fellow Greeks a contrary order to lead her away as his prisoner.

When Penthesilea can no longer cling to the possibility of living by the Amazon code, she declares herself ready to exchange it for the law of war, which she calls a "worthy chivalric custom." Having accepted this new code of behavior, she now curses her own people for rescuing her from Achilles' power:

> PENTHESILEA. I curse your winning, it dishonors me!
> I curse each tongue exulting over it,
> the air that bears the noise of it abroad,
> I curse that too! By every law of chivalry
> wasn't I fairly his, thanks to the luck
> of battle?
> (*Five Plays* 239)

> (Verflucht sei dieser schändliche Truimph mir!
> Verflucht jedwede Zunge, die ihn feiert,
> Die Luft verflucht mir, die ihn weiter bringt!
> War ich, nach jeder würdgen Rittersitte,
> Nicht durch das Glück der Schlacht ihm
> zugefallen?)
> (2298–2302/*SWB* 1: 400)

The High Priestess of the Amazons regards Penthesilea's disloyal curse on her rescuers as her third strike against the governing semiotic code, and responds by excommunicating the queen from her people: "In the name of our people, I pronounce you free" (Frei, in des Volkes Namen, sprech ich dich [2329/*Five Plays* 240/*SWB* 1: 401]). But Penthesilea, having affirmed the Amazon law with her own oath, is not free from it until she renounces it with a speech act of her own. "I/abjure the law of our women" (Ich sage vom Gesetz der Fraun mich los [3012/*Five Plays* 267/*SWB* 1: 426]), she resolves at the end of the drama, moments before taking her own life.

Penthesilea demonstrates the tragic consequences of a determination to live according to one's law and one's oath: necessary as these controlling performatives are to the definition of a valid social identity, they also make it impossible to assimilate new experiences, for the unknown future resists containment by speech acts of the past. If this is a paradox that citizens of most societies learn to live with, in Penthesilea's case it is extreme and ineluctable. She can live neither within nor outside of the Amazon code. Once she ceases to live according to the law of the Amazons, and fails in her attempt to substitute for it the "law of chivalry" in battle, she has no human law left by which to define herself; she is reduced to invoking the gods while behaving like a beast.

The grotesque fusion of verbal utterance and physical violence at the end of the drama is epitomized in the passage where Penthesilea characterizes her murder of Achilles, during which she tore his body with her teeth, as a kind of speech act. Delirious, she boasts that she has kept her word much more exactly than other women, who declare only figuratively that they love a man so much they could eat him up: "when I wound *my* arms around your neck/I did exactly that, devour you" (als ich an deinem Halse hing,/Hab ichs wahrhaftig Wort für Wort getan [2997–98/*Five Plays* 266/*SWB* 1: 426]). Literalizing words as physical actions in this way constitutes a kind of linguistic performance, but also a gross mistake—two connotations that come together when Penthesilea alludes to her act of *versprechen*. "Ich habe mich, bei Diana, bloß versprochen," she pleads to Achilles' corpse: "It was a slip—/ I swear it, by Diana—of the tongue" (2986/*Five Plays* 266/*SWB* 1: 426). The heavy irony of referring to her fatal "mistake"—tearing Achilles' flesh with her teeth when she intended to kiss him—as "a slip of the tongue" is compounded by the resonances between her verb *sich versprechen* 'to misspeak' and the non-reflexive verb *versprechen* 'to promise.' There are many kinds of oral confusion here. Penthesilea admits to a tendency to make hasty utterances—"I am remiss and fail to stand/guard over my rash mouth the way/I should" (weil ich der raschen Lippe Herr nicht bin [2987/*Five Plays* 266/*SWB* 1: 426])—but if she is not master of her tongue, her role as sovereign of her people nevertheless augments the public effect of her misguided speech acts, wrecking havoc on the Amazon campaign against the Greeks. Penthesilea's act of *(sich) versprechen* also alludes to the implied or incomplete promises she makes to Achilles over the course of the drama: that she will dedicate herself to him once she has brought him back, as her prisoner, to Themiscyra (1852–53/*Five Plays* 224/*SWB* 1: 385), or that (as he cries out, even as she is slaughtering him) she will celebrate the festival of roses, the Amazon mating ritual, with him (2664–65/*Five Plays* 267/*SWB* 1: 413). Penthesilea's most explicit act of promising herself to Achilles, and the only promise that she keeps, is her vow to follow him into death: "I/abjure the law of our women, I/will follow the young man who's lying here" (Ich sage vom Gesetz der Fraun mich los,/Und folge diesem Jüngling hier [3012–13/*Five Plays* 267/*SWB* 1: 426]). As Jakob Spälti points out (77–79), Kleist puns on *(sich) versprechen* as an ambivalent promise of marriage in his near-contemporaneous epigram "Das Sprachversehen" (The mistake in speaking, 1808):

> What! now you won't have her, and you were promised to the lady?
> Answer: forgive me, my friend! it happens that one mis-speaks.

> (Was! Du nimmst sie jetzt nicht, und warst der Dame versprochen?
> Antwort: Lieber! vergib, man verspricht sich ja wohl.)
>
> (SWB 1: 23)

Ultimately, though, *Penthesilea* suggests that the frame of reference for *(sich) versprechen* goes far beyond an individual's rash words. It encompasses the fundamental incompatibility of language with experience that de Man evokes when he puns, "die Sprache verspricht (sich)" (*Allegories of Reading* 277): language, insofar as its performative dimension always entails an implicit but untenable promise of future validity, mis-speaks. In the context of *Penthesilea*, the Amazon code and the speech acts that reaffirm it are the central mis-speaking promises: they purport to translate the physical experience of both past and future into a linguistic medium that is intrinsically incommensurate with experience.

The plight of Penthesilea, and the condition of the Amazons in general, constitutes a limit case of the conflict between individual identity, codes of behavior, and the inaugural speech acts that generate them. Like the testamentary contract in *Die Familie Schroffenstein*, the Amazon code has been read as an ironic commentary on the social contract of Enlightenment philosophers;[2] but, for the Amazons, a more particular significance attaches to their founding scene as a verbal and semiotic act. The Amazon state must distinguish itself from other states, in which the physical strength of men deprives women of a public voice. It must by its very existence stand for the possibility of living by a law that counters the "natural" hierarchy; it must constantly reaffirm the power of words over physicality. Thus Amazonian law subjects physical experience—sex, violence, and procreation—to the "first mothers' words" (1909/*Five Plays* 226/*SWB* 1: 387), and its inaugural scene incorporates gross savagery (Tanaïs's amputation of her breast) into verbal convention (an act of baptism). In other words, the Amazons' code and their identity are intensely performative, for their warrior code makes the women what they are: a distinct society dedicated to defending a constitution that defines the society as distinct, precisely because it successfully subjects physicality to a verbal code. Penthesilea gradually, and then precipitously,

---

[2]Hofmann connects the contract that defines the Amazon state with the Rousseauist tradition of social contract and contemporary issues of governance and constitution (142–43). While his article focuses on the conflict between the inhuman code of the Amazons and Enlightenment ideals, and especially on what happens when legal codes are internalized by specific characters, I would argue that Kleist's dramas also address the fundamental tensions caused by legal codes inasmuch as they are forms of language.

loses her identity as a queen, an Amazon, and even a human being as she loses her place in the code that defines her and her state.

Kleist's last play, *Prinz Friedrich von Homburg*, complicates—but also partially redeems—the tragic irony of Ottokar's and Penthesilea's situation by having Prince Friedrich confirm and challenge existing social discourses within the same utterance. In this drama, the Prince makes a first attempt to establish his identity, as the young hero of the battle of Fehrbellin, through a speech act that defies the code circumscribing his role as a military officer: he orders his unit to attack too early, when he has expressly been commanded to wait until the Elector himself gives the order. Condemned to death by a military tribunal for his act of disobedience, the Prince experiences in his own person the dilemmas that arose in eighteenth-century debates over the applicability of social contracts—especially the paradoxical relationship, famously identified by Rousseau, between their general validity and their specific referentiality. In conversation with his friend Hohenzollern, the Prince easily admits that the verdict against him is correct, and indeed necessary, in terms of the objective legal code: "The court had no choice but to find/for death; the law by which it acts requires/that" (Das Kriegsrecht mußte auf den Tod erkennen;/So lautet das Gesetz, nach dem es richtet [870–71/*Five Plays* 311/*SWB* 1: 670]). But in the traumatic night visit to the palace during which the Prince witnesses the digging of his own grave, he comes to realize the referential significance of the verdict—that it decrees *his own* bodily death. Finally, the Elector puts the Prince in a position where he must formally acknowledge, first in writing and then in a verbal declaration in the presence of the Elector and his generals, that the law justly applies *to him*.

When the Elector sends a message to Prince Friedrich in prison, offering to pardon him if he himself calls the verdict unjust, the Prince is well aware of the irony and self-reflexivity of his situation. "He leaves it up to me—*I* must decide!" he marvels (Mich selber ruft er zur Entscheidung auf! [1342/*Five Plays* 330/*SWB* 1: 688]), realizing that the "two words" with which he is called on to respond put him in the unusual position of passing sentence on himself, or becoming both subject and object of the act of judgment. His letter of reply—which is never heard by the audience, but which evidently contains an admission that "My offense,/I see it now, is heavy, very heavy" (Schuld ruht, bedeutende, mir auf der Brust,/Wie ich es wohl erkenne [1382–83/*Five Plays* 331/*SWB* 1: 690])—counterbalances the speech act with which he originally overstepped the martial law. If the Prince's order on the battlefield is an affirmation of subjective identity in defiance of the military code, the letter that he sends back to the Elector counts as a new, performative declaration of his identity as one who lives within the state and the military system delineated by its laws.

But by virtue of the fact that Prince Friedrich is made to pass judgment in his own case, his response is also a speech act that paradoxically creates the conditions of its own possibility. In affirming that he—as an accountable agent in a critical military situation, and despite being a relative and favorite of the Elector—*is* subject to the strictures of the law, the Prince also exercises the power of judging when and to whom the law should apply. One might even say that he demonstrates, in a particularly dramatic way, the situation that Bentham claims is typical of all general legislation, or legislation *de classibus*. Because "the legislator in the grouping of the persons things and acts which he takes for the subjects and objects of his laws is limited to such parcels as correspond to the generic names which are furnished by the language," the legislator's authority is limited by the need to determine exactly who is included in a given class, and by the subject's consequent ability to interpret his or her own position in relation to the class and the law (*Of Laws* 82). Prince Friedrich's response, affirming his approval of the court's verdict in his case, places him simultaneously in the position of law-breaker and law-maker; he is subject to the system, but he is also the one empowered to decide *who* is subject to the system.³ This empowerment is reflected in the language of liberty that the Prince adopts from the moment he approves the verdict; ironically, submission to the law will allow him to die a "free death" (1752/*SWB* 1: 704). More ironically still, when the Prince is finally pardoned instead of being executed, the Elector and the generals proclaim him aloud as the one "who conquered gloriously/At Fehrbellin" (1855/*Five Plays* 350/*SWB* 1: 709). He achieves, in the end, the identity that he first contended for when he challenged the military code with his unauthorized order, but only by confirming that code and his subjection to it.

Shrouded in enigma, this last act of Prince Friedrich's pardon and triumph is far from resolving the predicament of contractual language depicted so powerfully in *Penthesilea*. On the contrary, other elements of *Prinz Friedrich von Homburg*, such as the thoroughgoing confusion of

---

³See Hofmann: "But with this readiness, with his 'I will' that signals his resolve to suffer death as specified in the law, Homburg takes his place at the Elector's side as co-legislator in a patriotic government" (161). Hofmann relates the role of the Prince and the generals in the final verdict to the problematic position of the Elector himself, as an absolute monarch who nevertheless maintains that power resides in the "rule of law."

dream and reality, complicate the relationship of language and experience. But this drama does open up a new perspective on the performatives that shape the social order, by following up the implications of their interpretability and their self-reflexivity, or the fact that the speakers who affirm them are also those to whom they apply. Indeed, the very incommensurability of language and experience, that makes a perfect constitution or law-code impossible, also opens up a gap for interpretation, and thus signals a way—though hardly an easy one—in which universalizing linguistic structures might coexist with individual identity.

'AMPHITRYON' AND THE "I AM"

Kleist's most acute exploration of subjective and social identity is the earlier, darkly comic *Amphitryon*. This drama complicates the relationship between speech acts and human existence by suggesting that even private or subjective identity may be a function of specific, public speech acts and their reception. Not only do objective codes of behavior interact with, or even predominate over, individual will, but the individual's sense of self may have to yield to intersubjective negotiation. The play centers on the confusion between two characters who look identical—the hero Amphitryon, and the god Jupiter masquerading as Amphitryon—a situation that is itself doubled on a socially lower and more comic level by the confusion between Amphitryon's servant Sosias, and the god Mercury masquerading as Sosias. Early in the play, Sosias is compelled to admit that Mercury/Sosias probably has a better claim to "be" Sosias than he himself does; in the final act, Amphitryon is forced to admit the same about Jupiter/Amphitryon. Throughout the drama, characters utter the words "I am" and "you are" in strikingly ironic contexts, so as to evoke and problematize the meaning of these phrases in the philosophy and literature of Kleist's age. As is true, in different ways, of Fichte's, Humboldt's, and Coleridge's writing, so in Kleist's *Amphitryon* "I am" becomes a performative, and intersubjective, statement.

On the one hand, Sosias, whose dilemma provides a foil for his master Amphitryon's dilemma, affirms an intrinsic and inalienable sense of identity that seems independent of external influences—at least when "external influences" consist of physical compulsion. When Mercury/Sosias threatens to beat Sosias if the latter does not give up his claim to the name and identity of Sosias, Sosias affirms that a beating will not alter his conviction about his identity, even if it could eliminate his existence altogether:

Kleist and the Fragile Performative Order

> SOSIA. Let me go, I beg you. Your stick can make
> it so that I'm no more, but not that I'm
> not I, because I am.
> *(Five Plays* 11)
>
> (SOSIAS.   Ach laß mich gehn.
> Dein Stock kann machen, daß ich nicht mehr bin;
> Doch nicht, daß ich nicht *Ich* bin, weil ich bin.)
> (228–30 / *SWB* 1: 254)

By the end of this encounter, though, when it becomes evident that Mercury/Sosias possesses all the private knowledge that the real Sosias should possess, even Sosias begins to doubt his own identity:

> SOSIA. There's not a thing he doesn't know, the devil
> take him! I'm beginning to have doubts about
> myself. Already he was Sosia thanks
> to his bold face and stick, but now he's got
> good reasons, too, for being him, which makes
> his case complete. Yet when I pinch myself
> I'd swear this flesh here is pure Sosia.
> *(Five Plays* 15)
>
> (SOSIAS. Er weiß um alles.—Alle Teufel jetzt!
> Ich fang im Ernst an mir zu zweifeln an.
> Durch seine Unverschämtheit ward er schon
> Und seinen Stock, Sosias, und jetzt wird er,
> Das fehlte nur, es auch aus Gründen noch.
> Zwar wenn ich mich betaste, wollt ich schwören,
> Daß dieser Leib Sosias ist.)
> (341–47 / *SWB* 1: 257)

The experience of his own body—the factor that typically confounds the effect of verbal utterance in Kleist's plays—is the one reservation that Sosias still maintains against Mercury/Sosias's persuasions. In act 2, scene 5, though, the long interview between Amphitryon's wife Alkmene, and Jupiter disguised as Amphitryon, dismantles even this guarantee of identity. It begins to seem as if identity does not depend on subjective perception and personal conviction, but on *external* appearance and *other people's* convictions. Alkmene is desperate for an assurance from the figure she believes is her husband that it was indeed he who made love to her the night before:

> ALCMENE. Oh my dear husband, please
> do tell me, was it you or not? Speak, it
> was you, it was!
> *(Five Plays* 46)
>
> (ALKMENE. O mein Gemahl! Kannst du mir gütig sagen,
> Warst dus, warst du es nicht? O sprich! du warsts!)
> (1264–65 / *SWB* 1: 285)

"Ich wars," Jupiter answers; but his words, of course, mean different things to Alkmene ("It was I, Amphitryon") and to Jupiter himself ("It was I, Jupiter"). Jupiter/Amphitryon complicates his affirmation further when he continues, "Yes, it was me. But it's/no matter who it was" (Ich wars. Seis wer es wolle): speaking as Amphitryon, he tries to comfort Alkmene by affirming that it was Amphitryon that she slept with *if she took it to be Amphitryon*. The belief of the observer or addressee now determines the identity of the speaking subject, not the subject's own belief or inner feeling. This concept is far from comforting Alkmene at the time, though later in the same scene she herself grasps desperately at the new definition of identity, seeking to determine who Jupiter/Amphitryon is *for her*:

> ALCMENE.   The god—it's you, it's you?
> JUPITER.   For you
>   to say. Myself, I am Amphitryon.
> ALCMENE.   Amphitryon—
> JUPITER. For you, Amphitryon.
>   (*Five Plays* 55)
>
> (ALKMENE.   Bist dus mir? Bist dus mir?
> JUPITER.   Entscheide du. Amphitryon bin ich.
> ALKMENE.   Amphitryon—
> JUPITER.   Amphitryon, dir ja.)
>   (1543–45/*SWB* 1: 293)

The idea that one can *be*, not absolutely, but with respect to someone else, will become crucial in the final scene of the play. In speech-act terms, this idea gives new meaning to the notion of establishing identity through dialogue that is so important to the early Romantics and to linguistic philosophers like Humboldt. By the end of his dialogue with Alkmene, Jupiter/Amphitryon has established his identity as Amphitryon, and her last utterance in the scene is to call him by that name (1574/*Five Plays* 57/*SWB* 1: 294). The I-You relationship between Alkmene and Jupiter/Amphitryon, brought about by both sexual and verbal intercourse, gives dramatic expression to the new, pragmatic understanding of pronouns that characterized linguistic theory at the time *Amphitryon* was written. As Humboldt puts it, "*I* is not the individual invested with these particular characteristics, who is found in these particular spatial circumstances, but rather the one who, in this moment, takes up a position opposite another in consciousness, as a subject" (*GS* 6: 306). In Kleist's drama, however, this definition of the I is rendered ironic by being juxtaposed with an alternative definition— namely, the real Amphitryon's subjective awareness of his own identity. What counts is no longer Amphitryon's (or Jupiter/Amphitryon's) inner conviction of being Amphitryon, nor an objective reality in which the name "Amphitryon" consistently corresponds to an individual invested with particular characteristics, but rather Alkmene's belief that the one who says "I am Amphitryon" *is* Amphitryon. In other words, the utterance "I am Amphitryon" has become explicitly performative. Its effect or force in a dialogic context is more significant than its reference to reality; it needs to be judged by the standards of felicity (in persuading the addressee, in being appropriate to the occasion) rather than descriptive accuracy.

If this radically dialogic concept of identity makes "I am" statements into performatives, it also emblematizes the difference between the Romantic performative and the speech act of modern analytic philosophy. Austin and Searle analyze performatives such as oaths and promises based on the heuristic assumption of a stable, unified speaker. But the notion of speech acts that arose among Romantic writers, particularly in response to Kant's First Critique, is predicated on an I that is in the process of becoming. This processive—and therefore also unstable—status of the I is reflected in the utterances of Kleist's characters generally, but most explicitly, and to the point of tragicomic irony, in the dialogues of *Amphitryon*. The instability of first-person pronouns affects the operation of performative utterances, for illocutionary acts like promises or oaths depend on the assumption that the speaker is an integral, capable moral agent. Not only speech-act theorists, but also eighteenth-century moral philosophers recognize that the uniqueness of individual identity is crucial to commissive speech acts, for individual volition is the basis of moral responsibility. "Our exertions, our deliberations, our purposes, our promises, are only in things that depend upon our will," writes Thomas Reid in developing a theory of language as interpersonal action (2: 619).

In *Amphitryon*, however, the doubling of individual identity destabilizes speech acts like promises or oaths. During the same, long conversation with the god who is Amphitryon "for her," Alkmene, unable to be sure that she has not dishonored her husband, swears a solemn oath to leave him:

> ALCMENE. If that is your idea, I swear—
> and hear me, you immortal gods, you
> dread punishers of all false swearing—
> Sooner will I go down to my grave
> than come back, while there's breath still in
> my bosom, to your bed.
> (*Five Plays* 48)

> (ALKMENE. Nun dann, weil dus so willst, so schwör
> ich dir,
> Und rufe mir der Götter ganze Schar,
> Des Meineids fürchterliche Rächer auf:
> Eh will ich meiner Gruft, als diesen Busen,
> So lang er atmet, deinem Bette nahn.)
> (1328–32 / *SWB* 1: 287)

But what is the status of an oath when the identity of the swearer, or the person to whom the oath relates—or even the identity of the god by whom it is sworn—is unknown or illusory? Alkmene is not in fact addressing the man she thinks she is addressing as "you." In terms of her own intention, the oath, forceful as it is, will be broken soon after, for she continues to live with Amphitryon as his wife. Ironically, though, in the context in which it happens to be spoken it turns out to be both felicitous and fulfilled: Alkmene will not visit *Jupiter's* bed again. Because of the shiftiness of the term "you," the fact that it refers not to an individual invested with particular characteristics but to one who takes up a position opposite another in consciousness, the intended addressee of the oath switches places, as it were, with the being by whom it is sworn. Believing she is swearing *by* Jupiter and the other gods, Alkmene in fact swears *to* and *about* Jupiter. There is, then, a certain appropriateness in Jupiter's response. Through his "inborn power," Jupiter/Amphitryon immediately nullifies her speech act:

> JUPITER. The powers I
> possess are such, I'll break your oath and scatter
> all its pieces in the air.
> (*Five Plays* 48)
>
> (Den Eid, kraft angeborner Macht, zerbrech ich
> Und seine Stücken werf ich in die Lüfte.)
> (1333–34 / *SWB* 1: 287)

To compound the irony, Jupiter/Amphitryon explains why the oath is invalid by telling Alkmene the truth—that it was a god who visited her—although without revealing the full, pragmatic truth—that he who is speaking to her is that same god.

The complications surrounding these two performatives, the "I am" declaration and the oath, in Alkmene's dialogue with Jupiter/Amphitryon, foreshadow what happens in the climactic final scene. By the common consent of Amphitryon, Jupiter/Amphitryon, and all the bystanders, the impasse over which is the real Amphitryon will be decided by Alkmene's utterance. She is allowed, or rather compelled, to pronounce the word of power that will decide who is genuine and who the imposter:

Kleist and the Fragile Performative Order

FIRST GENERAL. Speak, Lady!
SECOND GENERAL. Speak!
THIRD GENERAL. Oh tell us!—
SECOND GENERAL. Princess, do!
FIRST GENERAL. If she continues silent, we are lost.
JUPITER. The truth, child, tell the truth.
ALCMENE. Friends, *this* one is
  Amphitryon.
  (*Five Plays* 80)

(ERSTER FELDHERR. Sprecht!
ZWEITER FELDHERR. Redet!
DRITTER FELDHERR. Sagt uns!—
ZWEITER FELDHERR. Fürstin, sprecht
  ein Wort!—
ERSTER FELDHERR. Wir sind verloren, wenn sie
  länger schweigt.
JUPITER. Gib, gib der Wahrheit deine Stimme, Kind.
ALKMENE. Hier dieser ist Amphitryon, ihr Freunde.)
  (2228–31/*SWB* 1: 316)

This extraordinary speech situation renders the utterance that is required of Alkmene explicitly performative: the man she declares to be Amphitryon *is* henceforth Amphitryon. When she chooses Jupiter, the "real" (or "former"?) Amphitryon is driven to an utterance that further alters existing circumstances and his relation to them:

AMPHITRYON. Every word she utters
  is the truth—not gold ten times refined
  is truer. More than oracles—than what
  the lightning writes upon the night, than what
  the thunder says—I trust the strict integrity
  of what her lips have just declared. I'll swear
  an oath upon the altar here and now,
  die ten times over if I'm not
  unshakably persuaded: to her he is
  Amphitryon.
  (*Five Plays* 81–82)

(O ihrer Worte jedes ist wahrhaftig,
Zehnfach geläutert Gold ist nicht so wahr.
Läs ich, mit Blitzen in die Nacht, Geschriebnes,
Und riefe Stimme mir des Donners zu,
Nicht dem Orakel würd ich so vertraun,
Als was ihr unverfälschter Mund gesagt.
Jetzt einen Eid selbst auf den Altar schwör ich,
Und sterbe siebenfachen Todes gleich,
Des unerschütterlich erfaßten Glaubens,
Daß er Amphitryon ihr ist.)
  (2281–90/*SWB* 1: 317–18)

Although Alkmene's utterance represents the triumph of performative effect over constative truth-value, Amphitryon ironically commits himself to its utter truth. He finally accepts the principle that identity may not be an essential quality, but an intersubjective effect relative to someone else's perception. Indeed, he accepts it so fully as to swear a solemn oath that, whoever he himself may be, his double is Amphitryon in relation to Alkmene. But, again, what status does this oath have? Can a speaker utter a performative disavowing his own identity, when the performative is of a kind that, by definition, derives its force from the speaker's identity as a unique, accountable agent?

Although Amphitryon seems to accept the usurpation of his identity in the end, he still shows no awareness that the manner in which that identity is taken away from him may simply be an extrapolation from his own overdeveloped sense of honor. For Amphitryon's identity has always been performative in a certain sense. From his pride in his military valor, his imperious way of addressing others, and the value he places on his own honor as a ruler and a husband, it is clear that his identity is heavily invested in other people's responses to him. Several times in the drama, he chooses to displace his Amphitryon-ness into external markers: he bends a feather on his helmet, expecting that it will distinguish him in the eyes of his followers from any rival; he sends Alkmene the diadem he has taken as booty and engraved with his initial (an object that betrays him, however, when the "A" on it mysteriously morphs into a "J"). As Amphitryon gathers his followers around him for an assault on the usurper who has occupied his palace, he demands their affirmation of his identity—"Who am I?"—and accepts their satisfying answer: "Good. Amphitryon. So it is" ("Wohlan. Amphitryon. Es gilt" [2111–12/*SWB* 1: 312]). Amphitryon, more than any other mortal in the play, depends for his position on what others think of him. His identity is, in this sense, a more *performed* identity than any other—although even Sosias begins the play with a rehearsal scene in which he performs himself presenting Amphitryon's news and his gift to Alkmene.

In a more narrowly linguistic sense, too, the radical performatives of the final scene are foreshadowed by the characters' acceptance of the principle that some speakers' utterances count for more than others. The dialogue between Amphitryon and Sosias in act 2, scene 1 demonstrates that the right to determine what is truth belongs to the master and not the servant. Sosias, at Amphitryon's command, tells the story of his arrival in Thebes, but reaches the limits of what is expressible in language when he tries to explain that his "other I" beat him and drove him from the palace. To avoid angering his master, Sosias offers to replace the improbable truth with something appropriate to say in the given situation: "Shall I speak from conviction—/like an honest man, you understand—/or speak as people do at court?" (Soll ich nach meiner Überzeugung reden,/Ein ehrlicher Kerl, versteht mich, oder so,/Wie es bei Hofe üblich, mit Euch sprechen? [623–25/*Five Plays* 24/*SWB* 1: 266]). Compelled to tell his story according to his conviction, Sosias nevertheless finds that Amphitryon's unaccepting reaction confirms his experience of how speech gets legitimated:

> SOSIA. That's the way it is. If it's my mouth
> it comes out of, it's childish nonsense, pay
> it no attention. But if it'd been a great
> one flogged himself, you'd hear the whole world
> crying miracle.
>
> (*Five Plays* 29)
>
> (So ists. Weil es aus meinem Munde kommt,
> Ists albern Zeug, nicht wert, daß man es höre.
> Doch hätte sich ein Großer selbst zerwalkt,
> So würde man Mirakel schrein.)
>
> (766–69/*SWB* 1: 270)

With these recurrent signs that identity and utterance *always* derive their validity from being acknowledged as appropriate in a given situation, it begins to seem as if the decision about Amphitryon's identity in the final scene is merely the extreme case of an already established performativity. In the context of that scene, Amphitryon's willingness to swear that "to her he is/Amphitryon" functions as the revelation that makes possible a breakthrough into a new order. As far as Jupiter is concerned, Amphitryon's admission that he may not be fully Amphitryon, or not the only Amphitryon, makes him into Amphitryon at last. His identity, now revealed as a performative rather than an essential quality, is given back to him in another series of "I am"/"you are" utterances:

> JUPITER. Just so! And you're Amphitryon.
> AMPHITRYON. I am—Then, awful spirit, who are you?
> JUPITER. Amphitryon. I thought you understood.
> AMPHITRYON. Amphitryon! But that's too much for mortal
> wits. Do make more sense.
>
> (*Five Plays* 82)
>
> (JUPITER. Wohlan! Du bist Amphitryon.
> AMPHITRYON.   Ich bins!—
> Und wer bist du, furchtbarer Geist?

> JUPITER. Amphitryon. Ich glaubte, daß dus wüßtest.
> AMPHITRYON. Amphitryon! Das faßt kein
>   Sterblicher.
>   Sei uns verständlich.)
>
> (2291–95 / *SWB* 1: 318)

Amphitryon's plea for clarity gets at the heart of the problem with speech acts and identity in this play. The mechanisms of performativity in language are now laid bare, because the system has been broken open by a being that linguistic conventions cannot comprehend. Jupiter, in his next speech, explains that he is not only Amphitryon, but also Greece, light, aether, that which was, that which is, and that which is to come. Neither the categories by which we make sense of reality, nor the linguistic norms that post-Kantian philosophers aligned with those transcendental categories, are so constructed as to be able to deal with a being who is identical with everything. The concept of absolute being, it now seems, can explode the logical and linguistic system—perhaps because being and the verb "to be," as we have seen with Herder, Bernhardi, and Humboldt, form the underpinnings of the Romantic idea of language. *Amphitryon* illustrates how verbal conventions are turned inside out by the intervention of divinity or transcendence: the most explicit performatives, such as oaths, lose their grounding in individual moral agency, and the most basic of referential or affirmative statements, such as Alkmene's "this one is Amphitryon," become explicit performatives.

Die gebrechliche Einrichtung der Welt—the fragile organization of the world—is an expression that, appearing repeatedly in Kleist's prose, has become idiomatic for his worldview. The phrase has a history in theological literature of the seventeenth and eighteenth centuries, where it refers to the establishment of a world-order in light of human fallibility or original sin. In Kleist's work (as in salvation history, though in a different sense) the organization of the world is brought about by performative utterances—the oaths, laws, and declarations by which speakers attempt to give their environment a lasting and universally valid construction. Yet these speakers come to realize that the same speech acts that organize the world render its organization fragile. Because the expression of temporality and subjectivity is an intrinsic problem for a universalizing and abstracting language, verbal formulas inevitably come a cropper with the unpredictability of the future and the diversity of individual experience. As he does with the unusually codified society of the Amazons in *Penthesilea*, in *Amphitryon* Kleist uses an extraordinary circumstance, the intervention of gods, to press the performative order of the world to its limits, disrupting our complacent acceptance of social institutions and the discursive conventions on which they rely.

SPEAKING, THINKING, AND THE BODY

Despite extensive traditional scholarship on Kleist's language, as well as on Kleist and language, his one brief essay on philosophy of language has only recently begun to have a real impact on the interpretation of his work.[4] "Über die allmähliche Verfertigung der Gedanken beim Reden," a manuscript of half a dozen pages probably composed in 1805–6, is dedicated and addressed to Kleist's friend Rühle von Lilienstern. In it, Kleist distinguishes between two types of speech: the rote kind, used to express or communicate a thought that has been formulated in advance, and a second kind that he values more highly and grants much more attention, in which the thought is only formed in the process of speaking to someone else. This brief contribution to the philosophy of language does not include any reference to the linguistic philosophy of Kleist's contemporaries; indeed, it runs counter to the new linguistics of his time inasmuch as Kleist affirms that thought *sometimes* proceeds independently of language, whereas for Herder or Humboldt cognition is *always* a verbal process. Interestingly, the writer with whom Kleist's essay is in close sympathy is William Godwin. While Godwin generally regards language as an instrument for communicating pre-existent thoughts, he affirms in both *The Enquirer* (1797) and *Thoughts on Man* (1831) that thoughts are completed in the process of writing—one "does not write because he understands the subject, but he understands the subject because he has written" (*PPW* 5: 93; 6: 74).

Kleist's recommendation that thoughts be shaped in the process of speaking needs to be distinguished from the valorization of dialogue that is so pervasive in the work of Humboldt and other contemporaries. The "gradual completion of thoughts while speaking" involves neither interpersonal conversation—Kleist stresses that it is not primarily verbal responses or questions on the part of the addressee that help the speaker's thought along—nor the typical Humboldtian dialogue between the mind and the object that the mind produces when it articulates a portion of the world as verbal utterance. Rather, Kleist focuses on the in-

---

[4]In the category of "traditional" scholarship, see Kommerell, Holz, and Spälti. More recent discussions of rhetoric, dialogue, intuition, and paradox, all of which include consideration of "Über die allmähliche Verfertigung der Gedanken beim Reden," can be found in essays by Gillespie, J. Smith, Gustafson, and Itoda.

teraction between the speaker and the *body*, not the words, of the listener. Facial expressions and gestures that signal the addressee's response, or that threaten interruption, challenge the speaker to continue speaking until the thought is complete.

Kleist's most important example of the way thoughts are formulated in the process of speaking—a telling example, in terms of the tremendous impact of the French Revolution and its distinctive forms of speech on Romantic ideas about language as action—is Mirabeau's pronouncement in the National Assembly on 23 June 1789, when he refused to dismiss the Assembly in accordance with the King's order and instead proclaimed the authority of the deputies as representatives of the nation. Reading the historical record of this speech, Kleist suggests that Mirabeau had no idea where his utterance was going when he got up to speak; but by articulating his thought in the charged public atmosphere of the Assembly, and especially in confrontation with the Master of Ceremonies who was attempting to execute the King's command, Mirabeau ended up announcing a new political order. "Perhaps it was in this manner finally the twitch of an upper lip, or an ambiguous toying with a cuff, that effected the toppling of the order of things in France," Kleist concludes (*SWB* 2: 321). This principle of the interrelation of speech acts with bodily experience proves crucial for the type of performative that characterizes his drama and fiction.

Kleist's primary point is that the conclusion of Mirabeau's thought only occurred to him after he began speaking, but he also analyzes Mirabeau's speech quite precisely as an utterance that alters the existing order of things. Phrase by phrase, he demonstrates how Mirabeau shifts the balance of power in responding to the Master of Ceremonies, who has come back into the room where the deputies are assembled in order to ask, presumably as a rhetorical question, whether they have heard the King's order to disperse:

> 'Yes,' answered Mirabeau, 'we have heard the King's order'—I am certain that at this considerate beginning, he was not yet thinking of the bayonets with which he closed; 'yes, my lord,' he repeated, 'we have heard it'—one sees that he doesn't even really know yet what he wants. 'But what gives you the right'—he continued, and now suddenly a spring of tremendous ideas wells up in him—'to intimate orders to us here? We are the representatives of the nation.'—That was what he needed! 'The nation gives orders and does not receive them.'—in order to launch himself right to the peak of presumption. 'And to make myself perfectly clear to you'—and only now he finds that which expresses the complete resistance for which his soul stands armed: 'you may tell your King that we

will not leave our places otherwise than by the force of the bayonets.'—At which he, self-satisfied, seated himself on a chair. (SWB 2: 320–21)

In speech-act terms, Mirabeau responds to the Master of Ceremonies by refusing uptake to his question on several levels at once. "Did you hear the King's order?" is clearly not intended as a question about whether the order was literally audible, but instead has the indirect illocutionary force of a command: "I order you, in the name of the King, to disperse!" Mirabeau temporizes by bracketing off the imperative force and answering the question on a literal level, offering only the minimal form of uptake by acknowledging that the King's order has indeed been heard. He then takes up the illocutionary force of the order separately, but only to destabilize the authority behind it. As Kleist notes, Mirabeau initially questions the Master of Ceremonies' authority to convey the King's orders, but shifts immediately to a challenge of the King's right to issue orders to the National Assembly at all, on the grounds that the members of the Assembly, as representatives of the nation, are not subject to commands from any source.

The transformation of the political structure occurs in the statement "we are the representatives of the nation," which Kleist recognizes as the crucial utterance in Mirabeau's speech ("That was what he needed!"). In terms of both Romantic and modern philosophy of language, "we are the representatives of the nation" can be described as a performative masquerading as a constative proposition. It is another "I am" statement (this time in the plural form) in which "to be" does not function constatively, but has performative effect. By declaring the deputies to be representatives of the nation, Mirabeau *makes them into* representatives of the nation—according to the terms by which he then defines "nation," namely as the authority that can issue orders but is not subject to them. To complete the devolution of authority, Mirabeau himself exercises the right previously exercised by the sovereign, by sending the Master of Ceremonies back with a message from the representatives to the King (now become "your King" rather than "our" or "the" King). He adds that, having lost the authority to issue felicitous commands to the Assembly, the King can only have recourse to the authority of physical force. Implicit in Mirabeau's final utterance may also be the awareness that military force, far from being an extra-linguistic authority, is also bound up with the ability to issue successful orders to the wielders of bayonets. To sum up: Kleist's analysis of the speech acts of Mirabeau places speech and the body in a reflexive relationship, with force moving in both directions through the middle term of performativity. The physical confrontation between Mirabeau and the Master of Ceremonies produces Mirabeau's ultimatum, but the act of uttering the ultimatum challenges the existing structure of authority among Mirabeau, the deputies, the Master of Ceremonies, and the King in ways that will manifest themselves in physical terms, ultimately as an altered relationship between the King and the soldiery (the "bayonets").

It requires only a minimal addition of speech-act terminology, then, to see that Kleist focuses on the pragmatic effect of Mirabeau's words within the particular speech situation. Indeed, he renders the speech as a much more explicit performative than it actually was, when compared with the extract from Mirabeau's *Works* that Kleist's editor Helmut Sembdner provides as his likely source.[5] Like British writers of the 1790s, Kleist is inspired by the inaugural utterances of the French Revolution to reflect on the way intersubjective speech acts operate. Mirabeau's utterance thereby becomes a model for Kleist's own utterance in "Über die allmähliche Verfertigung der Gedanken beim Reden." "Mir fällt jener 'Donnerkeil' des Mirabeau ein," he writes (*SWB* 2: 320): "That 'thunderbolt' of Mirabeau's occurs to me." Characterizing Mirabeau's speech as a thunderbolt, he relates it to his own cognitive process, for it is when Mirabeau's thunderbolt occurs to him (or, more literally, "falls into" his mind) that he can complete his own thoughts about the process of thinking. Throughout the essay, Kleist writes within the same context that he recommends to others, working out his thoughts in a sustained address to his friend Lilienstern—though not actually in dialogue with him, for the addressee never says a word. The same parallel between what Kleist recommends and what he does applies in the case of his syntax, when he describes, in convoluted sentences rich in subclauses and appositions, how the delays caused by conversational fillers or unnecessary appositions help him to formulate his point in the process of articulating it (*SWB* 2: 320). The form of "Über die allmähliche Verfertigung der Gedanken beim Reden" is, in other words, a performance of its content; indeed, the parallel between what the writer is saying and what he is doing is so conspicuous that one wonders whether the primary purpose of this short text is not performance rather than statement. The essay thus introduces what seems to be an inevitable component of Kleist's fiction: the parallel between the effects that utterances

---

[5]In the French original, Mirabeau challenges only the authority of the Master of Ceremonies to convey the King's order, without challenging the King's authority directly, and affirms only "nous sommes ici par la puissance du peuple," rather than using the significant term "representatives" or assuming for the nation the power to give commands (*SWB* 2: 925n).

and texts have within the story, and the effect of the story itself in its interaction with the reader.

In describing the gradual completion of thoughts while speaking, then, Kleist is evidently describing his own mode of writing sentences and paragraphs—but surely this process describes his mode of composing entire texts as well. The abrupt changes in the direction of the plot, the unexpected and often baffling shifts of attention to new characters or tangential details, the coincidences and contingencies that we recognize as characteristic of a Kleist novella are counterparts to the "unarticulated sounds," the drawn-out conjunctions, and the "apposition where none is needed" that Kleist adds to sentences when he is still thinking about where they will end (*SWB* 2: 320). Not merely a stylistic or biographical comment about his mode of writing, this temporizing is intrinsic to the worldview his novellas convey. For the gradual completion of thoughts while speaking is a process that can be observed in Kleist's characters as well; indeed, this type of thinking typifies the relationship of speech acts to speech situations throughout his fiction. The language of the narratives, as well as specific speech acts within the narratives, responds to physical experience, often to ambiguous bodily details such as the twitch of an upper lip or the toying with a cuff that Kleist suggests may have triggered the overthrow of the political order in France. Moreover, like the lip-twitching, cuff-toying Master of Ceremonies whose presence in the National Assembly is determined by a behind-the-scenes speech act (the King's order), the physical stimuli that motivate utterances are themselves dependent on other utterances. Neither speech acts nor physical experiences have clear priority in Kleist's fiction, and the two are always related in unexpected and contingent ways. Yet his texts represent the need to understand and untangle the mutual determination of speech acts and experience as an inescapable responsibility, or at least a pervasive obsession.

'MICHAEL KOHLHAAS': COAL-BLACK HORSES AND THE WHITE PAGE

Kleist's most spectacular exploration of speech acts and human experience is also his longest and most famous story: the 100-page novella *Michael Kohlhaas*, in which a sixteenth-century horse-trader is led by his quest for justice into legal and political conflict with three jurisdictions.[6]

---

[6]For another reading of this text in terms of performative utterance, with emphasis on the differences between speech acts in law and in literature, and the question of whether literature can posit law, see J. Hillis Miller (80–104).

The world of *Michael Kohlhaas* is inscribed by performatives, especially written ordinances, to an almost incredible degree—which is also to say that it is typical of the conglomerate of principalities and jurisdictions that made up central Europe in the sixteenth century, as it is of nineteenth-century Prussia. Virtually all communicative transactions in the story take place through letters or less neutral texts, including mandates, decrees, edicts, legal judgments, arrest warrants, briefs, and resolutions. These documents are so numerous, and referred to so insistently even in contexts where it hardly seems necessary to do so, that the scriptedness of Kohlhaas's world becomes one of the elements of dark humor in the narrative. Kleist's marvellously detailed prose delineates an environment in which physical and emotional activity (work, travel, family life, social affiliations) are so thoroughly interwoven with letters, laws, and other documents that it seems impossible to make a single move without sending vibrations through both the linguistic and the extra-linguistic order of things. Against this background, Kohlhaas's quest to intervene in the fragile organization of his world is also an attempt to establish a new basis for effective verbal utterance, by joining public proclamation with military action and legitimating his utterances by individual will rather than existing social conventions. His success in winning uptake, and the corresponding decline in the authority of speech acts emanating from the state, can be traced as far as the scene in the market square in Dresden, which marks the point at which Kohlhaas's speech acts, too, begin to succumb to the inherent fragility of any human linguistic order. Only the intervention of the mysterious gypsy woman, while far from resolving the vexed interaction between language and the body, opens up a new angle on this interaction—allowing us to see that there may be involuntary ties between language and being, though they cannot be manipulated in any way that would further human welfare.

A figurative inscription on the landscape is the original catalyst for the tragedy of Michael Kohlhaas. The old, hospitable Lord of Tronkenburg having died and been succeeded by the thoughtless Junker Wenzel von Tronka, the textual prescriptions or institutional facts that constitute the Tronkenburg domain have changed, so that where Kohlhaas has crossed into Saxon territory with his horses seventeen times in the past without incident, there is now a toll to be paid and a permit to be stamped. The new designation of the Tronkenburg estate as "territory not to be entered without a permit" generates a chain of responses in the form of further utterances and texts. The most immediate of these is an official certificate that Kohlhaas obtains from the chancellery in Dresden attesting that no document is necessary in order to enter Saxony, and that "the story about the permit was a mere fabrication" (*Stories* 118). Much later, Kohlhaas and the reader learn that—ironically, but perhaps not surprisingly in the world represented here—the import of horses from Brandenburg into Saxony is in fact prohibited after all, according to a twelve-year-old edict that had been generally forgotten but that no one had bothered to revoke (*Stories* 177). Kohlhaas's world is so densely inscribed that even apparently novel and apparently illegitimate speech acts eventually prove to be citations of earlier decrees.

During the days of Kohlhaas's guerilla campaign to enforce the justice that he believes the courts have denied him in his quarrel with the Junker, his physical environment seems to be literally, even parodically, scripted. The landscape of Saxony is gradually pasted over with the placards of Kohlhaas and his antagonists. Kohlhaas's four "writs" or "mandates" (Mandate), along with the responses of the authorities to them, are "distributed throughout the region by travellers and strangers," fastened to the doors of churches and town halls, or, like Martin Luther's placard condemning Kohlhaas's actions, "posted up in every town and village of the Electorate" (*Stories* 141, 149). The placarding of town and countryside may be a sixteenth-century version of mass media, but it also serves as a peculiar literalization of the idea that the world can only be experienced as a manifold of constantly changing and proliferating verbal acts—whether or not these can actually be deciphered by the mostly illiterate population, and whether or not their source can be identified.

If written guidelines for behavior are so readily available, not to say intrusive, it may seem that all one has to do to preserve the order of the world is try hard enough to discover and obey them; and this is, in fact, the first impulse of Kohlhaas and most of the sympathetic characters in the story. All the letters, pleas, and complaints Kohlhaas submits when he first tries to obtain justice through the courts, up to the point at which his wife is killed, are prepared "fully in accordance with what was required" (*Stories* 129). But *Michael Kohlhaas* is, among other things, a story about the incommensurability of human experience and the linguistic forms in which people try to contain it. The fragile organization of Kohlhaas's world breaks down under the force of two conditions that put pressure on it from opposite sides. These might be described as, first, the *limitedness*, and second, the *unlimitedness*, of verbal utterance. Even if language seems to be an inevitable component in shaping the experience of reality (for Kohlhaas as for post-Kantian philosophers), its power is limited by other formative components of experience. Coincidences, contingencies, and temporality—as well as illness, death, and familial ties—constantly interfere with the proper operation of performatives according to linguistic rules and sociopolitical conventions. On the other hand, any verbal utterance seems to entail unlimited links to other linguistic forms: signs lead to further signs, and present speech acts depend on prior speech acts, so that attention is constantly drawn away from immediate experience and into the mechanisms of the linguistic system itself.

Kohlhaas never really accepts the principle that the verbal, textual, or legal ordering of the world is limited by an inability to encompass fully either experience or temporality. His sense of justice is founded on the conviction that the law can be made to fit his case exactly and that the return of his original horses in their original state, despite the lapse of time, is literally feasible. Indeed, Kohlhaas's stubborn insistence on the return of *his* horses in *exactly* the condition in which he left them is symbolic of what might be called his theory of language, which is based on an ultimate, if unconscious, faith in the ability of language to transcend time. His behavior is predicated on the belief that amnesties will be honored and promises kept. Kohlhaas treats both laws and promises, in other words, as if the hypothetical future state they project were guaranteed, regardless of intervening time and experience. Similarly, he elides the difference between the abstract and the referential dimension of the law, the concern of eighteenth-century theorists from Rousseau to Godwin: the general law has meaning for Kohlhaas only if, and as, it refers to his particular case.

But Kohlhaas is thwarted in his attempts to identify the utterance of promises with their fulfilment, and the universal grammar of laws with their referential or (in de Man's terms) performative dimension. Time becomes an agent that intervenes between promise and fulfilment, as when the Prince of Meissen's oral promise that Kohlhaas will not be held as a prisoner in Dresden turns out to be good only as long as the Prince himself is in the city; once the Prince has "gone to his estates," it can be broken (*Stories* 162, 176, 178). The need for interpretation also introduces friction into promises: the Elector of Saxony grants Kohlhaas amnesty on the condition that the High Court at Dresden does not "dismiss" his complaint (*Stories* 160), but the ambiguity over whether "dismiss" means ruling against Kohlhaas, or refusing to hear his suit in the first place, can later help the Elector renege on the amnesty. Time intervenes also in the fulfilment of the "promise" that the law itself holds out. It seems to dictate the restoration of Kohlhaas's horses in their original condition, but instead the horses turn up as half-dead nags in the possession of the horse-slaughterer, or are even, according to rumors, dead already and "buried in the Wilsdruf carrion-pit" before Kohlhaas can obtain justice (*Stories* 165).

Delays and diversions are introduced into the operation of the law by its supposed enforcers, who are influenced by a network of private relationships that run counter to the objectivity of the law. Because Count Kallheim's identity is not completely circumscribed by his political office as the Prince of Brandenburg's chancellor, but also includes his being the brother-in-law of the Tronkas, he fails to deliver the petition that Kohlhaas prepared "fully in accordance with what was required" to the court at Dresden, but instead brings it to the accused, von Tronka himself, where it is inevitably detoured away from the court (*Stories* 129). Because the cupbearer and chamberlain of the Prince of Saxony are not just officials of the court, but cousins of von Tronka, they find further ways of delaying and interfering with the case. Unwritten lines of influence based on marital or blood relationships, personal obligation, and political expediency cut across and interfere with the fulfilment of legal performatives.

On the other hand, many of these "unwritten" influences that introduce temporal delay or spatial detour into the language of the law can themselves be traced back to sociopolitical speech acts. The marital alliances and class superiority that cause officials to interfere with the fulfilment of the law's promises are, like the von Tronkas' investiture with particular offices and titles, institutional facts. Thus, one might equally well identify the *unlimitedness* of performative language as the cause of Kohlhaas's predicament. The problem, in *Michael Kohlhaas*, is not only that rule-governed performativity is undermined by non-linguistic factors such as the movement of time, but also that the causes and effects of speech acts extend further than any individual character can fathom. These chains of utterances are always subject to infelicities, including lack of uptake and alienation from an authorizing source. Embodied in written documents—and the characters in *Michael Kohlhaas* seem to carry virtual file folders of documents around with them, which they produce to one another as occasion demands—performatives end up being read in unexpected contexts, where they generate unpredictable effects. Kohlhaas happens to receive the letter from his first attorney, containing the news about the refusal of his first petition to the court at Dresden, when he is, for entirely contingent reasons, in the presence of the local governor; the latter, noticing Kohlhaas's distress on receiving the letter, offers his help in preparing a second petition to take the case further (*Stories* 128). Later, the unsatisfying reply to the supplication that Kohlhaas's wife has carried to Dresden happens to reach Kohlhaas at the particularly sensitive moment of her funeral, spurring his resolve to respond with a much more radical speech act, by passing judgment in his own case and setting out to enforce it (*Stories* 137–38). Near the end of the novella, the servant sent by the rascal Nagelschmidt with a letter to Kohlhaas, proposing to help Kohlhaas escape from prison so that he can take up the leadership of the rebel band again, falls into the hands of the authorities when the servant happens to suffer an epileptic fit in a town near Dresden (*Stories* 183). As if in an attempt to control the proliferation of written performatives, the narrator of Kohlhaas's story almost obsessively notes when and where documents are produced, circulated, read, and occasionally returned to their owners. But the ironic effect of this documentation of documents is to intensify the reader's sense that the illocutionary (let alone the perlocutionary) force of texts is limitless, uncontrollable, and contingent on unforeseeable circumstances.

To modern readers, then, *Michael Kohlhaas* can seem like an exhibition of the poststructuralist performative that Derrida describes in "Signature Event Context," where he critiques Austin's model of the idealized, normative, and felicitous utterance. Not only is the "standard" performative, in Kleist's story as in Derrida's essay, a written rather than a spoken utterance, but its source is often indeterminate, the context in which it is interpreted is uncontrollable, it may fail entirely to secure uptake, and its defining condition is the ever-present possibility of failure. But in terms of Kleist's own philosophical context, especially his "Kant crisis," these uncertainties and contingencies might also be identified as interference caused by the Kantian transcendentals, space and time, that color our understanding of reality-in-itself—causing us to see it, Kleist wrote, as if distorted by green-tinted lenses (*SWB* 2: 634). The performative utterances in *Michael Kohlhaas* are generally explicit, intersubjective illocutionary acts of the kind Austin and Derrida have in mind (promises, declarations, legal judgments, and so forth); but their influence in the world of this and other Kleistian novellas is so pervasive that they also seem implicated in the subjective perception of reality. The landscape that is inscribed with written placards as well as with unwritten rules of procedure is one image for the involvement of language in cognition itself, as is Kohlhaas's extraordinary sense of justice, so thoroughgoing that it constitutes an interpretation of empirical reality in terms of the law. *Michael Kohlhaas*, in this reading, is one more text of the post-Kantian generation that illustrates—this time in a political as well as a cognitive context—the effects of inserting language into the Kantian system. Inasmuch as it also evokes a poststructuralist model of performative utterance, the novella implies a connection between the Kantian transcendental framework and Derrida's fallible speech act: the *differances* that cause utterances to miss their mark ultimately derive from the need to conceive reality through the lenses of space and (especially) time.

Kohlhaas's response to the frustration of his desire for exact correspondence between language and reality, or between promise and fulfilment, amounts to a quest to set performative utterance on a new foundation. Through his actions, he almost succeeds in overturning the conventions that legitimate utterances in his society—or in constructing a new kind of performative that establishes the conditions of its own possibility. This process begins with the resolution Kohlhaas composes after his wife's funeral, when he decides it is time to abandon the domain of sanctioned, sociopolitical performatives and establish a new basis for effective utterance:

> He sat down and drew up an edict in which, 'by virtue of the authority inborn in him,' he ordered Junker Wenzel von Tronka, within three days of sight of the document, to bring back to Kohlhaasenbrück the two black horses he had taken from him and worked to death on his fields, and fatten them in person in Kohlhaas's stables. (*Stories* 137–38)

Kohlhaas's appeal to "inborn authority" is a deliberate challenge to the authority of the state, and thereby to institutional speech acts. As he later avers in his interview with Luther, no one has given him this authority; he has seized it because, being denied the protection of the law, he considered himself excommunicated from the state and thereby exiled from civilization—driven "into the wilderness among savages" (*Stories* 152). Cast back, as it were, into a state of nature, Kohlhaas recognizes the right and the necessity of pursuing his ends by force, but also by establishing a new social contract; and these two components, violence and a new basis for authoritative utterance, are intertwined in all his ensuing actions. He frames his first public mandate, declaring a just war on Wenzel von Tronka and requiring inhabitants of the area to hand over him and his property, on the site of his first violent act, the fiery destruction of Tronkenburg (*Stories* 140). Composed in a room of the warden's tower that has survived the fire, the first "Declaration under the Writ of Kohlhaas" constitutes a new inscription on the Tronkenburg territory, decreed by a new authority. Yet Kohlhaas takes pains to treat it in the manner of an established law—making sure, for instance, that the abbess Antonia von Tronka at Erlabrunn, and the citizens of Wittenberg, have had a chance to read the writ before attempting to punish them for not obeying it.

Kohlhaas's three further writs frame his quest in increasingly religious terms; he declares himself to be "an emissary of the Archangel Michael," and his headquarters becomes "the seat of our Provisional World Government" (*Stories* 148). Like all performatives that attempt to found a state, Kohlhaas's mandates are felicitous to the extent that hearers and readers grant them uptake. Thus, in Kohlhaas's case, the growth of his armed band as well as the increasing antagonism of the crowds in Wittenberg and elsewhere toward the state officials are a measure of his newly assumed authority and the force of his decrees. Partway through Kohlhaas's campaign, the authority of his words is explicitly tested when the magistrate of Leipzig posts declarations affirming that Wenzel von Tronka is not in the city, but Kohlhaas posts contradictory declarations affirming that he is:

> It was in vain that the council had proclamations put up in the surrounding villages declaring categorically that the Junker was not in the Pleissenburg; the horse-dealer posted similar notices insisting that he was, and announcing that even if he were not in the fortress he, Kohlhaas, would continue to act as if he were until told where he really was. (*Stories* 148–49)

The warring placards mark the point at which Kohlhaas's speech acts are able to impose on the state's. For the threatened populace, Wenzel von Tronka is, to all intents and purposes, in Leipzig if Kohlhaas says he is, until the condition Kohlhaas specifies is met. His decree is persuasive enough to cause an anonymous informant to respond with yet another placard, that raises panic at the Saxon court by revealing what is apparently the truth (or, at least, what the court thinks Kohlhaas will act on as truth): that von Tronka is with his cousins at the court in Dresden. If Kohlhaas's declaration that he himself is a representative of the Archangel Michael does not literally make him into an archangel or the emissary of one, the narrator nevertheless affirms that since the publication of his last mandate Kohlhaas has the appearance of a messenger of God. His subjective identity may not be that of an archangel, but, in intersubjective terms, he counts as an archangelic avenger for the society around him. His altered public appearance (i.e., the fact that he travels with a contingent of fire and sword), and the failure of state officials to contradict his speech acts, are evidence of his success in establishing a new basis for the legitimation of performatives.

An ironic confirmation of Kohlhaas's authority lies in the fact that it can now be forged and abused. While Kohlhaas is negotiating with the court in Dresden, the outlaw Johann Nagelschmidt mimics his revolutionary actions by taking command of a group of Kohlhaas's followers, calling himself a representative of Kohlhaas (just as Kohlhaas called himself a representative of the Archangel Michael), and beginning to issue decrees "in proclamations which closely resembled those of Kohlhaas" (*Stories* 174). Kohlhaas is able to prove to the authorities that he has no involvement in these forgeries—which he does, typically for this story, by producing "some papers which he had with him" as evidence of his enmity with Nagelschmidt, and by writing a new declaration condemning Nagelschmidt's actions (*Stories* 175–76). But the incident underscores the all-important question of how the authority behind speech acts can be recognized or authenticated, as does another scene in the marketplace of Dresden that the narrative deliberately parallels with Nagelschmidt's forgery as two indications of the downturn in the fortunes of Kohlhaas.

The marketplace scene, the most farcical moment in the narrative but also a turning point for the operation of performative language, concerns the Chamberlain Kunz von Tronka's attempt to buy back two half-dead black horses, that Kohlhaas affirms are his own, from the horse-slaughterer in whose possession they have landed. Trying to save what is left of his dignity as royal chamberlain, as well as to elicit obedience to his orders, Herr Kunz deliberately throws open his coat in the marketplace to reveal his orders and chain of office before he speaks. When this proves ineffectual, he tries speaking while "holding his sword with pride and dignity under his arm" (*Stories* 169). The effect is lost on the horse-slaughterer, who is too busy watering his horses, urinating, and looking for a pub in which to have breakfast even to glance at Herr Kunz; but even when Kunz announces his identity as royal chamberlain, the horse-slaughterer fails to treat his words with the respect to which Kunz is accustomed. For the first time in the story, a nobleman and officer of the court finds that his utterances no longer have their intended effect on a hostile crowd in the public marketplace. Not only does the horse-slaughterer fail to recognize his authority or respond accordingly, but when Kunz attempts to buy the horses and order one of his servants to lead them away, his order is met by incipient rebellion. The servant's cousin, Meister Himboldt, issues a contrary order to the boy not to touch the horses; Kunz, furious, orders the guard to arrest Meister Himboldt; Himboldt protests that he was only instructing the boy in decent behavior; and violence breaks out:

> 'Ask him [cried Master Himboldt] if he's prepared to go against all custom and decency and touch the horses tied to that cart; if he'll do it after what I said, then let him! For all I care he can flay and skin them here and now!' At this the Chamberlain rounded on his groom and asked him if he took exception to carrying out his order to untether Kohlhaas's horses

and take them home. When the young man, retreating into the crowd, diffidently answered that the horses would have to be made decent again before that could be expected of him, the Chamberlain pursued him, snatched off his hat which bore the family's coat of arms, stamped on it, drew his sword, and raining furious blows on him with the flat of the blade, instantly drove the groom out of the square and out of his service. Master Himboldt cried out: 'Down with the murderous tyrant!' and as the people, incensed by this scene, pressed together and forced the guard back, he threw the Chamberlain to the ground from behind, tore off his cloak and collar and helmet, wrenched his sword out of his hand and with a savage sweep of the arm hurled it away across the square. In vain Junker Wenzel cried out to the other noblemen to help his cousin, as he himself escaped from the riot.... (*Stories* 170)

In the battle of words that precedes the physical riot, speech-act conventions go out the window. The royal chamberlain fails to get an underage servant-boy to obey his orders; instead, the boy's cousin is able to rouse his fellow citizens to an attack on Kunz. When the Junker Wenzel tries to order the guard to rescue *his* cousin Kunz, his words prove ineffective. Meister Himboldt completes the symbolic divestiture of authority by tearing off Kunz's coat, collar, and helmet, and throwing away the sword with which he had tried in vain to lend authority to his words. The loss of verbal authority in this scene is accompanied by a series of misidentifications and failed recognitions, as if the confusion of discursive conventions brings with it a loss of identities. Not only does the horse-slaughterer fail to identify Herr Kunz and the whole crowd fail to recognize his authority, but the Baron von Wenk, sent to the Chancellor's house in order to ask him to send Kohlhaas to identify the horses, fails to recognize that Kohlhaas is in the room with them. Even the identity of the horses about which the whole scene revolves remains in question, for the information about their provenance is uncertain and comes from an unauthenticated source.

The loss of Kunz's authority in the marketplace scene, and the concomitant misuse of Kohlhaas's authority by Nagelschmidt, mark a reversal in the narrative: where Kohlhaas seemed on the point of having his horses returned to him and Wenzel von Tronka compelled to restore them to their original state, the authorities now begin a renewed search for an alternative way to handle the situation than that which a strict interpretation of the law would require. The upheaval in the verbal organization of the world, it seems, has gone too far. The imprisonment of Kohlhaas at this point, in violation of the formal and public promise of amnesty that was made to him by the Elector of Saxony, is symbolic of the failure of accepted speech-act conventions:

Kohlhaas asked whether he was a prisoner, and whether he was to understand that the amnesty which had been solemnly vouchsafed to him before the eyes of all the world was now broken; whereupon the Baron suddenly wheeled round on him, his face flushing fiery red, and stepping close looked him straight in the eyes and exclaimed: 'Yes, yes, yes!' (*Stories* 181–82)

Once the old order has broken down so far that Kohlhaas's antagonists no longer even try to conceal their abuse of contractual language—even if they betray their consciousness of mis-speaking by a blush—a totally new form of speech act seems called for. The extraordinary twist in the story at this point is the arrival of the gypsy woman and the revelation that Kohlhaas has been carrying a scrap of paper containing her prophecy in a vial around his neck. In terms of the development of *Michael Kohlhaas* as a narrative about the relationship of language and experience, what happens here is analogous to the journey around the world to see if paradise can be entered again from the other side, an image Kleist uses in "Über das Marionettentheater" (On the marionette theater). The utterances of the gypsy woman represent, on the one hand, a radical violation of the conditions for sociopolitically authorized performatives. On the other hand, they also embody a new, absolute correspondence between language and reality which all of Kohlhaas's attempts to encompass desire and fulfilment in written documents have been unable to achieve. The gypsy's pronouncements issue from an unrecognized authority; no one knows her, no one can locate her, and when a person who has spoken to her tries to say something about her, a kind of fit prevents him from uttering a word (*Stories* 210). It is impossible either to affirm or to deny that she has some relation to Kohlhaas's dead wife. As a woman, a gypsy or stateless person, and a cripple, she is as much the contrary of the authoritative speakers in the story (the Princes and Electors, and even Kohlhaas) as it is possible to be. If she represents an extreme case of utterance that lacks an authoritative source, her written prophecy, which Kohlhaas delays reading until the moment before his execution, represents an extreme case of the temporal displacement of performative force. Indeed, the delay is so pronounced that the illocutionary force the paper possesses as an *unread* document becomes more important than the force it derives from a hearer's or reader's uptake. Time, which earlier interfered with the success of the performative by intervening between utterance and uptake or between promise and fulfilment, now becomes the most important factor in the effectiveness of the gypsy's prophecy: its power lies in the *potential* of being read.

By losing touch with the conventions and sources of authority on which performative force should depend, speech acts are somehow freed to enter into a new correlation with reality. The gypsy woman's utterances suggest the possibility of a correspondence (however unsettling) between language and experience, beyond, and by means of, the rupture of the sociopolitical performatives that maintain the world in a fragile order. What form exactly this correspondence takes remains mysterious. The gypsy's prophecies are evidently constative statements, but ones that have an uncanny perlocutionary effect on listeners; by virtue of being uttered, they bring about behavior that fits the world to the words. Her test prophecy about the stag that will appear in the marketplace causes the Elector of Brandenburg, through anxiety or arrogance, to order the stag to be slaughtered, thereby making it possible for the animal to come to the marketplace in the form of dinner. Similarly, it may be that her ominous but obscure prophecy about the impending downfall of the Elector of Saxony's house becomes self-fulfilling when the paranoia it awakens in him sends him into physical and mental decline and thereby weakens his regime. Although they contain no explicit promissory force, the gypsy's words seem to bridge the gap between present utterance and a future state of affairs. Kohlhaas's treatment of her written prophecy symbolizes the elision of another gap—that between speech acts and the body. By swallowing the scrap of paper containing the prophecy, he (re-)incorporates utterance, symbolically closing the rift between language and bodily experience. By submitting to execution a moment later, however, he demonstrates that the rift needs to be maintained in the ordinary functioning of society. In the narrative, and in the world that Kohlhaas leaves behind, the conventions and institutions governing performative utterance close in once again, and the Elector of Brandenburg regularizes the performative order when he utters the last, authoritative speech act of the story, ennobling Kohlhaas's sons and declaring that they are to brought up as pages in his court.

A postscript of sorts comes from an unexpected source. Bentham, in his critique of the 1791 Declaration of Rights issued by the French National Assembly, uses an almost prophetic metaphor to illustrate the pernicious way words change their meaning depending on time, context, and usage. The shift "from the language of utility and peace to the language of mischief," Bentham claims, is "no more than if you were to trust your horse with a man for a week or so, and he were to return it blind and lame: it was your horse you trusted to him; it is your horse you have received again: what you had trusted to him, you have received" (*Bentham's Political Thought* 287). Bentham, too, is writing in and about a context in which inaugural utterances establish the sociopolitical order; the French Declaration of Rights is a contemporary, real-world, felicitous equivalent of the Kohlhaasian mandates in Kleist's novella. Yet his evocative image suggests that not only Kohlhaas's declarations, but the fate of the horses that represent the catalyst for his whole adventure, may be read as an illustration of how the meaning and effect of words shift beyond the control of those who use them and those whose lives they alter. Could the horses, which the narrative so often refers to as "the blacks," stand for black ink on white pages? Kohlhaas's determination to have them returned to him in the identical condition in which he left them would then symbolize his desperate desire to control the meaning and the contexts of written performatives, which so often prove subject to a different uptake than he expects, and his insistence that a promise correspond with its fulfilment. Kohlhaas's own name—"coal-black hare"—links him with the blackness of horses and ink, and when the gypsy women writes on the paper that she gives Kohlhaas with *eine Kohle* 'a piece of (char)coal' (*SWB* 2: 92), she commits to some kind of connection between her speech act and Kohlhaas's intrinsic identity. Swallowing the paper with its coal-black inscription, Kohlhaas fulfils an identification between his name and the peculiarly felicitous speech acts that the gypsy represents.

A language that, like the horses, accompanies and facilitates one's negotiation of the world, yet neither deforms reality nor is deformed by it: this is the horse-trader Kohlhaas's fantasy. At the end of his story, the blacks, like the law by which their return is effected, are once again in their fit place. Yet—can we ever be sure that the restored horses *are* Kohlhaas's original horses? And if so, is the bequest by which he leaves them to his sons a bequest of the same, shifty, changeable language with which he grappled, which is not to be let out of one's sight lest it be worked into an unrecognizable state by others? If Kleist himself shares Kohlhaas's ideal of a stable language, he also recognizes some pragmatic truths: that speech acts are incommensurate with temporal experience; that human language cannot encompass the absolute or the transcendent; that utterances, and especially written texts, have effects that cannot be reined in.

CONVENTIONS, CONTINGENCIES, AND THE WILL OF GOD IN "DER ZWEIKAMPF"

The mutual interaction of language and experience takes on new dimensions in Kleist's last story, "Der Zweikampf" ("The Duel"), which may be read as an extreme case of the influence of the empirical over the verbal, and, equally well, as an extreme case of the influence of verbal pronouncements over physical experience. The duel of the title is a medieval trial by combat, in which a legal issue is decided by physical battle between two champions in the belief that God will grant victory to the one who has sworn to truthful testimony, and bring defeat on the one who has sworn falsely. As a legal proceeding, trial by battle was finally being abolished from the law codes of European nations about the time Kleist wrote "Der Zweikampf" in 1811. This form of legal decision is evidently outmoded in a modern European context because it gives physical force and empirical contingencies precedence over the verbal process of testimony, deliberation, and judgment according to written codes and precedents. Ironically, however, a more important motivation for abolishing trial by combat in the early nineteenth century was that, in its antiquated form, the law provided felons with a loophole whereby they could escape a guilty verdict: they could swear to the truth of their testimony and their readiness to defend that oath in combat, knowing that the antiquated custom of battle would never be carried out; the ordeal would end with the speech act. As the legal historian Helen Silvig writes, by the time "primitive procedures" such as trial by combat were abolished in England in 1815, they "were often advantageous to defendants and, accordingly, were prized as privileges, indeed, as civil liberties" because "the defendant could avoid all liability merely by taking an oath" (1365). In Kleist's story, performative utterance also comes to predominate over the battle itself, so that the text begins with one imperial decree (the edict that Wilhelm von Breysach has obtained from the Emperor legitimating his son and heir) and ends with another (the Emperor's order that the statutes governing trial by combat be altered). Read with attention to these and the many intervening speech acts, the entire narrative, ostensibly about a physical ordeal, can also be seen as a grotesquely amplified account of how a single phrase in the law-books comes to be amended.

The situation described in the first paragraph as the germ of the whole adventure is already a tangle of physical and verbal determinants. Duke Wilhelm von Breysach, returning from a meeting with the Emperor at which he has secured an act of legitimation for his illegitimately conceived son, is fatally wounded by an arrow. Though he loses his life, Wilhelm wins an important legal victory when his vassals at least provisionally accept the authority of the imperial edict that allows his son to inherit the throne, over the standing law that would grant the succession to his half-brother, Jakob der Rotbart. Within the convoluted sentences that set out the background of the story, temporality complicates the interrelation of physical and verbal levels. Presumably the very fact that Wilhelm rides out to meet the Emperor and obtain the edict gives his assassin the opportunity to shoot him. But the fact that he then lives just long enough to read out the imperial decree to his hastily assembled vassals, and witness their decision to support his son, determines the further course of his story, for the performative language of the edict now alters the line of succession. The all-important delay that allows Wilhelm to read out the proclamation is emphasized by the structure of the last sentence in the opening paragraph, which is improbably extended to include an account of the actions of his chamberlain, his wife, and his vassals, and of the significance of their decision, before concluding at last with the main clause announcing Wilhelm's death:

> His chamberlain Herr Friedrich von Trota, amazed and appalled by this event, managed with the help of some other knights to carry him into the castle, where his distraught wife, having hastily summoned a council of the vassals of the realm, held him in her arms as with his last remaining strength he read aloud the imperial deed of legitimation; and when, despite some lively opposition, for by law the crown should have passed to his half-brother Count Rotbart, the vassals had complied with his last express wish and, subject to the Emperor's approval, had recognized Count Philipp as successor to the throne under the guardianship and regency of his mother in view of his minority, the Duke lay back and died. (*Stories* 287)

The imperial edict read out by Duke Wilhelm and conditionally accepted by his vassals constitutes a kind of inaugural speech act that suddenly and radically re-orders the situation of the characters—and the new order it brings about is typically fragile. Not only is the reading of the edict contingent on Wilhelm's precarious physical condition, but its effect remains conditional on the Emperor's approval. The narrative also hints at how dependent Wilhelm, as the nominal speaker, and even the Emperor, as the ultimate origin of the edict, are on contingent circumstances, on bodily frailty, and on ancillary agents for the effect of the speech act. Wilhelm's vassals need to be "hastily assembled" just in time to hear his last will—a situation engineered, interestingly, by Wilhelm's socially inferior wife, who, "distraught" as she is, and though she is not herself an authorized speaker, takes control of the circumstances within which the reading of the imperial edict ultimately results in her election as Regent for her son.

As with Wilhelm's and his wife's hasty effort to win acceptance for the imperial edict, so in the duel itself, the key issue is the legitimation of utterances. This becomes an issue of life and death when Jakob der Rotbart is accused of murdering Wilhelm and defends himself with an alibi, claiming to have spent the night in question with the virtuous widow Littegarde von Auerstein. Jakob, defending himself against the accusation of fratricide, Littegarde, defending herself against the accusation of fornication, and the chamberlain Herr Friedrich von Trota, taking up Littegarde's cause as her suitor and champion, must achieve legitimation for their statements within the legal conventions of their late-fourteenth-century society, which require that truth be determined by combat. Trial by battle is introduced into the story in a scene that echoes the performance of Mirabeau in the National Assembly, in Kleist's "Über die allmähliche Verfertigung der Gedanken beim Reden." It is not clear whether Friedrich von Trota has any idea how he is going to prove Littegarde's innocence when he sets off for the imperial court at Basle. But when he arrives in the public courtroom where Jakob der Rotbart is about to be acquitted of the murder, on the basis of the testimony he and Littegarde's brothers have provided about her alleged rendezvous with him that night, Friedrich changes the direction of the proceedings with his verbal and bodily acts:

> The herald, in the great hall of the court, had just read aloud the letter from Rudolf von Breda and his brother, and the judges, with the accused man standing beside them, were about to give effect to the imperial decree and proceed formally to his honourable discharge, when Herr Friedrich von Trota advanced to the bar and, invoking the right of any impartial spectator, requested permission to look at the letter for a moment. Consent was given, and the eyes of the whole assembly were turned on him; but scarcely had the paper been handed to him by the herald than Herr Friedrich, after a fleeting glance at it, tore it from top to bottom and hurled the pieces, with his glove wrapped round them, into Count Jakob Rotbart's face, declaring him to be a vile and contemptible slanderer and vowing to prove before all the world, in a life and death ordeal by combat, the lady Littegarde's innocence of the offence of which he had accused her. (*Stories* 301)

Intervening just at the moment when the court is about to pronounce its verdict in Jakob's case, Friedrich shifts the whole proceeding to a new level. His actions demonstrate (like Mirabeau's) that the established hierarchy of legally authorized speakers and authoritative speech acts may be broken open by individuals in unpredictable speech situations. Friedrich is within his rights as a spectator to ask to examine the document submitted in evidence, but exercises his right in an unforeseen way, by the physical act of tearing up the evidence and using it to perform a ritual challenge against Count Jakob. By calling for an ordeal by battle, Friedrich proceeds to reinvoke the law, but at its most fragile point—where it tries to harness divine intervention.

At the heart of the story, therefore, is a physical battle between Count Jakob and Herr Friedrich that is completely circumscribed by speech acts. Not only does the duel take place according to the laws of the empire, but it counts as a form of divine utterance inasmuch as it allows God to speak out in favor of one or the other of the combatants. Both Friedrich and Jakob (a pious man despite his depravity) refer to the duel as the "speech" or "declaration" (Spruch) of almighty God (*SWB* 2: 248, 259), while Littegarde, though knowing herself to be innocent, accepts on the basis of God's judgment in the duel that she has been declared "guilty, convicted and cast out, judged and condemned in time and for eternity!" (*Stories* 310). Friedrich's mother, however, expresses a more precise intuition about the way divine authority enters into human jurisprudence, when she points out that God's judgment in the ordeal is completely circumscribed by the human laws that undertake to interpret it, and these "established and prevailing laws . . . whether rational or not . . . have the authority of divine commandments" (*Stories* 308). The disjunction between a presumably omniscient and infallible, yet inaccessible, divine command, and the human laws in which it must be mediated and represented, forms the crux of "Der Zweikampf."

Once the law of trial by combat is invoked, the crimes of murder and fornication are superseded by the verbal crime of blasphemy, or swearing a false oath; the party that loses the battle will be put to death for having called on God in vain, as witness in a false cause. The bodily acts at the heart of the story—Duke Wilhelm's assassination, an illicit act of sexual intercourse, and the battle itself—are transmuted by the legal system into acts of permitted or forbidden utterance. The incommensurability of divine command and human law codes, then, is matched by a disjunction between bodily acts and discursive acts. Friedrich von Trota appears to lose the battle when he trips over his spurs and gives Jakob the opportunity to fell him; yet he makes a miraculous recovery from his three mortal wounds, while Jakob, on the contrary, becomes mortally ill from the infection of a scratch he received on the wrist, early in the contest. A few weeks after the battle, it begins to seem as if the outcome embodies a truth that runs deeper than a simple yes/no verdict: Friedrich's recovery from death-wounds signals a divinely given strength and purity, while Jakob's rotting body looks like an externalization of his corrupted soul. But the legal practice in which the experience is circumscribed cannot deal with this kind of bodily logic. Even if Friedrich soon feels ready to continue the duel to the death in defiance of "arbitrary human laws," his mother reminds him that "according to the law a duel which has been declared by the judges to be concluded cannot be resumed in order to invoke the divine verdict a second time in one and the same case" (*Stories* 307–8). Despite what the bodies are saying, it is the judges who, like umpires calling a game, declare when the duel is over and what the divine verdict is—even if the verdict will then work itself out in the burning of the losers' bodies at the stake.

Yet, just as the execution of Littegarde and Friedrich for blasphemy is about to take place, another last-minute speech act changes the course of their lives (or deaths). Jakob der Rotbart is carried to the place of execution and exhorts the Emperor to hear his final statement and confession: that the woman he thought was Littegarde when he spent the night with her has really turned out to be her maid Rosalie, and that he did in fact hire an assassin to murder his half-brother Wilhelm. Behind both these revelations are further chains of interactions by which characters transmute raw physical experience into conventional—and thus comprehensible—verbal forms. The truth of Littegarde's story is ironically affirmed, for instance, by a distant and seemingly unrelated legal case, in which Rosalie's parents have brought a paternity suit against Count Jakob on behalf of the child that has been born to her as a result of his intercourse with the woman he took to be Littegarde.

Jakob's final confession repeats, in terms of the speech situation, the deathbed scene with which the story began. Indeed, the connection between the deathbed scenes of the two brothers is even closer than it first appears, for Duke Wilhelm's widow now reveals that Wilhelm survived even a bit longer than the narrative initially indicated—long enough to stammer out his testimony that the murderer was Jakob: "'Oh, then it was as my husband the Duke himself suspected!' cried the Regent, who was standing beside the Emperor. . . . 'He said so to me at the very moment of his death but with broken words which I then scarcely understood!'" (*Stories* 320). Had Wilhelm's words been legitimated as testimony at the time, this revelation suggests, the entire ordeal might have been averted. Alternatively, the belated revelation again shows how far the legitimation of utterances is from the speaker's own control, and how it is subject, rather, to hearers, interpreters, and those who engineer the speech situation. We are led to suspect that Wilhelm's ambitious wife, now the Regent who takes her place "beside the Emperor," found it in her interests at the time of her husband's death to win legitimation for the imperial decree by which her son inherited the throne—but *not* for the "broken words" with which Wilhelm accused his brother of murder.

The result of these intertwining accusations, testimonies, and confessions is a world in which all action, even the most apparently physical and non-verbal, turns out to be regulated, predicted, or circumscribed by language. The crucial and characteristic speech act for the ordering of this society is one that seems at first to be superfluous, for it is mentioned only in the final half-sentence of the narrative. After a happy ending, in which Littegarde and Friedrich obtain recompense for their suffering by being allowed to marry and being endowed with gifts by the Regent and the Emperor himself, the narrator reports a last action on the Emperor's part:

> as soon as he returned to Worms after the conclusion of his business in Switzerland, he gave orders that in the statutes governing sacred ordeal by combat, at all points where they assume that such a trial immediately brings guilt to light, the words 'if it be God's will' were to be inserted. (*Stories* 320)

These last words underline a central problem with the legal system the story portrays: in appealing to God as its ultimate authority and the guarantor of truth, it ironically attempts to contain God and his word within the law.

Far from being limited to the medieval setting, this paradox was a current issue when Kleist's story first appeared in 1811, in the context of campaigns for the abolition of courtroom oaths, oaths of investiture, and oaths of allegiance. According to Silvig, the French Revolution gave impetus to these campaigns throughout Europe: "the impact of the French Revolution, spiritually as well as geographically, introduced a decisive change of attitude toward the oath which has been the source of many reform movements aimed at limiting or abolishing the oath" (1352). Kant and Fichte both condemn the conventional use of oaths as an immoral imposition by the state on the freedom of the individual; but it is Bentham who argues for the abolishing of oaths in terms that are particularly relevant to "Der Zweikampf." In the tract *"Swear Not at All,"* which appeared two years after Kleist's story, Bentham stresses the absurdity of including God as a character in the process of carrying out secular legal decisions. The legal definition of an oath implicitly makes God subject to the human legislator, for God can be called in at will and required to act according to the criteria of human law:

> On the supposition that, by man, over the Almighty, *power* should, to this or any other purpose, be exercised or exercisable, an absurdity, than which nothing can be greater, cannot be denied to be involved: —man the legislator and judge, God the sheriff and executioner;—man the despot, God his slave.

If, in any given instance, on the part of the almighty executioner, any exception to the rule of obedience be supposed, in that instance the effect of the ceremony is nothing; the case is exactly as if there had been no such ceremony. But if in any one case it be thus inefficient, how comes it to be otherwise in any other case? (*Works* 5: 192)

The paradox of positing an ultimate, transcendent authority, yet assigning it a fixed role within the legal system, causes the law to rupture in a case like the one in Kleist's story. In fact, the case of Jakob, Friedrich, and Littegarde brings to light a more specific aspect of this general problem: namely, that the law limits its transcendent and omnipotent judge to exactly two choices. God can only validate the statement of one or the other of the two combatants; the law makes no room for a third alternative if, as in the present case, both combatants are telling the truth as they know it. Bentham, after arguing that invoking God by an oath is absurd in the first place, contends that the more complex absurdity arises when an oath is taken by "two swearers, swearing, and thus respectively engaging themselves, to direct their utmost endeavours to the production of two opposite and altogether incompatible effects," and God is compelled to lend his power simultaneously to both (*Works* 5: 193). Kleist's "Der *Zwei*-kampf," then, is a battle not only between two combatants, but between two incompatible alternatives in a case whether both are—or else neither is—right. This dilemma, in turn, reveals that the dualistic logic of language cannot encompass the unknowable, but apparently non-binary, "logic" of transcendence—or of physicality.

The Emperor's emendation of the statutes to include the words "if it be God's will" attempts to admit, as it were, a little bit more transcendence into the law. His emendation is presumably meant to qualify, primarily, the requirement that combat *immediately* reveal guilt and innocence; from now on, God will at least be given the choice of making revelation either immediate or drawn-out. Recognizing that God's testimony may be harder than expected to hear or to read, surmising that it may require interpretation rather than simple acknowledgment, the legislator attempts to make room for a certain temporality or delay in the process of trial by combat. Yet in complacently amending his statutes by five words, the Emperor remains blind to the paradox of using the legal performative to contain an incalculable power that transcends the conventions of human language. In fact, he arguably makes matters worse by writing God's will into the official language of the law. His emendation may undo the law of the empire completely, inasmuch as it now reads: holy combat will immediately bring guilt to light—*or not, if it be God's will*.

Of what value is a law phrased as conditional—a law that admits its dependence on the ultimate, incalculable, unknowable, and above all uncircumscribable provision of divine will? The last five words of the story, as a supplement to the imperial statutes, undo those statutes; as a supplement to the narrative, they deconstruct it as well. Kleist presents a society circumscribed by law, that translates or at least interweaves all physical experience into performative utterance. Yet his final sentence undoes the "statutes governing sacred ordeal by combat" by revealing that the circumscription of experience by language is incompatible with the presence of the guarantor of that language, God. By the end of the story the law of trial by combat survives only by formally admitting the possibility of failure. The Emperor's reasoning echoes that of Reid, whose analysis of promises explicitly takes account of the "condition implied in every promise, *if we live* and *if God continue with us the power which he hath given us*" (2: 617).

There is one further twist. Despite the Emperor's apparent deference to divine authority, it is he who retains control over the admission or non-admission of God's will into the law. Strictly speaking, the story is entirely circumscribed, not by the divine word, but by the Emperor's emendations to the imperial statutes. Events are set in motion when Wilhelm takes the unusual step of riding to the imperial seat in Worms to obtain an edict that alters the due process of law in his case, inasmuch as it displaces the legal heir, Jakob, in favor of Wilhelm's previously illegitimate son. The end result, once events have run their course—and once the Emperor has taken the time to see to his business negotiations with Switzerland—is a tiny, and yet global, amendment to the imperial statutes that, as it were, legalizes God's will. "Der Zweikampf" begins and ends with an appeal to the law, but more specifically to the need to stretch law to fit exceptional cases. The characters require a verbal ordering of the world, but one that, if it is not to be catastrophically fragile, must be infinitely flexible.

What causes this need for flexibility, the story suggests with its examples of how speech acts get legitimated, is the fact that the utterances even of supremely authoritative speakers are subject to the context in which they occur, and hence subject to people and events that exert control over the context. The behind-the-scenes role of Duke Wilhelm's wife, above all, reveals how individuals can manipulate the speech situation, and hence influence uptake and interpretation. Performatives in "Der Zweikampf," from Wilhelm's deathbed testament to Jakob's deathbed testimony, never appear to enact the exact correspondence between word and action or will and effect that we associate with divine utterance. In the end, the Emperor still emerges as the most privileged speaker, suggesting that it is neither divine will nor mutually accepted conventions that determine the course of human lives and fortunes so much as authoritative, political pronouncements made in stage-managed circumstances that render them felicitous.

"A law is a command," writes Bentham (*Bentham's Political Thought* 149)—thereby tracing the illocutionary force of laws back to basic directives uttered by speakers with sufficient power. Kleist's novella, too, demonstrates the necessary contextualization of the utterances that gain legitimacy as laws of the realm. Hanging the story of the duel on physical contingencies that affect key legal utterances (the ability of Wilhelm's wife to gather his vassals around his bed in time for him to read out the edict; the gauntlet Friedrich throws in Jakob's face just before his acquittal is to be pronounced; the apparently superficial wound Jakob receives; and the pregnancy of the otherwise invisible Rosalie), Kleist demonstrates the interimplication of discourse, performativity, and the body. His fiction exposes the bizarre aspects of this constellation of terms, but at the same time makes us realize that these performative constellations—the attempt to stabilize a social order precariously balanced around physical force and metaphysical faith by inserting five words into the law code, for instance—are not particularly unusual in themselves. "This is simply what [we] do," as Wittgenstein put it (85), as we try to come to terms with the incommensurability and interdependence of language and physical experience.

7

Godwin's Philosophy and Fiction: The Resistance to Performatives

A decade before the works on which his modern reputation rests, *Political Justice* (1793) and *Caleb Williams* (1794), William Godwin published his first novel, *Italian Letters, or The History of the Count de St. Julian* (1784). This early text already broaches the troubled relationship between experience and language, a theme that all of Godwin's subsequent novels and many of his essays will draw on in one form or another. As an epistolary novel, *Italian Letters* presents a set of relationships delineated by the pragmatic utterances characters address to one another. The characters construct and radically alter one another's realities through the news they exchange as well as the promises they make, the lies they tell, and the letters they prevent from reaching their destination. The story concerns the sympathetic St. Julian, who leaves his fiancée Matilda in the care of his best friend, the Marquis of Pescara, while he is away in Spain attending to the Marquis's business affairs. He returns months later to find he has been betrayed by Pescara, who, spurred on by the letters of a libertine friend, has intercepted the correspondence between St. Julian and his fiancée, persuaded her that St. Julian has broken his engagement in order to marry a Spanish noblewoman, and married the disconsolate Matilda himself.

Until the catastrophe of Pescara's betrayal, the social order of the novel is precariously held together by verbal agreements among the characters, the crucial ones being the engagement between St. Julian and Matilda, and Pescara's promise that he will take care of Matilda until St. Julian returns. Once he discovers his friend's treachery, St. Julian reproaches him in words that expose the contractual foundations of the social order:

> From this moment then, let the name of trust be a by-word for the profligate to scoff at! Let the epithet of friend be a mildew to the chaste and uncorrupted ear! Let mutual confidence be banished from the earth, and men, more savage than the brute, devour each other! . . .Yes, my lord,

from henceforth all contract between us is canceled. You have set us right upon our first foundations. (*CN* 2: 144)

St. Julian's allusions to "contract" and the "first foundations" of human relationships cut to the heart of the matter. *Italian Letters*—like all of Godwin's later novels—demonstrates the disastrous consequences of relying on promises, contracts, or vows. Yet without these alliances, human relationships are thrown back on first foundations, or into a state of nature. Once St. Julian, in the explicit performative utterance quoted above, cancels all verbal agreements between him and Pescara "henceforth" and "from this moment," his next act graphically demonstrates what it means to live without the "name of trust," the "epithet of friend," and a contract of mutual confidence. Challenging Pescara to a duel, he kills him.

The denouement of *Italian Letters* recapitulates the dilemma of a social order that is inadequately held together by contractual utterances, yet cannot do without them. After a period of despair and mourning, St. Julian writes to his estranged beloved Matilda, now the widowed Marchioness of Pescara and the mother of an infant son. He appeals to her to renew their shattered engagement with a single word from the heart: "Speak but the word, and time shall reverse his course, and a new order of things shall commence. Think how much virtue depends upon your fiat" (*CN* 2: 158–59). But Matilda, having once been persuaded to annul her engagement to St. Julian and suffering the consequences, cannot risk abandoning the verbal contracts she has now accepted, that circumscribe her status as a widowed noblewoman of the house of Pescara and the mother of its heir. She refuses to enter into a second marriage with the murderer of her husband because of the dishonor it would bring to the name of the family into which she has married. Wrecked by the failure of engagements and promises, yet unable to break free of burdensome contracts with a radically re-creative *fiat*, the society of *Italian Letters* ends in an unsatisfying but insoluble bind.

'POLITICAL JUSTICE,' PROMISES, AND PHANTOM LIMBS

Godwin thematizes the unreliability and the deleterious effects of promises in the *Enquiry Concerning Political Justice*, where performative utterances in general violate the role that he assigns to language in an ideal society. Like his contemporaries, Godwin devotes part of the tumultuous 1790s to reflection on social contracts, promises, laws, oaths, and declarations. Unlike Reid, Bentham, Coleridge, or most of the German thinkers, though, Godwin steadfastly resists the idea that language should be accorded anything but secondary status in relation to thought and external reality, or that it has any legitimate purpose other than the communication of truth. Godwin does not trust words to do things. Because of this, his contributions to the theory of language and its function in society have an unexpectedly conservative ring, as he tries to erect a bulwark against the encroaching opinion that language constructs cognitive and social reality through the type of verbal act that this book has dubbed the Romantic performative. Rooted in his political philosophy of the 1790s, Godwin's resistance to performatives manifests itself in his fiction over the next forty years—even if his novels also undermine the antinomian ideal of *Political Justice* by showing that speech acts inescapably determine social reality.

On the positive side, Godwin regards language as the instrument by which people are educated, misunderstandings resolved, society reformed, and enlightenment spread. Godwin is convinced of the necessity of free speech and debate among members of a society, to the extent that he opposes not only censorship, but any other form of governmental control over what is said and written, including libel laws and state-sponsored educational systems. His goal, a society regulated by reason and understanding, requires a language that is unfailingly constative—that is, a language dedicated to truth, sincerity, and correspondence with experienced reality. "Accuracy of language is the indispensible prerequisite of sound knowledge," Godwin proclaims (*PJ* 1: 385), and summarizes in five propositions the progress from reason to human improvement, by way of the communication of truth:

> Sound reasoning and truth, when adequately communicated, must always be victorious over error: Sound reasoning and truth are capable of being so communicated: Truth is omnipotent: The vices and moral weakness of man are not invincible: Man is perfectible, or in other words susceptible of perpetual improvement. (*PJ* 1: 86)

In a chapter devoted to the "perpetual improvement" of "human inventions," Godwin specifically illustrates his belief in human perfectibility by reviewing the origin of speech and writing. Summarizing the development of the refined, analytical language in which human beings now reason about their experience, Godwin argues that language itself is a prime example of improvement in human inventions. In addition, it is the instrument that will, if committed to accurate analysis and honest communication, bring about the perfection of political science.

Because a truthful, descriptive language is one of the foundations of his political philosophy, Godwin condemns non-constative utterances more severely than any of his contemporaries. In an implicit attack on the political theory stemming from Hobbes and Locke, Godwin denies that contractual utterances can be the basis for either moral behavior or a healthy society. "Promises and compacts are in no sense the foundation of morality," he declares at the beginning of his chapter "Of Promises" (*PJ* 1: 194), and repeats the claim several times after that.[1] Instead, "the foundation of morality is justice"; virtuous behavior results from our basic, reasonable inclination to balance people's needs and their abilities so as to promote "the welfare of intelligent beings" (*PJ* 1: 195). Promising is a second-stage behavior that, if properly applied, *expresses* our moral intentions; but looking to promises to *explain* morality amounts to taking an effect for the cause. Worse, it obscures the real motive for moral behavior by putting a temporary, contingent, and superficial verbal formula in its place. Promises "call off our attention from the direct tendencies of our conduct, and fix it upon a merely local and precarious consideration" (*PJ* 1: 202); that is to say, we should perform a virtuous action for its own sake, not because we happen to have pronounced a few words relating to that action at some point in the past. Worse still, promises offend against the normal process of improving and perfecting our behavior, which depends on the continual acquisition of new and better information over time. Even if a promise corresponds with virtuous behavior at the time I make it, that which I perceive to be good or evil may change when I acquire more information; but my promise works against improvement by locking my behavior into the pattern that was set when my information was still incomplete. All speech acts that attempt to exert control over future behavior ultimately work against the improvement of society because they institutionalize error, protect existing abuses, and prevent reform.

In critiquing the promise, Godwin actually anticipates quite closely some aspects of the modern analysis of it as a paradigmatic performative. He recognizes that it is not a specific verbal or grammatical formula that makes an utterance into a promise, but rather the speech situation—or, more specifically, the uptake of the hearer. Godwin's distinction between "perfect" and "imperfect" promises suggests that even sentences not intended as promises may count as promises depending on the context in which they are uttered:

---

[1] In the 1798 edition of *Political Justice*, quoted here, the chapter "Of Promises" agrees with but expands on the corresponding chapter in the first edition of 1793.

> A perfect promise is where the declaration of intention is made by me, for the express purpose of serving as a ground of expectation to my neighbour respecting my future conduct. An imperfect promise is where it actually thus serves as a ground of expectation, though that was not my purpose when I made the declaration. Imperfect promises are of two classes: I may have reason, or I may have no reason, to know, when I make the declaration, that it will be acted upon by my neighbour, though not assuming the specific form of an engagement. (*PJ* 1: 203–4)

Austin will use the identical example to distinguish between explicit (or "primitive") and implicit performatives: "'I shall be there' may or may not be a promise. . . . [I]n a given situation it can be open to me to take it as *either* one or the other" (33). Godwin's intuition of the distinction between speaker's intention, hearer's uptake, and grammatical form shows that he, like Austin, regards speech as interpersonal action, and meaning as a function of the pragmatic context.

But Godwin's primary concern is the effect of time on this context. He exposes the troubled relationship between promises and temporality by suggesting that promising is akin to spending money that we imagine we might receive in the future, but do not yet possess:

> Now one of the principal means of information, is time. We must therefore devote to that object all the time our situation will allow. But we abridge, and that in the most essential point, the time of gaining information, if we bind ourselves to-day, to the conduct we will observe two months hence. He who thus anticipates upon the stores of knowledge, is certainly not less improvident, than he who lives by anticipating the stores of fortune. (*PJ* 1: 198–99)

By bringing time into the picture, Godwin in effect moves beyond an Austinian analysis of the promise in terms of context and uptake, and toward a perspective that resembles the deconstructionist critique of performative language. When de Man considers the language of eighteenth-century political theory, he, too, finds it vulnerable—albeit unconsciously so—to the problematic temporality of promising. Because "the speech act of the contractual text never refers to a situation that exists in the present, but signals toward a hypothetical future," as de Man concludes from a reading of Rousseau's *Social Contract* (*Allegories of Reading* 273), all promises and social contracts perform a metalepsis by which they illegitimately found themselves on a future situation that does not yet exist. In a similar vein, Shoshana Felman refers to the perverse temporality of the promise, which is "constituted by the act of anticipating the act of concluding" and thus betrays "the noncoincidence of desire with the present." Godwin, although more interested in the ethical than the rhetorical or psychological aspects of this situation, also insists that the future must be revealed by time and experience, not preempted by a hypothetical linguistic construction of it. He affirms that promises are unnecessary anyway, as long as my conduct and that of my neighbor remain regulated by rationality and duty. While rejecting the promise as a formal declaration, in other words, Godwin reposes his faith in an unspoken or internal promise of consistency in human conduct.

Godwin's critique of promises is circumscribed by the rest of his analysis of human behavior in *Political Justice*, particularly his commitment to sincerity and his belief in necessity. Depending on the circumstances, these conditions sometimes indicate that a promise should be kept, but other times that it should not. On the one hand, promising when one has no intention of fulfilling the promise violates the requirement of sincerity, a foundation of moral conduct that runs much deeper than the mere conventions of promising. Insincere behavior of this sort "can scarcely in any instance take place, without fixing a stain upon the promiser" (*PJ* 1: 210). On the other hand, Godwin recognizes many instances in which it would be right *not* to keep one's promise, even if it was sincerely made, since both character and behavior are determined by external circumstances, and it is impossible to know which circumstances will obtain in the future at the moment one is making the promise. The vulnerability of behavior to external circumstances leads Godwin to argue that, strictly speaking, it is absurd even to say "I will do this" (*PJ* 1: 389), and that governments ought not to hold themselves bound by treaties (*PJ* 2: 173). Promising, it appears again, is first of all superfluous with regard to basic moral conduct, and, secondly, illegitimate with regard to temporality.

Both these objections are summed up in an odd image, which Godwin at first seems to be using as an example of pain and evil during a brief digression on these topics, but which turns into an analogy for promising. Making a promise, Godwin suggests, is like the amputation of a leg. Even if there are cases when the operation is medically advisable, we should never forget that it is an "absolute evil" in itself. "The case of promises," he continues,

> is considerably similar to this. So far as they have any effect, they depose us, as to the particular to which they relate, from the use of our own understanding.... There may be cases in which they are necessary and ought to be employed: but we should never suffer ourselves, by their temporary utility to be induced to forget their intrinsic nature, and the demerits which adhere to them independently of any peculiar concurrence of circumstances. (*PJ* 1: 202)

Godwin's Philosophy and Fiction

Just as amputation deprives us of the use of part of the body, promising deprives us of the full, healthy use of the mind. Godwin's objections to promises and other performatives are summed up in the image of the utterance as a gap or emptiness: these speech acts, for Godwin, are a *hollow* use of language. They are expressions that contain no truth, add no morality, and maintain no reliable correspondence with experienced reality. At best, they are benign but empty. At worst, these hollow words interfere with the behavior of real minds and bodies and impede the productive synthesis of reason and experience.

THE PROGENY OF PROMISES

Godwin's critique of promises recurs several times in *Political Justice*, since he believes that the promise is the paradigm for many of the structures that order existing society. Foremost among these are two hot topics of the 1790s: the social contract and constitutions. In his chapter "Of the Social Contract," Godwin sides with the reformist position for which Paine became the most famous spokesperson, arguing that a hereditary contract—even when it is a specific, written contract entered into by a generation of citizens—should not be considered binding on their descendants, who never had a say in the matter. But Godwin goes further than Paine, and insists that even the same generation of people who made the contract may have occasion to change their minds if circumstances change, or if they obtain better information. He doubts that anyone can give informed assent to a contract so large as to encompass "the laws of England in fifty volumes folio," and cites Rousseau's argument, in his *Social Contract*, that "the general will . . . cannot be represented": "The deputies of the people cannot be its representatives; they are merely its attorneys. The laws which the community does not ratify in person, are no laws, are nullities" (*PJ* 1: 191–92). Where Paine criticized the belief that the 1689 Declaration of Rights is binding on future generations of Englishmen, yet championed the new French constitution, Godwin claims that the French fell into exactly the same trap of attempting to legislate for all time:

> The French national assembly of 1789, pushed this principle to the greatest extremity, and seemed desirous of providing every imaginable security for rendering the work they had formed immortal. . . . It is easy to perceive that these precautions, are in direct hostility with the principles established in this work. 'Man and for ever!' was the motto of the labours of this assembly. Just broken loose from the thick darkness of an absolute monarchy, they assumed to prescribe lessons of wisdom to all future ages. (*PJ* 2: 284)

The French National Assembly attempted to frame a new social order in its Declaration of the Rights of Man and Citizen; but because this declaration promulgated a single set of principles as fundamental and unchangeable, Godwin judges it to be, like all constitutions, "founded in misapprehension and error" (*PJ* 2: 285).

The same holds true for laws, oaths, and tests (i.e., oaths of loyalty required of those who would accede to certain official positions). All these speech acts perpetuate and magnify the two fundamental flaws of promises: they are superfluous at best, and at worst they preclude improvement or reform. Oaths, Godwin claims, are equally useless whether they are required of a virtuous man, or a potential traitor. The former will swear sincerely, but he would have acted honestly in any case; the latter, if inclined to act dishonestly anyway, will not be deterred by the extra crime of swearing a false oath. To illustrate the absurdity of trying to bind people to future conduct by an oath, when the future is always uncertain, Godwin chooses another charged example from revolutionary France:

> It was required of all men, in the year 1791, to swear, 'that they would be faithful to the nation, the law and the king.' In what sense can they be said to have adhered to their oath, who, twelve months after their constitution had been established on its new basis, have taken a second oath declaratory of their everlasting abjuration of monarchy? (*PJ* 2: 257)

Systems of legislation, which Godwin analyzes as "a species of promises," sustain the same illegitimate conservatism. They prevent improvement or progress by imposing a "principle of permanence": "Law tends, no less than creeds, catechisms and tests, to fix the human mind in a stagnant condition, and to substitute a principle of permanence, in the room of that unceasing progress which is the only salubrious element of mind" (*PJ* 2: 403). Dedicated to a transparent, enlightened, and enlightening language that corresponds as far as possible to experienced reality, Godwin's system has no room for the large classes of performatives that reach into the future and attempt to alter the world to fit the words, rather than fitting words to the actual state of the world. Using Searle's taxonomy, we might identify these classes of speech acts as directives (i.e., attempts to get the hearer to do something, including orders and laws), commissives (i.e., expressions that commit the speaker to some future course of action, including oaths and promises), and declarations (i.e., official utterances, such as constitutions, that change existing states) (*Expression and Meaning* 13–17). By tracing more highly institutionalized performatives back to the basically misguided speech act of promising, Godwin gives a linguistic-pragmatic turn to his analysis of the body politic, and implies that his skepticism about laws, constitutions, and other political structures is inseparable from his belief that they represent a misuse of language. The incommensurability of language and experience, especially the experience of time and change, leads, in Godwin's case, to a position of philosophical anarchism—a belief that neither verbal formulas, nor the institutions that perpetuate and are perpetuated by them, should pretend to regulate social behavior better than the fundamental claims of reason and virtue. *Political Justice* has little tolerance for declarations that can, or should, or do shape the world.

And yet: the point of the *Enquiry Concerning Political Justice* is to suggest what society might become, in defiance of what it actually is. The reason that Godwin has to resist so adamantly the idea that language might shape reality is that it patently *does* shape reality, and Godwin is intensely aware of the extent to which laws, oaths, promises, social contracts, and other performatives constitute his sociopolitical experience. His novels are therefore full of the very speech acts that *Political Justice* condemns. In Godwin's theory, verbal utterances should be the expression of moral character, reason, and experience, but in practice, identity and experience appear to be products of utterance. Nowhere is this more evident than in *Caleb Williams*, a virtual showcase of interpersonal speech acts (including promises, laws, libels, rumors, and fictitious published biographies) that impinge on the protagonist's very identity. In this novel of "things as they are," it is clearly the pragmatic scenes in which words are spoken (the private study or the public courtroom, for instance), and the conventions governing public behavior (especially the conventions of social class), that determine whose speech acts will be effective and whose will not, regardless of their truth-value.

Godwin's later novels pick up and intensify the speech-act issues raised in *Caleb Williams*: *Fleetwood* and *Deloraine* both contrast marital relationships governed by frankness with those mediated by contracts, commands, and other power-based performatives; a secret and a promise form the basis of the hero's identity in *St. Leon*; and the relationship between physical identity and identity as a legal or textual construct is central to the plot of *Cloudesley*. On the one hand, all these novels confirm Godwin's suspicion of performative utterance by showing how lives are ruined by the futile adherence to promises, how relationships are soured by secrets, and how identities are deformed by fraudulent but effective testimony. On the other hand, Godwin's fiction undermines his philosophical dedication to constative language by portraying the performative as inescapable. This is not only because it constitutes the foundation of so many societal institutions, but because the potential separation of "superficial" verbal conventions from the "first foundations" of morality, a separation that *Political Justice* or even *Italian Letters* claims to make, proves to be impossible. Since the basic moral motivations of Godwin's characters are inextricable from their own and other people's illocutionary acts, it becomes very difficult to maintain that verbal utterances are simply a secondary reflection or communication of behavioral principles that are already fully formed. Thus, the oath by which Caleb Williams swears to keep Falkland's secret is a verbal convention, but it is also the only way he knows to express his essential moral character. Even though Caleb has learned much more about the conventions that govern public utterances by the time he pronounces his formal accusation of Falkland in the final scene, that accusation is even more dramatically wrapped up with his subjective identity—to the extent that Caleb's attitude toward Falkland undergoes a conversion as, and because, he attempts to accuse Falkland before a magistrate. The narrative perspectives and structures of Godwin's novels add a further complication: not only are sociopolitical speech acts inseparable from essential moral being, but they are inseparable from fictionality. The speech acts characters use to construct their social status and their relationships to others, those they use to create themselves as protagonists within a narrative of their own adventures, and those that constitute the novels themselves as works of fiction, work in surprisingly similar ways. Despite Godwin's theoretical resistance to performatives, his novels testify to the constitutive role of the forms of language that Reid called social acts and Bentham called linguistic fictions; yet Godwin goes beyond Reid and Bentham in revealing the extensive linkage of social and legal speech acts with those that produce *literary* fiction.

'CALEB WILLIAMS': TRUTH AND PERFORMATIVES

The novel that fascinates readers as a fictional counterpart to *Political Justice* and as a study of (among other things) obsession, ideology, despotism, violence, detective fiction, Calvinism, Gothic, and the family romance, also makes an absorbing subject for speech-act analysis.[2]

---

[2] Among the many readings *Caleb Williams* has received are several that focus on the role or status of language, and a few that identify, at least briefly, its specifically performative aspects. Jacqueline T. Miller reads the novel in the context of the theoretical reflections on language in Godwin's essays, and calls attention to the way it represents self and world as linguistic constructs. Hogle's more obviously poststructuralist reading, also from the late 1970s, identifies four levels of discourse in *Caleb Williams*, all of which "end up referring to the pure performance of signs that controls the speaker (and the writer) of the text" (262). A more recent poststructuralist

Things as They Are—the sub-title of *Caleb Williams*, which was its main title until the 1831 edition—appears to promise a constative text that orients itself according to existing circumstances in the external world. Yet what the novel delivers is a bewildering array of interrelated levels of speech acts. The same preface to the original edition of 1794 that introduces the phrase "things as they are" also presents the novel as Godwin's "performance" of the existing "constitution" of society, directed to the novel-reading public in order to instruct them about social injustice (*CN* 3: 279). From the beginning, this delineation of things as they are seizes a pragmatic context, addressing a popular audience for a political purpose. The pragmatic dimension threatens, in fact, to overwhelm the story, and Godwin's preface had to be withdrawn from the first edition, lest the book itself have an overly performative effect in the tense political context and draw on its author a charge of sedition.

Readers of *Caleb Williams* recognize that the ideal of truth, which Caleb champions as Godwin did in *Political Justice*, is nevertheless undercut by Caleb's own unreliability as a narrator.[3] Like Godwin in the preface, Caleb begins by characterizing his narrative as a performance in the "theatre of calamity" that is his life (*CN* 3: 5). But the novel undermines the concept of sincere communication on a much larger scale: far from describing things as they are, the various tales told and written within *Caleb Williams* cause reality to conform to previously composed texts. Utterances that we like to think of as the epitome of truth, particularly courtroom testimonies, turn out to be absolutely context-dependent. Truth becomes a function of speaker, context, and convention, and is evaluated according to effect rather than correspondence with reality. The performative—embodied, ultimately, in the image of

---

approach by Simms explores the many elements of both Caleb's and Godwin's narratives that destabilize the writing of one's life and the writing of what "is," including linguistic shifters, deferral, framing, and gaps of various kinds in the text. Warren historicizes the question of language and its instability, locating *Caleb Williams* at a historical juncture when some writers, Godwin among them, began to critique the eighteenth-century ideal of gentlemanly "conversational practice," but failed to find in writing a reliable replacement for conversation. Performative elements in the novel are touched on by Edwards at the end of his joint essay with Everest, and more explicitly addressed by Balfour, who focuses on the promise made by Caleb to Falkland in the context of Godwin's philosophical condemnation of oaths and promises.

[3]In addition to the studies mentioned in the previous note, all of which address the instability of language and truth in the novel, see Clifford, who compares *Caleb Williams* and *Frankenstein* as novels that expose the problems of writing the self, and Sheiber, who agrees that Caleb is unreliable but adds that, Falkland's voice being equally refutable, the novel offers no reliable yardstick by which to measure the narratives of the various characters.

Falkland's locked trunk—still suffers from the emptiness that Godwin attributed to it in *Political Justice*, yet it lies at the very heart of the novel and the experience of its characters.

I. World-To-Word Narratives

In one of the essays in his 1797 collection *The Enquirer*, Godwin confirms the representational theory of language that underlies *Political Justice*; the "just order" of things, he maintains, is "ideas first, and then words" (*PPW* 5: 101). But Caleb Williams, not to mention the reader of *Caleb Williams*, encounters a panoply of texts and utterances that impose themselves on people's ideas of the world so as effectively to alter their cognitive apprehension of reality, and of one another. The world of *Caleb Williams* seems dominated by utterances that fit the world to words, rather than fitting words to a previously conceptualized world. Caleb's own autobiography, and his very idea of himself, must contend against the oral and written versions of "The Adventures of Caleb Williams" that begin to circulate once he gains notoriety as the thief and jail-breaker "Kit Williams." Caleb's story intertwines with stories *about* Caleb, as he finds when he boldly asks the hostess at an inn to describe Kit Williams:

> She replied that, as she was informed, he was as handsome, likely a lad, as any in four counties round; and that she loved him for his cleverness, by which he outwitted all the keepers they could set over him, and made his way through stone walls, as if they were so many cobwebs. (*CN* 3: 211)

Later, he purchases a copy of "the Most Wonderful and Surprising History, and Miraculous Adventures of Caleb Williams" from a hawker (*CN* 3: 237), only to find that the broadsheet is a different kind of narrative again. Not simply a sensationalized fiction of his adventures, it is a frighteningly exact account of his movements and the disguises he has adopted—apparently a truthful rather than a "Miraculous" history, but one framed so as to influence Caleb's present behavior. As he eventually discovers, the text is not a "true and faithful copy of the hue and cry printed and published by one of his majesty's most principal secretaries of state," as the hawker claimed (*CN* 3: 238), but an invention of Falkland's minion Jones (or Gines), intended to smoke Caleb out of hiding. It becomes increasingly obvious that there are more verbal re-creations of self and world, constructed for a greater variety of pragmatic purposes, than Caleb is aware of or able to control. In trying to evade the construction that one narrative puts on his person and character, he simply becomes subject to another narrative instead. When he adopts the disguise of an Irishman in order to differentiate himself from the Kit Williams whose story has become infamous, two informers immediately arrest him under the pretext of a warrant for the arrest of an Irish robber: "They had a description of his person which, though, as I afterwards found, it disagreed from mine in several material articles, appeared to them to tally to the minutest tittle" (*CN* 3: 215).

The full power of these verbal constructions makes itself felt at the end of Caleb's story, when Falkland arranges for the criminal charge against Caleb to be withdrawn, yet determines to have him pursued from town to town by accusation and gossip. At the isolated market-town in Wales where he tries to begin a new life, Caleb—who has now undertaken a formal study of linguistics—finds that his appearance, behavior, and personal expostulation are no match for the tales being broadcast about him. Even the discerning Laura Denison reverses her opinion of Caleb once a copy of "the Wonderful and Surprising History of Caleb Williams" appears in town, and she finds its construction of Caleb and Falkland substantiated by some letters left to her by her father, "which spoke of Mr. Falkland in the highest terms of panegyric" (*CN* 3: 328). Nor is Caleb himself uninvolved in the enterprise of constructing character through published narratives. His writing of his own memoirs, as a pragmatic act of vindicating his reputation, is ironically anticipated by the first employment he finds on moving to London: translating and paraphrasing "the histories of celebrated robbers" (*CN* 3: 229).

The proliferating stories about Caleb Williams within the protagonist's own, autobiographical account of Caleb Williams create a tangle of narratives, meta-narratives, and feedback loops between narrative levels, that it is hard not to think of as postmodern. Yet the situation in which protagonists encounter versions of their own story recurs, not only in Godwin's later fiction, but even in his experience of current political events. In Godwin's last novel, a page torn from a French periodical chances to contain a distorted account of the protagonist Deloraine's adventures. When Deloraine himself finds it, it causes him to re-interpret his own actions, and when his landlord finds it, he revises his opinion of Deloraine's character, breaks the contract the two have made, and betrays him. The histories of Deloraine and Caleb reflect Godwin's own experience of the way speech acts proliferated in the public sphere during Paine's trial for sedition, after the appearance of the second part of *The Rights of Man* in 1792. On 8 February 1793, an open letter from Godwin to one Mr. Reeves, "Chairman of the Society for protecting Liberty and Property against Republicans and Levellers," appeared in the *Morning Chronicle*. In it Godwin charges Reeves with suppressing Paine's own writings and substituting for them a variety of false narratives designed to change the public perception of Paine:

> We all know by what means a verdict [against Paine] was procured: by repeated proclamations, by all the force, and all the fears of the kingdom being artfully turned against one man. As I came out of court, I saw handbills, in the most vulgar and illiberal style distributed, entitled, The Confession of Thomas Paine. I had not walked three streets, before I was encountered by ballad singers, roaring in cadence rude, a miserable set of scurrilous stanzas upon his private life. . . . No sooner were the cheap pamphlets of Mr Paine, and the hand-bills of his partisans suppressed, than pamphlets, printed sheets, and hand-bills without number issued from the press in answer to his reasonings. (PPW 2: 17)

Godwin insinuates that Reeves was involved in producing the vulgar handbills and scurrilous stanzas, accuses him of direct responsibility for the pamphlets countering Paine's arguments, and asserts that Reeves has done much more harm to the British Constitution by interfering with free speech than Paine ever did by speaking out against the Constitution. When similar events occur in the novel that Godwin began writing only weeks later, they provide a forceful illustration of the effects of public utterance as a political instrument, but also of the everyday truth that speakers constantly impose identities on one another through prejudice and gossip.

Both the political and the sociological axiom are built into the narrative structure of *Caleb Williams*, a novel which never allows us to forget that characters only exist as they are constructed in narratives. Godwin makes full use, in other words, of the range of meanings the term "character" had in the eighteenth century. Character comprises personal appearance, mental and moral constitution, and public reputation, as well as referring to an agent in a literary work; in *Caleb Williams*, these various forms of identity are superimposed on one another as all of them turn out to depend on illocutionary acts.

II. Pragmatic Truth

If readers are frustrated by the inability to judge the truth of characters' narratives in the face of so many conflicting accounts, Caleb is frustrated by the inability to make what he claims *is* truth count *as* truth in any of the contexts in which he finds himself, least of all in contexts where truth is traditionally held sacred. The novel features two sites in which, if anywhere, we would expect to find truth: the confessional autobiography and the courtroom. Yet precisely these two scenes of testimony undermine the idea that "truth" entails correspondence with objective reality. As one critic puts it, referring to Godwin's work as a whole, "we are only told what truth does . . . not what it *is*" (Simms 349).

Caleb Williams locates assertions of truth in plainly pragmatic contexts, where contingencies of time and place, the status of speaker and addressee, and prior and subsequent events, are none of them neutral factors. As a result, the meaningful measure for utterances is not the "truth" of the classical philosopher, but the speech-act philosopher's "felicity." Falkland's words count as true rather than Caleb's because the former is a squire and the latter a servant, and because Falkland has previously gained a reputation for virtue and honor, while Caleb is an unknown quantity in the public world. "I was ignorant of the power which the institutions of society give to one man over others," Caleb admits when reviewing his own history (*CN* 3: 319). He spends most of the novel striving to meet the conditions necessary for his utterances and his behavior to be accorded legal recognition.

During Caleb's first hearing before the magistrate Mr. Forester, and at the various other trial scenes that follow, he gradually learns to value the felicity of utterances rather than their truth. His initial response to the charge of robbery that Falkland has brought against him is an affirmation of his essential honesty, defined as a correspondence between internal disposition, external appearance, verbal utterance, and social behavior: "I appeal to my heart; I appeal to my looks; I appeal to every sentiment my tongue ever uttered" (*CN* 3: 150). At this point, Caleb's beliefs about the use of language echo Godwin's own assertions about truth and sincerity in *Political Justice*—even as we sense a dramatic difference between the abstract statement of these ideas in *Political Justice*, and Caleb's first-person application of them when his own credibility and welfare are at stake:

> Why have we the power of speech, but to communicate our thoughts? I will never believe that a man conscious of innocence, cannot make other men perceive that he has that thought. Do not you feel that my whole heart tells me, I am not guilty of what is imputed to me? (*CN* 3: 152)

In invoking the voice of his heart, Caleb attempts to assert a subjective, inward notion of identity as his legal and public identity, in opposition to the identity of "thief" or "felon" that others are seeking to impose on him. His appeal to his own sincerity and integrity contrasts with Falkland's much more intersubjectively oriented defense of himself against the charge of murdering Tyrrel—a defense that even takes the form of a public document, which, Mr. Collins affirms, Falkland once considered sending to the press. Instead of trying to communicate the voice of his heart, Falkland invokes the voices of his listeners to attest to his character, reputation, and honor. Although he affirms his innocence, his main concern is to gain the uptake of his listeners to the affirmation: "I have no fear that I shall fail to make every person in this court acknowledge my innocence" (*CN* 3: 89). Falkland appeals other people's consciousness of his innocence rather than his own consciousness of it; and the appeal not only absolves him, but redounds to his great credit. Caleb's defense, although it "made some impression," is not forceful enough to outweigh his lack of a public reputation, or the circumstantial evidence that the magistrate has before his eyes. But the importance of status and convention for the success of utterances becomes most evident when Caleb goes on to affirm that Falkland himself knows he is innocent. The implied accusation of Falkland shocks, and instantly turns everyone against Caleb. According to the social conventions of eighteenth-century England, it is unacceptable for a servant to accuse his master of lying; according to the legal conventions of a trial, it is unacceptable for the defendant to call the prosecutor in his own defense. Both these circumstances assure that Caleb's utterance counts neither as a true statement nor as a valid defense, but rather as a self-indictment even beyond what the material evidence would have caused.

The dependence of truth on context becomes painfully obvious to Caleb in the penultimate trial scene of the novel, when he is once again brought before a magistrate to answer the charge of robbery and resolves, at long last, to play his trump card. Breaking his promise to Falkland, he will finally declare the truth: that Falkland is the murderer of Tyrrel. To Caleb's astonishment, though, the court refuses to hear him, and the magistrate's response makes clear that his declaration fails because it does not meet the conventional requirements for lodging an accusation. As a "felon" (the identity imposed on Caleb by Falkland's charge of robbery), Caleb can only inform against his accomplices about a crime in which he was actually involved; as a servant, he cannot inform against his master. The hope that Caleb has kept in reserve throughout his trials, that his knowledge of Falkland's murder will finally exonerate him, turns out to be hollow:

> A man under certain circumstances shall not be heard in the detection of a crime, because he has not been a participator in it! . . . Six thousand a year shall protect a man from accusation; and the validity of an impeachment shall be superseded, because the author of it is a servant! (*CN* 3: 243)

Caleb's declaration fails to count as either the true statement or the accusation for which he intended it, but has other illocutionary and perlocutionary effects instead. The magistrate takes Caleb's utterance as the most impudent of provocations. Speaking first "as a magistrate," he affirms the inadmissibility of Caleb's accusatory statement; then, addressing Caleb again "in my own proper person," he warns him that the statement itself counts as a crime that could get him hanged (*CN* 3: 243). Ironically, the utterance Caleb believed would free him turns out to be the utterance that would convict him. But its effects go beyond the conditions of the courtroom; shortly afterward, it becomes clear that, although Caleb's statement failed to meet the legal requirements for an accusation, it has in fact damaged Falkland's reputation. Falkland has Caleb brought before him, and continues to confound the sphere of law with the sphere of reputation by insisting that Caleb sign an affidavit asserting that the accusation of murder is false. In doing so, Falkland unmistakably affirms his conviction that utterances—even the most "solemn," legally binding ones—should aim at producing "happiness" rather than "truth . . . for its own sake":

> I insist then upon our signing a paper declaring in the most solemn manner that I am innocent of murder, and that the charge you alleged at the office in Bow-Street is false, malicious and groundless. Perhaps you may scruple out of a regard to truth. Is truth then entitled to adoration for its own sake, and not for the sake of the happiness it is calculated to produce? (*CN* 3: 248)

Caleb refuses to sign the false declaration on the grounds that he would forfeit his reputation by doing so. Although he has already destroyed his reputation by uttering, in an improper context and under the wrong conditions, what he believes to be the truth, and although he has learned the extent to which the force of statements predominates over their referential accuracy, Caleb adheres in this instance to the strict principles of sincerity laid down by Godwin in the first edition of *Political Justice*. "Regardless of personal danger or of injury to my interests in the world," Godwin there affirms (*PPW* 3: 136), there is no exception to the rule that sincerity is the best course:

> We must not be guilty of insincerity. We must not seek to obtain a desirable object by vile means. We must prefer a general principle to the meretricious attractions of a particular deviation. We must perceive in the preservation of that general principle a balance of universal good, outweighing the benefit to arise in any instance from superseding it. (*PPW* 3: 139)

Yet when he appears before a magistrate one last time, as he relates in the "Postscript," Caleb has learned something about the conditions that must be met in order for a sincere statement to count as a legally valid statement. He now starts out by affirming to the magistrate his qualifications for lodging an accusation, as granted by the law:

> I was in every respect a competent witness. I was of age to understand the nature of an oath; I was in my perfect senses; I was untarnished by the verdict of any jury, or the sentence of any judge. His private opinion of my character could not alter the law of the land. (*CN* 3: 269)

But even when Caleb has the felicity conditions right, he cannot control the perlocutionary effects of his utterance. The final irony is that Caleb's decision to testify affects not just the reputation of Falkland and their relationship to one another, but his own innermost convictions. When he opens his mouth to speak, his accusation turns into its opposite, as if the very process of uttering the accusation alters moral values and private sentiment:

> I came hither to curse, but I remain to bless. I came to accuse, but am compelled to applaud. I proclaim to all the world that Mr Falkland is a man worthy of affection and kindness, and that I am myself the worst of villains! (*CN* 3: 275)

If the novel has inexorably seemed to chronicle the triumph of the performative over the true proposition, context over content, and the felicity of utterances over their correspondence to reality, this final scene reveals that something still more complex and disturbing has been happening with language. Rather than subordinating the language of truth, so that one could imagine recuperating it as Godwin urges in *Political Justice*, sociopolitical performatives have actually grafted themselves onto anything that could be called truth or sincerity. It is by telling his "artless and manly story" (*CN* 3: 275)—but in a carefully stage-managed context—that Caleb finally achieves legal and public recognition for his testimony. Yet the public success of his utterance immediately brings about an essential, emotional change in him, causing him to transform his half-told accusation into veneration. Moreover, Caleb's sudden self-reproach has the effect on Falkland that neither the unadulterated truth nor a public accusation ever did; he just as suddenly disclaims the reputation he has been guarding all his life and affirms Caleb's superiority. Speech, in this scene, acts out beyond all convention. Speech acts alter subjective as well as sociopolitical reality, and any attempt to separate the genuine motives for moral behavior that Godwin identified in *Political Justice* from the hollow, conventional, and unessential uses of language that he there condemned, now has to be abandoned.

III. Spoken And Unspoken Knowledge

As Godwin, in developing the adventure plot of *Caleb Williams*, worked backward from the third volume to the first,[4] it is also possible to move backward from the speech acts in the final trial scene to see how sociopolitical performatives come to be interwoven with identity and moral behavior in the course of the novel. The nature and timing of Caleb's accusation of Falkland in the last two courtroom scenes are determined by another explicit performative that occurs at the novel's center. In the act of confessing to Caleb that he is the murderer of Tyrrel, Falkland also swears Caleb to silence:

> You must swear, said he. You must attest every sacrament, divine and human, never to disclose what I am now to tell you.—He dictated the oath, and I repeated it with an aching heart. I had no power to offer a word of remark. (*CN* 3: 122)

Caleb's promise to keep Falkland's secret is a vow of silence in more ways than one. It keeps Caleb from speaking out, at least on the subject of Falkland's murder, until the end of the novel, but its performance is also related in an odd silence. The terms of the oath are not revealed to the reader, and, as happens so often in the novel (*CN* 3: 130, 138, 189, 263, 329), Caleb is "unable to utter a word" other than to repeat exactly what Falkland tells him he must say. As both a promise and an oath, this use of words offends against Godwin's sense of the proper relationship between language and reality. His condemnation of commissive speech acts in *Political Justice* is echoed by the most sympathetic characters in *Caleb Williams*: the honest servant Thomas (who exclaims to Caleb, "Pray, do not swear! for goodness sake, do not swear!" [*CN* 3: 156]), and especially the poet Mr. Clare, who disparages promises as "the fetters of superstition" and spurns other public performatives such as a will drawn up by an attorney (*CN* 3: 31–32). When Caleb swears, he is, moreover, allowing a social superior literally to dictate his use of language, and (although he presumably has a strong intuition of what he is about to hear) he swears to keep the secret before Falkland reveals to him what the secret is. These conditions create a situation in which, according to the principles of *Political Justice*, Caleb should be entitled—even obliged—*not* to keep his promise once he has new and better information. Although Caleb adheres to the Godwinian principle of sincerity when he refuses to sign Falkland's false affidavit, he does not realize that absolute sincerity, at least according to Godwin, extends to one's "duty"

---

[4] Godwin describes the composition of *Caleb Williams* in his preface to the 1832 edition of *Fleetwood* (*CN* 5: 7–12).

to disclose even the secrets of others, if society at large would benefit: "The facts with which you are acquainted are a part of your possessions, and you are as much obliged respecting them as in any other case, to employ them for the public good" (*PPW* 3: 140). According to this logic, it is Caleb's own determination to remain shackled by the "fetters of superstition" that causes his tragedy.

But the scene of Falkland's confession and Caleb's oath complicates Caleb's predicament, while it complicates Godwin's ideas about intersubjective speech acts as presented in *Political Justice*. It is Caleb's curiosity—or, seen in the most positive light, his desire to know the truth—that puts him in a position to learn Falkland's secret. When Falkland extracts a promise of concealment from him, to the extent that he has any choice at all, Caleb gives it sincerely out of a complex of subjective responses to Falkland that presumably include admiration, affection, awe, and fear. Caleb's promise is, to this extent, an expression of his essential moral character. Yet it is also an illocutionary act exchanged between a servant and his master, confirmed by a formal oath whose terms are literally dictated by the master; it is an act heavy with political implications, and its consequences will play themselves out in courtrooms and public hearings. Neither a purely subjective nor a purely intersubjective act, Caleb's promise testifies to the way both these spheres are entangled within performative utterances, even while they remain in conflict with one another.

Falkland's confession of his secret to Caleb points to a still more profound fusion of subjective and intersubjective spheres, inasmuch as it suggests there is a public, even performative dimension to knowledge itself. As he began to realize that even apparently constative utterances are some sense performative, Austin was tempted to include "I know that" and "I believe that" in the class of performative verbs, for, as he says, we can no longer assume that these expressions are "purely descriptive" (90). *Caleb Williams* demonstrates how and why knowing can be performative: knowledge comes to "count" in the world of the novel only when it is communicated in an interpersonal, conventional, or public context. Caleb suspects Falkland of involvement in Tyrrel's murder for a long time, but only when Falkland actually utters a confession (which he does because he has overheard Caleb utter his suspicions out loud while walking in the garden) does this knowledge restructure their relationship and dramatically alter Caleb's history. As long as Caleb's knowledge of the murder remains private, it is of no value to him in his attempts to improve his situation as a fugitive; and when he does try to render it pragmatically effective, he finds that his knowledge must take on a conventional, legally accepted form. Even apart from the conventions of the courtroom, Caleb's secret would not have any *narrative* value if he did not also "publish" it as the central fact in his autobiography. Knowledge, withheld and revealed, is an operative term in defining the relationship among characters as well as between narrator and reader. In this sense, *Caleb Williams* implies that the private, subjective condition of knowing may only be an abstraction from the public, intersubjective experience of expressing knowledge in words, publishing it in writing, or otherwise using it to negotiate one's own and other people's public status.

IV. The Secret of the Trunk

As the emphasis shifts from the constative fact of what is known, to the performative experience of acquiring and applying knowledge, that which is known increasingly becomes a product of discourse. With Mr. Collins's narrative and Falkland's confession, Caleb acquires knowledge of an act, a fact, or a murder that exists (for him and for us) only as it is narrated. "Reality" that is controlled or constructed by speech acts is associated by Godwin, as we have already seen in *Political Justice*, with hollowness or emptiness. In *Caleb Williams*, this condition is exemplified by the cavity of Falkland's mysterious trunk. Appearing once in each of the three volumes of the novel, the trunk itself is an artifact that gains meaning from the actions that are performed on and with it, rather than, as one might expect, from its contents. Although Caleb sees Falkland closing it, then breaks the lock himself and all but opens the lid, he never learns what it contains. Rather, the narrative turns on conjectures about its contents, and on Caleb's and Falkland's judgments when each catches the other in the act of opening the trunk.

In volume 2 of the novel, Caleb's foiled attempt to break into the trunk during the fire on Falkland's estate directly triggers Falkland's confession. That confession, in other words, and the attendant oath on Caleb's part, *substitute for* the act of viewing the contents of the trunk. This correlation between the trunk and verbal discourse is intensified in the third volume, when Caleb recalls that he was never able to determine the trunk's contents, but came to believe that it contained Falkland's written account of the murder:

> I am now persuaded that the secret it inclosed was a faithful narrative of that and its concomitant transactions to be reserved in case of the worst, that, if by any unforeseen event the guilt of Falkland should ever come to be fully disclosed, it might contribute to redeem the wreck of his reputation. (*CN* 3: 267–68)

"But it is no matter," Caleb continues (*CN* 3: 268); or, more tellingly, in later editions, "the truth or the falshood of this conjecture is of little moment" (*CN* 3: 334). In place of Falkland's posited narrative, which is never actually seen or read, Caleb leaves his own story, with its final swerve in praise of Falkland, to "redeem the wreck of his reputation."

The Iron Chest, a dramatic adaptation of *Caleb Williams* written by George Colman in 1796, not only makes Falkland's trunk the focal point of the action, but actualizes Caleb's conjecture that it contains a written confession: the iron chest is opened in the climactic scene of the play to reveal documents that testify to the murder. In Godwin's novel, though, it is never conclusively determined whether the trunk contains a written narrative or not. What *is* clear is that narratives and other speech acts substitute for its contents and for the act of viewing the contents. If the failure to see what is in the trunk forms a conspicuous lacuna in Caleb's story, it is a small step to the conjecture that the trunk itself is a lacuna—that it is, finally, empty. It would not be the only empty strongbox in Godwin's fiction, and perhaps there is an after-image of Falkland's trunk in the ebony box of *Fleetwood*, in which "titles and instruments" belonging to Fleetwood's fiancée Mary and representing her £60,000 fortune are to be stored when the family moves to Italy. But the papers are mistakenly placed in the wrong container, and instead of remaining in Fleetwood's safekeeping they are lost in a shipwreck along with Mary's family. Mary is left without an inheritance, Fleetwood holding an empty box. As, in *Fleetwood*, lawsuits ensue in an attempt to give legal significance to the empty box and the lost titles, so in *Caleb Williams* conjectures, confessions, oaths, and accusations arise from the emptiness of Falkland's trunk.[5]

The empty trunk is an apt image for Godwin's notion of the performative, reminiscent of the analogy of the amputated leg in *Political Justice*. Speech separated from thought, and acts separated from their moral foundation, reveal a lacuna behind them—or at best constitute hollow and superficial motives for virtuous behavior. Falkland himself, whose honorable reputation depends so heavily on the success of public speech acts such as his defense in the Tyrrel case, is described in the opening

---

[5]Uphaus, who also raises the possibility that the trunk may be empty, reads it as a figure for Falkland's psyche, the contents of which both Caleb and the reader desire to re-enact, raise to the level of meaningful speech, and transfer into their own consciousnesses. Thus, the trunk is "an analogue to the novel's narrative process" (290)—the movement from contemplation of an intriguing phenomenon to participation in it. Simms's deconstructive reading also treats the contents of the trunk as a "lacuna" which is filled in differently by different characters, so that it stands as "a constant deferral of representation of an impenetrable truth" (352).

pages of the novel as having degenerated into "nothing but the grosser part, the mere shell of Falkland" (*CN* 3: 9). Perhaps it is not going too far to hear in the term "trunk," and the word "chest" that Godwin used in the first version of *Caleb Williams*, a bodily metaphor. The heart within the trunk or chest should motivate speech and action, but an empty trunk produces only voice or resonating air—just as an amputated leg produces phantom pain unconnected with the real experience of nerves and flesh.

V. Sociopolitical Fictions

The crucial irony of Godwin's linguistic theory is that emptiness may be the condition of performative language, but this emptiness is inescapable, because as soon as knowledge, feeling, or morality gets expressed in an interpersonal context it becomes implicated in "hollow" illocutionary acts and subject to "empty" pragmatic conventions. When verbal transactions are committed entirely to writing—as is Mary's lost fortune, in the episode of *Fleetwood* referred to above—they can end up in unforeseen contexts, with indeterminable effects. But whether written or spoken, *uttered* knowledge or sentiment becomes public property. At the beginning of volume 2, when Caleb takes over the narrative in his own person after relating Mr. Collins's story, he embarks on his memoir as if it were a statement made before a court of law:

> I do not pretend to warrant the authenticity of any part of these memoirs except so much as fell under my own knowledge, and that part shall be stated with the same simplicity and accuracy that I would observe towards a court which was to decide in the last resort upon every thing dear to me. (*CN* 3: 95)

Caleb's story is both private testimonial and public act of testimony. Thomas Reid, we may recall, distinguished testimony, as a social act performed in the context of a courtroom, from (cognitive) judgment, as a solitary act of the mind (1: 413). These two kinds of utterance may look exactly the same, since both take the form of a proposition, yet we easily distinguish the social from the solitary act on the basis of context and common sense: is the proposition uttered in the presence of a judge and jury, or to a friend met by chance on the street? But Caleb's narrative stance blurs the distinction again, suggesting that the social act and the solitary act—like the performative and the constative—might be two dimensions of the same utterance, and not unproblematically intertwined.

Because Caleb's activity of narrating is inseparable from that which is narrated, Gavin Edwards calls *Caleb Williams* an "unrelentingly performative discourse." He points to the ambiguity between performative and constative dimensions that characterizes both the novel itself, and the law as represented in the novel:

> When people are 'found' guilty they are, in and from that moment, guilty; yet to 'find' people guilty is also, implicitly, to give them a name which is already written into the facts of the case. Godwin's novel underwrites this double claim so explicitly that the ambivalence becomes manifest; in the novel whoever is 'found guilty' is guilty, but is innocent too. (Everest and Edwards 144–45)

Edwards's example reveals the unstated assumption behind the conventional expression "to find someone guilty": that guilt is a constative and a performative condition at once. In a legal sense, guilt only attaches to the accused from the moment the verdict is pronounced; yet the idiom "find" suggests that the verdict is simply bringing guilt to light, or referring to a pre-existing, extra-linguistic condition of guiltiness. The ambiguity recalls some now-familiar performative paradoxes. When Derrida, Bourdieu, or Lyotard exposes the "scandal" of the performative, he points to the claim within performative utterances that what they instantiate is (also) already the case—that the utterance is both performatively felicitous *and* referentially true. Yet this paradox is virtually a commonplace of Romantic linguistics, expressed particularly by Humboldt, for whom speech always *instantiates* a relationship between self and world, or between speaker and addressee, while also *referring to* relationships that it assumes are already in place.

The legitimation of utterances in *Caleb Williams*, a process that draws on ideas about speech as public action which appear in different forms in the work of Reid, Bentham, and even Paine, allows for an alternative analysis of the paradox. In this view, the act of finding someone guilty does not necessarily elide temporality by pretending that the situation it brings into effect already exists; rather, what it elides is the distinction between an essential or private condition and an institutional or public condition. The accused is only guilty in a legal, political, or public context once the verdict of "guilty" is pronounced by a properly authorized official. But our desire for truth, defined as the correspondence of language with reality, encourages us to fantasize that public guilt is continuous with an already existing state of moral, essential, or private guilt. The latter may, for all we know, be inaccessible; or, to put it differently, even subjective guilt may, as soon as it is communicated in any intersubjective context whatsoever, become as much a verbal and institutional construct as guilt before the law. Godwin's novelistic technique reveals how frequently and easily the distinction between these spheres gets elided in the normal functioning of society—and in the normal process of reading. This is where Bentham's term "fictions" comes into its own; indeed, Godwin implicitly gives the word the same range of meanings. Fictitious entities, according to Bentham, can be legal (as with property, right, or guilt); they can be moral (as with identity, truth—or, again, guilt); they can be imaginative or literary. In *Caleb Williams*, fictions exist and are created, as often as not, on all three levels at once. Despite Godwin's theoretical dedication to a model in which language is the expression of thought and experience, the intersubjective, subjective, and narrative speech acts of his novels testify to Bentham's claim: "to language alone—it is, that fictitious entities owe their existence—their impossible, yet indispensable, existence" (*Works* 8: 198).

MARRIAGE AND THE DISINTEGRATION OF DISCOURSE ('DELORAINE,' 'FLEETWOOD')

The five other novels Godwin went on to write reflect and refract the array of performatives and constatives, public and private speech situations, history, story, and testimony that is *Caleb Williams*. If the later novels are still more loosely written than *Caleb Williams*, and none of them forms quite as close a complement to *Political Justice*, they nonetheless help to focus the issues raised by both these texts, because most of them highlight one or another of the illocutionary acts that figure in Godwin's social and political critique. Conversely, a focus on performative utterance can help illuminate these compelling but still insufficiently studied novels.

The attitude that Godwin adopts toward language and truth in his texts of the early 1790s persists throughout his career: the ideal purpose of language is full, sincere, and immediate disclosure of thoughts between one person and another. This ideal receives confirmation in one of the last texts Godwin published, the essay "Of Frankness and Reserve" in *Thoughts on Man* (1831), which continues to insist that the proper use of language in society involves perfect frankness—that is, honesty combined with full disclosure. Godwin's last novel, *Deloraine* (1833), provides the one striking example of a relationship in which this ideal is realized. In recounting his relationship with his first wife Emilia in the opening chapters of the novel, the narrator Deloraine dwells obsessively on the verbal confidence they shared. From the time of their courtship—which, Deloraine points out proudly, involved no "contract or precise anticipation" and so left each party perfectly free to change his or her mind on receiving new and better information (*CN* 8: 12–13)—the two told each other absolutely everything. Deloraine describes this discursive relationship at length in the second chapter of the novel, stressing again and again the complete frankness, the "most perfect unreserve," and the "habit of entire and unhesitating explicitness" that subsists between him and Emilia. Godwin's philosophical commitment to sincerity echoes throughout this part of Deloraine's narrative:

> Our hearts were ever on our lips. We considered the faculty of speech as given us to express our thoughts. We had no idea of those ambages and prevarications by which the majority of our species are ever seeking to defeat the curiosity, the one of the other, by which they are taught continually to look at their phrases before they are uttered, lest by any accident they might tell that which it was intended should remain unknown. (*CN* 8: 22)

Deloraine contrasts their discourse with that found in society at large, and in less perfect marriages, where frank communication is impeded by prejudice, mistrust, and fear that one's utterance will be met by indifference, hostility, or misinterpretation. Indeed, Deloraine and Emilia appear to converse in a perfectly neutral speech situation, where there are no contextualizing or qualifying circumstances to complicate the effect of their utterances or the meaning of their words.

As might be expected, this is an evanescent (not to say idealized) state. Emilia dies young, and Deloraine's account of their relationship serves mainly as a foil for the story of his second marriage to Margaret Borradale. Because Margaret is permanently afflicted by the loss of her first love, William, her relationship with the narrator is marked by silences that are all too obviously instances of repressed speech. Deloraine is hyper-conscious of "the meaning of her silence, the words that were for ever bursting their bounds, and forcing their way to her lips, but were never pronounced" (*CN* 8: 107). Margaret's reserve is symptomatic of the problems besetting Deloraine's second marriage, which leads to a tragedy brought about by a sequence of undelivered letters, secrets, and the partners' fatal misreadings of one another's behavior.

The anatomy of a disintegrating marriage is a still more prominent theme in Godwin's 1805 novel *Fleetwood*. In its first two volumes, Casimir Fleetwood recounts his upbringing and the flawed educational experiences that have led to his becoming a badly adjusted, dissolute, misanthropic individual. He nevertheless enters into marriage with a younger woman, Mary Macneil, hemming their union about with two solemn speech acts: besides the marriage vows themselves, Fleetwood makes a supplementary vow to Mary's father that he will always treat his bride well. Fleetwood wants to persuade himself and the reader that he and Mary communicate perfectly, indeed that their understanding transcends language: "We communicate with instantaneous flashes, in one glance of the eye, and have no need of words" (*CN* 5: 199). But the evidence indicates, rather, that the silences in their relationship are symptoms of repression and reserve. If Fleetwood believes that he and Mary communicate best without words, it is ironic that he depicts their relationship entirely in terms of discourse. On the positive side, they read and discuss works of literature together; more ominously, he agonizes over her utterances and how they should be interpreted; as his animosity toward her grows, he constantly talks himself back into love with her. Although Fleetwood represses many of the authoritative and injurious utterances that spring to his mind, by the time he and Mary argue over whether or not to attend a ball on a neighboring estate, his conversation with her has degenerated into a series of accusations, confessions, decrees, apologies, and, finally, horribly elaborate and explicit curses.

The story of Fleetwood's marriage builds toward a crisis in which he drives Mary from the house, persuaded by his deceitful kinsman Gifford that she has been having an affair with Gifford's half-brother, Kenrick. As his suspicions grow, Fleetwood ceases to attend to the truth-value of Mary's words, but instead becomes hypersensitive to their pragmatic value as contextualized acts. When she gives orders to have the tickets to the controversial ball returned, why does she do it in the breakfast room, where it will embarrass her husband in front of the servants? When she introduces Fleetwood to her dashing dancing partner, Mr. Matthews, do Matthews's words to her indicate his "smothered contempt" (*CN* 5: 206)? When Mary murmurs her husband's name in her sleep, do even her unconscious utterances need to be interpreted as attempts to deceive him, rather than as sincere expressions of love? The final proof of infidelity, as far as Fleetwood is concerned, is a letter he finds in Mary's jewelry box, on which he recognizes Kenrick's handwriting—but in judging it proof that Mary and Kenrick are lovers, he misconstrues its pragmatic value by mistaking both context and addressee of the utterance (it is, in fact, a letter to another young woman that Kenrick has given Mary for safekeeping).

Fleetwood becomes habituated to divorcing language from truth, using and interpreting it instead as a vehicle of power and authority. When he throws Mary out of his house, he effects their separation with a formidable array of performative documents: a bill of divorce, a declaration that her child is illegitimate, a formal adoption of Gifford as his heir, and a document that will allow Gifford to inherit Fleetwood's entire property. But this is not quite the end of the story. Instead, while the victorious Gifford puts his trust in the documents he has managed to acquire, Fleetwood's emotions are too complex to be contained by the written instruments; his persistent love for Mary allows him to begin to imagine that she might be innocent after all. Sentiment struggles, at the end of the novel, against the social order constructed by Fleetwood's documents and his perverse interpretation of Mary's speech acts. So does the bodily resemblance between Mary's son and Fleetwood himself: the boy "is as like you," Fleetwood is told, "as if you had spit him out of your mouth" (*CN* 5: 286). The novel upholds Godwin's belief that where language is not an instrument of truth, it will instead become an instrument of control that perpetuates harmful patterns of behavior, and brings about soulless relationships while devastating natural ones. Even performatives that appear benevolent, such as Fleetwood's solemn promise to Mary's father that he will always be good to her, fail to guarantee or even promote moral behavior. As Fleetwood writes his memoirs, after the catastrophe of his marriage, his broken promise has become only one more cause for regret and self-reproach.

THE FETTERS OF SUPERSTITION: PROMISES AND SECRETS ('DELORAINE,' 'ST. LEON')

Despite the mischief they cause—indeed, in order to expose the mischief they cause—promises are central to most of Godwin's novels. Even apparently benevolent promises seem to go awry because they are fundamentally incompatible with temporality, and therefore with the proper development of character and relationships. "Human character" should be "formed by experience" (as Godwin puts it in one of the chapter titles in *Political Justice*), but when language ceases to be a constative reflection of experience, speech acts become a counter-force that impedes the formation of character. While verbal commitments are not substantial enough to provide a genuine basis for moral action, they nevertheless tend to fix behavior in its present pattern. Once one utters a promise, a dilemma results: keeping the promise represents a refusal to learn and to revise one's opinions, while breaking the promise turns it, retroactively, into a lie. The only responsible alternative is not to promise at all. Yet most of Godwin's characters allow promises, vows, or contracts to determine the course of their lives; their histories expose the impossibility of keeping promises in the face of changing circumstances, and the destructiveness of attempting to do so.

Inserted into the story of Deloraine is the earlier history of his second wife Margaret, which provides both an illustration of and a recurring image for the disastrous effect of promises. Margaret's engagement to her childhood sweetheart, William, is broken twice: once on her father's insistence that she make a socially advantageous marriage into an elder branch of his family; and a second time when her father relents and summons William back from Canada to claim Margaret as his bride, but William is lost at sea on his way home. For Margaret and her family, the news that William has perished in a shipwreck seems to provide grounds for breaking her promise to him and accepting Deloraine's proposal of marriage instead. But while the promiser, Margaret, considers the contract canceled in the face of new information, the recipient of the promise clings to it and orients all his efforts toward its fulfilment. William, who is not dead after all, reappears four years later in the full expectation that circumstances are unchanged from the time that Margaret was promised to him. "I am William," he affirms, appearing before Margaret's father; "Did you not write to me, and invite me to return? Years have past since; but they have made no alteration in my sentiments" (*CN* 8: 122).

In fact, William seems to expect that everything will be in the state it was when he left England *because* he is returning in accordance with a promise: "He fancied that he should find every thing, just as it had been announced to him in his letters of recal written more than four years ago. He imaged to himself Margaret still standing on the cliffs at Plymouth looking out for his arrival" (*CN* 8: 111). It is as if he believes that the "firmness and solemnity" of the "pledge" that Margaret's father made to him, on recalling him from abroad, could in itself forestall any change in circumstances. But the narrator Deloraine reflects that, on the contrary, the verbal contracts that constitute human relationships are subject to the vicissitudes of time: "It is the condition of human life, that its connections and affairs, its changes and succession of property, its contracts and engagements, should go on in never interrupted succession" (*CN* 8: 278). Deloraine's image for time and change is the incessant motion of the sea: "Men succeed each other in the scene of human life, even as one wave on the shore rolls over and carries away another" (*CN* 8: 122). This sea of time undercuts language, exposing it as a fragile repository for stability and security. William places himself as much at risk of drowning when he orients his life according to a verbal pledge made years before as when he trusts a ship to bring him across the Atlantic. By preventing the fulfilment of Margaret's and William's engagement at the agreed date, then returning him to her when the engagement has been superseded by a new set of promises, the sea of time, symbolized by the real ocean, outperforms the supposed performativity of language.

The most common, and the most destructive, promise made by Godwin's characters is the promise to keep a secret; besides Caleb Williams, his St. Leon and Cloudesley are fettered by such a vow. If promises are fundamentally incompatible with Godwin's belief in human perfectibility, secrets are incompatible with his dedication to perfect frankness. Promises proleptically assert control over future experience, but secrets are equally damaging to moral behavior because they create a gap in experience, as it were, by suspending the publication of knowledge. Promises and secrets, both offenses against the progress of time, are in a way the inverse of one another; the promise illegitimately contracts time by pretending to knowledge of the future, while the secret illegitimately extends the time during which people's knowledge remains incomplete. Moreover, they compound one another's error: if I promise to keep a secret, I presume to predict that no one will ever suffer from my withholding of the information.

The most spectacular example of a character ruined by a secret and a promise is the protagonist of Godwin's 1799 novel, *St. Leon*. A mysterious stranger offers to bequeath to St. Leon the philosopher's stone and the elixir of life, on condition that he never reveal to anyone where and how he obtained these secrets. After deliberating over this contract—including the stranger's insistence that he thereby give up the perfect frankness he enjoys with his wife Marguerite—St. Leon agrees to its terms. He then finds that his newly purchased knowledge not only gives him wealth and eternal youth, but also plunges him into a new discursive relationship with his family, society, and reality itself. Alone among Godwin's characters, St. Leon experiences the power of an ideal, transcendent performative that would literally change the world: "He possesses the attribute which we are accustomed to ascribe to the Creator of the universe: he may say to a man, 'Be rich,' and he is rich. . . . Palaces, as if they were the native exhalations of the soil, rise out of the earth at his bidding" (*CN* 4: 138). But even this verbal power over the material world proves a poor substitute for the frankness and sincerity that St. Leon has bargained away for it. In material terms, his secret makes life unbearable for him and his family because his new, baseless wealth arouses suspicion and envy wherever he goes, rendering it impossible for him to live normally in a human community. Beyond this, his promise to keep the stranger's secret obliterates the frankness on which his social and domestic ties were based, and destroys his happiness. "Mystery," he laments at the end of his tale, "was the great and unconquerable bane of my situation" (*CN* 4: 318).

St. Leon's secret creates an emptiness at the center of both his existence and his narrative that is not unlike the impenetrable, for all practical purposes empty trunk in *Caleb Williams*. What exactly is the narrative value of St. Leon's encounter with the stranger—a conversation that cannot be repeated, and an event that cannot be clearly described? As St. Leon himself admits, the fact that he is prohibited from revealing his secrets even in his private confession generates gaps in his history, as when he cannot explain why he did not use the elixir of life to save Marguerite from dying (*CN* 4: 178). The baselessness of his wealth, and of his very existence as an eternally young man who appears from nowhere in different historical situations, finds a counterpart in the baselessness of his narrative. The central conversation in the novel, on which St. Leon's entire history is predicated, remains a lacuna—not only because it is inaccessible to everyone except St. Leon, but also because this elided event involves an exchange of promises, of "hollow" language that stands in a suspect relation to experience. What is exchanged between St. Leon and the stranger is, in some sense, only a verbal contract, without any substance behind it. The events of the novel are predicated on the central hypothesis that St. Leon can produce unlimited gold and rejuvenate himself, yet this information does not exist in any way that can be known by us.

The novel, in other words, or rather St. Leon's narrative of his own life, is essentially a verbal contract, in which we agree to take the narrator's word for what happened. St. Leon himself links the lacuna at the center of his narrative with his contractual relationship to the reader: because "the pivot upon which the history I am composing turns, is a mystery," he says, readers must "accept of my communication upon my own terms" (*CN* 4: 178). In taking St. Leon at his word, we wager on the truth of the narrative—thus repeating the practice of St. Leon himself, the gambling addict who relates how he lost enormous sums through playing on terms of honor with men who were unable to pay the money they played for, if they lost (*CN* 4: 55). The status of St. Leon's story as a first-person utterance is conspicuous; it is as if all the apparently constative statements of the novel need to be prefaced by an implicit "I state that..." that would make their performative quality explicit. This is not to deny the effect of the story, but rather to suggest that it *is* primarily an "effect": centering the novel on a secret and a promise that represent a gap in knowledge calls attention to the posited or fictional status of the entire text. The hollow center of the novel intensifies our awareness of its pragmatic value as the speech act of a single speaker, founded on the lacuna of an inaccessible private knowledge. As is the case with many of Godwin's narrators, the emphasis shifts from the constative truth of St. Leon's statement to the performativity and pragmatics of *making* a statement.

IDENTITY AS INSTITUTIONAL FACT
('DELORAINE,' 'CLOUDESLEY')

The title character of Godwin's 1830 novel *Cloudesley* is again self-victimized by the double disaster of a promise to keep a secret. Cloudesley is the repository of a secret concerning a crime his master has committed; but, unlike the secret Caleb is keeping, which is that of a physical murder, Cloudesley's secret concerns an essentially verbal crime. His master, Lord Danvers, is guilty of fraud: when Danvers's elder brother and his sister-in-law both died abroad, twenty years earlier, Danvers usurped the position of their newborn son by attesting that the baby was stillborn, contracting with his servant Cloudesley to dispose of it, and returning to Britain to assume the titles that rightfully belonged to the infant. The plot of *Cloudesley* thus layers one destructive speech act on top of another, and creates the conditions for profound reflection on the phenomenon of identity. Godwin's earlier novels already raised questions about the extent to which "identity" consists in physical existence (or what philosophers, especially Searle, call "brute facts") and the extent to which it depends on social institutions and the speech acts they generate (that is, "institutional facts") (Searle, *Speech Acts* 50–53). Caleb Williams finds his identity circumscribed by the narratives that circulate about him in the public sphere, and by his ability or inability to make his knowledge about Falkland count as a valid public statement. The young lover William, in *Deloraine*, finds that he has "no place among the sons of men" when he resurfaces after society and its legal system have pronounced him dead (*CN* 8: 125). Situations like these raise the question of what constitutes personhood—a burning topic in an age when the female half of the population has a narrowly circumscribed legal identity and very limited right to own property, and when the amount of property a man must own in order to count as a voting member of the community is under heated debate.

When Deloraine, near the end of his story, decides to elude his pursuers by resorting to disguise rather than flight, he is led to reflect on the importance of "identity" to the moral fabric of society. He is thinking mainly of identity in the sense of reputation, or the regulatory influence exerted on our behavior by the fact that other people know who we are and what we have done in the past:

> The moral government of man in society to a great degree hinges upon the question of identity, in other words, that every man is recognisable by his fellows. . . . But the mass of mankind . . . are held in awe by the opinions and censure of each other. Reputation is the breath of their nostrils, the element by which they respire. The construction that shall be made of their proceedings is the thought the awes them; and even the judgment they shall make of themselves is regulated by the judgment of their neighbours. We are members of a community, and can be scarcely said, any one of us, to have a rational existence independent of our fellows. (*CN* 8: 255–56)

Identity, in this sense, draws on the institutional fact of what constitutes proper behavior in a given society, as well as on the brute fact of physical appearance, or recognizability. If the pragmatic importance of reputation, as Deloraine describes it, already seems to qualify Godwin's ideal of behavior based on each person's innate conception of reason and justice, the context of Deloraine's reflections constitutes an even greater qualification: he is about to construct a new identity for himself by dressing up as a different person whenever he appears in public. This separation between essential self and public self grows increasingly acute in the closing pages of the novel, when the narrator finally reveals that even "Deloraine" is not his real name: the names in his story have been changed to protect the innocent, and "Deloraine" is a "veil" for a yet more "fatal name" (*CN* 8: 286). Although he leaves his written memoir to his daughter, the only person who knows his secret, and although he believes that no one else will ever read the text, he declines to reveal his true name even in its pages. When even a private, confessional autobiography perpetuates the fiction of an assumed name and identity, which is itself erected on a theory of public reputation as the basis for moral behavior, it becomes dubious whether there is any brute fact or essential identity at the base of the entire construct.

Cloudesley, as Godwin's most extended exploration of institutional identity and its performative grounding, is no doubt a flawed work, in which the narrative perspective is more complicated and less plausible than usual, the story both repetitive and rambling. Yet the novel deals with strikingly modern topics, ranging from problems of international jurisdiction to adolescent behavior and anxieties, and even to academic politics. *Cloudesley* is also full of compelling ironies about the nature and foundation of identity in society. The beginning and end of the story are narrated by the young commoner William Meadows, who, on returning to England after an adventuresome sojourn in Russia, is unexpectedly called into the presence of the neighboring nobleman, Richard Danvers, who recounts his life story and, at its center, his indelible crime of fraud. Assailed by grief and remorse after losing his own family to illness, Danvers commissions Meadows to travel to Italy in search of his dispossessed nephew, whom the servant Cloudesley has named Julian and raised as his own son. Meadows locates Julian Cloudesley, and Danvers himself arrives in Italy just in time to save him from being unjustly executed as a highwayman; before expiring, Danvers restores Julian to his rightful inheritance as an English and Irish peer.

The crime that Danvers commits involves a combination of brute and institutional facts. He needs the body of a dead infant, which Cloudesley somehow procures for him, to substitute for his infant nephew in order to promulgate the fiction that the latter was stillborn. But the more significant aspect of his transgression, as judged by the number of times he returns to it in his narrative, is the filing of false documents that attest to the death of his brother's son. When he first commits the crime, Danvers mitigates it in his own eyes by arguing that he is not depriving the infant of life, but only of legal fictions: "Their child was not dead. But he was, by my sole means, civilly dead to his property, his rank and his country" (*CN* 7: 106). This argument is relatively easy to maintain as long as the child himself is an unborn "fiction." Later, though, Danvers finds that the boy's bodily existence itself exerts a kind of pressure on his and Cloudesley's conscience: "The contract between Cloudesley and myself by which Julian was despoiled of his all, had been sealed before the child was born, when he was a creature of the understanding only, respecting which something might be affirmed or denied. The case was altered, when he had become an object of the senses" (*CN* 7: 175).

To William Meadows as he listens to this tale, and to the reader of the novel, successive events clarify what it means to deprive a person of his institutional identity, even if his physical being remains intact. Numerous situations in which characters are restricted in the exercise of their property or their rights because they travel into different legal jurisdictions underscore the importance of legal status within a given community. The most extreme example of existence beyond all jurisdictions is provided by the company of banditti led by the robber hero St. Elmo, a man without country or law who (in a phrase that echoes Paine) "regarded what is called civilised society as a conspiracy against the inherent rights of man" (*CN* 7: 217). The existence of the banditti, men from noble families who have chosen to live outside regular legal and political communities, constitutes a serious critique of societal institutions, because the outlaws' alternative lifestyle actually provides greater scope for behavior motivated by pleasure, pain, affection, and even justice—exactly the kind of behavior advocated by the political theorist Godwin. The outlaws gain the sympathy of both the reader and Julian Cloudesley, who innocently joins their band because he feels greater ties of affection with them than with anyone in the legitimate community. On the other hand, both legitimate social identity and outlawry are starkly contrasted with the brute fact of physical death by execution or disease, for each of which the novel provides spectacular examples. When Meadows traces Julian to Palermo, he arrives there just in time to witness the mass execution of half the banditti with whom Julian has been living—a scene that impresses Meadows as the most intense contrast possible between vibrant life and sudden extinction. Lord Danvers experiences the extinction of physical identity in his own family four times over, when each of his children, who have apparently inherited the same disorder, dies of an emaciating disease at about age eleven—that is, just before the onset of physical adulthood. Not surprisingly, Danvers regards the death of his children and his wife as divine retribution for figuratively murdering his brother's son before the infant could accede to his rights as an adult.

The fabricated identities of the main characters in *Cloudesley* are peculiarly performative identities, inasmuch as they are inseparable from the characters' behavior. Lord Danvers has placed himself in a position from which he is uniquely empowered to perpetuate that same position: "It is no trifling undertaking," he reflects, "to thrust from his place a nobleman, whose title is already authentically recorded, and who had been admitted to the possession of the estates and the income annexed to that title" (*CN* 7: 137). By villainously—but successfully—claiming the title of Earl Danvers, he ascends to a social status that effectively puts him out of reach of the charge of being a villain. Given the prejudice of the legal system in favor of property and privilege, the greater the extent of his fraud, the less likely it is that he would ever be found guilty of fraud. Moreover, his own consciousness of the exalted rank he has assumed through his crime makes him all the more determined that he must not allow himself to be dishonored by public exposure, even if he would otherwise wish to undo his actions. Cloudesley, the other party to the contract by which Julian is disinherited, unhappily puts himself in an inverse position. By helping to make Danvers powerful and wealthy, he has minimized his own ability to break or alter the terms of their contract, as both of them realize the first time Cloudesley threatens to expose the secret. For Danvers, breaking his side of the contract would simply involve cutting off Cloudesley's allowance of £500 a year; because "a poor suitor always labours under great disadvantages," this would render it much more difficult for Cloudesley to break *his* side of the bargain by persuading the courts that Danvers is a usurper (*CN* 7: 141). Julian's position is marked by an ironic performativity as well. As Cloudesley realizes in dismay when considering his options, if Julian were to regain his title, his uncle Danvers would simultaneously be exposed as a fraud and usurper, and the whole house would be exposed to scandal. The act of gaining a noble title would be inseparable from the act of casting dishonor on that title. "You would affix to the name of Herbert, and to the titles of Alton and Danvers, an everlasting disgrace," the usurper Danvers warns Cloudesley; "that disgrace would even contaminate the whole blood of the house, and rebound on your ward" (*CN* 7: 194). The resolution to all these paradoxes comes only when Danvers's physical identity and his assumed institutional identity are extinguished together. Before his death in Italy, he makes a will restoring property and title to Julian; he is then buried, at his request, in complete oblivion: "no stone told even his name to the passer by" (*CN* 7: 286).

"The rank I bore was a forgery; the income I spent was the property of another," Danvers ruminates, in one of many self-reproaching passages in his narrative (*CN* 7: 115). Rank and property are doubly fictitious in his case; they are always legal "fictions," in Bentham's sense, but here Danvers has constructed them for himself by manipulating laws and public perception. Danvers's rank, property, and identity are fictional in more senses still if we take into account that they appear within a series of interlocking narratives: Danvers's story is contained within Meadows's narrative, which is contained within Godwin's novel. As in Godwin's other texts, the multiple layers of fictionality attached to social structures cannot help but underscore the dependence of those structures on speech acts.

The dilatory structure of the narrative in *Cloudesley* makes the novel difficult to read at times, but also serves to confirm the principle that identity is shaped by performative utterance. New characters—including Julian's dead mother Irene, Cloudesley's friend Borromeo, and the outlaw St. Elmo—are constantly being introduced into the story, first by a simple mention of their name, then through an extensive flashback that covers their entire history up to the point where it intersects with the main narrative. Through his speech acts, the narrator (ostensibly Danvers, but also Godwin as novelist) constructs complete identities and histories for these characters. At the same time, such mini-narratives serve a pragmatic purpose for Danvers as he addresses himself to William Meadows: he offers them as a kind of proof of the identity and genealogy of Julian, as if a detailed cast of well-rounded characters will contribute to the persuasiveness of his story. These hastily called up characters serve the same purpose, one might say, as the anonymous "witnesses" that are called in from abroad at the end of the novel, when the British courts work through the lengthy process of establishing Julian's new institutional identity (*CN* 7: 286). There is, then, an ongoing parallel between the imaginative process of creating identity and character in literary fiction, and the institutional process of establishing identity, title, and property as legal fictions. Like Caleb Williams as he disseminates versions of his own history, Lord Danvers unites these activities in his person: as he confesses how he manipulated Julian's social identity and his own, he also controls the creation of their identity as characters in a story.

The novel's title provides a final comment on the ironies involved in both these forms of fiction. As the only one of Godwin's six mature novels in which the title character is not the narrator, *Cloudesley* is already something of an anomaly in terms of narrative structure. Beyond this, it is never quite clear to whom the title refers. Is it named for Cloudesley the servant (who does not seem to have a first name)—Julian's assumed father, who is an important but never the central character in the story? Or does the title refer to Julian Cloudesley, who *is* a central character, and probably the hero insofar as the novel has one—but who merits this status precisely because he is *not* really a Cloudesley? Does it refer, perhaps, to the assumed and shifting quality of all names and titles, and thus to the way they "cloud" true identity? William Meadows confronts the dilemma of the name "Cloudesley" at the end of the story, when he seeks out the Neapolitan government minister who alone can save Julian from execution as a bandit. How can he request pardon for Julian, "a being without a name," when the name that was stolen from him at birth, "one of the first names in the records of his country" (*CN* 7: 279), would instantly obtain his release, yet all the circumstantial evidence identifies him with the name "Julian Cloudesley" that is printed in the list of arrested banditti (*CN* 7: 265–66)? "I should have been instantly asked," Meadows reflects, "'How am I to know this? Why am I to believe you? Here is the calendar of the offenders: his name is Julian Cloudesley. Is that the name of one of the first families in Britain?'" (*CN* 7: 279). Even if, in the end, Julian's physical identity is saved by the timely conversion of his social identity from "Cloudesley" to "Danvers," the novel ironically perpetuates the act of usurpation by memorializing, not the noble, institutional title of Danvers, but the name of the fallible yet good-hearted foster father, Cloudesley.

FICTION AS TESTIMONY AND TESTAMENT

The recurrent analogy between the speech acts that take place within the legal and social world of the narratives, and the speech acts that constitute the narratives, is perhaps Godwin's most intriguing contribution to the idea of the performative. In an essay that uses Searle's speech-act theory to talk about fictionality, Gérard Genette suggests that the difference between everyday, social performatives ("The meeting is in session" or "You're fired"), and the speech acts of literary fiction ("Once upon a time there was a little girl . . .") may finally be quite small, since both kinds of utterances bring about "collective mental states" in their hearers or readers (42). Novels can be considered performative utterances just as the more explicit declarative utterances of ordinary language can; conversely, the states that result from ordinary, sociopolitical performative utterances have a great deal in common with the mental constructs that we associate with literary fiction.

A similar conclusion might be drawn from the Godwinian novel, which is (from *Caleb Williams* onward) always presented as a first-person utterance; each novel-length "utterance" counts as a specific illocutionary act by the narrator. The pragmatic aspect of these narratives, in other words, tends to be conspicuous: the writer is not simply recording his memoirs, but performing a specific act within a specific intersubjective context in the hope of thereby positioning himself differently within his own history. Lord Danvers's story, which makes up most of *Cloudesley*, is specifically addressed to Meadows as a confession, as a vindication of his desire to find and help Julian, and in order to persuade Meadows to exert himself in the unusual commission with which Danvers charges him. Even a text that no one is ever expected to read, such as the confession of St. Leon, has an interpersonal or dialogic aspect, for St. Leon addresses his journal as his only friend:

> Senseless paper! be thou at least my confidant! To thee I may impart what my soul spurns the task to suppress. The human mind insatiably thirsts for a confidant and a friend. It is no matter that these pages shall never be surveyed by other eyes than mine. They afford at least the semblance of communication and the unburthening of the mind; and I will press the illusion fondly and for ever to my heart. (*CN* 4: 137)

The act of writing is intrinsic to the events of the story: it is because St. Leon has just vowed not to reveal his secret to another human being that he writes (to) his book. In this and other novels, the experiences that Godwin's characters relate in their stories themselves form the pragmatic context for the writing of the story; the act of narrating and the narrated events are inseparable, and mutually dependent.

Most of these narratives perform the past-directed illocutionary act of *confessing*—an illocution in which neither the performative nor the constative dimension can be neglected. The convention of confessing, one might say, has a built-in requirement of correspondence to experienced reality; that is, it belongs to the definition of confessing that what is confessed be the truth. Some of Godwin's narrators, such as Caleb Williams and Mandeville, radically undercut that convention when their narratives accentuate the subjectivity of "truth," and the lack of an objective criterion by which to measure it. But even when the truth of the confessed events is not especially called into question, confessing remains a manifestly *contextualized* act. It is the only act Fleetwood or Deloraine can still perform that might alter the effect of the narrated events, by placing either the narrator himself, or other participants or observers, in a different relation to those events. As Fleetwood testifies, the act of putting his history into words is itself an event in his history: "The proper topic of the narrative I am writing is the record of my errors. To write it, is the act of my penitence and humiliation" (*CN* 5: 21). The confession is not only a pragmatic use of language, but a self-reflexive one, whereby Fleetwood interacts with his own history in the process of verbalizing it.

But when the narrator puts his life into writing, he also generates the possibility that his utterance will have unpredictable and uncontrollable perlocutionary effects. "To write," according to Derrida, "is to produce a mark that will constitute a sort of machine which is productive in turn, and which my future disappearance will not, in principle, hinder in its functioning, offering things and itself to be read and to be rewritten" (*Limited Inc* 8). In the case of the Godwinian novel, the narrator typically writes as if he never expects his narrative to be read—and yet his act of writing makes the text vulnerable to as many different kinds of uptake as there are potential readers and contexts. The conclusion of *Deloraine* spotlights this situation, for Deloraine explicitly raises the question of the pragmatic value of the history he has just produced:

> I am now arrived at the last page of my scroll.... I leave it behind me to be disposed of by my successors as they please. I do not forbid them to destroy it. If it never see the light, it will yet have served a temporary purpose to myself. Catherine has a child, a boy, beautiful, lovely, and of seraphic innocence. As long as she or her offspring see the light, these papers must never be divulged. I have changed the names indeed; but the story is too full of particulars, many of them well known, for it to be pos-

> sible that it should not be brought home. Yet, if Catherine and her husband so please, let this narrative be preserved! It may surely be kept in perfect security. And, such is the endless vicissitude of human things, a century, or even half a century may pass, and all things connected with my tale may be obliterated; and Deloraine, and the fatal name to which that appellation serves as a veil, may have perished from the memories of men; and this story may no more be a libel, than the records of Haroun Al Raschid, or the fortunes of Ahasuerus, Vashti and Haman. (*CN* 8: 286)

Deloraine's last paragraph converts his testimony into a testament, whereby he bequeaths his life in written form to his heirs, to do with as they think best. The legacy highlights what is implicitly true for all of Godwin's novels: that life as an act of writing or utterance has consequences separate and different from life as it is lived. Godwin's warning in *Political Justice*—that language is incommensurate with time and experience—is borne out by the narrators in his fiction, whose contextualized, conventionalized, pragmatic speech acts reveal that experience is one thing, its verbal form another. But Godwin's theoretical urgings that language should remain secondary to experience give way, in his novels, to the fact that verbal structures do exert control over experience. The proliferation of promises and oaths, courtroom situations and other forms of testimony, publicly circulating texts, and confessions that reconstruct history in Godwin's fiction makes clear how thoroughly verbal utterances shape private identity as well as the public sphere—for these performative utterances, though suspect, represent the only way we have of bringing subjective feeling into play in intersubjective negotiations. In both the novels and the society they depict, it appears again and again that verbal fictions are the only form of reality accessible to our reading eye.

Conclusion

This study has sought to locate the roots of the performative in late-eighteenth-century epistemology and political philosophy, especially in Kant's account of the mental faculties and the intellectual aftermath of the French Revolution. In response to Kant's theory that the mind actively produces phenomena by processing intuitions in accordance with *a priori* forms of understanding, both his critics and his followers speculated that language must be intimately involved in this process. More accurately—and more radically—philosophers like Hamann, Herder, and Humboldt recognized that language must *be* the process through which we articulate and conceptualize elements of the material world. While they defined cognition as essentially verbal, they also defined verbalization as essentially communicative. The mind's dialogue with the external world, and one speaker's dialogue with another, are bound together at the very origin of Romantic philosophy of language.

The German synthesis of cognition and communication was enacted contemporaneously, but with a different emphasis, in Britain. Reid, Kant's less successful British counterpart in proposing a response to the impasse of empiricism and idealism, based his Common-Sense philosophy of mind heavily on the evidence of ordinary language. Reid's emphasis on the communicative function of language led him to a proto-speech-act theory that, while not overly influential in itself, epitomized the orientation of the British school toward verbal utterance as social action. Drawing on a strong tradition of social-contract theory as well as on topical debates over declarations and constitutions, Tooke, Bentham, and Godwin gave British philosophy of language a strong political and legal inflection, while Coleridge synthesized the political, philosophical, and theological frames of reference.

While they share an emphasis on oral speech and the dialogic situation, the German and British lines of linguistic philosophy emphasize complementary aspects of the speech act. In Germany, Humboldt articulates the need for uptake from a conversational partner, in order to validate the speaker's attempt to conceptualize an object in language. But, as Herder indicates fleetingly in his language-origin essay, the utterances that one speaker tests out on another can also impose a worldview on the Other. These instances of imposition are more prominent in British philosophy, where Paine, Coleridge, and Bentham consider the various circumstances in which institutions and hierarchies authorize the utterances of one speaker to constitute the parameters of another's world. With Bentham's theory of fictions, linguistic philosophy broaches the rather modern idea that institutions and power structures themselves are nothing but the effect of previous speech acts—a record, as it were, of their relative success.

In exploring the interaction of cognition and communication, both German and British philosophers demonstrate that the effect of speech goes beyond the control of the speaker. Humboldt, Coleridge, and their contemporaries constantly return to the idea that the internal structure, grammar, and sound patterns, the autonomy and the very materiality of language, affect the operation of any individual speech act. The Romantic speech act is thus, typically, an utterance that embodies a speaker's cognitive process, that seeks a listener's legitimating uptake, and that gives language itself an opportunity to manifest its agency. Depending on the hierarchy at work in the speech situation, the utterance may also inform, or deform, the listener's conception of reality. The paradoxes involved in this analysis of language as act, whereby each dimension of the process (the existence of the linguistic system, the establishment of an interpersonal relationship, the stabilizing of the speaker's subjectivity, and the utterance-event itself) seems to be prior to the others and yet to affect the others, is what I have called the Romantic performative, an utterance that founds the conditions of its own possibility.

What is its relevance for the reading of Romantic literature, and, conversely, what is literature's relevance for linguistic philosophy? To begin with, I have hoped to show how often the effects of speech on the construction of reality, the legitimation of utterances in social contexts, and the coincidence of cognition with communication are thematized in Romantic poetry and fiction. In dramas and novels, characters construct worlds for one another through their words, enveloping one another in their own (often institutionalized) fictions. These fictional interactions can have more or less direct relevance to the relationship of author and reader. A close relationship between fictional dialogue and the poet's address to the reader obtains in the case of Hölderlin, since the ambiguous or partial success of the illocutionary acts performed by his Hyperion and Empedokles (poet-philosopher and philosopher-poet, respectively)

Conclusion

serve as a challenge for Hölderlin himself, a poet with a troubled sense of his role in shaping a community. His lyric poetry presents itself as gapingly open-ended dialogue—a daring attempt, as he makes clear in the foreword to "Friedensfeier," to actualize new cognitive constructions in an unconventional language that he ventures to hope will receive sympathetic uptake. Coleridge, too, offers his poetic construction of a renewed English landscape in "Fears in Solitude" as a substitute for the authoritative, but destructive, public speech acts that shape 1790s England, and tests the limits of language's creative power in poems like "Hymn before Sun-rise" and "Frost at Midnight."

Kleist and Godwin, with their prominent legal themes and contexts, intensify the scrutiny of speech acts and their legitimation. Both bring the body into play (for Kleist, the absent-minded toying with a shirt cuff can inspire a revolutionary declaration), as well as the materiality of writing itself (the gypsy-woman's prophecy, in *Kohlhaas*, gains its performative value from being written with charcoal, worn around the neck, and finally ingested by the protagonist whose very name is "coal"). Problematizing the idea of language as a cognitive act by exploring the physicality and contingency involved in acts of communication, Kleist also shows how linguistic practices in the human world fail to take account of our rule-breaking conceptions of the supernatural. For Godwin, whose rationalism leads him, unlike the others, to reject the performative aspect of language in favor of sincerity and referentiality, the performative speech act is an amputation of reference, a frustrating source of discomfort like the ache in a phantom limb. From the 1790s until the 1830s, his novels, while bearing out the dangers of speech acts that impose on human freedom, also demonstrate the utter inevitability of performative language in social relations. Ironically, it is Godwin who, with his promising, testifying, confessional first-person narrators, brings to view some of the most profound observations about the parallels between sociopolitical fictions and literary fiction.

My hope is, then, that a detailed study of Romantic philosophy of language leads outward in several important directions. For intellectual history, it brings about a recognition of how and why speech-act theory and the concept of performativity is rooted in eighteenth-century, above all in Kantian epistemology. For a general theory of reading, it throws a spotlight onto the dialogic aspect of poet-reader relationships as a conscious and crucial aspect of many Romantic texts. Products of cognitive activity, yet subject to the conventions of interpersonal discourse as well as the autonomy of the language system, the poet's speech acts pose a bid or a challenge for the reader's uptake. For a general theory of social relations, finally, the Romantic performative opens up a new perspective on the *tenuousness* of speech acts, since the acts of cognition embodied in uttered words always need to be tested out in unpredictable and contingent speech situations, where there is no guarantee that they will be taken up or legitimated. But Romantic philosophy of language also draws attention to the *tenacity* of speech acts: as soon as they *do* achieve legitimation, they begin to subject the addressee to the worldview they have formed, imposing terms and limitations on the listener's cognitive process. This never-ending chain of discursive actions and reactions amounts to a performative notion of history and, equally, a performative model of reading.

Reference Matter

Bibliography

Aarsleff, Hans. *From Locke to Saussure: Essays on the Study of Language and Intellectual History*. Minneapolis: U of Minnesota P, 1982.
——. *The Study of Language in England, 1780–1860*. 1967. Minneapolis: U of Minnesota P, 1983.
Acton, H. B. "The Philosophy of Language in Revolutionary France." *Proceedings of the British Academy* 45 (1959): 199–219.
Aspetsberger, Friedbert. *Welteinheit und epische Gestaltung. Studien zur Ichform von Hölderlins Roman 'Hyperion.'* Munich: Fink, 1971.
Austin, J. L. *How to Do Things with Words*. Ed. J. O. Urmson and Marina Sbisà. 2nd ed. Cambridge: Harvard UP, 1975.
Balfour, Ian. "Promises, Promises: Social and Other Contracts in the English Jacobins (Godwin/Inchbald)." *New Romanticisms: Theory and Critical Practice*. Ed. David L. Clark and Donald C. Goellnicht. Toronto: U of Toronto P, 1994. 225–50.
Barker, Francis, et al. *1789: Reading Writing Revolution. Proceedings of the Essex Conference on the Sociology of Literature, July 1981*. Colcester: U of Essex, 1982.
Barrell, John. *English Literature in History, 1730–80: An Equal Wide Survey*. London: Hutchinson, 1983.
Baum, Richard. "Systemlinguistik und Sprechakt." *Indogermanische Forschungen* 82 (1977): 1–38.
Behler, Constantin. "Humboldts 'radikale Reflexion über die Sprache' im Lichte der Foucaultschen Diskursanalyse." *Deutsche Vierteljahresschrift für Literaturwissenschaft und Geistesgeschichte* 63 (1989): 1–24.
Behler, Ernst. *German Romantic Literary Theory*. Cambridge: Cambridge UP, 1993.
Benjamin, Walter. *Der Begriff der Kunstkritik in der deutschen Romantik. Gesammelte Schriften*. Ed. Rolf Tiedemann and Hermann Schweppenhäuser. 12 vols. Frankfurt: Suhrkamp, 1980. 1: 11–122.
Bentham, Jeremy. *Bentham's Political Thought*. Ed. Bhikhu Parekh. London: Croom Helm, 1973.
——. *Bentham's Theory of Fictions*. Ed. C. K. Ogden. London: Kegan Paul, 1932.
——. *An Introduction to the Principles of Morals and Legislation*. Ed. J. H. Burns and H. L. A. Hart. London: Athlone, 1970.
——. *Of Laws in General*. Ed. H. L. A. Hart. London: Athlone, 1970.

———. *The Theory of Legislation.* Ed. C. K. Ogden. London: Kegan Paul, 1931.
———. *The Works of Jeremy Bentham.* Ed. John Bowring. 11 vols. 1838–43. New York: Russell, 1962.
Benveniste, Emile. "Le langage et l'expérience humaine." *Problèmes de Langage.* N.p.: Gallimard, 1966. 3–13.
———. *Problems in General Linguistics.* Trans. Mary Elizabeth Meek. Coral Gables FL: U of Miami P, 1971.
Bernhardi, August Ferdinand. *Anfangsgründe der Sprachwissenschaft.* Berlin: Frölich, 1805.
———. *Sprachlehre.* 1801–3. Hildesheim: Olms, 1973.
Bierwisch, Manfred. "Humboldtsche Themen in der Linguistik des 20. Jahrhunderts." *Sprache, Mensch und Gesellschaft. Werk und Wirkungen von Wilhelm von Humboldt und Jacob und Wilhelm Grimm in Vergangenheit und Gegenwart.* Proc. of the Humboldt-Grimm-Konferenz. 22–25 Oct. 1985. Ed. Arwed Spreu and Wilhelm Bondzio. 2 vols. Berlin: Humboldt U, 1986. 1: 114–25.
Binder, Wolfgang. *Hölderlin-Aufsätze.* Frankfurt: Insel, 1970.
Blakemore, Steven. "Burke and the Fall of Language: The French Revolution as Linguistic Event." *Eighteenth-Century Studies* 17 (1984): 284–307.
———. *Burke and the Fall of Language: The French Revolution as Linguistic Event.* Hanover: UP of New England, 1988.
———. "Revolution in Language: Burke's Representation of Linguistic Terror." *Representing the French Revolution: Literature, Historiography and Art.* Ed. James A. W. Heffernan. Hanover: UP of New England, 1992. 3–23.
Böhler, Michael. Nachwort. *Schriften zur Sprache.* By Wilhelm von Humboldt. Stuttgart: Reclam, 1973. 223–54.
Borsche, Tilman, ed. *Klassiker der Sprachphilosophie. Von Platon bis Noam Chomsky.* Munich: Beck, 1996.
———. *Sprachansichten. Der Begriff der menschlichen Rede in der Sprachphilosophie Wilhelm von Humboldts.* Stuttgart: Klett-Cotta, 1981.
———. *Wilhelm von Humboldt.* Munich: Beck, 1990.
Boulton, James. *The Language of Politics in the Age of Wilkes and Burke.* London: Routledge, 1963.
Bourdieu, Pierre. *Language and Symbolic Power.* Ed. John B. Thompson. Trans. Gino Raymond and Matthew Adamson. Cambridge: Harvard UP, 1991.
Breitinger, J. J. *Fortsetzung der Critischen Dichtkunst, worinnen die poetische Mahlerey in Absicht auf den Ausdruck und die Farben abgehandelt wird.* Zürich, 1740.
Burke, Edmund. *A Philosophical Enquiry into the Origin of Our Ideas of the Sublime and Beautiful.* Ed. James T. Boulton. Notre Dame: U of Notre Dame P, 1968.
———. *The Writings and Speeches of Edmund Burke.* Gen. ed. Paul Langford. 6 vols. to date. Oxford: Clarendon, 1981–.

Burke, Kenneth. *A Grammar of Motives*. Berkeley: U of California P, 1945.

———. *Language as Symbolic Action: Essays on Life, Literature, and Method*. Berkeley: U of California P, 1966.

Burkhardt, Armin. "Der Dialogbegriff bei Wilhelm von Humboldt." *Sprache und Bildung. Beiträge zum 150. Todestag Wilhelm von Humboldts*. Ed. Rudolf Hoberg. Darmstadt: Technische Hochschule Darmstadt, 1987. 141–73.

———, ed. *Speech Acts, Meaning and Intentions: Critical Approaches to the Philosophy of John R. Searle*. Berlin: Gruyter, 1990.

Butler, Judith. *Excitable Speech: A Politics of the Performative*. New York: Routledge, 1997.

Cassirer, Ernst. *Language*. Trans. Ralph Manheim. New Haven: Yale UP, 1953. Vol. 1 of *The Philosophy of Symbolic Forms*. 4 vols. 1953–96.

Chomsky, Noam. *Cartesian Linguistics: A Chapter in the History of Rationalist Thought*. New York: Harper, 1966.

Christmann, Hans Helmut. "Neue Beiträge zur Geschichte der These vom Weltbild der Sprache: 'Praktische' Anwendungen in Frankreich und Deutschland am Ende des 18. Jahrhunderts." *Logos Semantikos. Studia Linguistica in Honorem Eugenio Coseriu 1921–1981*. Ed. Horst Geckeler, Brigitte Schlieben-Lange, Jürgen Trabant, and Harald Weydt. 5 vols. Berlin: Gruyter, 1981. 1: 87–99.

Clemit, Pamela. *The Godwinian Novel: The Rational Fictions of Godwin, Brockden Brown, Mary Shelley*. Oxford: Clarendon, 1993.

Clifford, Gay. "*Caleb Williams* and *Frankenstein*: First-Person Narratives and 'Things As They Are.'" *Genre* 10 (1977): 601–17.

Coleridge, Samuel Taylor. *Aids to Reflection* (= *AR*). Ed. John Beer. Princeton: Princeton UP, 1993. Vol. 9 of *The Collected Works of Samuel Taylor Coleridge*. 1969–.

———. *Biographia Literaria* (= *BL*). Ed. James Engell and Walter Jackson Bate. 2 vols. Princeton: Princeton UP, 1983. Vol. 7 of *The Collected Works of Samuel Taylor Coleridge*. 1969–.

———. *Coleridge on Logic and Learning* (= *L&L*). Ed. Alice D. Snyder. New Haven: Yale UP, 1929.

———. *Collected Letters of Samuel Taylor Coleridge* (= *CL*). Ed. Earl Leslie Griggs. 5 vols. Oxford: Clarendon, 1956–71.

———. *The Complete Poetical Works of Samuel Taylor Coleridge* (= *CPW*). Ed. Ernest Hartley Coleridge. 2 vols. Oxford: Clarendon, 1912.

———. *The Friend* (= *F*). Ed. Barbara Rooke. 2 vols. Princeton: Princeton UP, 1969. Vol. 4 of *The Collected Works of Samuel Taylor Coleridge*. 1969–.

———. *Inquiring Spirit: A New Presentation of Coleridge from His Published and Unpublished Prose Writings* (= *IS*). Ed. Kathleen Coburn. London: Routledge, 1951.

———. *Lay Sermons* (= *LS*). Ed. R. J. White. Princeton: Princeton UP, 1972. Vol. 6 of *The Collected Works of Samuel Taylor Coleridge*. 1969–.

———. *Lectures 1795 on Politics and Religion* (= *LPR*). Ed. Lewis Patton and Peter Mann. Princeton: Princeton UP, 1971. Vol. 1 of *The Collected Works of Samuel Taylor Coleridge*. 1969–.

———. *Lectures 1808–1819: On Literature* (= *LL*). Ed. Reginald A. Foakes. 2 vols. Princeton: Princeton UP, 1987. Vol. 5 of *The Collected Works of Samuel Taylor Coleridge*. 1969–.

———. *Logic* (= *L*). Ed. J. R. de J. Jackson. Princeton: Princeton UP, 1981. Vol. 13 of *The Collected Works of Samuel Taylor Coleridge*. 1969–.

———. *Marginalia* (= *M*). Ed. George Whalley and H. J. Jackson. 4 vols. to date. Princeton: Princeton UP, 1984. Vol. 12 of *The Collected Works of Samuel Taylor Coleridge*. 1969–.

———. *The Notebooks of Samuel Taylor Coleridge* (= *CN*). Ed. Kathleen Coburn. 4 vols. London: Routledge, 1957–90.

———. *Opus Maximum* (= *OM*). Microfilm ms. Victoria University Library, Toronto.

———. *The Philosophical Lectures of Samuel Taylor Coleridge* (= *Phil.Lect.*). Ed. Kathleen Coburn. London: Pilot, 1949.

———. *Shorter Works and Fragments* (= *SWF*). Ed. H. J. Jackson and J. R. de J. Jackson. 2 vols. Princeton: Princeton UP, 1995. Vol. 11 of *The Collected Works of Samuel Taylor Coleridge*. 1969–.

———. *Table Talk* (= *TT*). Ed. Carl Woodring. 2 vols. Princeton: Princeton UP, 1990. Vol. 14 of *The Collected Works of Samuel Taylor Coleridge*. 1969–.

Colman, George [the Younger]. *The Iron Chest: A Play, in Three Acts*. London: Cadell, 1796.

Conte, Maria-Elisabeth. "Semantische und pragmatische Ansätze in der Sprachtheorie Wilhelm von Humboldts." *History of Linguistic Thought and Contemporary Linguistics*. Ed. Herman Parret. Berlin: Gruyter, 1976. 616–32.

Corrigan, Timothy J. "Coleridge, the Reader: Language in a Combustible Mind." *Philological Quarterly* 59 (1980): 76–94.

Culler, Jonathan. "Apostrophe." *Diacritics* 7.4 (1977): 59–69.

Davies, Lindsay. "The Poem, the Gloss and the Critic: Discourse and Subjectivity in 'The Rime of the Ancient Mariner.'" *Forum for Modern Language Studies* 26 (1990): 259–71.

Degrois, Denise. "Coleridge on Human Communication." *Coleridge's Visionary Languages: Essays in Honour of J. B. Beer*. Ed. Tim Fulford and Morton D. Paley. Cambridge: Brewer, 1993. 99–109.

De Man, Paul. *Allegories of Reading: Figural Language in Rousseau, Nietzsche, Rilke, and Proust*. New Haven: Yale UP, 1979.

———. *Blindness and Insight: Essays in the Rhetoric of Contemporary Criticism*. 2nd rev. ed. Minneapolis: U of Minnesota P, 1983.

———. "Sign and Symbol in Hegel's *Aesthetics*." *Critical Inquiry* 8 (1982): 761–75.

Derrida, Jacques. "Admiration de Nelson Mandela, ou Les lois de la réflexion." *Psyché. Inventions de l'autre*. Paris: Galilée, 1987. 453–75.

———. "Declarations of Independence." Trans. Tom Keenan and Tom Pepper. *New Political Science* 15 (1986): 7–15.

———. "Force of Law: The 'Mystical Foundation of Authority.'" *Deconstruction and the Possibility of Justice*. Ed. David Gray Carlson, Drucilla Cornell, and Michael Rosenfeld. New York: Routledge, 1992. 3–67.

———. *Limited Inc.* Trans. Samuel Weber and Jeffrey Mehlman. Ed. Gerald Graff. Evanston: Northwestern UP, 1990.

———. *Otobiographies: L'enseignement de Nietzsche et la politique du nom propre*. Paris: Galilée, 1984.

———. *Speech and Phenomena, and Other Essays on Husserl's Theory of Signs*. Trans. David B. Allison. Evanston: Northwestern UP, 1973.

Di Cesare, Donatella. "Die aristotelische Herkunft der Begriffe ἔργον und ἐνέργεια in Wilhelm von Humboldts Sprachphilosophie." *Das sprachtheoretische Denken Eugenio Coserius in der Diskussion (1)*. Ed. Harald Thun. Tübingen: Narr, 1988. 29–46. Vol. 2 of *Energeia und Ergon: Sprachliche Variation—Sprachgeschichte—Sprachtypologie*. 3 vols. 1988.

Essick, Robert N. "Coleridge and the Language of Adam." *Coleridge's Biographia Literaria: Text and Meaning*. Ed. Frederick Burwick. Columbus: Ohio State UP, 1989. 62–74.

———. "William Blake, Thomas Paine, and Biblical Revolution." *Studies in Romanticism* 30 (1991): 189–212.

Esterhammer, Angela. "Calling into Existence: *The Book of Urizen*." *Blake in the Nineties*. Ed. Steve Clark and David Worrall. London: Macmillan, 1999. 114–32.

———. *Creating States: Studies in the Performative Language of John Milton and William Blake*. Toronto: U of Toronto P, 1994.

Everest, Kelvin, and Gavin Edwards. "William Godwin's *Caleb Williams*: Truth and 'Things As They Are.'" Barker et al. 129–46.

Fava, Elisabetta, ed. *Speech Acts and Linguistic Research: Proceedings of the Workshop, July 15–17, 1994*. Padua: Nemo, 1995.

Felman, Shoshana. *The Literary Speech Act: Don Juan with J. L. Austin, or Seduction in Two Languages*. Trans. Catherine Porter. Ithaca: Cornell UP, 1983.

Fichte, Johann Gottlieb. *Fichtes Werke*. Ed. Immanuel Hermann Fichte. 11 vols. 1834–46. Berlin: Gruyter, 1971.

———. *Introductions to the Wissenschaftslehre and Other Writings (1797–1800)*. Ed. and trans. Daniel Breazeale. Indianapolis: Hackett, 1994.

———. *Science of Knowledge (Wissenschaftslehre) with the First and Second Introductions*. Ed. and trans. Peter Heath and John Lachs. New York: Meredith, 1970.

Fiesel, Eva. *Die Sprachphilosophie der deutschen Romantik*. Tübingen: Mohr, 1927.

Formigari, Lia. *Signs, Science and Politics: Philosophies of Language in Europe 1700–1830*. Trans. William Dodd. Amsterdam: Benjamins, 1993.

Funke, Otto. *Englische Sprachphilosophie im späteren 18. Jahrhundert*. Bern: Francke, 1934.

Furet, François. *Interpreting the French Revolution*. Trans. Elborg Forster. Cambridge: Cambridge UP, 1981.
Gaier, Ulrich. "Übertragen. Zu Hölderlins Sprachphilosophie." *Hölderlin-Jahrbuch* 29 (1994–95): 22–46.
Gall, Ulrich. *Philosophie bei Heinrich von Kleist. Untersuchungen zu Herkunft und Bestimmung des philosophischen Gehalts seiner Schriften.* 2nd rev. ed. Bonn: Bouvier, 1985.
Gasché, Rodolphe. *The Wild Card of Reading: On Paul de Man*. Cambridge: Harvard UP, 1998.
Genette, Gérard. *Fiction & Diction*. Trans. Catherine Porter. Ithaca: Cornell UP, 1993.
Gillespie, Gerald. "Kleist's Hypothesis of Affective Expression: Acting-out in Language." *Seminar* 17 (1981): 275–82.
Gipper, Helmut. "Sprachphilosophie in der Romantik." *Sprachphilosophie. Ein internationales Handbuch zeitgenössischer Forschung*. Ed. Marcelo Dascal, Dietfrid Gerhardus, Kuno Lorenz, and Georg Meggle. 1 vol. to date. Berlin: Gruyter, 1992–. 197–233.
———. "Wilhelm von Humboldt als Begründer moderner Sprachforschung." *Wirkendes Wort* 15 (1965): 1–19.
———. "Wilhelm von Humboldts Bedeutung für die moderne Sprachwissenschaft." *Die Brüder Humboldt heute*. Ed. Hans Hartman. Mannheim: Humboldt-Gesellschaft, 1968.
———, and Schmitter, Peter. *Sprachwissenschaft und Sprachphilosophie im Zeitalter der Romantik*. Tübingen: Narr, 1979.
Godwin, William. *Collected Novels and Memoirs of William Godwin* (= *CN*). Ed. Mark Philp. 8 vols. London: Pickering, 1992.
———. *Enquiry Concerning Political Justice and Its Influence on Morals and Happiness* (= *PJ*). Ed. F. E. L. Priestley. 3 vols. Toronto: U of Toronto P, 1946.
———. *Political and Philosophical Writings of William Godwin* (= *PPW*). Ed. Mark Philp. 7 vols. London: Pickering, 1993.
Goodson, A. C. "Coleridge on Language: A Poetic Paradigm." *Philological Quarterly* 62 (1983): 45–68.
———. *Verbal Imagination: Coleridge and the Language of Modern Criticism*. New York: Oxford UP, 1988.
Gorman, David. "The Use and Abuse of Speech-Act Theory in Criticism." *Poetics Today* 20 (1999): 93–119.
Grice, H. Paul. "Logic and Conversation." *Speech Acts*. Ed. Peter Cole and Jerry Morgan. Syntax and Semantics 3. New York: Academic, 1972. 41–58.
Guilhaumou, Jacques. *Sprache und Politik in der Französischen Revolution. Vom Ereignis zur Sprache des Volkes (1789 bis 1794)*. Trans. Kathrina Menke. Frankfurt: Suhrkamp, 1989.
Gustafson, Susan E. "'Die allmähliche Verfertigung der Gedanken beim Reden': The Linguistic Question in Kleist's *Amphitryon*." *Seminar* 25 (1989): 104–26.

Haberer, Brigitte. *Sprechen, Schweigen, Schauen. Rede und Blick in Hölderlins "Der Tod des Empedokles" und "Hyperion."* Bonn: Bouvier, 1991.
———. "Zwischen Sprachmagie und Schweigen. Metamorphosen des Sprechens in Hölderlins 'Hyperion oder Der Eremit in Griechenland.'" *Hölderlin-Jahrbuch* 26 (1988–89): 117–33.
Habermas, Jürgen. "Entgegnung." *Kommunikatives Handeln. Beiträge zu Jürgen Habermas' 'Theorie des kommunikativen Handelns.'* Ed. Axel Honneth and Hans Joas. Frankfurt: Suhrkamp, 1986. 327–405.
———. "A Reply." *Communicative Action: Essays on Jürgen Habermas's The Theory of Communicative Action.* Ed. Axel Honneth and Hans Joas. Trans. Jeremy Gaines and Doris L. Jones. N.p.: Polity, 1991. 214–64.
———. *Theorie des kommunikativen Handelns.* 2 vols. Frankfurt: Suhrkamp, 1981.
———. *The Theory of Communicative Action* (= *TCA*). Trans. Thomas McCarthy. 2 vols. Boston: Beacon, 1984.
———. "Vorbereitende Bemerkungen zu einer Theorie der kommunikativen Kompetenz." *Theorie der Gesellschaft oder Sozialtechnologie.* Frankfurt: Suhrkamp, 1971. 101–40.
———. "Was heißt Universalpragmatik?" *Sprachpragmatik und Philosophie.* Ed. Karl-Otto Apel. Frankfurt: Suhrkamp, 1976. 174–272.
———. "What Is Universal Pragmatics?" *Communication and the Evolution of Society.* Trans. Thomas McCarthy. Boston: Beacon, 1979. 1–68.
Hamann, Johann Georg. *Schriften zur Sprache.* Ed. Josef Simon. Frankfurt: Suhrkamp, 1967.
Hamlin, Cyrus. *Hermeneutics of Form: Romantic Poetics in Theory and Practice.* New Haven: Schwab, 1998.
———. "The Task of Interpretation: The Hermeneutics of Hölderlin's *Patmos.*" Unpublished ms.
Harding, Anthony John. *Coleridge and the Idea of Love: Aspects of Relationship in Coleridge's Thought and Writing.* London: Cambridge UP, 1974.
Harris, James. *Hermes, or a Philosophical Inquiry Concerning Universal Grammar.* 4th ed. 1786. New York: AMS, 1975. Vol. 1 of *Works by James Harris.* Ed. Karl D. Uitti. 3 vols.
Havens, Michael Kent. "Coleridge on the Evolution of Language." *Studies in Romanticism* 20 (1981): 163–83.
Hegel, Georg Wilhelm Friedrich. *Phenomenology of Spirit.* Trans. A. V. Miller. Oxford: Clarendon, 1977.
———. *Werke.* [Theorie-Werkausgabe.] Ed. Eva Moldenhauer and Karl Markus Michel. 21 vols. Frankfurt: Suhrkamp, 1969–79.
Heidegger, Martin. *Erläuterungen zu Hölderlins Dichtung.* Frankfurt: Klostermann, 1981. Vol. 4 of *Gesamtausgabe.* 1975–.
Heintel, Erich. "Einleitung des Herausgebers. Herder und die Sprache." Herder, *Sprachphilosophische Schriften* xv–lxvii.
———. "Sprachphilosophie." *Deutsche Philologie im Aufriss.* Ed. Wolfgang Stammler. 2nd ed. 3 vols. Berlin: Schmidt, 1966–69. 1: 563–620.

Henrich, Dieter. *Der Grund im Bewußtsein. Untersuchungen zu Hölderlins Denken (1794–1795).* Stuttgart: Klett-Cotta, 1992.
Herder, Johann Gottfried. *Essay on the Origin of Language* (= *EOL*). Trans. Alexander Gode. *On the Origin of Language.* New York: Ungar, 1966. 85–166.
―――. *Sprachphilosophische Schriften* (= *SS*). Ed. Erich Heintel. 2nd ed. Hamburg: Meiner, 1975.
Hobbes, Thomas. *Leviathan.* Ed. Richard Tuck. Cambridge: Cambridge UP, 1996.
Hofmann, Hasso. "Individuum und allgemeines Gesetz. Zur Dialektik in Kleists 'Penthesilea' und 'Prinz von Homburg.'" *Kleist-Jahrbuch* 1987: 137–63.
Hogle, Jerrold E. "The Texture of the Self in Godwin's *Things as They Are.*" *boundary 2* 7 (1979): 261–81.
Hölderlin, Friedrich. *Poems and Fragments.* Trans. Michael Hamburger. Cambridge: Cambridge UP, 1980.
―――. *Sämtliche Werke.* [Stuttgarter Ausgabe = *StA*.] Ed. Friedrich Beissner. 8 vols. Stuttgart: Kohlhammer, 1946–85.
Holz, Hans Heinz. *Macht und Ohnmacht der Sprache. Untersuchungen zum Sprachverständnis und Stil Heinrich von Kleists.* Frankfurt: Athenäum, 1962.
Hornbacher, Annette. *Die Blume des Mundes. Zu Hölderlins poetologisch-poetischem Sprachdenken.* Würzburg: Königshausen, 1995.
Humboldt, Wilhelm von. *Gesammelte Schriften* (= *GS*). Ed. Albert Leitzmann. 17 vols. 1903–36. Berlin: Gruyter, 1968.
―――. *On Language: The Diversity of Human Language-Structure and Its Influence on the Mental Development of Mankind* (= *OL*). Trans. Peter Heath. Cambridge: Cambridge UP, 1988.
―――. *Über die Sprache: Reden vor der Akademie* (= *ÜS*). Ed. Jürgen Trabant. Tübingen: Francke, 1994.
―――. *Wilhelm von Humboldts Briefe an Karl Gustav von Brinkmann.* Ed. Albert Leitzmann. Leipzig: Hiersemann, 1939.
―――, and Friedrich Schiller. *Der Briefwechsel zwischen Friedrich Schiller und Wilhelm von Humboldt.* 2 vols. Berlin: Aufbau, 1962.
Hume, David. *A Treatise of Human Nature.* Ed. L. A. Selby-Bigge. 2nd ed. Oxford: Clarendon, 1978.
Iser, Wolfgang. *The Fictive and the Imaginary: Charting Literary Anthropology.* Baltimore: Johns Hopkins UP, 1993.
Isermann, Michael. *Die Sprachtheorie im Werk von Thomas Hobbes.* Münster: Nodus, 1991.
Itoda, Soichiro. "Die Funktion des Paradoxons in Heinrich von Kleists Aufsatz 'Über die allmähliche Verfertigung der Gedanken beim Reden.'" *Kleist-Jahrbuch* 1991: 218–28.
Jackson, H. J. "Coleridge, Etymology and Etymologic." *Journal of the History of Ideas* 44 (1983): 75–88.

Jacobs, Carol. *Uncontainable Romanticism: Shelley, Brontë, Kleist.* Baltimore: Johns Hopkins UP, 1989.
Jakobson, Roman, and Grete Lübbe-Grothues. "Ein Blick auf *Die Aussicht* von Hölderlin." *Hölderlin. Klee. Brecht. Zur Wortkunst dreier Gedichte.* Ed. Elmar Holenstein. Frankfurt: Suhrkamp, 1976. 27–96.
Janke, Wolfgang. "Enttönter Gesang—Sprache und Wahrheit in den 'Fichte-Studien' des Novalis." *Erneuerung der Transzendentalphilosophie im Anschluß an Kant und Fichte. Reinhard Lauth zum 60. Geburtstag.* Ed. Klaus Hammacher and Albert Mues. Stuttgart: Frommann-Holzboog, 1979. 168–203.
Kant, Immanuel. "An Answer to the Question: What Is Enlightenment?" *Practical Philosophy.* Trans. and ed. Mary J. Gregor. Cambridge: Cambridge UP, 1996. 11–22.
———. *Critique of Pure Reason* (= *CPR*). Trans. Norman Kemp Smith. New York: St. Martin's, 1965.
———. "Die falsche Spitzfindigkeit der vier syllogistischen Figuren erwiesen." *Kants Gesammelte Schriften.* Ed. Königlich Preußische Akademie der Wissenschaften. Berlin: Reimer, 1910–. 2: 45–61.
———. "The False Subtlety of the Four Syllogistic Figures." *Theoretical Philosophy, 1755–1770.* Trans. and ed. David Walford and Ralf Meerbote. Cambridge: Cambridge UP, 1992. 85–105.
———. *Kritik der reinen Vernunft* (= *KrV*). Ed. Wilhelm Weischedel. 2 vols. Frankfurt: Suhrkamp, 1996.
Kirchner, Werner. "Hölderlins Entwurf 'Die Völker schwiegen, schlummerten.'" *Hölderlin-Jahrbuch* 12 (1961–62): 42–67.
———. "Hölderlins Patmos-Hymne: Dem Landgrafen von Homburg überreichte Handschrift." *Hölderlin. Aufsätze zu seiner Homburger Zeit.* Ed. Alfred Kelletat. Göttingen: Vandenhoeck, 1967. 57–68.
Klancher, Jon P. *The Making of English Reading Audiences, 1790–1832.* Madison: U of Wisconsin P, 1987.
Kleist, Heinrich von. *Five Plays.* Trans. Martin Greenberg. New Haven: Yale UP, 1988.
———. *The Marquise of O— and Other Stories* (= *Stories*). Trans. David Luke and Nigel Reeves. Harmondsworth: Penguin, 1978.
———. *Sämtliche Werke und Briefe* (= *SWB*). Ed. Helmut Sembdner. 7th rev. ed. 2 vols. Munich: Hanser, 1984.
Knapp, Steven, and Walter Benn Michaels. "Against Theory." *Critical Inquiry* 8 (1982): 723–42.
Kommerell, Max. *Geist und Buchstabe der Dichtung. Goethe—Kleist—Hölderlin.* 1940. Frankfurt: Klostermann, 1953.
Kroeber, Karl. "Coleridge's 'Fears': Problems in Patriotic Poetry." *Clio* 7 (1978): 359–73.
Kurz, Gerhard. "Hölderlins poetische Sprache." *Hölderlin-Jahrbuch* 23 (1982–83): 34–53.
Lacoue-Labarthe, Philippe, and Jean-Luc Nancy. *The Literary Absolute:*

The Theory of Literature in German Romanticism. Trans. Philip Barnard and Cheryl Lester. State U of New York P, 1988.

Land, Stephen K. *From Signs to Propositions: The Concept of Form in Eighteenth-Century Semantic Theory*. London: Longman, 1974.

———. *The Philosophy of Language in Britain: Major Theories from Hobbes to Thomas Reid*. New York: AMS, 1986.

Larkin, Peter. "'Fears in Solitude': Reading (from) the Dell." *The Wordsworth Circle* 22 (1991): 11–14.

Liebrucks, Bruno. *Sprache*. "Wilhelm von Humboldt." Frankfurt: Akademische Verlagsgesellschaft, 1965. Vol. 2 of *Sprache und Bewußtsein*. 7 vols. 1964–79.

Liu, Alan. "Wordsworth and Subversion, 1793–1804: Trying Cultural Criticism." *Yale Journal of Criticism* 2.2 (1989): 55–100.

Lyotard, Jean-François. *The Differend: Phrases in Dispute*. Trans. Georges Van Den Abbeele. Minneapolis: U of Minnesota P, 1988.

Macovski, Michael. *Dialogue and Literature: Apostrophe, Auditors, and the Collapse of Romantic Discourse*. New York: Oxford UP, 1994.

Magnuson, Paul. "The Politics of 'Frost at Midnight.'" *The Wordsworth Circle* 22 (1991): 3–11.

———. "The Shaping of 'Fears in Solitude.'" *Coleridge's Theory of Imagination Today*. Ed. Christine Gallant. New York: AMS, 1989. 197–210.

Markis, Dimitrios. "Das Problem der Sprache bei Kant." *Dimensionen der Sprache in der Philosophie des Deutschen Idealismus*. Ed. Brigitte Scheer and Günter Wohlfahrt. Würzburg: Königshausen, 1982. 110–54.

McHoul, Alec. "Kant's Pragmatics." *Journal of Pragmatics* 25 (1996): 587–92.

McKusick, James C. *Coleridge's Philosophy of Language*. New Haven: Yale UP, 1986.

McLean, William Scott. "Private Song and the Public Sphere: Some Remarks on the Development of Hölderlin's Later Poetry." *Goethezeit. Studien zur Erkenntnis und Rezeption Goethes und seiner Zeitgenossen*. Ed. Gerhart Hoffmeister. Bern: Francke, 1981. 265–80.

Meiner, Johann Werner. *Versuch einer an der menschlichen Sprache abgebildeten Vernunftlehre oder philosophische und allgemeine Sprachlehre*. 1781. Stuttgart: Frommann, 1971.

Menninghaus, Winfried. *Walter Benjamins Theorie der Sprachmagie*. Frankfurt: Suhrkamp, 1980.

Menze, Clemens. *Wilhelm von Humboldts Lehre und Bild vom Menschen*. Ratingen: Henn, 1965.

Meschonnic, Henri. "Le langage chez Habermas, ou: Critique, encore un effort." *Critique de la théorie critique. Langage et histoire*. Ed. Henri Meschonnic. Saint-Denis: Presses Universitaires de Vincennes, 1985. 153–99.

Miller, Jacqueline T. "The Imperfect Tale: Articulation, Rhetoric, and Self in *Caleb Williams*." *Criticism* 20 (1978): 366–82.

Miller, J. Hillis. *Topographies*. Stanford: Stanford UP, 1995.

Morris, Charles W. *Foundations of the Theory of Signs.* Chicago: U of Chicago P, 1938.

Morton, Michael. *Herder and the Poetics of Thought: Unity and Diversity in On Diligence in Several Learned Languages.* University Park: Pennsylvania State UP, 1989.

Müller-Sievers, Helmut. *Epigenesis: Naturphilosophie im Sprachdenken Wilhelm von Humboldts.* Paderborn: Schöningh, 1993.

Müller-Vollmer, Kurt. "From Poetics to Linguistics: Wilhelm von Humboldt and the Romantic Idea of Language." *Le Groupe de Coppet: Actes et documents du deuxième Colloque de Coppet, 10–13 juillet 1974.* Ed. Simone Balayé and Jean-Daniel Candaux. Société des Etudes Staëliennes, 1977. 195–215.

———. "Thinking and Speaking: Herder, Humboldt and Saussurean Semiotics." *Comparative Criticism* 1989: 193–214.

Myers, Victoria. "The Other Fraud: Coleridge's *The Plot Discovered* and the Rhetoric of Political Discourse." *Romanticism, Radicalism, and the Press.* Ed. Stephen C. Behrendt. Detroit: Wayne State UP, 1997. 65–82.

Nägele, Rainer. *Text, Geschichte und Subjetivität in Hölderlins Dichtung. "Uneßbarer Schrift gleich."* Stuttgart: Metzlersche Verlagsbuchhandlung, 1985.

Nerlich, Brigitte. "The 1930s—at the Birth of a Pragmatic Conception of Language." *Historiographia Linguistica* 22 (1995): 311–34.

———. "Einführung in die Geschichte der Pragmatik." *Zeitschrift für Semiotik* 18 (1996): 413–21.

———. "Language and Action: German Approaches to Pragmatics in the 19th and Early 20th Centuries." *History of Linguistics 1993.* Ed. Kurt R. Jankowsky. Amsterdam: Benjamins, 1995. 299–309.

———. "The Notion of 'Speech Act' in German Linguistics, Philosophy and Psychology between 1830 and 1970." Fava 1–20.

———. "Sprachliche Darstellung als Prozeß. Die Pragmatisierung eines Begriffs von Kant bis Bühler." *Zeitschrift für Semiotik* 18 (1996): 423–40.

Nerlich, Brigitte, and David D. Clarke. "Language, Action and Context: Linguistic Pragmatics in Europe and America (1800–1950)." *Journal of Pragmatics* 22 (1994): 439–63.

———. *Language, Action, and Context: The Early History of Pragmatics in Europe and America, 1780–1930.* Amsterdam: Benjamins, 1996.

Neumann, Werner. "Sprachhandlungsauffassungen an der Wende vom 18. zum 19. Jahrhundert." *Sprachtheorie. Der Sprachbegriff in Wissenschaft und Alltag.* Ed. Rainer Wimmer. Düsseldorf: Schwann, 1987. 121–42.

———. "Über die Aktualität von Humboldts Sprachauffassung." *Erbe, Vermächtnis und Verpflichtung. Zur sprachwissenschaftlichen Forschung in der Geschichte der AdW der DDR.* Ed. J. Schildt. Berlin: Akademie, 1977. 101–18.

Novalis [Friedrich von Hardenberg]. *Schriften. Die Werke Friedrich von Hardenbergs.* Ed. Paul Kluckhohn and Richard Samuel. 2nd rev. ed. 5 vols. Stuttgart: Kohlhammer, 1960–88.

Nüsse, Heinrich. *Die Sprachtheorie Friedrich Schlegels*. Heidelberg: Winter, 1962.
O'Brien, William Arctander. *Novalis: Signs of Revolution*. Durham: Duke UP, 1995.
Ozouf, Mona. *Festivals and the French Revolution*. Trans. Alan Sheridan. Cambridge: Harvard UP, 1988.
Paine, Thomas. *The Complete Writings of Thomas Paine*. Ed. Philip S. Foner. 2 vols. New York: Citadel, 1945.
Parker, Andrew, and Eve Kosofsky Sedgwick, eds. *Performativity and Performance*. New York: Routledge, 1995.
Parker, Reeve. *Coleridge's Meditative Art*. Ithaca: Cornell UP, 1975.
Perkins, Mary Anne. "Coleridge, Language and History." *Coleridge's Visionary Languages: Essays in Honour of J. B. Beer*. Ed. Tim Fulford and Morton D. Paley. Cambridge: Brewer, 1993. 181–94.
———. *Coleridge's Philosophy: The Logos as Unifying Principle*. Oxford: Clarendon, 1994.
Petrey, Sandy. *Realism and Revolution: Balzac, Stendhal, Zola, and the Performances of History*. Ithaca: Cornell UP, 1988.
Pfau, Thomas. "Immediacy and Dissolution: Notes on the Languages of Moral Agency and Critical Discourse." *Intersections: Nineteenth-Century Philosophy and Contemporary Theory*. Ed. Tilottama Rajan and David L. Clark. Albany: State U of New York P, 1995. 222–42.
Pfefferkorn, Kristin. *Novalis: A Romantic's Theory of Language and Poetry*. New Haven: Yale UP, 1988.
Pratt, Mary Louise. "Ideology and Speech-Act Theory." *Poetics Today* 7 (1986): 59–72.
Prickett, Stephen. "Radicalism and Linguistic Theory: Horne Tooke on Samuel Pegge." *Yearbook of English Studies* 19 (1989): 1–17.
Rajan, Tilottama. *The Supplement of Reading: Figures of Understanding in Romantic Theory and Practice*. Ithaca: Cornell UP, 1990.
Reid, Thomas. *Philosophical Works*. Ed. William Hamilton. 2 vols. 1897. Hildesheim: Olms, 1967.
Ricoeur, Paul. *The Conflict of Interpretations: Essays in Hermeneutics*. Ed. Don Ihde. Evanston: Northwestern UP, 1974.
Rosaldo, Michelle Z. "The Things We Do with Words: Ilongot Speech Acts and Speech Act Theory in Philosophy." *Language in Society* 11 (1982): 203–37.
Rousseau, Jean-Jacques. *Discourse on Political Economy and The Social Contract*. Trans. Christopher Betts. Oxford: Oxford UP, 1994.
Ruoff, Gene W. *Wordsworth and Coleridge: The Making of the Major Lyrics, 1802–1804*. New Brunswick: Rutgers UP, 1989.
Ryan, Lawrence. *Hölderlins Hyperion. Exzentrische Bahn und Dichterberuf*. Stuttgart: Metzler, 1965.
Sandor, Andras. "Signification, Meaning, and the Text Level of Language." *Indogermanische Forschungen* 94 (1989): 45–66.
Scarry, Elaine. "Die Kriegserklärung: Sprechakt, Repräsentation und mate-

rielle Welt." Trans. Jürgen Blasius. *Was heißt 'Darstellen'?* Ed. Christiaan L. Hart Nibbrig. Frankfurt: Suhrkamp, 1994. 268–339.

Scharf, Hans-Werner. "Chomskys Humboldt-Interpretation. Ein Beitrag zur Diskontinuität der Sprachtheorie in der Geschichte der neueren Linguistik." Diss. Düsseldorf, 1977.

———. "Das Verfahren der Sprache. Ein Nachtrag zu Chomskys Humboldt-Reklamation." *History of Semiotics.* Ed. Achim Eschbach and Jürgen Trabant. Amsterdam: Benjamins, 1983. 205–49.

Schelling, Friedrich Wilhelm Joseph. *Schellings Werke.* Ed. Manfred Schröter. 6 vols. 1927. Munich: Beck, 1958–59.

Schlegel, August Wilhelm. *Vorlesungen über Ästhetik I.* Ed. Ernst Behler. Paderborn: Schöningh, 1989. Vol. 1 of *Kritische Ausgabe der Vorlesungen.* Ed. Ernst Behler and Frank Jolles. 1 vol. to date.

Schlegel, Friedrich. *Kritische Friedrich-Schlegel-Ausgabe* (= *KFSA*). Ed. Ernst Behler with Jean-Jacques Anstett, and Hans Eichner. 27 vols. to date. Munich: Schöningh, 1958–.

Schleiermacher, F. D. E. *Hermeneutik und Kritik.* Ed. Manfred Frank. Frankfurt: Suhrkamp, 1977.

Schlieben-Lange, Brigitte. "Elemente einer pragmatischen Sprachtheorie in den Grammaires générales um 1800." *Zeitschrift für Literaturwissenschaft und Linguistik (LiLi)* 19 (1988): 76–93.

———. "Die Französische Revolution und die Sprache." *Zeitschrift für Literaturwissenschaft und Linguistik (LiLi)* 11 (1981): 90–123.

———, et al., eds. *Europäische Sprachwissenschaft um 1800. Methodologische und historiographische Beiträge zum Umkreis der "idéologie."* 4 vols. Münster: Nodus, 1989–94.

Schuhmann, Karl, and Barry Smith. "Elements of Speech Act Theory in the Work of Thomas Reid." *History of Philosophy Quarterly* 7 (1990): 47–66.

Searle, John R. *Expression and Meaning: Studies in the Theory of Speech Acts.* Cambridge: Cambridge UP, 1979.

———. *Intentionality: An Essay in the Philosophy of Mind.* Cambridge: Cambridge UP, 1983.

———. *Speech Acts: An Essay in the Philosophy of Language.* Cambridge: Cambridge UP, 1969.

———. "A Taxonomy of Illocutionary Acts." Searle, *Expression and Meaning* 1–29.

Seeba, Hinrich C. "Der Sündenfall des Verdachts. Identitätskrise und Sprachskepsis in Kleists 'Familie Schroffenstein.'" *Kleists Aktualität. Neue Aufsätze und Essays 1966–1978.* Ed. Walter Müller-Seidel. Darmstadt: Wissenschaftliche Buchgesellschaft, 1981. 104–50.

Shaffer, E. S. *"Kubla Khan" and* The Fall of Jerusalem: *The Mythological School in Biblical Criticism and Secular Literature 1770–1880.* Cambridge: Cambridge UP, 1975.

Sheiber, Andrew J. "Falkland's Story: *Caleb Williams'* Other Voice." *Studies in the Novel* 17 (1985): 255–66.

Silvig, Helen. "The Oath: 1." *Yale Law Journal* 68 (1959): 1329–90.

Simms, Karl N. "Caleb Williams' Godwin: Things as They Are Written." *Studies in Romanticism* 26 (1987): 343-63.
Slagle, Uhlan V. "The Kantian Influence on Humboldt's Linguistic Thought." *Historiographia Linguistica* 1 (1974): 341-50.
Slakta, Denis. "L'acte de demander dans les Cahiers de doléances." *Langue française* 9 (1971): 58-73.
Smith, John H. "Dialogic Midwifery in Kleist's *Marquise von O* and the Hermeneutics of Telling the Untold in Kant and Plato." *PMLA* 100 (1985): 203-19.
Smith, Olivia. *The Politics of Language 1791-1819*. Oxford: Clarendon, 1984.
Spälti, Jakob. *Interpretationen zu Heinrich von Kleists Verhältnis zur Sprache*. Bern: Lang, 1975.
Spranger, Eduard. "W. v. Humboldt und Kant." *Kant-Studien* 13 (1908): 57-129.
Stammen, Theo. "Kleist als politischer Denker." *Freiburger Universitätsblätter* 25.91 (1986): 59-74.
Stephens, Anthony. *Heinrich von Kleist: The Dramas and Stories*. Oxford: Berg, 1994.
Stetter, Christian. "'Über Denken und Sprechen': Wilhelm von Humboldt zwischen Fichte und Herder." *Wilhelm von Humboldts Sprachdenken. Symposion zum 150. Todestag, Düsseldorf, 28.-30.6.1985*. Ed. Hans-Werner Scharf. Essen: Hobbing, 1989. 25-46.
Stewart, Dugald. *Outlines of Moral Philosophy*. Edinburgh: Creech, 1793.
Stierle, Karlheinz. "Die Friedensfeier. Sprache und Fest im revolutionären und nachrevolutionären Frankreich und bei Hölderlin." *Das Fest*. Ed. Walter Haug and Reiner Warning. Munich: Fink, 1989. 481-525.
Streitberg, W. "Kant und die Sprachwissenschaft. Eine historische Skizze." *Indogermanische Forschungen* 26 (1909): 382-422.
Surber, Jere Paul. *Language and German Idealism: Fichte's Linguistic Philosophy*. Atlantic Highlands NJ: Humanities, 1996.
Thomas, Keith G. "Coleridge, Wordsworth and the New Historicism: 'Chamouny; The Hour before Sun-Rise. A Hymn' and Book 6 of *The Prelude*." *Studies in Romanticism* 33 (1994): 81-117.
Trabant, Jürgen. *Apeliotes, oder Der Sinn der Sprache. Wilhelm von Humboldts Sprach-Bild*. Munich: Fink, 1986.
―――. "Gedächtnis und Schrift: Zu Humboldts Grammatologie." *KODIKAS/CODE* 9 (1986): 293-315.
―――. "Habermas liest Humboldt." *Deutsche Zeitschrift für Philosophie* 41 (1993): 639-51.
―――. *Traditionen Humboldts*. Frankfurt: Suhrkamp, 1990.
Turner, John. "Burke, Paine, and the Nature of Language." *Yearbook of English Studies* 19 (1989): 36-53.
Ulman, H. Lewis. *Things, Thoughts, Words, and Actions: The Problem of Language in Late Eighteenth-Century British Rhetorical Theory*. Carbondale: Southern Illinois UP, 1994.

Underwood, Ted. "Productivism and the Vogue for 'Energy' in Late Eighteenth-Century Britain." *Studies in Romanticism* 34 (1995): 103-25.
Uphaus, Robert W. "*Caleb Williams*: Godwin's Epoch of Mind." *Studies in the Novel* 9 (1977): 279-96.
Wagner, Johann Jacob. *Von der Natur der Dinge*. 1803. Brussels: n.p., 1968.
Wallace, C. Miles. "Coleridge's Theory of Language." *Philological Quarterly* 59 (1980): 338-52.
Warnock, G. J. *J. L. Austin*. London: Routledge, 1989.
Warren, Leland E. "*Caleb Williams* and the 'Fall' into Writing." *Mosaic* 20 (1987): 57-69.
Welke, Klaus, ed. *Sprache—Bewußtsein—Tätigkeit. Zur Sprachkonzeption Wilhelm von Humboldts*. Berlin: Akademie, 1986.
Wheeler, Kathleen. "Coleridge's Theory of Imagination: A Hegelian Solution to Kant?" *The Interpretation of Belief: Coleridge, Schleiermacher and Romanticism*. Ed. David Jasper. New York: St. Martin's, 1986. 16-40.
Wild-Schedlbauer, Roswitha. "Reflexionen über A. F. Bernhardis Leben und sprachwissenschaftliches Werk." *Neuere Forschungen zur Wortbildung und Historiographie der Linguistik. Festgabe für Herbert E. Brekle zum 50. Geburtstag*. Ed. Brigitte Asbach-Schnitker and Johannes Roggenhofer. Tübingen: Narr, 1987. 367-85.
Wittgenstein, Ludwig. *Philosophical Investigations*. Trans. G. E. Anscombe. 2nd ed. Oxford: Blackwell, 1958.
Wordsworth, William. *The Prose Works of William Wordsworth*. Ed. Alexander B. Grosart. 3 vols. London: Moxon, 1876.
Zimmermann, Klaus. "Sprachliche Handlungen in den Cahiers de doléances von 1789." *Zeitschrift für Literaturwissenschaft und Linguistik (LiLi)* 11 (1981): 52-69.
Ziolkowski, Theodore. *German Romanticism and Its Institutions*. Princeton: Princeton UP, 1990.
Žižek, Slavoj. *Enjoy Your Symptom!: Jacques Lacan in Hollywood and Out*. New York: Routledge, 1992.
Zuberbühler, Rolf. *Die Sprache des Herzens. Hölderlins Widmungsdichtung*. Göttingen: Vandenhoeck, 1982.

Index

In this index an "f" after a number indicates a separate reference on the next page, and an "ff" indicates separate references on the next two pages. A continuous discussion over two or more pages is indicated by a span of page numbers, e.g., "57–59." *Passim* is used for a cluster of references in close but not consecutive sequence.

Aarsleff, Hans, 4, 23n
accusations, 284, 298–310 *passim*
Adams, John Quincy, 52
agency, 11–14, 40, 59, 77, 84, 131, 167, 214, 257–62 *passim*, 270; of language, 20–21, 162, 164–67, 181n, 330
American Revolution, 54
analytic philosophy, 2, 19, 33, 125, 142, 257
Apel, Karl-Otto, 15, 68
apostrophe, 172f, 201, 216f, 234, 236f
apperception, 74–75, 176. *See also* perception; understanding
Aristotle, xii, 33–34, 39, 42–43, 47, 81–82, 109
Aspetsberger, Friedbert, 200
assertions, 43, 48, 72–73, 126, 153–55, 158, 160, 178, 185. *See also* statements
Ast, Friedrich, 139
Austin, J. L., xi–xii, 2, 10–15, 19, 28n, 31, 43, 46, 58–59, 77, 96, 99, 125, 188, 198, 214, 257, 272, 293, 308; relation to Reid, 33–39 *passim*, 67; relation to Kant, 69–75 *passim*; relation to Coleridge, 158, 176, 184–85. *See also* ordinary-language philosophy; speech-act theory
authority and authorization, 18, 20, 29–30, 33, 43–51 *passim*, 55–66 *passim*, 82n, 140f, 145, 155, 167, 180, 312, 330; in Hölderlin's work, 188–89, 196–98, 203, 208, 211–14; in Kleist's work, 240–46 *passim*, 253, 264–88 *passim*

Bacon, Francis, 78
Bakhtin, Mikhail, 19, 136n, 179n

Balfour, Ian, 299n
baptism, 196–202 *passim*, 247, 251
Barrell, John, 5
Barthes, Roland, 133
Baum, Richard, 126n
Beaumont, George, 170
Behler, Constantin, 106
Behler, Ernst, 4
being, xiii, 83–85, 96–99, 104, 110, 118, 121, 175, 187–89, 216f; and language, 8, 79–81, 91–95, 159–68 *passim*, 231f, 262
Bentham, Jeremy, xi, 1, 5, 18, 24, 32, 41–51, 63, 64n, 67, 242, 278, 291, 312, 324, 329f; on law, 43–46, 54, 58, 253, 288; theory of fictions, xiii, 19, 42f, 47–51, 150, 298, 313, 330; critique of oaths, 46n, 152, 285–86
Benveniste, Emile, xii, 14, 29n, 125–33 *passim*, 188–89
Berkeley, George, 39f, 182n
Berlin Academy, 106n, 120, 142f
Bernhardi, August Ferdinand, xiii, 1f, 40, 48, 83, 87–96, 100, 104, 108, 117f, 122, 127, 143, 162, 175, 218, 232, 242, 262
Bible, 5, 60–61, 65, 127, 205, 215, 234–38 *passim*; Coleridge's view of, 145, 151–72 *passim*, 178, 185–86; Book of Genesis, 65, 85, 147, 164, 167, 171, 190
Bierwisch, Manfred, 106n
Binder, Wolfgang, 226–27
Blake, William, 23, 54, 57, 109n, 199
Blakemore, Steven, 28n, 52, 150n
blasphemy, 147, 149, 203, 207, 210, 283f
body (and language), 242–43, 249, 252,

255, 263–65, 267–68, 278, 281–84, 288, 295, 311, 316, 322, 331
Böhler, Michael, 109n
Bopp, Franz, 4
Borsche, Tilman, 135
Boulton, James, 28n
Bourdieu, Pierre, xii, 18, 214, 312
Breitinger, Johann Jacob, 82n
Brentano, Franz, 6, 115
Brun, Friederike, 169–72
Büber, Martin, 136n
Burke, Edmund, xiii, 24, 28n, 50–67 *passim*, 109n, 148, 150–51
Burke, Kenneth, 166
Burkhardt, Armin, 6, 129n, 136n
Butler, Judith, xi, 20–21

Cahiers de Doléances, 27
censorship, 23, 29, 291
charters, 54–55, 62. See also Magna Carta
Chomsky, Noam, 106
Christmann, Hans Helmut, 28n
Clarke, David D., 6f, 14f, 23n, 34n, 69, 100n, 102, 150n
Clifford, Gay, 299n
cognition, 100–104, 108, 329–32; and language, 3f, 7f, 16f, 20f; in German idealism, 68, 75–89 *passim*, 95; Humboldt's analysis of, 114, 126, 128, 136–37, 141–42; Coleridge's analysis of, 144, 146, 162–65, 169, 173, 176, 180–81
Coleridge, George, 155
Coleridge, Samuel Taylor, xiii–xiv, 1–8 *passim*, 23, 71ff, 75, 88, 96f, 99, 121f, 125, 144–86, 190f, 216, 240, 254, 291, 329–31; *Aids to Reflection*, 145, 162, 166–67, 185; *Biographia Literaria*, 176–77; "Destiny of Nations," 145–46; "Fears in Solitude," xiii, 147n, 149, 151–55, 157, 180, 331; "France: An Ode," 147–51, 155, 157, 180; "Frost at Midnight," xiii, 147n, 180–84, 331; "Hymn before Sun-Rise," xiii, 169–73, 331; *Logic*, 72, 163, 166, 173–85 *passim*; *Statesman's Manual*, 155–61, 165–66, 185
Colman, George, 310
commands, 33ff, 42–47 *passim*, 63, 66, 171, 197, 200, 209, 220, 222, 264f, 283, 297; relation to laws, 43–44, 50, 288

commissives, 11, 257, 296, 307. See also promises
Common Law, 33, 49f. See also law
Common Sense philosophers, 33–40 *passim*, 329. See also Reid, Thomas
communication, 4, 7–8, 11, 14–16, 20, 35–40 *passim*, 76–78, 83–89 *passim*, 95, 100n, 102–3, 108, 242, 263, 329–31; Humboldt's analysis of, 124, 135–37, 141–42; in Coleridge's work, 162–69 *passim*, 179f; in Hölderlin's work, 191, 200, 218, 220, 226, 230, 233, 238; in Godwin's work, 291, 299, 303, 308, 312, 314f, 326
Condillac, Étienne Bonnot de, 28, 87
confession, 284, 302, 307–10, 315, 319, 321, 325–28, 331
constatives, 10, 18f, 34, 38, 43, 52f, 55, 61, 72, 84n, 99, 140, 155–61 *passim*, 167f, 170, 176, 184–86, 189, 232, 234, 260, 265; in Godwin's work, 291f, 297, 299, 308–20 *passim*, 327. See also statements; truth
constitutions, xiii, 5, 17, 23f, 26f, 32, 41–45 *passim*, 51–66, 150, 157, 167, 254, 295–97, 302, 329
Continental Philosophy, xiii, 14, 67, 134. See also *individual philosophers by name*
contracts, xiii, 23f, 29–39 *passim*, 59–67 *passim*, 243, 245, 253, 277, 289–97 *passim*, 313–23 *passim*, 329. See also social contract
copula (verb), 75, 81–83, 90, 99, 101, 121, 124, 128, 159–60, 176. See also verb-substantive
covenant, 29–30, 32, 64–67, 245
Crosby, John F., 6
Culler, Jonathan, 173

Darstellung, 16, 89f, 93, 95, 102
De Man, Paul, 17, 36–37, 64n, 84n, 134–35, 140f, 188, 242, 251, 270, 293
De Quincey, Thomas, 169
declarations, xiv, 17–18, 25, 27, 32, 45, 51–67 *passim*, 140–41, 150, 185, 199, 202, 242f, 247, 252f, 258, 262, 272–75, 283, 291, 297, 304f, 329, 331; Declaration of Independence (U.S.), 17, 51, 54, 147; Declaration of Rights (1689), 32, 54–55, 58, 65f, 295; Declaration of the

Rights of Man and Citizen (1789, 1791), 18, 49, 51–58 *passim*, 63f, 147, 278–79, 296; as illocutionary act (Searle), 11, 159, 188f, 197, 200, 205, 211, 231–32, 296, 326
deconstruction, 17, 20, 34, 36–37, 64n, 115–16, 293, 310n. *See also* Derrida, Jacques
Degrois, Denise, 179n
deictics, 15, 113, 127f, 153–54, 180, 187–88, 198, 216, 218, 233, 236
Derrida, Jacques, 16–18, 20, 36f, 46, 55–56, 106, 107n, 116, 140–41, 242, 272–73, 312, 327
Descartes, René, 12, 39, 106n, 167
dialogism, 19, 21, 96, 102
dialogue, xi–xiv, 7f, 14, 40, 81, 127, 326, 329–31; related to cognition, 8, 20, 40, 103, 329; Humboldt's views on, 108, 114, 129, 135–39, 142, 144; Coleridge's views on, 146, 164, 170, 173, 179–83; in Hölderlin's work, 191–202 *passim*, 212–39 *passim*; in Kleist's work, 241–42, 256–57, 263, 266
Di Cesare, Donatella, 109n

Edwards, Gavin, 299n, 311–12
empiricism, 12, 35, 39f, 67f, 329
energeia, xii, 106n, 108–10, 175
Enlightenment, 26, 28n, 32, 60, 76, 145, 167, 245, 251
epistemology, 6, 21, 68, 70, 77, 80n, 90–97 *passim*, 108, 177, 184, 224, 227, 243, 329; Kantian, 3, 70, 76, 108, 133, 139, 227, 241, 331
Essick, Robert N., 150–51
Esterhammer, Angela, 57n, 159n
etymological linguistics, 4, 29, 48, 162, 166, 168, 174, 181, 182n. *See also* Tooke, John Horne
Everest, Kelvin, 299n
excommunication, 45, 141, 191, 210–12, 248f, 273

"fabulous retroactivity," 16–18, 21, 140–41. *See also* Derrida, Jacques
Fava, Elisabetta, 6
Felman, Shoshana, 140, 242, 293
festivals, 25f, 196, 225–30, 232, 250
Feuerbach, Ludwig Andreas, 136n
Fichte, Johann Gottlieb, xiii, 1f, 9, 68, 73, 83–104 *passim*, 118, 128, 133, 135, 140, 143, 175, 179, 205–6, 242, 254, 285
fiction, xiv, 73, 177, 226, 298, 313, 319, 324–31 *passim*
Fiesel, Eva, 184n
Foucault, Michel, 20
Frege, Gottlob, 2, 19, 93
French Revolution, xiii, 3, 6, 40, 51ff, 54, 62–63, 67, 81, 148–51, 157, 190, 226–28, 285, 296, 329; and linguistic pragmatics, 24–29, 52, 56, 264, 266
Funke, Otto, 23n
Furet, François, 24

Gadamer, Hans-Georg, 106
Gasché, Rodolphe, 84n
Genette, Gérard, 326
George III, 57
Gillespie, Gerald, 263n
Gipper, Helmut, 88n, 106n
Godwin, William, xi, xiv, 1, 23, 109n, 144, 150, 152, 162, 242, 263, 270, 289–329, 331; *Caleb Williams*, xiv, 289, 297–313, 318ff, 325ff; *Cloudesley*, 17, 297, 318, 320–26; *Deloraine*, 297, 301–2, 313–21 *passim*, 327–28; *Enquirer*, 263, 300; *Fleetwood*, 297, 307n, 310–16 *passim*, 327; *Italian Letters*, 289–90, 298; *Mandeville*, 327; *Political Justice*, 152, 289–300, 303–16 *passim*, 328; *St. Leon*, 297, 318–20, 326–27; *Thoughts on Man*, 263, 313
Goethe, Johann Wolfgang von, 111f, 143
Goodson, A. C., 162n, 181n
Göriz, Carl August, 28n
government, 29f, 51–55, 59–60, 62–66, 149, 251n; Bentham's views on, 42, 49–51, 58
Grice, H. Paul, 41
Grimm, Jacob, 4
Guilhaumou, Jacques, 26–28
Gustafson, Susan E., 263n

Haberer, Brigitte, 192n, 193n, 194–95, 200, 204n
Habermas, Jürgen, xii, 13–15, 19, 26, 68, 107–8, 207, 220
Hamann, Johann Georg, 69, 76, 87, 227, 329
Hamlin, Cyrus, 202n, 236n

Harris, James, 43, 109
Hegel, Georg Wilhelm Friedrich, 123–24, 133–35, 227
Heidegger, Martin, 2, 136n, 159, 160n, 187–88, 227
Heintel, Erich, 69
Henrich, Dieter, 206n
Herder, Johann Gottfried, xiii, 5, 8, 17, 40, 48, 69, 76–83, 86f, 92, 96, 100, 104, 108–17 *passim*, 143, 174n, 179, 191, 227, 262f, 329f
Hermann, J. G. J., 175
hermeneutics, 17, 68, 87, 106f, 127, 139, 160, 227, 238
Hessen-Homburg, Friedrich Ludwig, Landgrave of, 234, 237f
Heyne, Christian Gottlob, 144
historical-comparative linguistics, 4f, 102, 143
Hobbes, Thomas, 24, 29–30, 64, 245, 292
Hofmann, Hasso, 251n, 253n
Hogle, Jerrold E., 298n
Hölderlin, Friedrich, xi, xiv, 84, 141, 187–240, 242, 330f; early poems, 218–20, 233–34; "Friedensfeier," xiv, 226–33, 331; "Germanien," xiv, 221–25, 233; *Hyperion*, xiv, 191–203, 211, 217–20, 222, 226, 239; "Patmos," xiv, 234–40; *Tod des Empedokles*, xiv, 17, 191, 203–17, 222, 239
Holz, Hans Heinz, 263n
Humboldt, Wilhelm von, xi, xiii, 1, 4f, 14f, 17f, 48, 68f, 87, 89n, 96–145 *passim*, 164, 169, 175f, 189–91, 195, 206, 216, 238, 240, 254, 256, 262f, 312, 329f; synthesis and "synthetic positing," 9, 71, 83–85, 109, 114, 117–20, 190, 231–33; relation to Benveniste, 14, 126, 129–30; linguistic relativity, 28, 117; on dialogue, 40, 136–38, 179, 218, 220; relation to Kant, 75, 117–18, 242
Hume, David, 12, 24, 30–42 *passim*
Husserl, Edmund, 2, 6, 19, 115–16, 136n

"I am," xiii, 8f, 97–99, 101, 146, 157, 164, 168, 175, 178, 184, 205–7, 216, 243, 254–58, 261, 265. See also verb-substantive
idealism, German, xiii, 2, 8–10, 23, 68, 70, 78, 83f, 89, 96f, 99f, 104, 123, 128f, 133, 135, 140, 227, 329. See also individual philosophers by name
idéologues, 28
imagination, 74f, 95, 101, 111–12, 165, 177, 181n
Inchbald, Elizabeth, 23
infelicity, 43, 46, 58, 271
Institut National (France), 28
intentionality, 11, 31, 39, 69, 102, 116, 179, 240, 293
Isermann, Michael, 29n
iterability, 20–21, 37–38
Itoda, Soichiro, 263n

Jackson, H. J., 162n, 182n
Jakobson, Roman, 219n
Janke, Wolfgang, 101
Johnson, Samuel, 52

Kant, Immanuel, xiii, 3–15 *passim*, 23, 58, 83, 85, 90–100 *passim*, 104f, 144, 166, 177, 182n, 184, 186, 227, 232, 329, 331; "Was Ist Aufklärung?" 60–61; *Critique of Pure Reason*, 68–76, 78–81, 174, 176, 257; relation to Humboldt, 108–24 *passim*; relation to Kleist, 241–42, 262, 269, 272–73, 285
Kepler, Johannes, 167
Kirchner, Werner, 190n, 237
Kleist, Heinrich von, xiv, 141, 240–88, 331; *Amphitryon*, xiv, 243, 254–63; *Familie Schroffenstein*, 243–45; "Griffel Gottes," 240–41; *Michael Kohlhaas*, xiv, 243, 267–79, 331; *Penthesilea*, xiv, 243, 245–53, 262; *Prinz Friedrich von Homburg*, 243, 245, 252–54; "Über die allmähliche Verfertigung der Gedanken beim Reden," 263–67; "Zweikampf," xiv, 243, 279–88
Klopstock, Friedrich Gottlieb, 169
Kommerell, Max, 211n, 263n
Kurz, Gerhard, 217–18

Lacoue-Labarthe, Philippe, 12–13
Land, Stephen K., 5, 23n, 34n
language, origin of, 4f, 8, 32, 40, 76–79, 81, 86–89, 91–92, 102, 179, 291, 330
langue (and *parole*), 109n, 113, 125, 139
law, 17–18, 32–33, 37, 41–51, 53–54, 64–67, 253–54, 295–96, 310–12; in Kleist's

fiction, 267n, 270–73, 280–88 *passim*.
  See also Common Law
Leibniz, Gottfried Wilhelm, 109
Leighton, Robert, Archbishop, 166
Levinas, Emmanuel, 19, 136n
liberty, 47, 53, 63, 146–51, 155, 220f, 224
Lilienstern, Rühle von, 263, 266
Liu, Alan, 20
Locke, John, 6, 29, 292
logos, xiii, 69, 101, 145–46, 157–65, 167–69, 173, 184
Louis XVI, 24, 52
Löwith, Karl, 136n
Lübbe-Grothues, Grete, 219n
Luther, Martin, 236n, 269, 273
Lyotard, Jean-François, 17–18, 45, 56, 140f, 312

Macovski, Michael, 179n
Magna Carta, 33, 54
Magnuson, Paul, 147n, 151
Markis, Dimitrios, 69n
McKusick, James C., 162n, 174, 182n
McLean, William Scott, 218
Meiner, Johann Werner, 82
Menze, Clemens, 110n
Meschonnic, Henri, 1
Miller, Jacqueline T., 298n
Miller, J. Hillis, 267n
Milton, John, 145, 169, 172, 195
Mirabeau, Honoré Gabriel, Comte de, 264–66, 282
Morris, Charles, 5
Müller-Sievers, Helmut, 119n
Müller-Vollmer, Kurt, 3, 106n
Murray, Alexander, 175–76
Myers, Victoria, 150n

Nägele, Rainer, 226–27
naming, 24, 48, 57n, 77–78, 92, 148, 162, 187f, 193–96, 223f, 226, 246f, 325
Nancy, Jean-Luc, 12–13
Napoleon Bonaparte, 190
National Assembly, 24, 26, 51, 55, 63, 264f, 267, 278, 282, 295–96
natural rights, 27, 32, 49–66 *passim*, 148, 150
Naturphilosophie, 100, 140
Neohumboldtians, 106, 109
Nerlich, Brigitte, 6f, 14f, 23n, 31n, 34n, 69, 100n, 102, 150n

Neumann, Werner, 106n
new historicism, xi, 20, 28
Newton, Isaac, 167
Nietzsche, Friedrich, 13
nouns, 47–48, 77, 80f, 88, 91–94, 101, 119, 127, 174f, 233
Novalis (Friedrich von Hardenberg), 84, 87, 101, 104, 184n, 206, 227
Nussbächer, Konrad, 219n

oaths, xiv, 5, 24–26, 62f, 66, 192, 195–97; of allegiance, 32, 113, 220, 245, 285; Romantic-period critiques of, 41, 43, 46n, 58, 60, 149, 151–52, 285–86, 296; in Kleist's work, 242–45, 249, 257–60, 262, 280, 283, 285–86; in Godwin's work, 290, 296–99, 306–10, 328. See also vows
obligation, 24, 31n, 37, 39, 47, 49f
Ogden, C. K., 42, 49n
ordinary-language philosophy, 14, 33, 40. See also Austin, J. L.
Otherness, 19, 114f, 128f, 136–39, 141f, 189, 193f, 201f, 216–19, 222, 224, 239, 330
"outerance" and "outness," 163–65, 181, 184
Ozouf, Mona, 25, 226

Paine, Thomas, xiii, 24, 51–67, 150, 295, 301–2, 312, 322, 330; *Rights of Man*, 52, 54–65, 296, 301
Parker, Andrew, 12
Parker, Reeve, 171
perception, 12, 43, 48, 68, 70, 74, 76, 91, 93ff, 100, 114, 118, 133, 162, 179, 189, 241, 272
Perkins, Mary Anne, 179n
Petrey, Sandy, 28n
phenomenology, twentieth-century, 6, 19, 107–8, 115–16, 169n, 227
pietism, 218
Pindar, 226
Pitt, William, 51
Port-Royal grammar, 81, 120
positing, xiii, 8f, 71, 73–74, 83–86, 93–94, 96f, 107, 118–24, 131, 137, 140–42, 146, 153, 173, 177, 183, 189f, 218, 225, 319. See also self-positing
post-colonial theory, 20

poststructuralism, 17–18, 20, 133–134, 138, 140–41, 241–42, 272, 298n
Pratt, Mary Louise, 12
predication, 47, 75, 80ff, 91, 94, 101, 104, 120–26, 128, 142, 163, 176f, 231–33. *See also* verbs
Prichard, Harold A., 31n
promises, xiv, 10–11, 24, 30–31, 49, 67, 99, 113, 125, 140f, 155, 158, 185, 200, 221, 250f, 257, 270f, 273, 276f, 279, 287; Reid's theory of, 33–37, 39–40; Godwin's critique of, 289–99 *passim*, 304–8, 316–20, 328, 331. *See also* commissives
pronouns, 38, 81, 98f, 120, 126–35, 141, 206, 218, 256f
prophecy, 57, 61, 156–58, 161, 182, 185, 212, 230, 277–78, 331
propositions, 33, 70–76, 83, 85f, 92, 96–99, 122–28, 141, 160, 167, 174, 176–78, 183, 231–32, 265, 306, 311. *See also* statements

Radcliffe, Ann, 109n
Reid, Thomas, xi, xiii, 1, 5f, 24, 32–42, 46, 67, 109n, 257, 287, 291, 298, 311f, 329
Reinach, Adolf, 19, 34n
representation, xiii, 7–8, 11, 19ff, 25f, 68, 81–103 *passim*, 108, 300; Kantian, 13, 70, 73–75, 134, 140; political, 55f, 140, 264–66, 295; in Humboldt's work, 115, 117f, 122, 142; in Coleridge's work, 159, 175, 177
Ricoeur, Paul, 107–8
Rosaldo, Michelle Z., 12
Roth, Georg Michael, 100
Rousseau, Jean-Jacques, 36f, 58, 63f, 77f, 251f, 270, 293, 295
Runge, Philipp Otto, 184n
Ruoff, Gene, 171
Russell, Bertrand, 2
Ryan, Lawrence, 200

Sandor, Andras, 126n
Sapir, Edward, 106
Sartre, Jean-Paul, 136n
Saussure, Ferdinand de, 106, 126n
Scarry, Elaine, 18
Scharf, Hans-Werner, 117n
Schelling, Friedrich Wilhelm Joseph, xiii, 1, 68, 83, 86n, 96–101, 104, 133, 135, 140, 143f, 178
Schiller, Friedrich, 112–14, 143, 227
Schlegel, August Wilhelm, 2–3, 84–89 *passim*, 102–4, 109–10, 143
Schlegel, Friedrich, 2ff, 71, 84–89 *passim*, 102–4, 109–10, 137, 143, 164, 179, 206
Schleiermacher, Friedrich, 87, 127, 139, 191
Schlieben-Lange, Brigitte, 26–27, 81
Schuhmann, Karl, 34n
Searle, John R., 2, 10–19 *passim*, 33f, 39, 70, 72–73, 77, 93, 99, 125, 128, 141, 146, 159, 177–79, 188, 220, 257, 296, 320, 326
secrets, xiv, 204n, 223, 297f, 307–9, 314, 318–26 *passim*
Sedgwick, Eve Kosofsky, 12
Seeba, Hinrich C., 241, 244n
self-positing, 9, 84f, 100f, 103f, 130, 206. *See also* "I am"; positing
Sembdner, Helmut, 266
Shaffer, E. S., 238n
Shaftesbury, Lord, 30
Shakespeare, William, 77, 112
Sheiber, Andrew J., 299n
Shelley, Percy Bysshe, 149
signatures, 17, 56, 140f
silence, 171, 173, 192n, 198, 205, 222, 307, 314f
Silvig, Helen, 280, 285
Simms, Karl N., 299n, 310n
Sinclair, Isaak von, 234
Slagle, Uhlan V., 117n
Slakta, Denis, 27n
Smith, Barry, 6, 34n
Smith, John H., 241–42, 263n
Smith, Olivia, 5, 23n, 57
social contract, 5, 29–37 *passim*, 42, 49–51, 53, 61–64, 67, 245, 251f, 273, 290–97 *passim*, 329. *See also* contracts
Spälti, Jakob, 250, 263n
speech situation, xii, 15, 81, 96, 108, 120, 137, 224, 259, 266f, 282–87 *passim*, 292, 314, 330, 332
speech-act theory, 9–14, 19, 29–30, 33, 41, 59, 192n, 257, 303, 326, 331; background in Romantic period, xii, 2, 6, 26f, 33–34, 39, 71–55, 83f, 93–99 *passim*; in relation to Humboldt, 107–8,

125, 137f, 142. *See also* Austin, J. L.; Searle, John R.
Spranger, Eduard, 117n
statements, 18, 33, 42, 50, 69, 73, 176, 178, 200, 232, 257, 262, 265f, 278, 305, 319–20. *See also* assertions; constatives; propositions
Stewart, Dugald, 41
Stierle, Karlheinz, 226f
Streitberg, W., 69n, 117n
subject, 68, 74–75, 96–102 *passim*; founding of subject-positions, xii, 180–84, 218; in Humboldt's work, 108, 115, 130–32, 135, 141–42; in Hölderlin's work, 188–89, 191, 227
subjectivity, xiii–xiv, 12–13, 262, 330; in language, 7ff, 14f, 20, 180, 216
Surber, Jere Paul, 88
synthesis, 9, 73–75, 94–97, 231–33; Humboldt's theory of, 9, 71, 83–85, 109, 114, 117–25, 131, 135, 142, 190, 231–32; Coleridge's theory of, 174, 176–77, 183

Taylor, Charles, 107n
temporality, 67, 113, 128, 132, 135, 198, 262, 269–71, 281, 286, 293–94, 312, 316; paradoxical, in performatives, 9, 17–18, 104, 138–40; transcendence of, 156–57, 159, 185–86
testimony, 37–38, 41, 48, 280, 284, 297, 299, 302, 306, 311, 313, 328
Thomas, Keith G., 171
Thomson, James, 169
Tieck, Ludwig, 2, 89
Tooke, John Horne, 4–5, 28–29, 48, 144, 162, 166, 168, 174f, 181, 329
Trabant, Jürgen, 107n, 119n, 120
truth, 57, 146, 156ff, 161, 163, 167f, 241, 280, 282–86; Godwin's view of, xiv, 291–320 *passim*, 327; as goal of statements, 10, 15, 33, 71ff, 125, 151, 155, 178, 185, 260
Turner, John, 150n

understanding (as mental faculty), 34, 69–76, 79–83, 90–92, 95–96, 100–101, 104, 117–18, 162–66, 169, 174, 177, 183, 186, 241
Underwood, Ted, 109n
universal grammar, 5, 33, 38–39, 41, 43, 69, 71, 81–82, 121, 124–26, 174, 270
universal pragmatics, 13–16
Uphaus, Robert W., 310n
uptake, 19, 37, 43–47 *passim*, 59, 102, 108, 121, 137, 160, 292–93, 304, 327, 329ff; in Hölderlin's work, xiv, 188, 194, 198–213 *passim*, 220–25, 232–33, 239; in Kleist's work, 246, 265–79 *passim*
utilitarianism, 42

Vater, Johann Severin, 102
verbs, xiii, 8, 10, 15, 38, 73–83 *passim*, 88, 90–95, 101, 104, 120–28 *passim*, 135, 144, 174–82 *passim*, 202n, 231f, 250, 262. *See also* predication
verb-substantive, 8, 82f, 88, 91, 122, 166, 175–76, 178, 182, 231. *See also* copula; "I am"
Vincent, William, 175
vocatives, 218
vows, 191, 196–98, 200–202, 248, 250, 282, 290, 307, 314–18 *passim*, 326. *See also* oaths

Wagner, Johann Jacob, 100–102, 137
Warnock, G. J., 12
Warren, Leland E., 299n
Weisgerber, Leo, 106
Welke, Klaus, 106n
Wheeler, Kathleen, 160n
Whorf, Benjamin Lee, 106
Wittgenstein, Ludwig, 2, 19, 29n, 127, 138, 288
Wollstonecraft, Mary, 23, 109n
Wordsworth, William, 144, 172

Zimmerman, Klaus, 27n
Žižek, Slavoj, 140
Zuberbühler, Rolf, 219